Pusey Rediscovered

Pusey Rediscovered

Edited by
PERRY BUTLER

First published in Great Britain 1983
SPCK
Holy Trinity Church
Marylebone Road
London NW1 4DU

ACKNOWLEDGEMENTS

Extracts from *The Letters and Diaries of John Henry Newman*
(ed. C. S. Dessain and T. Gornall)
are reprinted by permission of Oxford University Press.

'Dr Pusey's Marriage' by David W. F. Forrester
was first published in *The Ampleforth Journal* 78 (1973),
and is reprinted by permission.

British Library Cataloguing in Publication Data

Pusey rediscovered.
   1. Pusey, E.B.   2. Church of England—Biography
   I. Butler, Perry
   283'.092'4   BX5199.P9

   ISBN 0 281 04054 0

Printed in Great Britain at
the Alden Press, Oxford

Contents

Contents

The Contributors

PERRY BUTLER is the author of *Gladstone, Church State and Tractarianism* (1982). Ordained in 1980, he is Curate of St Nicholas, Chiswick.

LEIGHTON FRAPPELL is Senior Lecturer in British History at Macquarie University, New South Wales. He is an Associate Editor of the *Journal of Religious History*.

MARTIN ROBERTS is Lecturer and Chaplain in the West Sussex Institute of Higher Education, Chichester.

DAVID JASPER is Chaplain and Harris Research Fellow at Hatfield College, University of Durham. He is currently writing a book on Coleridge.

ALAN LIVESLEY is Vicar of Beighton, Sheffield.

DAVID W.F.FORRESTER was ordained to the Roman Catholic priesthood in 1972 and is now Parish Priest of Bishop's Waltham, Hampshire. He is the author of two books of spirituality, and his biography of the young Pusey is shortly to be published.

ROGER JUPP is Assistant Priest of the parish of Cowley St John, Oxford.

ROBERT HARVIE GREENFIELD ssje, formerly Dean of St John's Cathedral, Portland, Oregon, is now a member of the Cowley Fathers in Cambridge, Massachusetts.

RUTH TEALE is an Associate of the Research School of Social Sciences in the Australian National University, and the author of many articles on colonial churchmen and church politics. She is married to Leighton Frappell.

The Contributors

KEITH DENISON is Vicar of Mathern and Mounton, Gwent, and Diocesan Adviser for Post-Ordination Training.

GABRIEL O'DONNELL OP is an American Dominican priest, and Assistant Professor of Spiritual Theology and Liturgy at the Dominican House of Studies, Washington D.C.

PETER NOCKLES is Assistant Librarian at the John Rylands University Library of Manchester. He has contributed to a volume of studies on the Catholic revival in the Church of England in the nineteenth century, to be published in 1983.

IEUAN ELLIS is Senior Lecturer and Head of the Department of Theology, University of Hull. He is the author of *Seven Against Christ: A Study of Essays and Reviews* (1980).

RODERICK STRANGE is the Catholic Chaplain at Oxford University and a priest of the Shrewsbury diocese. He is the author of *Newman and the Gospel of Christ* (1981).

PETER G.COBB is Vicar of Midsomer Norton, Bath. He was Librarian of Pusey House, Oxford from 1969 to 1971 and Custodian from 1976 to 1978. He is currently writing a biography of Pusey.

A.M.ALLCHIN is Canon Residentiary of Canterbury Cathedral. He was Librarian of Pusey House from 1960 to 1969, and Editor of *Sobornost* from 1960 to 1977. He has written several books, including *The Kingdom of Love and Knowledge* (1979) and *The Dynamic of Tradition* (1981).

Introduction

Although by the late 1830s the followers of the Oxford Movement were popularly known as 'Puseyites', Pusey has been the most neglected of the Tractarian leaders. Of the writing of books on Newman there is, apparently, no end. Keble too has found modern biographers. But for an appraisal of Pusey's life and significance we are still almost totally dependent upon the four volumes of H. P. Liddon's *Life*, published between 1893 and 1897.

Liddon's biography is monumental. In preparation for it he amassed, transcribed and organized a hugh amount of material. He wrote both as a warm admirer and a rigid adherent of his master. However, he also wrote to a preconceived plan which looked at Pusey solely in terms of the Oxford Movement. In the words of the editors of the posthumously completed and published fourth volume, 'Liddon . . . regarded that long life chiefly in its relation to the Oxford Movement. It would fall, he used to say, into four parts, to be entitled the Preparation, the Movement, the Struggle, the Victory.'[1]

Some aspects of Pusey's life were, therefore, neglected or treated in too superficial or misleading a manner. For example, Liddon shied away from discussing many personal matters such as Pusey's relationship with his wife and family. Other matters such as his interests in church building and the erection of colonial bishoprics were not adequately dealt with. Again, Pusey's intellectual and religious development was presented in too linear a fashion, in a way which perhaps smoothed over difficulties and ambiguities, seeing it too easily in terms of a steady progression to mature Anglo-Catholicism.

Subsequent scholarly neglect of Pusey may not, however, be due simply to the scale of Liddon's massive biography and its enormous documentation. Pusey was and remains an enigmatic,

ix

complex and controversial figure whom many have found uncongenial both theologically and personally. As Dr Colin Matthew has recently written in an article not noticeably sympathetic to its subject, 'Dr Pusey: even today the name provokes a reaction and an image—for some of Anglican sanctity, for others of ecclesiastical deceit.'[2] T. A. Lacey, an Anglo-Catholic of the next generation, wrote that when he went up to Oxford in 1871, 'Pusey stood in his lone eminence respected by almost all, disliked by most.'[3] And something of the depth of that hostility is caught in the remark of a Student of Christ Church, York Powell, who on Pusey's death dismissed him as, 'this miserable little man' who had been one of 'the fighters against the light.'[4]

For many people today their picture of Pusey is still either that of scholar and saint, heroic leader of the Anglo-Catholic movement, confessor and spiritual writer, or that of a man whose scholarship and teaching were marred by his lack of a free intelligence, a life-denying joyless man whose austere piety bordered upon the pathological.

To commemorate the centenary of Dr Pusey's death Canon Cheslyn Jones (Principal of Pusey House 1971–81) invited a number of scholars to contribute to a book of essays, based largely on unpublished or little-known sources, discussing as fully as possible those aspects of Pusey's life and work which have not been given adequate attention hitherto. In the event these essays are appearing not in the centenary year but, with no less appropriateness, during the year commemorating the 150th anniversary of the Oxford Movement. Any fresh appraisal of the significance of that Movement, and of catholic Anglicanism, will have to take greater cognizance of the contribution of Edward Bouverie Pusey. I hope that these studies, dealing as they do in different ways with such a many-sided and unusual individual, will help stimulate greater scholarly interest in Pusey in the future and to an extent atone for the astonishing neglect of the past.

In conclusion, I would like to thank all those who have contributed in many different ways to the making of this commemorative volume and to acknowledge with gratitude the generous subsidy towards the publication made by the

Governors of Pusey House from the fund left to them in memory of Dr F. L. Cross, sometime Librarian of the House and latterly Lady Margaret Professor of Divinity in the University.

Perry Butler

NOTES

1   Henry Parry Liddon, *The Life of Edward Bouverie Pusey*, ed. J. O. Johnston and R. J. Wilson, 4 vols. (1893–7), IV, p. iii.

2   H. C. G. Matthew, 'Edward Bouverie Pusey: from Scholar to Tractarian', *Journal of Theological Studies*, 32 (1981), 101–24.

3   T. A. Lacey, *The Anglo-Catholic Faith* (1926), 42.

4   O. Elton, *Frederick York Powell: A Life* (1906), I, 66–7, quoted in J. Newton, *Search for a Saint: Edward King* (1977), 113.

Abbreviations

CCC	*Colonial Church Chronicle*
JEH	*Journal of Ecclesiastical History*
JTS	*Journal of Theological Studies*
n.s.	*new series*
SCH(L)	*Studies in Church History*

1

'Science' in the Service of Orthodoxy: The Early Intellectual Development of E. B. Pusey

LEIGHTON FRAPPELL

1

The course of mental and spiritual development which at length brought E. B. Pusey into the Tractarian fold has long been an object of speculation. In later life he was at pains to account for his tardy accession to the Movement, which occurred only in 1835–6, and Newman's silence on the subject in the *Apologia*[1] caused him to take up his pen in mild remonstrance: for it seemed to lend credence to the common opinion that well into the 1830s Pusey had been of a very different spirit from that of his future associates. But the letter was never sent, indeed never finished, for he evidently despaired of explaining himself even to one formerly so close.[2] How then could he look for understanding from his opponents, who refused to believe that he had not fundamentally changed his religious course, and delighted to throw up against him the charge that he had once entertained markedly liberal opinions in theology as in politics? Made in the face of repeated denials, Pusey came to regard such suggestions as scandalous,[3] but they were only fuelled by what was taken to be his attempt to conceal the evidence of those opinions by withdrawing from sale in 1848 his early work on German theology and assiduously acquiring the remaining copies.[4]

Not surprisingly, the publication of Pusey's biography was eagerly anticipated as the occasion when all would be made clear. What Newman had done to explain himself to an interested public, Liddon would now accomplish on Pusey's behalf.[5] Yet such expectations were doomed to disappointment: the faithful custodian of his master's reputation was not about to admit the possibility that the man who had symbolized Anglo-Catholicism for fifty years had not from the outset been ordained by providence to his role, or that the root of the matter, High Church orthodoxy leavened by patristic and Caroline divinity, had not always been in him. Thus for Liddon, viewing Pusey's career teleologically, the association with Keble and Newman in the Movement was not only inevitable but an act of spiritual self-realization after fruitless wanderings in the wasteland of continental Protestant divinity, engaged in well-intended but vain attempts to meet infidelity on its own ground, that of the so-called higher criticism.[6]

Perhaps surprisingly Liddon's assertion long went unchallenged, due not least to the very bulk and detail of the *Life*, which hides its subject under 'a pile of paper';[7] but as other weighty Lives of the great Victorians have at length come under scrutiny, so too did Liddon's. In 1958 Geoffrey Best described a fresh biography, dealing especially with Pusey's early career, as a desideratum,[8] and in 1967 this need was met in part with the completion by Forrester of an important thesis, still unpublished, on Pusey's religious and emotional development down to 1850.[9] In setting aside Liddon's account, Forrester lends critical weight to the persistent belief, found for example in Tulloch,[10] that Pusey was indeed early an advanced religious thinker, whose liberalism was both considered and to a point coherent and not just, as Liddon implies, a case of temporary unsettlement; that it was hence antecedently improbable that he would subsequently join ranks with Keble and Newman. In that very occurrence therefore Forrester sees no 'homecoming' but an intellectual and emotional revolution (subsequently confirmed by another in 1845, divesting him of any remnant of his former opinions) which represents the victory of his craving for emotional security: a craving engendered by the unnatural strictness of his father, resulting in a failure to achieve self-reliance and confidence in his own judgement, and satisfied at last by the surrender of his intellect to a dominant personality (Newman) and an authoritarian creed. In a recent article, moreover, Matthew has echoed this judgement, citing, like

2

Forrester, the transformation of Pusey's relationship with his wife and children during the course of the 1830s as a symptom of his changing beliefs.[11]

It is the contention of the present paper that in the last resort neither of these contrasting accounts of the young Pusey is satisfactory; that whereas Liddon's apologetic standpoint leads him to pass quickly over the years before the Movement and to offer no real explanation of his adherence to it, it is inadequate to describe Pusey's opinions during the 1820s and beyond as 'liberal' or 'liberal Anglican', especially when the effect is to exaggerate the divide which separates the Tractarian from the doctrinally orthodox scriptural Protestant: for it is chiefly as the latter that the pre-Tractarian Pusey appears before us, as Liddon, Forrester and Matthew have all failed adequately to grasp. If the distance between that standpoint and Tractarianism is significant, it is by no means the gulf depicted by those who write in reaction against Liddon; a gulf whose traversing can only be explained finally by resort, in the case of Forrester, to a species of psychological analysis.

2

At the end of his life Pusey recalled that he had been brought up a Prayer Book Christian in the High Church tradition, that he had learned the doctrine of the Real Presence from his mother, and that in natural sequence he had been directed to the Fathers and the Caroline divines.[12] There is no occasion to doubt the claim, especially that his mother influenced him deeply with her emphasis on the immanence of God and the prayerful fulfilment of duty as his fitting service. However, together with his inner zeal and devotional bent, Pusey developed most likely in contact with his stern father that outward reserve and gravity which struck his acquaintances, and which distinguishes him so signally from that other Oxford High Tory, Hurrell Froude, whose 'manly' and ironic nature could not be cowed by a similarly severe parent.[13] Froude entered with alacrity and pride of intellect into his religious inheritance, and in due course would bring out its latent fervour; Pusey's more introverted nature found difficulty in reconciling the warmth of his religious feeling with the 'High and Dry' formalism, with its abhorrence of 'enthusiasm', in which he was expected to express it. From the outset, therefore, he was potentially a refugee from his formal religious inheritance, which he would later and in another context come to associate with chilling 'orthodoxism'; yet in outlook dependent and impressionable, he would remain always uncomfortable in his wanderings from it. In this he stands in contrast with Newman, who relished the intellectual and spiritual odyssey that took him through uncharted and exotic landscapes of the soul. For Newman change (development) was a natural process, for Pusey a perilous voyage to be looked back upon only with alarm at the dangers encountered, once the safety of the harbour had been reached.

At Eton Pusey's religious training (like Froude's) was singularly neglected,[14] and at Christ Church he developed those habits of solitary reading and scholarship, which remained with him always: indeed his father's interdict in 1821 upon his union with Maria Barker threw him still more deeply into his books in an attempt to fend off the despair which seemed to threaten even his sanity.[15] As he later wrote, all his great industry 'was partly intended to cure or at least to stupify' his distress of mind,[16] and until the age of 27 (when the interdict was finally lifted), he lost all hope of earthly happiness and even came to love his own grief.[17] The stifling of emotion and the relief sought in study engendered an intellectualism and critical boldness, which was reflected in his questioning of the political and religious prejudices of his class. Pusey's 'Whiggery' is well known;[18] he was staunch for Catholic Emancipation and deplored the Test and Corporation Acts as inflaming party spirit among Christians who were agreed about the essentials of the faith.[19] This tolerance reflected at once an almost Latitudinarian disdain for the divisions engendered by religious passion and his own attempt to rise above emotional involvements, and for many years a certain 'rationalism' overlay and obscured the warmth of his hidden feelings, including his religious feelings. Froude, struggling for self-control in 1826, wished for himself that he could 'start up into a Pusey and regulate my conduct on rational principles',[20] and Maria still thought her Edward 'formidable' in 1827, although she alone could pierce his reserve. The Noetics of Oriel (of which Pusey became a Fellow in 1823) regarded him as one of themselves, although his grave aloofness distanced him as much from Whately, Hawkins and Copleston as from Froude and Keble (who left residence this same year), so that his subsequent Tractarianism was viewed by them almost as an apostasy from their ranks.[21] Indeed, closest to him in the years 1823 and 1824 was Newman, whose Evangelicalism was no barrier to the approbation of one so free of party spirit and who looked chiefly for indications of religious seriousness and deep moral earnestness.

Pusey's intellectualism drew him naturally to the study of the Christian evidences, that assertion of the plausibility of the Christian claims judged by the lights of reason and history which had been elaborated in response to the assaults of the eighteenth-century deists and anti-Christian philosophers. A knowledge of the evidences was part of the mental culture of any well-read religionist, and Pusey was thoroughly versed in the arguments for Christianity from probability, analogy, the fulfilment of prophecy and even prudence. So too were the Noetics; indeed this was their stamping ground, but unlike them Pusey's omnivorous reading and anxious earnestness acquainted him more fully with the arguments of recent and (in England) largely unfamiliar infidelity where their deficient scholarship and reliance on dialectic bred in them a false sense of security as they embroidered old 'proofs'. Between Pusey and the Noetics was a difference of tone and 'seriousness', although they were united especially in their distaste for sectarianism.[22] The latter would never have gone to Germany to reconnoitre the enemy's current positions!

The zeal transcending love of intellectual display, which Pusey brought to the defence of revealed religion, is reflected in his correspondence during 1823 and 1824 with an old Eton acquaintance, Julian Hibbert, discreetly referred to by Liddon as 'Z'.[23] Hibbert was an avowed atheist steeped in the works of such French 'infidels' as Volney, Dupuis, Voltaire, Diderot and D'Holbach. He dismissed the arguments for theism from design and probability, and his case against Christianity rested on a denial that it was either unique or inexplicable in historical terms alone, that miracles and the fulfilment of prophecy attest to its truth, and that the moral tone of the Scriptures is more

than humanly elevated. He declared the Koran of equal merit
with the Bible, rejected the inspiration of Scripture, and viewed
theology as mere perplexity, warning Pusey against devoting
his life to it.[24] By bringing prominently before him the subtlety
and boldness of modern unbelief, with its recourse to the
weapons of textual criticism and comparative religion, Hibbert
undoubtedly alarmed Pusey, who could not but reflect on the
unpreparedness of English religion, whether the unreflecting
orthodoxy of the 'High and Dry', the 'enthusiasm' of the
Evangelicals or the superficiality of the Noetics, to face the new
threat. Yet significantly he was not dismayed; indeed his
response to the challenge represented by Hibbert was one
almost of exhilaration since it opened before him the prospect of
'usefulness'—of serving the cause of religious truth in a bold
and timely way, which was to become his almost obsessive
preoccupation for years after and afford the measure by which
he anxiously sought to gauge his own worth.

In a flurry of activity, in which he involved also his brother
Philip, Dupuis, Volney and many more were digested, together
with the Koran, and even a start made on the study of Arabic in
order to evaluate Dupuis' claim[25] that the Old Testament is but
part of a large body of Semitic and Egyptian religious literature
and reflects its common themes. Yet despite endless pains and
unfailing courtesy, Hibbert's warning that Pusey was 'plough-
ing in the sand' in trying to reclaim him for supernaturalism[26]
had to be heeded at last. Liddon characteristically attributes
Hibbert's stubbornness to moral turpitude,[27] and certainly
Pusey was shocked that the demonstration of all the traditional
'evidences' had failed to carry the day.[28] As well, however, he
had been made all too aware of the deficiency of his own
scholarship confronted with the craft of Hibbert's masters, and
the episode was important in fixing his attention upon the
interpretation of Scripture, especially the Old Testament, as the
field on which the next trial of strength with unbelief had
already been joined. It would be in the context of his efforts to
place that interpretation on a sounder footing, less vulnerable to
critical objection, that he would in due course acquire his
reputation as a liberal theologian, for that preoccupation
necessarily involved him in a reconsideration of received

attitudes toward inspiration and the relationship of Scripture to the creeds and formularies of the Church. Nor was that preoccupation unique: while Newman pursued the Anglican controversy with Rome, Pusey would find himself increasingly engaged in the more critical struggle by Protestantism to maintain its scriptural foundation by disputing the sceptics' boast that they alone were scientific exegetes.

Pusey composed (at Hibbert's urging) a formal refutation of Dupuis and Volney in part-fulfilment of his desire to contribute something original 'in defence of Religion', conscious however that he had nothing really new to say;[29] for his enquiries had revealed to him a body of French and German apologetic literature of which the Noetics were ignorant and which bore directly on the claims of the latter-day unbelievers.[30] Accordingly he had made a start on learning German, and his half-formed purpose of studying in Germany would soon find encouragement from a man who became to him a mentor and decisively influenced the course of his career. This was Charles Lloyd, Regius Professor of Divinity and briefly Bishop of Oxford, whose theological lectures, delivered between 1823 and his death in 1829, are widely acknowledged as having contributed strongly to the re-establishment of 'Church principles' in the decade before the Movement. Especially revealing was his demonstration through textual comparison of the continuity and surprising uniformity of witness to essential truths among estranged churches, for example by showing the derivation of the Anglican Prayer Book from the Roman Missal and Breviary and the close links between the Articles of Religion and the continental Protestant confessions. Newman later drew what he considered the appropriate conclusion in Tract 90,[31] when he claimed the right to hold the Articles in their Catholic sense, and although Lloyd's learning predictably left Froude unmoved[32] its example fixed Pusey in his emerging resolve to devote himself to the cause of Christian scholarship rather than the cure of souls. At the same time, Lloyd was no mere dry-as-dust but a man of wit and urbanity whose personal likes and dislikes were roundly declared and who evoked in most of his students a determination to apply the insights gained at his feet to the critique and amendment of the English Church. Lloyd's practical, reforming purpose was never in doubt, and the vigour of his anti-sectarian and anti-Erastian teaching later led Pusey to award him the palm of being the Oxford Movement's father.[33]

For all of this, however, Lloyd was clearly inadequate as a leader in the war with unbelief. It was not his study, any more than Romanism was Pusey's,[34] and he wisely encouraged his charge's thoughts of Germany. Of course, he could rehearse the traditional 'evidences', and did so in his lectures; but drawn from Paley, Lardner, Routh and such like they did not touch the heart of Pusey's concern, and his supposition that atheism was a rarely encountered and untenable position must have seemed ironic in the wake of the Hibbert affair.[35] Lloyd's immediate service to Pusey therefore, touching that matter which chiefly preoccupied him, was in providing the encouragement necessary to launch the hesitating young man on the hazardous German venture, encouraging him in the hope that therein lay his best chance of 'usefulness', and generally acting towards him *in loco parentis*.[36]

Pusey went to Germany in June 1825 for 'the critical and scientific part of Divinity',[37] and informed by the current view, with which the Hibbert affair had familiarized him, that the defence of revealed religion in its uniqueness and moral superiority involved the establishment of more accurate translations of the Scriptures; for it was commonly held that the claims of unbelievers were encouraged by faulty and misleading texts, producing for example Dupuis' false comparisons of aspects of Hebrew belief and practice with those of other ancient religions. Accurate scholarship was to be an effective solvent of infidelity, and already perhaps the thought had crossed Pusey's mind of revising the Authorised Version of the Old Testament.

During his first stay in Germany (to October 1825) Pusey completed his mastery of the language and established many of the scholarly contacts which he would exploit when he returned the following July to embark on an arduous year's study of Syriac, Chaldee and Arabic: cognate dialects of Hebrew, which were held to be essential to the better understanding of its words and constructions. Yet more importantly for his religious development, he at once encountered the phenomenon of religious rationalism in the persons of his Göttingen and Berlin professors, and was profoundly shocked. He had left England naively confident of finding abroad Christian scholars employing their learning to uphold the complete range of revealed truth and eager to learn at their feet, only to find that such eminent and supposedly orthodox men as Eichhorn and Pott[38] scoffed at Balaam's ass and indeed rejected all scriptural miracles apart from the resurrection. They had long since yielded up as indefensible part of the citadel which Pusey had come eager to secure! If these were counted among the foremost of Christianity's friends in Germany, what need had it of enemies? Pusey was at once thrown on the defensive. Was this the outcome of too cerebral an approach to the defence of religion, of attempting to meet the sceptics on their own ground? In the phenomenon of religious rationalism he saw, as in a distorting mirror, the danger inherent in his own course. His instinctive reaction was to fall back on safe ground: when Newman wrote seeking assistance from German books for use in preparing his *Essay on Miracles* (1826), Pusey warned against the rationalizing implication of distinguishing apostolic from post-apostolic miracles on the basis that the former served uniformly moral ends where the latter did not. For, apply this to Scripture and what becomes of the 'immoral' miracles of Elijah and Elisha?[39]

If, however, the encounter with Eichhorn and Pott checked Pusey in his course and posed a dilemma concerning the tendency of his own studies, Germany also disclosed the key to its resolution by opening to him a new line of apologetic; withdrawing Christianity from the scrutiny of superficial reason, calling to witness the hitherto despised testimony of religious sentiment and emotion, offering protection against the inroads of rationalism. The agents of this delivery were the great Friedrich Schleiermacher, professor of theology in the University of Berlin, and August Tholuck.

If Schleiermacher was himself a rationalist (indeed virtually a pantheist in Pusey's considered opinion[40]), who indulged a freedom of speculation for which he was chiefly known in England, thanks to Connop Thirlwall's translation of his minor treatise, *St Luke*,[41] he was more significantly the great regenerator of the pietist impulse in German Lutheranism.

Descending from Arndt, Spener and Francke, this drew more immediate inspiration from the patriotic romanticism of the years of Prussia's liberation struggle against Napoleon and rejected the 'French' philosophy of rational enlightenment and religious scepticism. In his *Der christliche Glaube*, 1821–2, Schleiermacher had located the grounds of religious assent in the feelings rather than the reason, or rather in the 'feeling' (*Empfindung*), religious reason, which he distinguished from 'feelings' (*Gefühl*), religious sentiment or emotion, as well as from the critical faculty. The distinction became important to Pusey[42] as to others, for it provided an answer both to religious rationalism and 'enthusiasm' by locating religious conviction neither in the formal reason nor in the affective sentiments but in a distinct faculty which partook of elements of both and which Coleridge, following his German masters, called the 'Understanding'. Moreover, beyond contributing to Pusey's religious development by first encouraging him not to distrust on principle the promptings of the heart, Schleiermacher afforded in his own practice a living example of religion's warmth. Pusey was moved by his simple reverence for the person of Christ and his Moravian-inspired quietism, which looked not to be busy in the affairs of God, lest selfish motives intrude, but to wait always for a call. Pusey would later recognize that quality in Newman also, and compare it self-reproachfully with his own anxious quest for 'usefulness'.

For all this, Pusey naturally remained in dread of Schleiermacher's rationalism—he questioned even the historical reality of the resurrection—which, as Faber says, he reconciled with his pietism by a remarkable *tour de force* of religious genius.[43] That resolution was altogether too personal for imitation, and his lack of any presumption in favour of the inspiration of Scripture left weaker men, who required some external warrant for the faith that was in them, without grounds of assurance. Certainly, his indifference to the call for a Christian science of biblical interpretation was a stumbling block;[44] yet what was wanting in the master, Pusey found in the disciples, among certain representatives of that group of theologians, known as the mediating school, which drew inspiration from him. As its name implies, the *Vermittlungstheologie* combined on a pietist

10

basis elements in the Lutheran tradition in what was intended to be a more balanced apprehension of the Christian faith than had prevailed in Germany since the eighteenth century, when the Protestant appeal to Scripture had degenerated into rationalising on the texts, when dogmatic theology, cut loose from its scriptural foundation, had presented the aspect of a barren, scholastic orthodoxy, and when in reaction pietism had taken on an increasingly 'enthusiastic' appeal to the sentiments as the essence of Christian belief.

Not surprisingly, in view of its broadly-conceived standpoint, the mediating school displays a range of emphases in its membership, from those such as Tholuck, whose pietism was associated with a general disregard for doctrine and ecclesiastical ordinances, to those like E. W. Hengstenberg, whose Evangelical faith was linked to dogmatism and an emphasis on church authority. Pusey had met and been impressed by Tholuck in Oxford before leaving for Germany, and renewed the acquaintance at Berlin in 1825. Transferring to Halle as professor of theology in 1826, Tholuck was the man who perhaps supremely embodied the genius of the mediating theology, for whom its *via media* between stale orthodoxy, rationalism and 'enthusiasm' was no mere compromise but a veritable 'Theology of the New Life'.[45] It was in Tholuck's immediate circle (which included F. Lücke, K. I. Nitzsch, and K. H. Sack) that Pusey, on the rebound from fear of rationalist excess, found his *niche* in Germany, subsequently corresponding with its members after his return to England. There is every reason to believe that for a time he entered into the ethos of this group, and sought to assimilate its insights to his own unshaken orthodoxy.

Tholuck was of Pusey's own age. Strongly devotional, again reflecting Moravian influence, which had been reinforced through contact with Schleiermacher's disciple, the Jewish convert and Church historian Neander, his missionary drive to proclaim the Christian experience of renewal has led him to be compared with Wesley.[46] On the other hand, his linguistic scholarship (he was a noted Orientalist) reassured the troubled Pusey that the pietist impulse was not incompatible with reverence for the Word of God and the desire to establish its text on a surer foundation. Indeed, the mediating position held implications for the interpretation of that Word that were not lost on Pusey. By 1827, and almost certainly before, he had rejected 'dictation', belief in the most plenary inspiration of the text, as unspiritual and the source of much scholastic elaboration of non-essential doctrine, which, as we shall see, he came to identify as the prime cause of Protestantism's decline. Rather, he dwelt on the superior religious understanding and inerrancy of the scriptural writers as moral guides and interpreters of fundamental doctrine. In company with his pietist friends, he emphasized the practice of the religious virtues inculcated in Scripture, and in reaction against 'scholastic' dogmatism showed himself eager to resolve apparently conflicting views as to the doctrinal implications of texts.[47] Yet if this is 'liberal', it is the opposite of rationalistic; for by conceding the existence in Scripture of non-religious elements he sought to obviate the effect of rationalist criticism of them, which tended to throw doubt upon the whole. To cling to a literal assertion of plenary inspiration was to commit Christians to the defence of Balaam's ass as much as the resurrection. Pusey's liberalism was entirely at the service of his orthodoxy.

It was presumably because he found this truly spiritual principle of interpretation exemplified in Luther that Pusey acknowledged him as the greatest Christian since St Paul;[48] and as for the mediating theologians, he subsequently wrote in the same spirit,

> I have found myself at once more united with the friends whom I acquired in Germany, than I ever did in a similar space in England: it seemed as if we at once knew and had long known each other.[49]

How this general approach to the sacred writings related to the textual analysis and explication, for which Pusey's great expenditure of time and effort on languages was intended to fit him, is a critical question. His reverence, which led him to reject an unspiritual view of inspiration, was bound similarly in due course to reject a text criticism whose inevitable tendency was to stress the historical circumstances of the Bible's composition, and to that degree explain away, even unintentionally, its supposed higher significance. Not for Pusey Schleiermacher's, or even Tholuck's, paradoxical effort of belief; and even as he pursued relentlessly his apprenticeship in biblical 'science', the while asserting its powers of clarification and its potential to serve as the handmaiden of renewed faith, one wonders in the last analysis just how far he really believed this. The very boldness with which he proclaimed it, only to flee subsequently from its consequences at the first blast of criticism, suggests a man desperate to convince himself that his long-cherished hope for 'usefulness' in the field of Christian scholarship was not vain after all. When, at the end of 1826, he was offered an Oriel tutorship he declined, daunted at the prospect of its mind-narrowing routine, but eagerly offered to return instead in the capacity of theological lecturer, guaranteeing to teach nothing unorthodox.[50] Evidently he would have welcomed release from a course of study at once uncompromising in its demands and far removed from practical divinity. Unfortunately the offer was declined.

The full ramifications of his espousal of 'science' would be brought out in the context of a dispute concerning the causes of religious rationalism in Germany. The mediating school afforded him with a ready-made historical account of the phenomenon which rang all too true in his own private experience. Distinguishing between rival theological extremes, it justified its own assertion of a middle course as truly Scriptural in a way not dissimilar to Anglican apologies of the *via media*. Where Anglicans saw to the right the 'human system' of Rome and to the left the individualistic principle of 'private judgement' offered by continental Protestantism, the mediating theologians discerned in their own, Lutheran, tradition the crushing scholastic orthodoxy of the late sixteenth and seventeenth century and found in it the root cause of the rationalist reaction of the *Aufklärung*. As the fault of the one had been its spiritually blind belief in 'dictation', which led it to elaborate from Scripture and impose non-essential and indefensible dogma, the fault of the other lay in its retaliatory resort to mere reason, which proved the solvent of even justifiable doctrine. In the impulse stemming from Schleiermacher the mediating theologians saw the dawn of a second Reformation, when, just

13

as the first had dispelled the scholastic mists of Rome, they would expose the virtual infidelity of rationalism in all its irreverent superficiality.

What did Pusey make of all this? In 1825 he had heard Tholuck deliver a course of lectures informed by this attitude on German Protestantism in the eighteenth century. He could attest to the chilling effect on the religious affections of an excess of orthodoxy, and the reaction against its lack of genuine spirituality had distanced him from the 'High and Dry' formalism of his own upbringing; so much so, indeed, that he had, as he now concluded in retrospect, been thrown into the way of implicit rationalism, even without knowing it. On the other hand, the distinction for Pusey between justifiable orthodoxy and scholasticism was bound to be a much finer one than for Tholuck, and it was on this critical distinction that the Rose affair would hinge. By putting to trial his ability to reconcile his pietistic warmth and trust in 'science' with an insistence on a strong doctrinal position the latter would mark the next turning point in his intellectual development; for inasmuch as he failed that trial, and his orthodoxy was called in doubt as a consequence, he moved to distance himself from his German friends. Yet in moving he would, as we shall see, in a sense hold his ground.

Early in 1828, turning aside from the Old Testament revision, which he had begun the previous year, Pusey published the first part of *An Historical Enquiry into the probable causes of the Rationalist Character lately predominant in the Theology of Germany*. Originally conceived as an anonymous pamphlet, it was a response to the High Churchman Hugh James Rose's *The State of the Protestant Religion in Germany* (1825), which had appeared in German translation in 1826 and been roundly condemned for superficiality and ignorance of the German religious scene.[51] Pusey's motives were mixed: the suggestion that he should write against Rose was probably Lücke's,[52] and for his own part he saw the opportunity, as he frankly confessed to Maria, of enhancing his reputation following his return to England.[53] Fundamentally at issue between the antagonists was the question of authority in matters religious. To Pusey, Rose appeared to be asserting that creeds and Church formularies,

enforced by episcopal government, are critical to the very
survival of Christianity; and certainly the latter held that laxity
with respect to the former and absence of the latter had been the
cause of Germany's lapse of late into religious rationalism.[54]
This Pusey dismissed as *a priorist* and jejune and offered instead
an historical account by way of explaining the phenomenon to
which Rose had drawn attention. Having recourse to Tholuck's
lectures, and subsequently acknowledging his debt also to
Neander, he retorted that lack of 'control' had no bearing on the
case, which illustrated rather the dire effects of scholastic
orthodoxy; for he predictably traced the root cause of rationalism to the ultra-defining Lutheranism which had overwhelmed
the genuine spirituality of Luther. Misled by an unreflecting
regard for Scripture, the outcome had been the creation of what
Pusey calls 'orthodoxism', bastard orthodoxy, a 'human system'
which in its confusion of essentials and non-essentials became a
burden to conscience and an affront to belief, and whose
principal monument was the Formula of Concord, 1580.[55] In
the second half of the seventeenth century came the pietist
reaction which for a time revivified faith and restored its critical
link, always broken in a scholastic age, with morality; yet for
want of a 'scientific' hold on Scripture this in turn degenerated
into 'enthusiasm', whose excesses provoked the rationalist
response which Pusey deplored no less than Rose.[56]

Even from this brief rehearsal of its argument it is obvious
that the *Historical Enquiry* is a faithful expression of the
mediating school's perception of historical Lutheranism, and
Pusey's encomiums fall especially on Arndt and Spener. Yet the
work is, above all, a tract for the times, since its message at last is
that their spirit is kindled anew in the Germany of Schleiermacher and secured this time against degeneration by virtue of
its alliance with 'science'. The result, Pusey proclaims, is a 'new
era of theology', superseding that which the Reformation had
inaugurated and holding promise of a more highly realized
divinity.[57]

It is difficult to avoid the conclusion that in many matters
Pusey had written incautiously, conveying more than he
intended or believed, and with the ardour of a neophyte. The
extent of his reliance on Tholuck was soon discovered,[58] and he

was indebted to Neander for his organizing concept of 'eras' (such as apostolic times and the Reformation) which determine for an interval the subsequent course of Christian history. Its power to shock an English audience lay precisely in the paradoxical claim that the parent of rationalism was excess of orthodoxy. To the incautious the conclusion seemed obvious: Pusey eschewed orthodoxy on principle; and indeed if commitment to episcopacy was any test, the young author's silent dismissal of Rose's prime contention was revealing. Still more damning, however, was his proclamation of Christian renewal in a country where Englishmen were accustomed to detect only speculative boldness and irreligion, not least in Schleiermacher himself, his use of expressions apparently redolent of rationalism such as the 'blending of belief and science', and his claim that the reign of reason had benefited theology by obliging it to take stock of itself, with the result that 'the essential has been separated from the non-essential and accidental, the indifferent and unimportant has been brought back to its true value . . .'.[59]

Pusey was resigned to being misunderstood, expecting to be taken for 'one third mystic, one third sceptic, and one third (which will be thought the worst imputation of all,) a Methodist, though I am none of the three'.[60] Critical of course were the first two charges. Blanco White was one who discovered in the book a defence of intuition and 'feeling' in religion, but far from deploring this 'mysticism' he wrote in grateful appreciation that the *Historical Enquiry* had strengthened his faith by enabling him to 'seize the citadel without stopping to raze every outwork of the enemy'.[61] Pusey was puzzled, and only learned with pain years later that his Oriel colleague's 'enemy citadel' had been dogma and the dogmatic principle no less! Rose on the other hand discerned, what was no less than the truth, a certain idealism which in its apparent suspicion of creeds and indifference to church authority threatened what it would affirm: the supremacy of Scripture. For what were Pusey's 'human systems'? As Rose remarked pointedly when he returned to the fray with his *Letter to the Bishop of London*, all reasonings on Scripture involve a human element,[62] to exclude which is to deny the possibility of a systematic theology, much as Hampden later did in his notorious Bampton Lectures when he seemed to stigmatize all attempts to give expression to the Christian message as unwarranted scholasticism.[63] Here potentially was the outcome of Pusey's thinking: religious relativism, which raised the Protestant claim to private judgement in matters of faith to the level of a categorical imperative.[64]

The charges undoubtedly struck home: not just in the *Historical Enquiry* but in private correspondence, Pusey had shown an incautious tendency to overestimate the ability of 'science' to become the arbiter of justifiable doctrine by its supposed powers of discrimination in relation to Scripture, and by implication had linked the proclaimed renewal of vital religion with progress of scholarship, the 'more enlarged views' of the times,[65] which promised to establish divinity on a higher level than that even of the Reformers. This seemed close to the opinions of Semler, who had taught the 'accommodation' of Christianity to the successive ages which mark the course of human enlightenment.[66] Tholuck himself regarded the Reformation as representing the adult understanding of the Christian message where the early Church had understood as a child. Clearly, Pusey was trespassing on dangerous, relativist ground, led on by the logic of his anti-scholastic polemic; and when during 1828 the question arose of his suitability for the chair of Hebrew he feared for his prospects, and was at pains to re-affirm his substantial orthodoxy and the conservative tendency even of his view of inspiration, which he professed to find widely held in the Church of England.[67] Relieved of those fears by his ordination and professorial appointment, and married at last to Maria, confidence returned, and with it the determination to restate his views with due circumspection and appropriate citing of unimpeachable authorities.

Part 2 of the *Historical Enquiry* is the fruit of that resolve, and cost its author great pains. Up to the very eve of its publication in 1830 he was rewriting difficult passages and trying to find support for his view of inspiration among the Fathers and standard Anglican divines.[68] He was finally obliged to relinquish the former on the advice of Hawkins[69] and also Tholuck, who was surprised that his friend was seeking allies in such a dubious quarter and directed him instead to the Reformers.[70]

The new book rejects comprehensively the charges laid against its author on the strength of its predecessor: that he was an apologist of rationalism, indifferent to episcopacy, impatient of articles, a hater of 'human systems', opposed to the idea of plenary inspiration, and of great liberalism on theological subjects.[71] Its preoccupation is, however, with the central issue of the relationship of Scripture to the creeds and articles in which doctrine is expounded. In denying that he had intended to reject all attempts at reasoning on Scripture, he explains that he wished only to re-assert the Protestant hold on its primacy, so that doctrine justifiable in its terms was alone insisted on. His strictures had been against the practice of seventeenth century Lutheranism, for example, which had reversed the due process by first erecting a 'human system' of dogma which it had then imposed upon Scripture by torturing its texts and refusing to discriminate essentials from non-essentials. The original Lutheran 'system' had, by contrast, been truly scriptural and to that extent proof against the rationalist reaction which overtook its 'supplementary', scholastic form.[72] Considered historically, however, that reaction had nevertheless brought forth good; for just as the 'human system' of Rome prepared the way for 'the glorious bursting of the light' which was the Reformation, so the ravages of rationalism preceded the contemporary revival: for 'the spiritual world of Germany is putting off the dreary garb of winter; it is starting up in the fresh vigour of renovated life'.[73] Moreover, in writing of a 'new era of theology' in Germany, Pusey insists that he had thought not of the discovery of new truths or the discarding of old, but only of 'the illustration and vindication of all the doctrines of Scripture . . .'.[74]

The new book shows Pusey withdrawing from the more exposed position which he had seemed to adopt in its predecessor into a traditional Protestant assertion of a fixed body of scriptural doctrine. The role of 'science' is reduced to that of a verifying agent, 'proving' the scriptural basis of the seminal Christian teachings and distinguishing them from the local and unwarranted additions made by particular churches and historical periods. In all likelihood, he had never meant to affirm more; and what is remarkable in Pusey's position is his valiant attempt under mounting pressure to uphold the Protestant assertion of the pre-eminence of Scripture, self-authenticating and requiring no 'human' authority to interpret its meaning. His resort to 'science' was his faltering attempt to reinforce that claim in the face of those to the right who would appeal to an interpreting authority and those to the left who claimed the right to private judgement or like Semler saw the Christian message in terms of relativist historicism. Not alone in his day it would be Pusey's lot to experience the difficulty inherent in this position, with its tenuous distinction of justifiable deductions from 'human additions', and its appeal to an elevated biblical 'science' to serve as arbitrator. In this perspective, his approaching intellectual crisis was but a particular instance of the general crisis of identity which was overtaking Protestantism, and which served to give impetus to the resurgence of Church principles in England, France and Germany during the 1830s.

Pusey emerged from the 'German war' with Rose profoundly dissatisfied, reflecting misgivings about his motives in launching it and doubts about his own controversial standpoint. His intense moralism accused him of having preferred intellectual display to personal improvement.[75] In all the debate about 'science' and 'human systems' he had failed to urge the ultimate end of Scripture, moral reformation and the inculcation of humility, which was the message both of the pietists and Keble, to whom he had drawn closer since 1828, and who had rebuked him for arguing in the *Historical Enquiry*, without regard to moral consequence, that truth is served by admitting difficulties in all their force.[76] He had forgotten his own advice in his first sermon (1828) that the quest for holiness is all-important; delay is perilous, as the season of repentance passes too soon and the unholy man remains so forever.[77] He had already delayed too long, and 1830 and 1831 would witness a private struggle, precipitated by a breakdown in health, in which the disappointments of the Rose affair and the example of Keble's and Newman's 'humility' confirmed in him that quietist idea of religion as a voiding of self in surrender to God, the while awaiting his call to service in vigilant self-scrutiny. 'Practical duties' as 'the great object of life, and self-denial, in order to discharge them', became his ruling principle.[78] It was the reaction of the disappointed activist, who had come to the conclusion that his very striving for 'usefulness' in the affairs of God had rendered him deaf to God's promptings in the heart. As he later wrote to Newman,

> I fear that often the desire of attaining some which I thought a great end, and the consciousness of being engaged in a good cause, has engrossed me too entirely, and made me think of my existence too much in reference to what might be accomplished by my means here, instead of looking preeminently to the preparing myself to meet my God.[79]

Critical to this reaction, which was but the exaggeration of an important element already present in his religious make-up, was the impact on him of political upheavals in France and some of the German states during 1830, which revealed the unsuspected capacity of freedom to degenerate into licence, but still more the emergence of severe strains within the mediating school. Its *via media* seemed to be disintegrating as men like H. F. W. Gesenius, an associate of Tholuck's at Halle and, like him, a noted Orientalist, reportedly fell into speculative rationalism, while Hengstenberg withdrew into a species of Lutheran scholasticism, based on a strong doctrine of church authority and an assertion of plenary textual inspiration.[80] Either way, the moral leaven of pietism was dissipated, and Pusey wrote to Tholuck concerning the prediction of a 'new era in theology' that 'I may have been too sanguine'.[81] By 1834 the transformation of his attitude toward the mediating school would be complete. Hearing in that year that Tholuck, too, was disheartened by the developments of recent years, he wrote rebuking those who still tried to maintain the *juste milieu* as 'essentially a cold, self-conceited, and withal Rationalistic party', which might nevertheless serve as a means of

> inviting over from Rationalism many, who when they shall have been brought thus far, will find no rest for the sole of the foot in it, and at last, betake themselves from the weary waste to the Ark, which is still open to receive them.[82]

Just what was Pusey's 'Ark' by 1834 we shall consider

directly; clearly, however, the shift of his opinions in the interval had been significant, in order to entail a general charge of rationalism against men whom he had once extolled as the restorers of vital belief after the rationalist blight. The notion of a 'reverent science' had proved in practice a chimera, a contradiction in terms; for was not 'science' itself a method whose outcome must be a new 'human system' lacking genuine affinity with the religiously inspired minds of the Scriptural authors? Pusey's definition of a religious rationalist had been expanded to embrace, not just those theologians and their methods so designated in the German tradition, but all who would make the historical and critical study of Scripture the foundation of their divinity. His thinking reflected the polarizing pressures of the times, and although Tholuck must have been irked by the tone of Pusey's letter, his own confidence was destined to suffer further blows. In 1835 appeared Strauss' *Leben Jesu*, arguably the great dividing line in nineteenth-century theology,[83] and he wrote back in prophetic despondency that in Germany a hundred years hence 'only Pantheists and Faithful will be opposed to each other, Deists and the old Rationalists will entirely disappear.'[84]

Pusey's changed attitude to 'science' is of course reflected in the fact that when at last he was free to return to his Old Testament revision he could no longer subscribe to its guiding assumption or believe in its beneficial effect.[85] But what was to supply the place of 'science'? The answer in brief was the mode of interpretation which he found exemplified in the Fathers; a mode holistic in its assumption of the allegorical and prophetic unity of the Scriptures, where 'science' stressed their differentiation in terms of authorship and historical circumstance. As Pusey had come to see in the latter an implicit denial of any higher, metaphysical or moral purpose, the former detected that purpose on every page of Holy Writ. His growing sense of affinity with the Fathers is difficult to trace in its development,[86] as the years after 1830 were very private ones, taken up with the duties of his Chair and the inherited labour on the catalogue of Oriental manuscripts at the Bodleian Library. They were years of withdrawal before his clear identification with Tractarianism and the return to an activist role at the time of the Hampden controversy: an activism proof this time against discouragement, since based on the conviction that in it was nothing of self, doing no other than as duty directed and leaving the issue to God.

Forrester points out that Pusey appears to have been little read previously in the patristic *corpus*,[87] due to his absorption in very different studies, but by 1836, when *The Library of the Fathers* was launched, he had made up somewhat the deficiency in his knowledge and by 1845 professed himself at home in their Church.[88] Also in 1836, in his unpublished 'Lectures on Types and Prophecy', he demonstrated the influence on his thinking of the Greek Fathers and Christian Platonism, and laid the foundations of the Tractarian 'typological' approach to biblical exegesis, in contrast both to that of the text critics and (significantly) old orthodoxy, with its mechanical theory of inspiration and belief in the literal fulfilment of prophecy.[89] That is, fleeing from the rationalism of the one he had by no means embraced the 'orthodoxism' of the other, and to that extent no doubt conceived himself as holding that *via media* between the two extremes which had been the ideal of the mediating school, but one which they had failed to realize in practice. For this reason, indeed, we must be wary of the hasty conclusion that his identification with the Movement represented a marked theological shift to the right and a flight to the haven of authority. In his estimate it was his German friends, not he, who had moved, and in rejecting 'science' he had but discarded a principle incompatible with their anti-rationalist profession. The Tractarians were for him a new, this time a genuine, mediating school, eschewing on principle both the 'human system' of Rome—the prime example of 'orthodoxism'—and the rationalism of the modern Protestants. In absolute terms he had of course moved, and moved considerably; yet relatively speaking he had held his ground. In this fact lay his own conviction, which seemed to his critics disingenuous, that his course had been constant in the last resort; for his commitment to 'science' was one of the head not the heart, and its rejection dictated by a sense of constancy to the promptings of the latter.

The 'Lectures on Types and Prophecy' illustrate the truth of the observation that Pusey repaired to the Fathers originally in search of a method rather than an authority.[90] The attribution to them of superior spiritual insight in no way impaired his belief in the primacy of Scripture, or his preoccupation with biblical exegesis as the foundation of a sound theology. Yet the distinction is in a sense meaningless because the critical service which the Fathers performed for Pusey was precisely in bridging the gap which had always existed in his thought between his High Church orthodoxy and his Protestant scrupulousness in demanding that all doctrine be seen to arise from and find its warrant in the pure Word of God. Unlike Anglicans of an older generation, he could no longer take the scriptural basis of his faith for granted, and the resort to 'science' had been an unsuccessful attempt to 'prove' doctrine from Scripture. The Fathers succeeded where 'science' had failed, for they supplied at once an approach to the sacred text which was 'reverent' and free of rationalist overtones, and whose cumulative, deductive wisdom was encapsulated in doctrinal form in the seminal creeds of the patristic Church. Of course, Pusey had never doubted the binding authority of those creeds: what he had been unsure of was the ground of their authority, and despite Tholuck's warning, he found in the Fathers the assurance—so vital to him—that the ground was indeed scriptural. For now he saw Scripture with new eyes, with its doctrinal treasures fully disclosed.

We arrive then at the paradoxical conclusion that Pusey was driven back on the Fathers in defence of his Protestant principles, and thereby rediscovered for himself and under Keble's influence, the great unifying idea underlying the theology of the Caroline divines. Likewise he found it in Tractarianism; and far from its being antecedently improbable that he would make common cause with the Movement,[91] there is every reason to conclude that it was likely to attract him to its ranks sooner or later. His newly discovered sense of continuity with the Anglican past on the shared basis of a divinity at once patristic and scriptural, and his certainty that the patristic norm was Catholic since scriptural, kept him always unshaken in his ecclesiastical allegiance and substantially free from doubts about the Anglican claim, especially doubts stemming from fears about the status of the English Reformation. As a rejection of Roman 'orthodoxism' the latter was, as Newman himself had shown, eminently justifiable; nor could Pusey honestly say less of its continental counterpart, and he always resisted that association of Reformation with heresy and implicit infidelity which was among Froude's polemical legacies to the Movement. He would indeed go part of the way, identifying religious rationalism as modern heresy in its irreverence and indifference to the patristic standard,[92] but baulked at defining heresy simply in terms of 'separation'. If in time he came to regard the continental Protestant churches as effectively heretical it was because their practice and belief was so much further removed from the patristic model than either England's or Rome's. Those among them who were not rationalists were, like Hengstenberg, 'orthodoxist'. Nevertheless, his grateful memory of the mediating pietists remained always with him; for here were men struggling heroically against the twin evils of scholasticism and rationalism, armed, alas, with defective weapons which would betray them at last, but filled with a zeal and a devotion to God that would do honour to Catholics.[93] He could never bring himself to stigmatize their masters of the sixteenth and seventeenth centuries as bold schismatics and heresiarchs.

Critical to the claim that Pusey's transition from 'scientific' Protestantism to Tractarianism is marked more by continuity than by upheaval must be the evidence afforded by changes in his pattern of formal, doctrinal belief. Do these indicate either dramatic re-appraisal or a doctrinaire narrowing of vision? Of course there was re-appraisal, but it was neither dramatic nor was the effect constrictive. In the later 1820s Pusey's open-minded attempt to look anew at the teaching of Scripture, without regard to the 'scholastic' constraints of degenerate Protestantism, links him clearly with men like Hawkins and Whately. His correspondence with Maria shows him at that time impatient of distinctions of justification and sanctification, faith and works, and eager to reduce to simplicity apparent complexities in the writings of St Paul.[94] To Lloyd he confessed his opposition to the idea of original sin conceived as a mechanical, disabling inheritance.[95] In company with Keble and Newman he came subsequently to discover an organizing focal point for his theology in the incarnation, expressing his sense of mystery and awe at God's condescension in a developed sacramentalism; and the effect was to illuminate and inform the intuitive judgements of earlier years. Thus, finding in the Fathers an assertion of man's dignity united with Christ, his idea of original sin as predisposing yet resistible rather than predetermining and irresistible was confirmed,[96] and with it his sense of the perversity of a system which separated faith and works even to the point of 'fearing' the latter as if detracting from the former. Justification became not as it were a trophy to be won, but a gift bestowed in baptism and nourished by works done in the power of faith, that is through Christ.[97]

In all of this Pusey was conscious of completing and realizing fully the beliefs of his pietist years, which appeared increasingly one-sided: for in throwing all upon God Evangelicalism too often shrugged off in practice the duty of watchful self-scrutiny and the purification of affections and desires. He had added to his faith and forsworn nothing, teaching now the whole duty of man as the counterpart of God's boundless grace. The broadening and strengthening of the theological vision is undoubted: here was the study to which he had always aspired, but from which his preoccupation with the Christian evidences and textual criticism had too long detained him.[98]

In later years, after the 'judgement' of Maria's death in 1839, the censure of Tract 90 and Newman's eventual secession, there was perhaps a contraction of vision: an unscriptural forgetfulness of the message of grace, a tendency to confuse scrupulousness with the performance of duty, a blatant appeal to church authority as the ultimate sanction of Christian truth. The last point is significant of the change. By 1845 he was so far persuaded that the Fathers *per se* were as powerless as 'science' to stem the course of popular irreligion and practical unbelief that nothing short of a system of 'positive truth', systematically proclaimed and inculcated by the Church of England and the universities, seemed to him likely to prevail. The Fathers afforded but one possible measure of such truth, as he observed to Hook in 1845; for the system more than its contents was critical.[99] If this sounds calculating, we are reminded of

Matthew's contention that Pusey's career became at last that of an ecclesiastical statesman intent on erecting an Anglican 'system', single-minded and unshakeable in its affirmations, proof against subversion.[100] Whether such statesmanship is compatible with the retention of a balanced spirituality, capable of drawing together important elements in Evangelical and High Church traditions, is at least doubtful; and it may be that the really difficult but critically important question to be answered about Pusey is not why he became a Tractarian, but why he seemed in the 1840s to lose his grasp on what to him had been the heart of Tractarianism: its appeal to a spiritual reality at once scriptural and patristic, transcending sectarian divisions and discredited 'human systems', bearing witness to the poverty of rationalism and unbelief. Here was a liberating message: yet by constraining it within the attempted revival of an ecclesiastical authoritarianism which had always been foreign to his outlook, and whose effect could only be to re-affirm the exclusiveness of the Church of England as a fortress built against infidelity and dissent, he associated it all but fatally with institutional bigotry and obscurantism.

This is not the place to pursue this problem, other than to suggest that the answer is almost certainly bound up with the undoubted fact of Newman's growing ascendancy over his opinions as the ever-present tendency to distrust his own judgement became chronic. To the extent that he became, as William Palmer of Worcester claimed, Newman's *alter ego*,[101] he also became a party to that debate about the identity of the true Church: a debate which had never been his, but was rather the concern of Tractarianism's right wing, but which involved him increasingly in an obsessional promotion of Anglicanism's claim as measured by the standard (Ward's standard, in *The idea of a Christian Church*) of holiness of life; and while this was no unworthy enterprise, we may wonder whether it was not intended to answer the doubts of one who had been lost irredeemably to that communion in 1845, the while neglecting those of so many others who were looking for the Church of England to reach out to Dissent and unbelief and show them a more excellent way. It is a strange irony that the one man of his generation so well equipped in training and natural sympathy to be the great advocate of vital Catholic religion to those alienated by 'orthodoxist' pedantry or rationalist sterility should have broken off the dialogue. It was his distinctive brand of Tractarianism, and the distinctive route by which he had arrived at it, which made him capable of such dialogue. Newmanism, by contrast, had nothing to contribute, and its ascendancy over Pusey's mind was a grievous blow to the Movement's prospects of acting as a general religious leaven. Had there been more of original Puseyism in it, James Anthony Froude would have been less justified in describing it as 'the Oxford Counter-Reformation'.[102] Its character as Reformation would have been more in evidence.

3

To return at last to the problem of interpreting Pusey's early intellectual development, with which this paper began: as between the viewpoints of Liddon on the one hand and Forrester and Matthew on the other, where does the truth about Pusey's Tractarian 'conversion' appear to lie? Each conveys a part of the truth, Liddon by insisting that Pusey was both in fact and in intention doctrinally orthodox in his High Church upbringing and undeviating in his commitment to creeds and articles, Forrester and Matthew by pointing to his liberal attitudes toward the interpretation of Scripture, his rejection of 'human systems' and commitment to 'science'. Insofar as Liddon acknowledges Pusey's liberalism he interprets it as 'unsettlement', but Forrester and Matthew identify him in spirit with the 'Liberal Anglicans' and characterize his subsequent Tractarianism as evidence of an intellectual upheaval which involved his flight to the haven of dogmatism. In fact, however, the dogmatic principle had always been strong in him, alongside a reverence for Scripture and an earnest Protestant sense of the duty to prove doctrine against it: a duty the more pressing in view of its long neglect, leading to the proliferation of scholastic subtleties on the one hand, provoking in turn their rationalist rejection on the other. The key to Pusey's preoccupations and course lies in the fact that he was acutely aware that Protestantism was in decay and under mortal challenge.

It was of course to be his experience that the tools of the

textual critics, with which he optimistically expected to discredit pernicious scholasticism and expose presumptuous rationalism, were not merely unfitted to the task but, as he concluded in his reaction against the 'higher criticism', themselves the effective agents of unbelief. His liberalism had always been at the service of his orthodoxy, employed against the original enemy, 'orthodoxism', which was the parent of rationalism. Thus his advanced view of inspiration had as its object the identification of credal and scriptural essentials, disentangled from the weeds of orthodoxist glosses which had overgrown them. The failure of 'science' in its allotted task, and the revelation indeed of its relativist and historicist tendencies as a result of the Rose controversy, brought on a time of intellectual and emotional crisis, in 1830 and 1831, which marks a turning point in Pusey's course, not in terms of his preoccupation, which was still with the problem of finding a scriptural warrant for fundamental doctrine, but in terms of his approach to solving that problem. The withdrawal from his quest for 'usefulness' and the active pursuit of religious knowledge, which he now associated with deafness to the promptings of God in the heart, established the mental framework of teachable humility in which he would discover the long-sought answer.

Indeed, his recovery from that crisis in the years following, and accession to the ranks of the Tractarians in 1835, is best seen not as revolution but as resolution. For as we have noted, in his growing immersion in the Fathers, and acknowledgement of their superior insight and spirituality as biblical exegetes, he found the link forged between Scripture and creeds which it had always been his endeavour to assert, whether against Rose on the one hand, or Semlerian liberalism on the other. As he saw Tractarianism as the timely re-assertion of patristic principles, embodying the vital harmony of Scripture and creeds, so he was drawn to it as a campaign for renewal which understood instinctively that Protestantism's salvation from dissolution at the hands of liberalism and secularism depended on its capacity to recognize that its own foundation principle—the primacy of Scripture as interpreted by the undivided Church—was quintessentially Catholic, and that in its re-affirmation lay its prospect of recovery. If all too soon he drifted from this insight, coming under the influence of his associates to see rationalism and 'private' judgement as pertaining to the very ethos of Protestantism rather than as a cancerous growth upon it, the point is nevertheless worth repeating that not a desire to flee from the disease but the hope of effecting a cure made Pusey a Tractarian. The step was a positive one, in fulfilment of his previous course, not a negative act of self-quarantine.

NOTES

1   *Apologia*, ed. M. J. Svaglic (Oxford 1967), pp. 64–5.

2   Uncat. MSS, Pusey House, Chest B, drawer 7.

3   See, e.g., his correspondence with the *Record* (10, 22 April 1841), in reply to its article 'Dr Pusey's views of the Inspiration of Scripture' (27 March 1841). The latter explained Pusey's absence from the Hadleigh conference in 1833 by claiming that he then questioned even the divine inspiration of Scripture.

4   Pusey to Francis Rivington, 10 January 1848, Uncat. MSS, Pusey House, Chest B, drawer 3.

5   Thus, Principal John Tulloch looked to Liddon to throw light on the 'comparatively obscure' period of Pusey's life from 1828 to 1835. See *Movements of Religious Thought in Britain during the Nineteenth Century* (1885, repr. Leicester 1971), p. 109 n.

6   Liddon adjudges accordingly that no permanent addition to Pusey's religious opinions was made as a result of his German experience, but only to his scholarship and appreciation of the dangers of religious rationalism. See *Life of Pusey* (4 Vols, 1893–7), vol. 1, p. 114. He does, of course, admit the affective influence of the Pietists and their successors.

7   O. Chadwick, ed., *The Mind of the Oxford Movement* (London 1960), p. 48.

8   G. F. A. Best, 'A Letter from Pusey to Bishop Maltby', *Theology*, 61 (1958), pp. 18–21.

9   David W. F. Forrester, 'The Intellectual Development of E. B. Pusey, 1800–50' (unpublished thesis, Oxford 1967).

10   Tulloch (1885), pp. 89–91.

11   H. C. G. Matthew, 'Edward Bouverie Pusey: from Scholar to Tractarian', *JTS* n.s. 32 (1981), pp. 101–24.

12   Pusey to the Revd A. C. Hall, Boston, U.S.A., 16 June 1879. Uncat. MSS, loose letters, Pusey House.

13   P. Brendon, *Hurrell Froude and the Oxford Movement* (London 1974), pp. 19–25.

14   Liddon, vol. 1, 11; cf. Brendon, p. 17.

15 Richard Jelf to Pusey, 21 August 1821, 'Jelf to E.B.P.', 1821–65 (Liddon bound vol., Pusey House).

16 Pusey to Maria, 28 November 1827. 'E.B.P. to Miss Barker 1827–8', pp. 330–31 (Liddon bound vol., Pusey House).

17 Pusey to Maria, 16 May 1828. 'E.B.P. to Miss Barker 1828', p. 273 (Liddon bound vol., Pusey House). Pusey and Maria often corresponded about the dangerous allurements of 'Byronism'.

18 Liddon, vol. 1, p. 18.

19 Pusey to Maria, 21 February 1828. 'E.B.P. to Miss Barker 1828', p. 104.

20 Cited in Brendon, p. 70.

21 See e.g., Whately to Hawkins, 3 April 1836, on Pusey's 'back-sliding'. 'Edward Hawkins Correspondence', vol. 3, Oriel College Library.

22 For this Pusey later praised Whately as 'a most uncouth person, but most valuable'. Pusey to Maria, 8 January 1828, 'E.B.P. to Miss Barker 1827–8', p. 474.

23 Liddon, vol. 1, pp. 44–9.

24 Hibbert to Pusey, 20 November 1823. Uncat. MSS, Pusey House, Chest B, drawer 5.

25 In his *L'origine de tous les cultes* (1794).

26 Hibbert to Pusey, 11 December 1823; see 24 n. above.

27 Liddon, vol. 1; 47.

28 Pusey to Richard Salwey, ? 1825. 'E.B.P. to Salwey: 20 letters, 1821–80', letter no. 10. Uncat. MSS, loose letters, Pusey House.

29 Pusey to Philip Pusey, 1 December 1823. 'E.B.P. and Philip Pusey, 1821–54', p. 46. (Liddon bound vol., Pusey House.)

30 Pusey was especially impressed by Gottfried Less, *Wahrheit des christlichen Religion* (Göttingen 1795).

31 *Apologia*, pp. 101, 538.

32 Brendon, p. 69.

33 Pusey to William Ince, 18 November 1878. Uncat. MSS, Pusey House, Chest B, drawer 7.

34 As Pusey could still write of himself as late as 1839. Pusey to H.E.Manning, 4 December 1839. 'E.B.P. to Manning, 1837–50' (Liddon bound vol., Pusey House).

35 A brief notice of the subject matter of Lloyd's lectures is in E.S.Ffoulkes, *A History of the Church of S. Mary the Virgin, Oxford* (London 1892), pp. 400–4.

36 Even so, Pusey took the step only with trepidation. Pusey to Salwey, 23 November? 1825. 'E.B.P. to Salwey: 20 letters, 1821–80', letter no. 11.

37 Pusey to J.Parker, 25 May 1825. Loose letters, transcribed, Pusey House. Perhaps the fullest account of his reasons for going to, and the nature of his studies in, Germany, was given by Pusey to Hawkins in

1827. 'Edward Hawkins Correspondence', vol. 8, no. 757, Oriel College Library.

38 Respectively professors of philosophy and theology at Göttingen.

39 Pusey to Newman, 9, 11 August 1825. 'E.B.P. to Newman', vol. 1, 1823–36, pp. 20–3 (Liddon bound vol., Pusey House). In the event Newman did adopt this 'rationalizing' distinction, derived from Less.

40 Pusey to Lloyd, 29 August 1826. 'E.B.P. to Bishop Lloyd, 1826–28'. (Liddon bound vol., Pusey House.)

41 See I. Ellis, 'Schleiermacher in Britain', *Scottish Journal of Theology*, 33 (1980), pp. 422–3.

42 See e.g. his exposition of it to Keble, 18 April 1829. 'E.B.P., Correspondence with Keble', vol. 1, 1823–45, pp. 18–19. (Liddon bound vol., Pusey House.)

43 Geoffrey Faber, *Oxford Apostles* (1933, repr. Penguin 1954), p. 138.

44 On Schleiermacher's failure to root his pietism in a reverent biblical science, see Tulloch, *Theological Tendencies of the Age* (Edinburgh 1885), pp. 23–7.

45 A. L. Drummond, *German Protestantism since Luther* (London 1951), p. 132.

46 Ibid., p. 127.

47 See generally Pusey's letters to Maria, 4 October 1827 to 8 January 1828, but especially that of 3 January 1828. 'E.B.P. to Miss Barker, 1827–8'.

48 Pusey to Maria, 19–21 October 1827. Ibid., p. 76.

49 Pusey to Tholuck, 29 June 1829. 'E.B.P. and Professor A. Tholuck' (Liddon bound vol., Pusey House).

50 Pusey to Newman, 25 November 1826, 9 January 1827. 'E.B.P. to Newman', vol. 1, pp. 43–8, 65–6.

51 Pusey to Lloyd, 26 February 1827. 'E.B.P. to Bishop Lloyd, 1826–8'.

52 Lücke to Pusey, 22 February 1827. 'German Correspondence of E.B.P.', pp. 195–8. (Liddon bound vol., Pusey House.)

53 Pusey to Maria, 4 October 1827. 'E.B.P. to Miss Barker, 1827–8', p. 50.

54 *The State of the Protestant Religion in Germany*, Cambridge 1825, pp. 10–18. For a recent account of the Pusey-Rose controversy see Ellis, pp. 420–2, 426–7.

55 *An Historical Enquiry*, pt 1 (London 1828), p. 14 *et seq.* On his use of Neander, see pt 2 (London 1830), p. 399.

56 Ibid., pt 1, p. 53 *et seq.*

57 Ibid., pp. 179–86.

58 Pusey's use of Tholuck's unpublished lectures briefly strained relations between the friends, since Tholuck had forgotten giving permission to draw upon them, and the publication of an English translation of them in America in 1827 provoked Rose to hint that his antagonist was guilty

of unacknowledged plagiarism. See Tholuck to Pusey, 23 March, 3 June 1829, and Pusey to Tholuck, 28 April, 29 June 1829, 'E.B.P. and Professor Tholuck'. Tholuck later published works entitled *Vorgeschichte des Rationalismus*, 2 vols. (Halle 1853–62), and *Geschichte des Rationalismus* (Berlin 1865), which are still standard references in seventeenth and eighteenth century Lutheranism. See too Liddon, vol. 1, pp. 161–2.

59   *An Historical Enquiry*, pt 1, p. 185.

60   Pusey to Maria, 30 May 1828. 'E.B.P. to Miss Barker, 1828', p. 315.

61   Blanco White to Pusey, 10 June 1828. Uncat. MSS, Pusey House, Chest B, drawer 3.

62   *A Letter to the Lord Bishop of London* (London 1829), p. 59.

63   *The Scholastic Philosophy considered in its Relation to Christian Theology* (Oxford 1833).

64   *A Letter to the Bishop of London*, pp. 64–7.

65   Pusey to Maria, 4 October 1827. 'E.B.P. to Miss Barker, 1827–8', p. 41.

66   Tholuck to Pusey, 3 September 1839. 'E.B.P. and Professor Tholuck'. On the idea of 'accommodation', see too D. Forbes, *The Liberal Anglican Idea of History* (Cambridge 1952), pp. 75–82.

67   Pusey to Lloyd, 6 October 1828. 'E.B.P. to Bishop Lloyd, 1826–8'.

68   Pusey to Newman, 29 September 1829. 'E.B.P. to Newman', vol. 1, 1823–36, pp. 155–6.

69   Pusey to Newman, ? October 1829. Ibid., pp. 168–9.

70   Tholuck to Pusey, 23 August 1829. 'E.B.P. and Professor Tholuck'.

71   *An Historical Enquiry*, pt 2, pp. 11–13.

72   Ibid., pp. 35–42.

73   Ibid., pp. 403–12.

74   Ibid., p. 95.

75   Newman too had feared the consequences of preferring intellectual to moral excellence. *Apologia*, p. 26.

76   Keble to Pusey, 19 April 1829. 'E.B.P., Correspondence with Keble', vol. 1, 1823–45, pp. 12–14.

77   On Heb. 12, 14. Uncat. MSS, Pusey House, Chest B, drawer 2.

78   Pusey to Benjamin Harrison, 1 August 1832. 'E.B.P. to Archdeacon Harrison', vol. 1, 1831–3. (Liddon bound vol., Pusey House.)

79   Pusey to Newman, 1 February 1831. 'E.B.P. to Newman', vol. 1, 1823–36, pp. 175–7.

80   Lücke to Pusey, 28 May 1830; Chevalier Bunsen to Pusey, 20 December 1830. 'German Correspondence of E.B.P.', pp. 206–8, 55–63.

81   Pusey to Tholuck, 8 November 1830. 'E.B.P. and Professor Tholuck'.

82   Pusey to Tholuck, 4 August 1834, ibid. Cited by Liddon, vol. 1, p. 296.

83 H. Harris, *David Friedrich Strauss and his Theology* (Cambridge 1973), p. 41.

84 Tholuck to Pusey, 21 February 1836. 'E.B.P. and Professor Tholuck'.

85 Liddon, vol. 1, pp. 120–1.

86 Prestige writes of his theological liberalism 'imperceptibly' merging into 'an affectionate reliance on the Fathers'. G. L. Prestige, *Pusey* (London 1933), p. 46.

87 Forrester, pp. 160–8.

88 Pusey to Manning, 22 January 1845. 'E.B.P. to Manning, 1837–50'.

89 A. M. Allchin, 'The theological vision of the Oxford Movement', J. Coulson and A. M. Allchin, eds., *The Rediscovery of Newman* (London 1967), pp. 56–7.

90 Matthew, p. 114.

91 Forrester, thesis abstract.

92 Pusey defended the Tractarian 'persecution' of Hampden to Tholuck as the appropriate way of dealing with heresy. Pusey to Tholuck, 6 March 1837. 'E.B.P. and Professor Tholuck'.

93 Liddon, vol. 1, p. 174.

94 See 47 n above.

95 Pusey to Lloyd, 6 October 1828. 'E.B.P. to Bishop Lloyd, 1826–28'.

96 Pusey to Harrison, 16 April 1835. 'E.B.P. to Archdeacon Harrison', vol. 1, 1831–3.

97 Pusey to Maria, 11 November 1835. 'E.B.P. to Mrs Pusey, 1828–38', pp. 122–6 (Liddon bound vol., Pusey House).

98 Pusey contrasted his own wayward progress with Newman's 'steady course', seeing in the one self-indulgent busyness and in the other self-denial and tranquillity. Pusey to Maria, 4 November 1835. Ibid., pp. 77–8.

99 Pusey to W. F. Hook, 22 September 1845. 'E.B.P. to Dr Hook, 1827–48', pp. 275–7. (Liddon bound vol., Pusey House.)

100 Matthew, pp. 101, 119–20.

101 *A Narrative of Events* connected with the publication of the *Tracts for the Times* (London, 1843, repr. 1883), p. 67.

102 *Short Studies on Great Subjects*, 4 vols. (1891 edn), vol. 4, pp. 231–360.

2

Coleridge as a Background to the Oxford Movement

MARTIN ROBERTS

Whatever one makes of that highly complex thinker, poet, and social critic, there can be no doubt that S. T. Coleridge has charmed the sensibilities of diverse thinkers over the last two hundred years and still appeals to us today as fresh and relevant to contemporary problems and concerns. His seminal mind produced no system and founded no movement and yet it did plant (and continues to plant) seeds in many different soils, so that whatever growth emerged in some measure carried his mark.

It is therefore not inappropriate that an attempt should be made to assess his significance for the rise and development of the Oxford Movement, bearing in mind that he died in 1834 and that his poetic intelligence was congenial to such Tractarian figures as Keble and Newman, even though the latter denied explicitly 'Coleridgean' elements in his thought. In fact, Coleridge was peculiarly well placed, historically and intellectually, to have at least an unconscious influence on the development of the Tractarian tradition (it might be difficult to locate precise and specific influences), inasmuch as he stood at the cross-roads of what may be called, in very broad terms, eighteenth-century rationalism and nineteenth-century romanticism. He understood both the Kantian critiques of human reason, with the corresponding enlightenment scepticism about the 'status' of the supernatural in relation to human concerns, and the romantic quest for a spiritual liberation of man through the use of the imagination and poetic intelligence. In fact, concern about the supernatural would of necessity be crucially important to rationalists, romantic poets and Tractarian

34

thinkers alike, the latter of whom saw problems in a purely man-centred view of religion and spirituality. For any given view of the supernatural inevitably has important consequences not just for faith, but for a theory of knowledge generally. Now Coleridge himself, by the circumstances of his life, was obliged to face the issue of the supernatural both in rational and poetic terms. His thoughts are therefore likely to be germane to Tractarian perspectives on this and related issues.

Our present concern then, will be to unfold the ways in which Coleridge approached the supernatural so that his belief in a transcendent personal God, who discloses himself definitively in the person of Christ and the Church, may shed some light on the Tractarian concern for the Church as the 'focus' of the supernatural precisely as the 'body of Christ'.

1

Coleridge's concern with the supernatural is something essentially practical, directed towards the formation and coherence of his own self-consciousness, rather than towards an esoteric 'occult' knowledge of some kind. For Coleridge, belief in and commitment to the supernatural had to 'work' in terms of illuminating his life and filling it with purpose and direction. It is his quest to penetrate the foundations of religion and morality in a way that prevents any separation of speculative thought on the one hand, and moral behaviour on the other, that led Coleridge to retire to Somersetshire, where the sheer vastness of the supernatural broke in upon him precisely in his efforts to sort out his own life.

> I retired to a cottage in Somersetshire at the foot of Quantock, and devoted my thoughts and studies to the foundations of religion and morality. Here I found myself all afloat. Doubts rushed in; broke upon me 'from the fountain of the great deep' and fell 'from the windows of heaven.' The fontal truths of natural religion and the books of Revelation alike contributed to the flood; and it was long ere my ark touched on Ararat, and rested. The idea of the Supreme Being appeared to me to be as necessarily implied in all

particular modes of being, as the idea of infinite space in all the geometrical figures by which space is limited. . . .[1]

It will be evident that Coleridge's working from the standpoint of his own self-consciousness, obliges him to begin to ascend to the idea of the Supreme Being, which is necessarily involved in the formation and coherence of his *own* self-consciousness. The idea of the Supreme Being, far from being a merely speculative notion, is, says Coleridge, 'necessarily implied in all particular modes of being'. In other words, Coleridge cannot *be* the Coleridge he is, apart from his dependence upon the Supreme Being; for it is only by beginning to ascend to the latter, as a sort of 'apex' of his own self-consciousness, that Coleridge can start to make some sense of his own life. Apart from such a willingness to 'admit' the Supreme Being into his own consciousness, Coleridge's very consciousness as such would forever be in danger of dissipating itself into a formless stream of sensations. The point is, it is not only the coherence of consciousness which is at stake with his concern for the supernatural, but more fundamentally, the ability to *form* consciousness at all. Coleridge seems to be feeling his way towards a 'centre', around which he can form himself and thereby establish his own coherence, and this centre is something which can only be known at all, insofar as he dynamically 'admits' the idea of the Supreme Being into his own life. We can begin to see then, that for Coleridge, the supernatural is crucial not merely for arriving at a religious faith, but more importantly, for the *formation* of consciousness in its most essential and basic requirements.

Furthermore, an important feature of Coleridge's experience of the supernatural, in the way we have described it, is the sense of awe and wonder and reverence, which must in some way be present, if the Supreme Being is to be admitted and consciousness moulded and shaped. Coleridge's sense of the vast or infinite is no cosy arm-chair speculation but rather, a deep feeling (even a fight) which is central to the dynamic *constitution* of his own personality and its coherence. (Such constitutive power here removes Coleridge from a more Kantian 'regulative' notion of the categories of knowledge.) Infinity and personality must somehow go together, so that the *personality* of the Supreme Being, admitted into his own consciousness, is the condition of Coleridge becoming and remaining a *person*. The following citation is perhaps illuminating:

> For a very long time indeed I could not reconcile personality with infinity; and my head was with Spinoza, though my whole heart remained with Paul and John. Yet there had dawned upon me, even before I had met with the *Critique of Pure Reason*, a certain guiding light. If the mere intellect could make no certain discovery of a holy and intelligent first cause, it might yet supply a demonstration that no legitimate argument could be drawn from the intellect *against* its truth. . . .[2]

We can see Coleridge's consciousness so forming and cohering that it is becoming aware of itself as standing in another person's *presence*, that of the Supernatural as personal and not abstract.

Now if it is objected that Coleridge's 'path' to the supernatural via his own self-consciousness is merely *subjective*, it will have to be noted that subjectivity, in the Coleridgean sense, is rather more 'objective' than might at first be supposed. For it is only by dependently 'admitting' the Supernatural into consciousness that the latter's formation can begin in a way that involves purposeful *direction* and coherence, and it is only at a certain level of formation, growth and commitment to this directional formation, that consciousness comes to 'behold' itself in the *presence* of the infinite as personal, so that to deny the 'objectivity' of that encounter would necessarily involve committing intellectual and moral suicide, by denying the reality of that which had brought consciousness into the *presence* of the supernatural as personal. To put it crudely, it would involve cutting-off the branch on which one was sitting.

Coleridge actually forces us to ask just what is present or given in self-consciousness, and his concern with the supernatural, subjective though it is, obliges us to view our religious faith in rather more 'objective' terms. What we believe about God cannot be confined to the private sector, but is something which must be thrown open to the most rigorous investigations of all

men, obliging us to ask just what conditions must be present if
we are to evaluate our common humanity.

Furthermore, Coleridge insists that we must 'admit' the
supernatural as personal by an act of the *moral will*, apart from
which, a mere intellectual ascent is no better than a cold
mechanism:

> I became convinced that religion, as both the corner-stone
> and the key-stone of morality, must have a moral origin; so
> far at least, that the evidence of its doctrines could not, like
> the truths of abstract science, be wholly independent of the
> will. . . .[3]

The willingness to ascend volitionally to the Supreme Being
is an indispensible *condition* of achieving the sort of coherent and
directed consciousness, which Coleridge describes. Actually,
Coleridge pushes us still further in the direction of 'admitting'
the supernatural as personal when, in one of his notebook
entries, he asserts that all human virtue *depends* on obedience to
God who reveals himself as legislator, by appealing to the
universal reason in us all:

> Conditions of human virtue [That there is a Being, whose will
> comprises in itself Goodness, & power in the plenitude of
> perfection—that Man is not that Being—that Man possesses
> a free will separable from perfect Reason, & yet by the very
> act of separating ceases to be *free*, and retaining one sole
> releict of freedom, *Guilt*! the Guilt of Suicide!—God
> manifests himself to Man, as Legislator, by the Law of
> Universal Reason, the *obedience* to which is not only perfect
> Freedom, but the only possible Freedom: The law appealing
> to the Free Will, i.e., Reason with the consciousness of will is
> conscience] where there is no Law, there must be Tyranny—
> and this will be either *ab extra*, or *a se*—the tyranny of satanic
> pride, or of bestial Sensuality. Without God Man ceases to be
> Man, & either soars into a Devil or sinks into a Beast-
> Spasm. . . .[4]

Coleridge is again practical rather than merely speculative,
this time forcing us to account for our *freedom* as human beings
and to recognize what conditions must be present for its

exercise. As far as Coleridge is concerned, man only learns what freedom means by experiencing, in the act of separating himself from perfect (supernatural) Reason, the crippling effects of *guilt*, and thereby working back from guilt towards the possibility of freedom via *obedience* and conformity to the One who alone is free and the source of all freedom. In fact, the enlightenment tendency towards a man-centred subjective individualism is here repudiated in a severely practical way, since the achievement of human virtue simply cannot happen until one admits, by experiencing guilt, that one is *not* that Being who contains all goodness and power in himself. If the supernatural belongs only to man's imaginative or poetic capacities, if the vast and the infinite is nothing more than his dream, then the formation and coherence of man's consciousness towards the production of the 'good', is just not possible. As Coleridge says, *without* God (as the 'personal' supernatural, in his own right) man literally ceases to be himself and soars into a devil or sinks into a beast-spasm.

Coleridge gives eloquent expression to his deep conviction that Man is nothing without God, and that his maturing subjectivity propels him through his existence into his essential and eternal union with God in whom alone his restless yearnings cease (like Augustine), in a letter written to his friend, Poole, at the latter's bereavement due to the death of his mother:

> . . . As all things Pass away & those Habits are broken up which constitute our own peculiar Self, our nature by a moral instinct cherishes the desire of an unchangeable Something, & thereby awakens or stirs up anew the Passion to promote *permanent* Good, & facilitate that grand business of our Existence—still further, & further still, to generalise our affections, till *Existence* itself is swallowed up in *Being*, & we are in Christ even as he is in the Father.[5]

To recapitulate so far: We are contending that Coleridge's 'path' to the supernatural is one which engages the most searching questions about human nature. He does not retreat into a private 'religious' sector to settle the problems of his own identity and coherence, but sees the need to inquire into the identity of human nature in specifically *theological* terms. This theological investigation is one which involves a perpetual ascent of the whole man, intellectually and volitionally, apart from which one cannot even get started with the business of self-understanding. Furthermore, the notion of *commitment* to the supernatural as personal is central to the whole enterprise. There can be no standing back morally and emotionally, since a mere intellectual ascent does nothing to shape and direct the human *person*, who, in the first place, is trying to come to terms with himself. Coleridge also obliges us to ask deep questions about the nature of subjectivity and what 'happens' when one puts into practice the necessary conditions (such as ascent, commitment and faith) without which consciousness can never be formulated, directed and organized around a 'centre' which is capable of producing man's ultimate 'good'. The experience of encounter in our consciousness, and the presence of the infinite as other than self and yet personal, obliges us to consider the possibility of an 'objective' ground and source of our consciousness, growth and coherence, precisely *within* its subjectivity. And to the extent that Coleridge offers us a 'path' to the supernatural which claims 'objective' status for the supernatural as that which is personal (in fact, super-personal) in its own right, he provides an alternative perspective on man's imagination and poetic intelligence which makes significant departures from the man-centred subjective individualism of many romantic and idealist thinkers. It is perhaps this new perspective which can be regarded as one of the background influences on the Oxford Movement with its specifically theological and ecclesiastical concerns, as far as the supernatural is seen to be indispensable to the achievement of the 'good' life, or growth in holiness.

2

So much for the theological thrust of Coleridge's experience of the supernatural, but what of the ecclesiastical dimension insofar as the latter (as the Tractarian tradition was well aware) focuses or makes concrete and visible the theocentric character of the supernatural? What was Coleridge's estimation of the Christian Church in his experience of the supernatural as personal? Did he simply idealize or internalize the concrete visibility of the Church by some poetic or imaginative device, which finally regards the Christian Church as little more than a human institution which, at best, articulates the highest aspirations of a man-centred spirituality? Or did he regard the Church as of divine (i.e., supernatural) origin (albeit it a human institution as well) and dependent for its on-going life upon supernatural resources?

Given our exposition of Coleridge's view of the supernatural one might expect to find him taking a somewhat 'human' view of the Church, bearing in mind his essentially subjective approach to the supernatural. But deeper reflection will make such a view unlikely, especially if Coleridge's subjectivity is, at its centre, formed and directed by an 'objective' (i.e., having its own non-human status) supernatural (personal) power which must be obeyed if human freedom is to be attained. And if so, as we have seen, Coleridge insists on human obedience to God who reveals himself as legislator through the law of universal human Reason, then we may legitimately ask him just where the *focus* of that divine revelation is to be located in a concrete and visible way. *Where*, in other words, is God's legislation to be found and obeyed?

Is there an implicit gathered community which is brought into existence by the revelation of God through the law of universal human Reason? One might well expect so, and one could not be blamed for wanting a concrete and visible expression of the interaction of God's revelation and Man's obediential response and consequent spiritual growth. Coleridge's grasp of the supernatural could well imply (for its viability) a concrete and visible community in which human Reason, in its response to divine revelation, is *articulated* as such in the world, and spiritual growth nurtured. The church could then be understood as a divinely appointed community in which society at large is able to focus its response to God and live explicitly in the presence of the supernatural. This community would not be a merely *human* invention (though it would have a considerable poetic and imaginative thrust to its life, which incidentally, is evident in a number of Tractarian Churchmen) since its identity would issue out of the objectivity of the supernatural, as the latter's concrete and visible human focus.

The difficulty, of course, is to know just how to formulate such a view of the Church so that the divine initiative and sustaining principle of its life is safeguarded and not reduced into a merely human institution.

Now for Coleridge this is again a very practical issue concerning the ultimate *authority* of the Church and in his book *On the Constitution of the Church and State: according to the Idea of Each*,[6] he addresses himself to this problem by asking just how the life-style of the Christian Church achieves a progressive civilization of the human community at large.[7] This he does by distinguishing four marks or qualities which must be present if the idea of the Christian Church is to be capable of fulfilling its vocation and not degenerating into a mere human institution along with all sorts of other human institutions.

First, he says that the Christian Church is not a kingdom or realm or state of the *world*. It is rather the 'appointed opposite of them all *Collectively*—the *sustaining, correcting, befriending* Opposite of the world!'.[8] It completes and strengthens the edifice of the State, without interference or commixture and helps bring about the highest good of society (here Coleridge's poetical and imaginative component in the life of the Church is to be discerned).

The second characteristic of the Christian Church is that it is objective in its nature and purpose: a visible, not secret, community consisting of visible and public communities.[9] The Church has both a hidden identity, issuing as it does from the supernatural (hence it is the opposite of the world), and a visible and concrete expression, insofar as it exists to 'befriend' and bring the world to its highest dignity. The Church is then, both ideal and real, invisible and concrete, human and divine, other-worldly and yet in this world existing in concrete communities. That is why Coleridge insists that the true identity of the Christian Church cannot be identified *exclusively* with any one of its concrete manifestations (e.g., Anglican, Roman, and so on[10]) without giving up its 'ideal' and divine nature and origin.

Now this leads directly into the question of the *authority* of the Church and where it is to be located. Coleridge says, thirdly, that the Christian Church, as both human and divine, must necessarily lack any visible head or Sovereign, or personal centre of unity, or any single source of power.[11] Thus:

> . . . the unitive relation of the churches to each other, and of each to all, being *actual* indeed, but likewise equally *IDEAL*, i.e., mystical and supersensuous, as the relation of the whole church to its one invisible Head, the Church with and under Christ, as one kingdom or state, is hidden. . . .[12]

The invisibility of the Church's authority or Headship is crucially important for Coleridge and in saying that such authority must be both real and ideal, human and divine, he points to the 'focus' of this dialectical authority and thereby to the focus of divine revelation in the person of Christ, as both divine and human. There, in Christ's *personhood*, the supernatural (as personal) can be seen to authenticate itself in a way which is personal, and which issues in a concrete and visible expression of itself in the Christian Church, the latter of which only lives in the dialectic of its real and ideal nature.

The fourth characteristic of the Christian Church is its universality or catholicity:

> . . . it is neither Anglican, Gallican, nor Roman, neither Latin nor Greek. Even the Catholic and Apostolic Church *of* England is a less safe expression than the churches of Christ in England: though the Catholic Church *in* England, or (what would be better still) the Catholic Church under Christ throughout Great Britain and Ireland, is justifiable and appropriate: for through the presence of its only head and sovereign, entire in each and one in all, the Church universal is spiritually perfect in every true Church, and of course in any number of such Churches, which from circumstance or place, or the community of country or of language, we have occasion to speak of collectively. . . .[13]

Given such catholicity of the Christian Church with its one true head, perfect in all 'true' churches, Coleridge expresses both the authority of the Church and its universality of application as follows:

> There can be no such head but Christ, who is not mere man, but God in the Divine Humanity, and therefore present with

every part of the Church; and every member thereof, at what distance soever.[14]

Now given these four necessary marks of the Christian Church it is possible to appreciate in Coleridge's theological grasp of the supernatural, a necessary ecclesiastical focus in the life of the Christian Church, that divine/human institution whose communities and members express the single life of its head in the divine humanity of Christ. His view of the supernatural leads naturally and inevitably into membership of the supernatural community of the 'body of Christ' in which alone *commitment* to and growth in the supernatural as personal, becomes possible. And in this grasp of the supernatural, at once theological and ecclesiastical, rather than man-centred and individualistic, Coleridge's poetic intelligence and imagination is harnessed in the service of the supernatural in the same way as those later poetic intellects of the Oxford Movement, who were to find their home within the supernatural 'body of Christ'. Actually, Coleridge's vision of the Church is one which seeks to vindicate its divine origin and power in terms of the necessary 'inner' conditions of man's consciousness, imagination and quest for self-identity. And to this extent it inevitably lifts the concerns of history and tradition into a wider and more imaginative life in the 'idea', to use a Coleridgean word. In such a living and imaginative 'idea', all opposites meet and are reconciled dynamically; church and world, human and divine, ideal and real, converge and dialectically live out and dependently express the hidden head and source of all things in God, focused definitively in Christ who is 'God in the Divine Humanity'. Of course, Coleridge's views provide no easy solutions to contemporary 'ecumenical' debates (they probably even complicate matters), but he does offer a rather distinctive, living and imaginative approach to these issues which not only questions the *ways* in which ecumenical debates are to be adequately formulated and by what criteria they are to be assessed, but actually (and perhaps more importantly) offers a defence of the supernatural nature of the Church, which is capable of speaking effectively to those people who have little knowledge of or interest in the historical Christian tradition.

3

To recapitulate the argument so far. We have contended that it is possible to discern in Coleridge two broad areas of concern (that of the ascent of consciousness and its concrete ecclesiastical focus or shape) which indwell each other and suppose each other if both man's consciousness and the Church are to relate to each other necessarily. Perhaps it is just this double concern of Coleridge's which prefigures some of the basic concerns and interests of the Oxford Movement. In fact, the remainder of this essay will be devoted to this 'double concern', as we have called it, and to view it, in relation to the thought of E. B. Pusey, as relevant to some of the interests of the Oxford Movement. Our aim is clearly not to trace any direct influences of Coleridge upon Pusey, but rather to see whether the sort of Coleridgean 'ethos' which we have described, is in some ways echoed within the spirituality of the Tractarian tradition.

For the sake of clarity and conciseness, attention will be devoted to one of Pusey's University Sermons.[15]

In this Sermon, it is quite remarkable to see how the structure of the text moves (in a sort of Coleridgean fashion) from a general consideration of the nature of human consciousness (in a somewhat speculative and philosophical way) towards a rather more concrete, ecclesiastical 'focus' of the movement of consciousness towards God and a genuinely theological self-understanding. In fact, Pusey, as we shall demonstrate, begins to unfold something very like Coleridge's ascent of consciousness in which God is seen as indispensible to *man's* authentic self-understanding, as a sort of 'apex' to man's moral and intellectual development. Pusey goes on to say that the 'natural' and the 'supernatural', far from opposing each other, are actually 'co-ordinate'[16] with each other. So let us see how this Coleridgean pattern of ascent, moving towards an ecclesiastical focus, is developed by Pusey in this sermon.

First, Pusey is preaching this sermon to the *University* of Oxford, and at the outset, paints a very broad picture of 'God', largely in terms of the necessity of the idea of God for epistemology in general. 'God' and the University have to be seen together from the *start*, necessarily (i.e., epistemologically)

45

before the 'logic' of the specifically *Christian* focus of God in Christ can be understood. Thus—

> ... The University includes within its range, the knowledge of God, the Author of all, as He has revealed Himself unto us, and then of that all, which He has displayed before us or laid up within us; their laws and their principles; that concentrated world within us, our mind, our conscience, our moral and intellectual being, in itself and as bearing on our fellow men. ... [17]

Pusey seems to be saying that all true knowledge, belonging to the intellect, the conscience, morality, society and so on, is contained within God and flows from God, so that 'God' is discovered *within* man's subjectivity as the immanent principle of the possibility and coherence of all knowledge. If a university is concerned with the intellect, conscience, morality, and so forth, then the notion of *God* functions as the 'other side' of the 'university' as the *condition* of the very growth and creativity of all knowledge. God, for Pusey, is 'the direct contradiction of that system of "non-intervention"'.[18] Pusey is clearly concerned with a God who *acts* in human affairs, in the sense that epistemology generally (if it is to 'work' coherently) must take seriously the idea of God as something immanent to itself. Pusey also follows Coleridge's (and post-enlightenment) willingness to locate the sphere of God's activity within the *human subject* (the 'natural' and the 'supernatural' are *co-ordinate*).[19]

Let us see how Pusey continues his broad 'epistemological' line of theological thinking:

> Even that strange form of Atheism, which would make to itself a god out of past, present, future, humanity, while it means to deify itself, what does it but own one continuous, eternal, all-pervading intelligent, self-existing Life, which alone gives oneness to the manifoldness of human existence, present to each, animating each? It denies the personality of God, but it, so far, bears witness to His presence with the Soul. It cannot conceive of the soul, as independent of God. ... Pantheism, strictly, denies its own personality, but asserts emphatically the Presence of God within the human

46

being. Man's consciousness of his God, in Whose Image he was made, bursts forth uncontrolably from the bonds of his false systems. Insanity itself, it is said, never wholly destroys the consciousness of the 'I'; Man's personal being, apart from all which he may imagine of himself. . . .[20]

Here, Pusey concentrates his thinking upon the presence of God in man's subjectivity, or the co-inherence of the natural and the supernatural, by considering the difficulties and self-contradictions which arise from pantheism and types of atheism which deny personality to the principle of 'oneness' in the multiplicity of life. That is to say, the *life* of the multiplicity of things, its givenness, or oneness (in the sense that the multiplicity of life actually *does* cohere before we consider just *how* it does) turns out to be *less* than personal, *less* than the multiplicity of life, if it is impersonal. And then, that which is 'lower' (oneness, in the a-theistic sense) is supposed to support what is presumably the 'higher' multiplicity of life. The result is a self-contradiction of life against itself. And Pusey therefore concludes that if an adequate 'oneness' (which can *support* multiplicity) is to emerge in life, this can only happen if the human soul (or subject) is *not* conceived of as independent of a living 'personal' God.

Perhaps the clearest statement of Pusey's intents here is to be found in a passage where he speaks about the co-inherence of the natural and the supernatural, nature and grace:

The natural and the supernatural, nature and grace, the ever-present creation of God's creatures involved in their continuous preservation, and the superadded beneficence whereby God bestows upon us continually what is beyond the exigencies and powers of nature, to prepare us for our supernatural end, Himself, the perpetual concurrence of God's upholding power in conformity to our natural being, whereby He sustains and supplies every power of thought, the strength of our frames, the clearness of our understandings, . . . whereby He lifts the soul above nature . . . *these two systems do not contradict, they are co-ordinate with one another*. . . .[21]

Notice the phrase 'perpetual concurrence' in respect of God's

47

activity. Pusey (like Coleridge) wants to hold Man and God together so that *God* indwells Man, or the supernatural is the immanent principle of the 'continuous preservation' of the natural, supplying and sustaining every power of human thought. God is 'immanent' in the sense that He is the living principle of *continuity* and the *sustaining* power in every human act. But more than this, Pusey goes on to say that God not only continues and sustains, but he *elevates* Man's soul *above* nature, to a participation in the *supernatural*. Here then, we discern a dynamic *ascent* of Man to a theological apex in which human identity is definitively disclosed. That is to say, the 'natural' is dynamically contained *within* the all-inclusive 'supernatural' (via a Coleridgean type of spiritual ascent of consciousness) so that there is for Man, continuity *with* purposeful progression (towards the supernatural, through a spiritual ascent of consciousness). And this *concurrence* of continuity and progression (so close to Coleridge's heart) enables Pusey to affirm that 'these two systems (the natural and the supernatural) do not contradict each other, they are co-ordinate with one another.'

So much for Pusey's 'Coleridgean' (epistemological and spiritual) ascent of consciousness. But what of its ecclesiastical focus?

Towards the close of this sermon, Pusey begins to 'focus' his vision both christologically and ecclesiastically, connecting the two by the dynamic biblical notion of 'the body of Christ'.

First, Jesus Christ, God and Man, is the 'cause', 'pattern', and 'end' of Man's spiritual life or ascent of consciousness, as we have described it. Pusey tells us why Christ is all these things, in the following citation:

> Jesus Christ, God and Man, is Himself, the Cause, the Pattern, the End of the supernatural life of man; the cause, in that the merits of Christ are the source of all grace to us, and from Him it flows to us; the Model, for He received all, that it might pass to us, and '*that* mind might be formed' in the members 'which was also in Christ' our Head; the End, for, as the glory of God is the end of all Creation, so all the graces of the Redeemed are to the praise of the glory of Christ. . . .[22]

The notion of the 'members' of Christ, who have the *mind* of

48

Christ, and in whom Christ is the *Head*, enables a bridge to be constructed between the christological 'focus' of the revelation of God in man's spiritual life (or ascent of consciousness, as we have also described it) and the *ecclesiastical* embodiment of the supernatural, spiritual life which flows from Christ as Head. And Pusey expresses this explicitly in terms of 'the Body of Christ':

> He gives them [i.e., spiritual gifts] us in common, as members of the Body of Christ, to bind us the more to one another. But what He gives to all, He gives individually to each . . . in the Holy Eucharist, by the miracle of His love, you eat the Flesh (He says) of the Son of Man, and drink His Blood; you dwell in Christ and Christ in you; are one with Christ and Christ with you. . . .[23]

Thus, finally, we find a full 'pattern' of spiritual ascent (in this Sermon) which, starting with the 'givenness' of consciousness (the co-inherence of the natural and the supernatural) finally focuses itself in Christ and his Body, the Church. The latter is thereby the supernatural community living the spiritual life, but a spiritual *life* which is *continuous* (yet progressive) with the life of the human spirit generally and its ascent.

Perhaps we could appropriately close this essay by saying that Pusey, like Coleridge, seems to be striving after a grasp of the spiritual life which is capable of addressing itself directly to man's ascent of consciousness in general; to this end, the creative use of imagination and of a 'poetic' sensibility may be regarded as a real contribution to human concerns common to all men, as well as a possible form of Christian apologetics. In this sense, perhaps both Pusey and Coleridge share something of the same spiritual 'ethos' and both alike are well aware of the disastrous consequences which will follow, both for the church and the world, if the two drift apart and man's 'spiritual' life is pushed into the purely private sector.

NOTES

1 Coleridge *Biographia Literaria*, ed. G. Watson (London, J. M. Dent, 1977), p. 111.

2 Ibid., p. 112.

3 Ibid., p. 113.

4 Coleridge *Collected Notebooks of STC*, ed. K.Coburn, 3 vols. (London, Routledge, 1973), vol. 3, 3866 n.

5 Coleridge *Collected Letters of STC*, ed. E.L.Griggs, 6 vols. (Oxford, 1956), *Letter 412*, vol. 2, p. 758.

6 Coleridge *On the Constitution of the Church and State: according to the Idea of Each* (London, J.M.Dent, 1972).

7 Ibid., p. 97.

8 Ibid., p. 98.

9 Ibid., pp. 99–100.

10 Ibid., p. 106.

11 Ibid., p. 101.

12 Ibid., pp. 103–4.

13 Ibid., pp. 106–7.

14 Ibid., p. 108.

15 E. B. Pusey, *Sermon 2, Sermons preached before the University of Oxford between 1859 and 1872* (Oxford, James Parker, 1872).

16 Ibid., p. 44.

17 Ibid., p. 33.

18 Ibid., p. 33.

19 Ibid., p. 44.

20 Ibid., pp. 36–7.

21 Ibid., pp. 43–4.

22 Ibid., p. 47.

23 Ibid., p. 50.

3

Pusey's 'Lectures on Types and Prophecies of the Old Testament'

DAVID JASPER

The manuscript of Pusey's 'Lectures on Types and Prophecies', bound in a slim red volume of some 125 leaves, once formed part of the library of Pusey's biographer, H. P. Liddon, and is now lodged in the library of Pusey House, Oxford. The fly-leaf informs us that the lectures were written 'mainly in July–August, 1836'. In his four-volume *Life of Edward Bouverie Pusey* (London, 1893–5), Liddon grants them but the briefest mention and never quotes from them. He remarks that they were written during the Long Vacation of 1836, concurrent with Pusey's interest in the Library of the Fathers, and the frequent and detailed references to patristic theology in the lectures are evidence of his contemporary concerns.

The manuscript is fragmentary, and it seems that Pusey was never completely satisfied with it. Liddon quotes from a letter written on 15 September, to the Revd B. Harrison, later archdeacon of Maidstone:

> I have not yet got through the types and prophecies of the Pentateuch, or, rather, I am but just commencing the types of the ritual, so that I hardly suppose that during the vacation I shall get beyond the Pentateuch. And then I shall have, if possible, to prepare lectures for the next term, even if I have enough for this.[1]

While apparently only 29 people attended the lectures during the following term, the class included John Henry Newman and Isaac Williams, and other influential figures in the Oxford

Movement were interested at a distance. In November, John Keble wrote to Pusey:

> I want to hear your lectures on types and prophecies, and whether Jeffreys[2] is right in saying that you are *always* against a *double sense*.[3]

The theme of the lectures continued to exercise Pusey for the rest of his life, material from them being incorporated into the later editions of his Tract 67 on *Scriptural Views of Holy Baptism* (first published in the second volume of *Tracts for the Times*, 1835), and appeared as late as 1878 in his last sermon on prophecy before Oxford University.

Liddon is eager to point out Pusey's admission that his notion of types was inadequate, and his sense that their mystery was not easily grasped in words; he quotes Pusey's remark, 'I cannot give any principle in a few words'.[4] His slight regard for the lectures is not difficult to understand. Pusey sharply attacks the old 'orthodoxism' of the previous age, which used individual prophecies as specific predictions of a Christian revelation. It was a refined form of such 'orthodoxism', which Liddon himself employed in his Bampton Lectures of 1878, *The Divinity of Our Lord*.[5] Pusey, claiming apostolic precedent and with echoes of Coleridge, takes the Old Testament as a coherent whole as prophetic, and he compares modern criticism with the Apostolic Fathers:

> We are anxious indeed, to trace up fulfilments of prophecy, but in a way wholly distinct; we wish to find predictions clear, apparent and undeniable, which we more sort with the events, and which on the very surface shall indisputably correspond; they had Christ always in their thoughts, and so with the full persuasion that the whole of the Old Testament, the law, the prophets and the psalms, [shared] before of Him, they read and understood of Christ therein, whatever naturally harmonized with His dispensation, whether it would appear itself to a more rigid understanding or no.[6]

Despite Liddon's disregard, Pusey's interpretation of prophecy had other adherents among influential figures in the Oxford Movement. Isaac Williams (1802–65), author of Tracts 80 and

87, on *Reserve in Communicating Christian Knowledge* (1838 and 1840), declared in his *Devotional Commentaries on the Gospel Narrative* (8 vols, London 1842–9) that 'prophecy pervaded and was imperceptibly interwoven throughout the letter of the Old Testament, rather than it was confined to distinct and palpable declarations of things future'.[7]

But the general neglect of the lectures among Pusey's contemporaries has been matched by their widespread disregard among modern scholars. No complete transcription of the manuscript has been published. The first to consult it and quote from it is Alf Härdelin in his book *The Tractarian Understanding of the Eucharist* (Uppsala 1965). Following his lead, A. M. Allchin deals with the lectures in more detail, quoting them at length, in his essay, 'The Theological Vision of the Oxford Movement', published in *The Rediscovery of Newman: an Oxford Symposium* (London 1967), edited by John Coulson and A. M. Allchin. Since then, only O. W. Jones in his book *Isaac Williams and his Circle* (London 1971), has referred to them, and it is clear that his knowledge of them depends wholly upon Allchin's work. There are, it seems, no other modern references to the manuscript.

The 'Lectures on Types and Prophecies of the Old Testament' open with a long section simply entitled, 'On "Prophecy"', of which the opening words set the tone:

The notion, and uses of Prophecy have, in these latter days, been much narrowed and obscured by the apologetic character which our Theology has so largely assumed.[8]

Pusey's purpose is to criticize and question contemporary orthodox assumptions of biblical inspiration, the nature of history and revelation, and evidences for the truth of Christianity in miracle and prophecy, by which was meant the God-given power of foreseeing future events.[9] He believed that the narrow intellectualism of such orthodoxy neglected the imaginative depth and grasp of Scripture as a whole which characterizes the ancient, catholic faith of the Church:

Let anyone compare our theology at the present day with that of Bishop Bull[10] and the ancient Church, and he will find that we have altogether lost sight of and forgotten out of mind, much which they dwelt on habitually as part of the Catholic Faith; we have the outline of the truth, but have lost much which gives to it substance and reality, and opens to us a safe and deepening range for our contemplation.[11]

The prophetic nature of the Old Testament is to be understood as a coherent whole and not simply as 'an accumulation of single facts' considered apart from their religious context and meaning, as particular predictions of New Testament events and personalities.[12] Pusey insists repeatedly that prophecy consists in the Old Testament being regarded as a complex yet organically connected 'system' whose impression depends 'not so much on single objects as on their combination',[13] and which is not intended as evidence for unbelievers, but rather as a guide for believers in matters of faith and the mysteries of God's Providence. Nor does it operate to narrow the Divine Mystery to distinct and logical propositions ('becoming clear, it became also shallow'), but rather to illuminate its depths and infinitude. Of 'orthodox' theologians he complains that:

> They wished to grasp the whole evidence of prophecy and to collect it into one frame, and so narrowed their own conception of it; They were content with nothing but the mid-day sun and so lost sympathy for the refreshing hues of its rising or setting light, or those glimpses into a far distant land, which, indistinct though they be, open a wider range of vision. The natural world is an impress of the spiritual; We see further with diminished light: noon-day beams contact our sphere of vision, although they heighten the intensity of the objects close at hand to us. God and His ways and his Nature we can of course know but in part; and our highest knowledge must be our indistinctest; for that which is most dearest must most surpass our comprehension; it belongs to another sphere and just touches, as it were, upon that wherein we dwell; its centre is not in this world, and so we cannot surely it encompass; its very proportions we can discern only here and there, so we see 'parts of His ways' bearing one upon another; as a whole we see nothing, because we are not at the centre whence it may be seen. Our most spiritual faculties are

just allied to it, and we are in the flesh. Because we are of God, and born of God, we have some sense for beholding the things of God; but because we are in the flesh, and 'no man can see God and live' (sic). The light but parts from between the cloud, lest we are bestruck down to the earth and blinded. Whatever then we gain in distinctness and precision we lose in depth; our furthest point of vision is just where 'light and darkness part'. The soul, through that which is divine in it, just putteth forth itself, and half-seeth things invisible, but cannot declare them or embody them in words. St Paul's highest revelations and visions were 'unspeakable words which it is not lawful for a man to utter'.[14]

It is with such presuppositions that Pusey embarks upon his programme of biblical exegesis in the lectures. His appeal is to the apostolic age and to the Fathers, among whom only the 'notoriously unsound' school of Antioch provides any precedent for the literalism of contemporary 'orthodox' exegesis.[15] The Fathers, instead of following their own predilections, were prepared to 'follow out the hints which God has given', and learn from apostolic teaching, putting Christ and not themselves at the centre.[16] The Scriptures should be allowed to speak for themselves and not fitted into the straightjacket of *a priori* assumptions or apologetical programmes.

A. M. Allchin remarks that one of the outstanding features of the lectures is their romantic quality and their stress on the power of the imagination.[17] It is possible to indicate in more detail the significance of this observation, and illustrate thereby something of the importance of the Romantic Movement for Tractarian theology. First should be noted Pusey's belief that 'the natural world is an emblem of the spiritual'. He writes in the lectures:

Nor indeed would external nature convey such direct interests to the soul, and that, stronger in proportion to the purity of each, unless it had in it somewhat of God; for it acts upon us not by reflection of the understanding, but by direct impression, not by our own reasoning about the wisdom of contrivances and the like, whereby men now deem, (as I said) that they 'ascend from nature up to nature's God', but by immediate influence, so that nothing exercises so congenial an influence over man's soul or so harmonized with it as the visible works of God.[18]

Everything in this world can be a type or symbol of heavenly realities. But this agreement with the general tendency of Romanticism should not be taken to imply any form of Tractarian pantheism. Nature, in much Tractarian writing, could be said to be sacramental only in a strictly limited way,[19] natural things being, in Keble's words, 'pledges to assure us of some spiritual thing, if they were not means to convey it to us'.[20] Pusey is careful at this point to designate the role of the imagination in the contemplation of nature:

> . . . the province of the true poet has been not to invent likenesses, but to trace out the analogies, which are actually impressed upon the creation.[21]

The distinction is extremely important. Pusey grants to the imagination a capacity for recognition, and not (as some romantics would) a creative power. The imagination might read in nature the 'book of God's works', while the effectual means of grace are to be found in the sacramental actions revealed in the typology of the Old Testament: the sacrifice of Isaac, the Passover, or the Day of Atonement. In the earlier poetry of Wordsworth and Coleridge, however, is to be observed a sacramental view of nature, a pantheism (or pan-sacramentalism) which was later deserted as both poets turned to a more definite Christianity. The rejection of nature for a non-sacramental Christianity, at least in the case of Coleridge, was accompanied by the growth of a doctrine of the creative imagination of which the 'living edicts'[22] in the Scriptures actually shape our world in metaphor and symbol.

The replacement of the sacramental mysteries by an organizing imagination, the discovery that nature was a problem and an obstacle, and the decline of his poetic powers, suggest that at the end of his life Coleridge was not at home emotionally in the abstract world of spiritual Christianity into which he had thought himself.[23] For Pusey, on the other hand, the imaginative recognition of the analogy between God's natural and revealed works, and of the likeness of the spiritual in the natural world is expressive of an awareness of the symbolical character of nature as intimating what is true and of a sense of the God-given quality of nature itself.[24]

Pusey's lectures also draw upon the 'organic' aesthetics of Wordsworth and Coleridge, rooted both in England and Germany, which conveyed a theory of symbolism and the unconscious and which provided an alternative and creative tradition to the contemporary 'Paleyite' apologetic which Pusey designates 'orthodoxism'.[25] For Pusey, as for Coleridge, a symbol 'always partakes of the Reality which it renders intelligible',[26] both of them sharing a Platonism which insists that a symbol is actually a part of the totality which it represents. Thus, Pusey writes:

> I have dwelt longer upon the character of types in themselves, even while we are considering only the general works and Providence of God, and antecedently to examining the peculiar system of His revelation, on account of the extreme importance of the subject, and in order to efface, if it might be, that types are in themselves anything arbitrary or uncertain . . . it seemed important to show how deeply and widely-rooted types were in the whole constitution of things, and the hold which they have taken upon man's nature might have been illustrated much more largely by reference to this extensive use of symbols, or artificial types, throughout all Heathen antiquity. Secondly, this way of looking upon things as in themselves significant, adds much to the vividness and force of typical language and may occasionally remove difficulties, of interpretation, which have been occasioned by the great boldness of the figure.[27]

The symbol (or type) is necessarily an element in that which it symbolizes (the archetype), as described by Coleridge, 'ὁ ἔστιν ἀεὶ ταυτηγόρικον', and 'is characterized by a translucence of the Special in the Individual or of the General in the Especial or of the Eternal through and in the Temporal'.[28] This sense of the importance of the particularity of the symbol and of the irreduceable nature of the type/archetype relationship is well understood by Pusey:

When moderns then attempt to translate into plain terms the figurative language of Holy Scripture, and to substitute abstract, and as they would fain have it, clearer terms for the types or typical language of the Old Testament, they uniformly by this transmutation evaporate much of their meaning. We have not, it is true, visible propitiatory sacrifice, a visible theocracy, a visible temple; but it is still through the medium of these figures that we understand, (as far as we do understand) the reality: we have no better way of understanding the main truths of the Gospel than through these very figures, 'the sacrifice of Christ' 'the kingdom of God', 'the temple of the Holy Ghost'; and he who would lay aside these types and typical language, and understand the mysteries of God without them, will be acting contrary to the teaching of Scripture and so very wrongly and foolishly. Men think that they gain in clearness, but they lose in depth; they will employ definite terms, in order to comprehend that which is infinite![29]

At one point in his lectures, Pusey compares the mysterious significance of the type with the natural wisdom of the child:

The words of the child are constantly typical of the future developed being. They speak greater truth than they them-selves (the outward organ of that truth) know: they speak it in reference to some particular occasion but indefinitely; they are aware of something kindred to that whole truth and have some glimmering of it, but it they grasp not. And yet they who hear it, will rightly wonder at it, and they who understand it better than the child itself, will yet confess that they could not have uttered it so simply or so forcibly. Its very indefiniteness adds to its reality, comprehensiveness, energy. It comes not from the child itself, but from a power within it; they are in truth the words of God, in the manner, the sayings of the Old Testament. . . .[30]

Wordsworth had been saying something very similar in his poetry in his awareness, not only of childhood as the 'seed-time' of the 'soul',[31] but of the relationship between the child and nature (in the broadest sense) as fundamental in the growth of the moral and spiritual personality. 'The child was in fact an essential part of the "wisdom" he sought to convey'.[32] But just as the growth into Anglican orthodoxy desiccated Wordsworth's poetic harmony with nature, indicative of an emotional lack in such orthodoxy, so also the Ode *Intimations of Immortality* laments the loss in adulthood of the child's 'visionary gleam'. Pusey is significantly different. While his sympathies with Wordsworth are clear, he develops the notion of the child uttering truths beyond its comprehension with a similar experience in adulthood, suggestive, in Allchin's words, of 'the sense of holding a shared secret which must have characterized the Oxford men at this time, and also their love of reticence and reserve in speaking of the things which moved them most'.[33]

> Thus every one has been aware, how in mixed society, he has often had pleasure in uttering words, which in his own mind related to some holier subject, than he thought it expedient either for himself or others to speak of more plainly: yet one, who knew him well, would know that the veiled meaning was his most real one, and that it was for the sake of that, that the words were uttered, although he intended also that which lay upon the surface of his words. And so again, when we are under strong emotions, words we often utter which are fuller than we ourselves are at the time fully aware; we feel only that we have uttered truths beyond ourselves; and it is upon reflection only that we find how much the Spirit within us, which gave us those emotions and the words too, meant by them.[34]

That which for Wordsworth was 'a sleep and a forgetting', is found in Pusey as denotative of that peculiarly Tractarian attitude towards the religious life—a secretiveness and sobriety of manner which is summed up in the Tractarian doctrine of Reserve.[35]

In one more important way in his lectures, Pusey identified his concerns with those of romantics like Coleridge. He suggests that the Providences of God are to be discerned not only in nature but also in the general history of mankind. History is a science which depends to a great extent on things which can only be discovered and verified by insight, sympathy and imagination,[36] and it is the imagination which recognizes that the key to the profane is sacred history:

> ... the history of mankind, in general, is typical, far more than we even now understand, although not so *to us* independently and originally when the light of the sun of revelation has been cast upon it, it also has its distinct, though dependent, light, which clears up the general outline of things but even these by the constant supply only of the original light. Sacred history is the key to profane. The veil is there raised, which ordinarily covers the connection of events with God, their First Cause, and the meaning and significance of these events in themselves, and their relation with each other. The principles of the history of God's Providences, and the harmony of His creation whereby one first corresponds with, and represents another, are there developed, so that one may apply them to what would in itself be obscure in profane history.[37]

Nevertheless, in examining the typology of the Old Testament, Pusey was careful to maintain that the records of history must be allowed to speak for themselves, from within their historical setting, and not have a pattern and meaning imposed on them retrospectively from future events:

> The question of interpretation then relates to the precise meaning of the words, not to the fulfilment of prophecy for the general result is not affected by it.[38]

For Pusey, as for Coleridge, and in Germany Johann Herder (1744–1803) and Johann Eichhorn (1752–1827), it was fundamentally important to understand the particular historical circumstances of the Scriptures, and primarily of the Gospels towards which the history of the Old Testament was directed.[39] By examining the sacred writings in their historical setting, one became aware both of the importance of 'profane' history as typological and also as an enabling milieu for sacred events, and of 'sacred' history as the working of the divine through the common affairs of mankind. Pusey was groping tentatively towards a theology of history.

In various ways, therefore, in these lectures, Pusey was proving himself to be open to influences which were shaping and directing the Romantics. In describing the work of the imagination, he refers at one point to Wordsworth and Keble as 'religious poets', and later quotes a stanza from Keble's *The Christian Year* (1827).[40] Coleridge, with whom the lectures have so much in common, is guilty of 'flippancy and arrogance',[41] when he interprets the story of Eden as an allegory, although his observations on the universality of the elements of the story ('trees of life and knowledge', 'talking and conversable snakes') are valuable. Where, it seems, Pusey disagrees with men like Wordsworth and Coleridge is in what he regards as their tendency to subjectivism, that is transforming that revelation which is clearly a gift graciously bestowed by God, into an artificial and man-made conceptual scheme.

As an illustration of Pusey's central thesis that the biblical revelation is given through the use of types, symbols and sacramental actions, may be taken his extended discussion of the Fall as 'prophetic'.[42] Significantly, he begins by claiming patristic support from Origen, St Chrysostom and St Augustine. Describing the events in Eden as 'the prophecy', Pusey writes:

The prophecy in its fulfilment, is a remarkable instance, how much and how varied meaning is comprised in God's word, and how manifold its fulfilment. Each interpretation has its place; only men err, when they mistake the lowest for the highest. Even they, then, who see nothing further than that man shall destroy the literal serpent's actual brood, are so far right. The words are even thus fulfilled. Man's implanted antipathy, the lesser but [remediable] inquiries, which he receives, if timely heeded, and his destruction of his enemy, are a visible type and an earnest, as it were, of that essential conquest. For our first parents, the image became more striking: if, as seems implied by the words of Scripture, the serpent's form was changed, upon the curse; and when creation bore the curse, it, which was cursed, above all, was most degraded; until now. . . . The Image is re-enacted continually, as a memento of the reality.

61

Then, as to the question, whether the seed of the woman 'contain the whole human race, or the one who was eminently so, as being the 'seed of woman' only, it might be safely answered, both: for both are fulfilled, and both are in the first one; since *we* triumph in and through Christ, and He in us, His members. And He has deigned to consider His victory over death and hell not complete, until what He had done for us, be also perfected in us, His Church; so such victory over Satan in any of God's faithful servants before the Redeemer's coming, was a petty type of that great conquest,—and an earnest also, in that it shewed that God had not forsaken the woman's seed, but the emnity, which He had placed, He was carrying on to victory—every victory since, as it is a fruit, so also is it a reflection of that great Archetype, and an earnest also of the fulfilment of His promise that His disciples shall tread on serpents and on all the power of the Enemy, that God shall bruise Satan under our feet shortly. Only, from these words it will appear that they are mainly fulfilled in Christ, who is the centre, in Him wholly, in us partially; in Him primarily, in us, whether before or after, secondarily and derivatively. And in His special and primary fulfilment, it is remarkable how words, which in the more general fulfil-ments have a more general meaning, have in the [closer] fulfilments a closer and more specific meaning.[43]

The Old Testament stories, such as that of the Fall, can and should be taken literally. To see no further than the actual enmity with the serpent is at least to be aware, in the type, of something of the essential truth being expressed. Underlying this literalism is, in fact, the Platonic assumption, common in patristic writings, and already noted in Coleridge, that the symbol is less real than the thing it symbolizes, but shares in its reality.[44] However, the types and images in which God speaks to us have more than one interpretation. Indeed, the complexity of the image reflects the energy and comprehensiveness of the reality, and it is on the point of the similarity of the nature of the type and the archetype that Pusey relates his discussion to the matter of the sacramental system of the Church:

It has been well said that God has appointed, as it were, a sort of sacramental union between the type and the archetype, so that as the type were nothing, except in so far as it represents, and is the medium of conveying the archetype to the mind, so neither can the archetype be conveyed except through the type. Though the consecrated element be not the sacrament, yet neither can the soul of the sacrament be obtained without it. God has joined them together, and men may not and cannot put them asunder. We find ourselves in no danger of the fleshly system, which clung to the types, without looking at the archetype; but, in truth, in looking to separate the archetype from the type, by this pseudo-spiritual system, we are adding this error to that which is more peculiarly our own. For whereas the type never did exist for itself, but always bearing the character of the Archetype impressed upon it, we by separating it therefrom, do as thoroughly empty it of its meaning, as they who saw nothing in it beyond its outward form. The pseudo-spiritualist and the carnal man alike see in the water, the bread or the wine nothing but the base element, and thereby each alike deprives himself of the benefit intended for him: the carnal will live on bread alone, the pseudospiritualist without it: the carnal mistakes the clouds and darkness for him who is enshrouded within it, the pseudo-spiritualist would behold Him whom 'man cannot see and live', the 'light inapproachable whom no man hath seen or can see'; the carnal neglects the revelation, the pseudo-spiritual will know the unrevealed God.[45]

The types of nature and history are not simply the creations of the human imagination. The imagination only recognizes what is actually in them expressive and indicative of the operation of the divine glory in the universe and in history. The work of the imagination is to draw into focus the type and the archetype into that 'sacramental union' which cannot be put asunder, and thus the necessity of the outward forms in type and sacrament is maintained, in Keble's words, 'the real efficacy of material sacraments, in opposition to the refinements of philosophy and vain deceit'.[46]

It will be helpful here to understand what Pusey means by the terms 'pseudospiritual' and 'carnal'. The former clearly designates the Evangelicals of his day, who seek to dispense with the mediation of the type in their regard for the 'soul of the sacraments'. They see no intrinsic significance in the elements of bread and wine. 'Carnal' is descriptive of Latitudinarians, who regard only the material of the type and who follow only a 'fleshly system', to the neglect of spiritual realities. The truth lies between the two, for the outward and earthly are knit indissolubly with the inward and heavenly. By participation the symbol conveys the reality of that of which it is the figure.

Various strands may now be drawn together. Pusey plays down the predictive element in Old Testament prophecy and warns of the dangers of a narrowing precision which fails to appreciate Scripture as a whole in all its complexity. Equally, claiming apostolic precedent, his Old Testament exegesis is consistently christocentric. He compares the present age with 'Origen and his school', who read the Scriptures in 'the apostolic mode':

> We are anxious indeed, to trace up fulfilments of prophecy, but in a way wholly distinct; we wish to find predictions clear, apparent and undeniable, which we more sort with the events, and which on the very surface shall indisputably correspond; they had Christ always in their thoughts, and so with the full persuasion that the whole of the Old Testament, the law, the prophets and the psalms, [shared] before of Him, they read and understood of Christ therein, whatever naturally harmonized with His dispensation, whether it would appear itself to a more rigid understanding or no.[47]

This centrality of Christ becomes in the lectures an assertion of the christological aspect of the Church, an expression of Tractarian theology which centred upon the Eucharist in Christ, the Church being a reflection of Christ incarnate. Pusey writes that:

> with this sacrifice of the Eucharist, the Ancients immediately connected other sacrifices, as the sacrifice of prayer, of thanksgiving, of alms and oblations, of ourselves our souls and bodies, of the whole Church, which is the body of Christ, yet it follows (not as some timid Protestants have persuaded

themselves) that therefore the Ancients thought of no other sacrifices than these; rather they are parts of the sacrifice, or connected with it, in that all things in Christian faith are connected with Christ; it is not accidental that the Christian Church is called by the same name as the Eucharist—the Body of Christ, for Christ dwelleth in the Church, and it visible exhibits Him, and He imparteth Himself through [the] Eucharist, as the outward and visible sign, and that mystical food, giving life to all the members, and running, as it were, through the veins of the whole Church gives it unity in that it keeps it united to Christ. . . .[48]

A few lines later, Pusey concludes his exposition of the Eucharist by quoting Augustine's statement on the Church, 'in that thing which she offers, she herself is offered'.

The whole of the Old Testament is centred upon and directed towards Christ. The sacrifice of the Day of Atonement, the Passover, the sacrifice of Isaac, Abraham, Noah and the story of the Fall are all both illustrative and typical of the situation which Christ came to attend to and of the restoration which he effected. Nevertheless, while the active presence of God in all creation and history is symbolically evident, that which may act as an instrument for the conveyance of grace may not be itself a sacrament, an effectual means of grace. Herein, therefore, lies the central importance of the sacramental mysteries, pre-eminently those designated by Christ in the Eucharist, and foreshadowed in their type, the Passover. In examining the role of the eucharistic elements, Pusey is highly critical of Reformation theology:

> . . . many Protestants have lost sight of the original doctrine of the Church, that the Lord's Supper, was, in the whole compass of its institution a commemorative act, that the offering up of the elements, which in one Church is retained in the lifting them up during the prayer of consecration, is a *commemorative* sacrifice; and so losing sight of that wherein the commemoration mainly consists, and to which the Ancient Church applies the words, 'Do this in remembrance of Me', they have applied it exclusively to the 'participation' which is not commemorative principally but Sacramental. As in the

Passover, so in the Eucharist; 1st that whereof the Sacrifice consists in the Passover the lamb, in the Eucharist, the bread and wine, both alike symbolic of the Body and Blood of Christ are first offered to God; in the language of the liturgy of [   ], 'we offer to Thee of thine own', [   ] and then God gives them back in nourishment to His people, only to the Jews in type, to Christians in reality, to the Jews to the nourishment of the body, to Christians to the strengthening and refreshing of the soul also, through the Body and Blood of Christ.[49]

Pusey teaches a doctrine of the Real Presence, but one which 'affords no countenance to the Romish errors'.[50] It is, in fact, founded upon his understanding of biblical typology as worked out in the lectures deriving very clearly from his patristic studies, and his conclusions are of importance in our understanding of the Tractarian teaching on the Eucharist.[51] One of the clearest patristic statements of Pusey's theology may be found in a work which he almost certainly knew, the *De Sacramentis* of St Ambrose. During his description of the epiclesis, Ambrose describes the bread and wine as the 'figure' of Christ's Body and Blood, with the implication that the elements are merely symbolic. Earlier, however, he clearly states that 'at the consecration this bread becomes the Body of Christ'.[52] There is, it seems, nothing incompatible between the Real and the symbolic presence, and, indeed, the use of figure-terminology to express Real Presence in symbols was widespread in patristic theology.[53]

In the Eucharist we are offered, by means of the bread and wine, the body and blood of Christ. But it is also a commemorative sacrifice which we offer to God, so that the Eucharist itself is, in a sense, a type of the whole Church, a living part of the totality which it represents, just as the elements are a type, both real and symbolic, of the Body and Blood of Christ:

> The Eucharist in so far *as it is offered to God* is a commemorative sacrifice, whereby we plead the death of His Son, and in that we plead it, we are accepted; in as far as *it is given us by God*, it is the Body and Blood of Christ, imparted by God by the means of the Bread and Wine.

In one way there is [   ] a difference between the offering of the symbols of Christ's Body and of His mystical Body the Church; and in another they take place together. . . .[54]

It is difficult to be precise in an examination or assessment of these early lectures of Pusey. Newman, indeed, was aware of his imprecision, but saw it as also a strength:

It is *very* difficult, even for his friends . . . to enter into his originality, full-formed accuracy, and unsystematic impartiality.[55]

Certainly the views expressed in them on the nature of the Church, the sacraments and Eucharist, as well as their approach to Old Testament exegesis, are important statements of Tractarian theology from a young Pusey more optimistic than he later became. The indistinction and mystery even, noted by Newman is an important element in Pusey's sense of language, literary form in the Old Testament, and typology, arising out of the recovery of a sensibility and a sense of unity in creation and history which links the lectures with what might loosely be called the Romantic Movement. Stephen Prickett, in his study of the influence of Coleridge and Wordsworth on the Victorian Church, notes three elements in their ideas which could equally be applied to the 'Lectures in Types and Prophecies' and which illustrate the importance of a sensitivity to literary forms and criticism in an attempt to understand the theology of the Tractarians:

Firstly, that of the ambiguity of human experience: a sense of the continuing co-existence and conflict of the natural and secular 'outer' world with the 'inner' world of religious experience, sacred and felt as super-natural. Secondly, and growing from this . . . a linguistic tradition that saw language itself as *expressing* this ambiguity. Language was seen as metaphorical, 'bi-focal', or 'stereoscopic', and in Coleridge's special sense of the word, 'symbolic'. Finally, we shall see how closely these two notions became associated with ideas of creativity and development. It is no accident that the writers who figure most prominently in this minority tradition—which we may conveniently, and not unfairly, call 'the tradition of Coleridge'—people like Keble, Newman, Maurice and MacDonald, should be both what we now call 'creative writers' (usually poets) *and* also theologians.[56]

There is one profound difference between this analysis and Pusey, which serves to establish a separation between the Romantic poets and the Tractarians. Something has already been said of why Coleridge and Wordsworth, as they grew into Anglican orthodoxy, felt a conflict and antithesis between the natural world and the supernatural. There is in them a lack of understanding of the doctrine of participation, of a sense of the indwelling of the divine in the particularities of the created order and history. Pusey on the other hand, was aware of the spiritual power of natural things as *verba visibilia*.[57] But more than this, his study of the Old Testament, of the Fathers and of the theology of Germany, led him to a sense of history and an understanding of typology and prophecy which pointed towards a principle of divine unity in the Church and an approach to a sacramental theology which was of profound importance for Tractarians and Catholic-minded Anglicans in the nineteenth century.

NOTES

1 Liddon, *Life of Pusey* vol. 1, p. 399.

2 The Revd H. A. Jeffreys, a former student of Christ Church, was then Keble's curate and later vicar of Hawkhurst in Kent. His academic life was severely curtailed by blindness.

3 *Life of Pusey*, Liddon, vol. 1, p. 400.

4 Ibid.

5 Lecture 2 'Anticipations of Christ's Divinity in the Old Testament'.

6 Unpublished manuscript of lectures, p. 10. Pusey's abbreviations have been expanded, although his spelling and punctuation have been retained.

7 *Devotional Commentaries on the Gospel Narrative* (1882), vol. 1, p. 189.

8 MS, p. 1.

9 See V. F. Storr, *The Development of English Theology in the Nineteenth Century, 1800–60* (London 1913), pp. 178–9.

10 George Bull (1634–1710), bishop of St David's. His defence of Catholic doctrine, particularly in the treatise *Defensio Fidei Nicaenae* (1685) was commended by Bossuet and other French theologians.

11 MS, p. 9.
12 Ibid., pp. 1–2.
13 Ibid., p. 5.
14 Ibid., pp. 2–3
15 Ibid., p. 9.
16 Ibid., p. 12.
17 *The Rediscovery of Newman*, p. 56.
18 MS, p. 16.
19 See H. N. Fairchild, *Religious Trends in English Poetry*, vols 3–4 (New York 1949–57), vol. 4, pp. 250 ff.
20 Tract 89, *On the Mysticism Attributed to the Early Fathers of the Church* (London 1841), p. 148.
21 MS, p. 15.
22 S. T. Coleridge, *The Statesman's Manual* (1816), in *Lay Sermons*, ed. R. J. White, *Collected Works*, vol. 6 (Princeton 1972), p. 29.
23 See J. D. Boulger, *Coleridge as Religious Thinker* (New Haven 1961).
24 See A. Härdelin, *The Tractarian Understanding of the Eucharist*, pp. 62–5.
25 See Stephen Prickett, *Romanticism and Religion. The Tradition of Coleridge and Wordsworth in the Victorian Church* (Cambridge 1976).
26 *The Statesman's Manual*, p. 30.
27 MS, pp. 20–1.
28 *The Statesman's Manual*, p. 30.
29 MS, p. 24.
30 Ibid., p. 14.
31 *The Prelude* (Edition of 1805) bk 1, 305.
32 Peter Coveney *The Image of Childhood. The Individual and Society: a Study of the Theme in English Literature* (Harmondsworth 1967) pp. 68–83.
33 Allchin, p. 60.
34 MS, p. 19. Allchin also quotes this passage, but his reading of Pusey's script is slightly different from the one suggested here.
35 Isaac Williams, *Tracts 80 and 87, On Reserve in Communicating Religious Knowledge* (London 1838, 1840).
36 See Herbert Butterfield, *Christianity and History* (London 1949), pp. 17 ff.
37 MS, p. 25.
38 Ibid., p. 78.
39 See E. S. Shaffer, '*Kubla Khan*' *and the Fall of Jerusalem: the Mythological School in Biblical Criticism and Secular Literature, 1770–1880* (Cambridge 1975), p. 32.
40 MS, pp. 17, 50.
41 Ibid., p. 46.

42 Ibid., pp. 42–50.

43 Ibid. p. 45

44 For a note on patristic usage, see Edward Yarnold *The Awe-Inspiring Rites of Initiation: Baptismal Homilies of the Fourth Century* (Slough 1972), pp. 93–4.

45 MS, p. 23. Härdelin, p. 100, compares this passage with Pusey, *A Letter to the . . . Bishop of London, in Explanation of Some Statements Contained in a Letter by W. Dodsworth*, 4th ed. (Oxford and London 1851), p. 153.

46 *Tract 89*, p. 46.

47 MS, p. 9.

48 Ibid., pp. 107–8. See also Pusey's Tract 67 on *Scriptural Views of Holy Baptism* where he writes that 'the Ancient Church had her eye specially fixed upon such as related to His Sacraments, the means whereby He originally united her to Himself', 4th ed. (London 1842), p. 272.

49 MS, p. 104. (Square brackets indicate blank spaces in MS.)

50 Ibid., p. 105.

51 See Härdelin, pp. 135–6.

52 The text used is that of Yarnold, p. 133.

53 See Darwell Stone, *A History of the Doctrine of the Eucharist*, 2 vols (London 1909), vol. 1, pp. 29–37, 58–123.

54 MS, pp. 105, 108. (Square brackets indicate blank space in MS.)

55 *Letters and Correspondence of John Henry Newman during his life in the English Church*, ed. Anne Mozley, 2 vols (London 1811), vol. 1, p. 186.

56 *Romanticism and Religion*, pp. 7–8.

57 Keble, *Tract 89*, p. 148.

4

Regius Professor of Hebrew

ALAN LIVESLEY

1

At the date of [Dr Pusey's] appointment, [declared *The Times* obituary], his chair was of no great significance. Very few read Hebrew. Bishop Burgess had in vain been urging the study on all the clergy who came to him for institution. It was only here and there that a clergyman in some remote parish beguiled his solitude with this unearthly, unfathomable, incommunicable tongue, and got quizzed accordingly. . . . All the general public expected from the new Professor was that he would save the credit of Oxford for learning, and add some bulky volumes to the numerous Oxford libraries. . . . The Regius Professors of Hebrew have, as a rule, been theologians as well as scholars, and have sometimes been best known in the former capacity.[1]

Apart from the strange distinction made between scholars and theologians, *The Times* obituary seems to give support to the opinion that many late eighteenth- and early nineteenth-century professors were of little consequence as scholars, and produced little of lasting importance. This was certainly not the case with Pusey's recent predecessors in the Hebrew Chair. When Pusey was born, Benjamin Blayney had been Regius Professor of Hebrew since 1787. He had produced a new version in 1769 from the Authorised Version, which might have had greater influence, had not a large part of the impression been lost in a fire at the Bible Warehouse in London.[2] Blayney's successor was Joseph White, DD, Fellow of Wadham, formerly Laudian Professor of Arabic, whose greatest work endures to the present day in the edition of the Philoxenian (or rather Harclean) Syriac version of the New Testament.[3]

When Pusey went up to Christ Church in January 1819,

71

White had been dead for nearly five years, and Richard Laurence, later Archbishop of Cashel, was Regius Professor of Hebrew.[4] Laurence, too, was interested in the revision of the Authorised Version, and we learn a great deal about his views on the subject from a lively controversy which arose from John Bellamy's *New Translation* of the Bible.[5] Bellamy's translation was not well received, and brought forth a number of pamphlets critical of it.[6] Laurence's pamphlet, *Remarks upon the Critical Principles and Practical Application of those Principles adopted by Writers who have at Various Periods recommended A New Translation of the Bible as Expedient and Necessary*, published anonymously (Oxford 1820), provoked a reply from Samuel Lee, Professor of Arabic at Cambridge, which in its turn brought forth a rejoinder from Laurence, *A reply to 'Some Strictures' of Samuel Lee, A.M. . . . On a Tract entitled 'Remarks upon the Critical Principles &c. Oxford MDCCCXX', by the Author of the Remarks* (Oxford 1821).[7] There is not space here to go into the details of the controversy between Laurence and Lee, nor does it seem, in Oxford at least, to have aroused the interest it deserved, since the copy of Laurence's *Reply to 'Some Strictures'* in the Bodleian Library was, until June 1981, uncut after page 9. Its value for this present essay is in indicating the background to Pusey's plan to revise the Authorised Version in the summary by Dr Laurence of the principles which he considered should guide those who undertake such a revision:

> The distinguished writers [Lowth, Blayney, Kennicott and others] who at various periods urged the necessity of a new translation, grounded their reasoning upon the supposed existence of an improved Hebrew text, in consequence of the improved state of Hebrew criticism, and of a more extended cultivation of Oriental literature. On the other hand, I contend that no such improved Hebrew text existed, that the modern Critics, who had laboured most at improving the text, had only corrupted it, and that the more extended cultivation of Oriental literature had produced little or no *practical* effects. My object was to shew, that a translation of the Scripture should not be conducted upon principles of theoretical criticism, unsanctioned by established usage; as

72

well as to point out some of the many difficulties and hazards which surrounded the path of the translator, who in search of novelties wanders from the beaten track of exposition. I did not so much consider, whether this or that theory was more or less founded upon apparently correct principles when abstractedly considered, as what had been in point of fact its *practical results and utility*. What I principally had in view, is thus briefly summed up in my recapitulation, '*I am disposed to give full scope to every display of critical investigation*; but I cannot admit, that a public version of the Scriptures should be cast in a mould accommodated to individual fancy and conceit.' [*Remarks*, p. 158].

The sole object then of my Tract was to oppose the vanity of innovation; and I deprecated the idea of undertaking to improve it by the rejection of the present vowels and the annexation of new ones, as individual caprice may dictate; by conjectural emendation; and by an indiscriminate selection at pleasure of various readings unclassed and unarranged. . . . I maintained that the translator of a version for public use should not suffer himself to be seduced from the plain path of his duty by ingenious theories; but conduct his interpretation upon principles of criticism, which have long been firmly established and universally approved.[8]

Laurence's remarks combine a warning against too great a readiness in a version for public use to admit conjecture, with a willingness 'to give full scope to every display of critical investigation'. That this is a warning which revisers in any age ought to heed, is illustrated in Professor Emerton's obituary of Sir Godfrey Driver,[9] by the identity of his conclusion with that of Dr Laurence, 'Moreover, while it is legitimate to register theories and suggestions in scholarly journals, it is arguable that greater caution should be exercised before a lexicographical theory is used in an official Church translation of the Old Testament'.[10]

A year after the publication of his *Reply to 'Some Strictures'* Richard Laurence accepted the archbishopric of Cashel. In the same year Pusey took a first class in the Schools. The way lay open for him to stand for a Fellowship at Oriel, an ambition which he had formed nearly a year before taking his degree. The following year was spent reading for his fellowship, struggling meanwhile with ill-health.[11] In the meantime Alexander Nicoll, sub-librarian of the Bodleian, and a former pupil of Laurence, succeeded Laurence in the Hebrew Chair.[12]

Pusey was elected to a Fellowship of Oriel College on Friday 4 April 1823. Apart from the information in Liddon's *Life* there is available some direct, and much indirect evidence of Pusey's Semitic interests and studies from this time until he succeeded Nicoll in 1828. The chief sources are these:

1   The Borrowers' Register of Oriel College Senior Library from April 1823 to August 1831.[13] The records are complete for this period, and although some books have been moved since 1831, the vast majority are still to be found under the same shelfmarks.

2   The manuscript letter from E. B. Pusey to Dr Nicoll in March 1827 from Bonn.[14]

3   Pusey's corrections in the small Bible (see Liddon *Life*, 1, pp. 117–22), now preserved at Pusey House.[15]

4   The list of Dr Pusey's books compiled after his death, on approximately 470 foolscap sheets, which is preserved at Pusey House. These sheets are in a variety of hands, and the sets of sheets are each numbered consecutively from 1 by their writers. These sheets are now jumbled together, and the various series of numbered sheets do not follow one another. The listings give the appearance of having been copied from the books as they were arranged on the shelves, not in any particular order, except that there is a tendency for a number of works by an author to follow one another. For example, six works of Gesenius follow one another on sheets numbered 95, 96: other works by him in the same series of sheets appear at sheet 166 and sheet 202. The only indication of where these books were listed is the heading on a sheet numbered 54: 'Tower Study'. This probably refers to the tower on St Aldate's of Pusey's lodgings in Christ Church, which could have been used as a study in which these books were shelved.[16] The books listed range in date from the

eighteenth century and earlier to 1882, the year of Pusey's death, but there is no indication when he acquired them.

Pusey lost no time after his election to a Fellowship at Oriel in making use of the College Library. The first entry under his name in the Borrowers' Register is dated 4 April 1823, the day of his election. Unfortunately this first borrowing is marked 'missing' in the Handlist, and its title is not given. The earliest borrowings that can be identified were two volumes of Graves, *Lectures on the Pentateuch*, borrowed on 16 April. These, together with Lowman, *On the Hebrew Ritual* (borrowed on 20 May), and Prideaux, *The Old and New Testaments connected in the History of the Jews* (borrowed on 5 December) were among the books upon which Dr Lloyd lectured when Pusey began to attend his lectures in May 1823.[17] The two works of Lowman on which Lloyd lectured, *On the Hebrew Government*, and *On the Hebrew Ritual*, Pusey later acquired for himself, for they appear on the Pusey House lists at a page 66, in editions dated respectively 1745 and 1816.

On 21 April 1823 Pusey borrowed N. G. Schroeder, *Institutiones ad fundamenta Linguae Hebraeae*. This was the text-book used by Dr Nicoll for his elementary course, lecturing three times a week through most of the academic year.[18] With this Grammar Nicoll used the Lexicon of Simonis, edited by Eichhorn, Halle, 1793.[19] Schroeder was a follower of the great Dutch orientalist Albert Schultens (1686–1750), 'distinguished, like his successors, by a most extensive erudition in classical and oriental literature, [who] endeavoured to prove the close connection between Hebrew and Arabic'.[20] Simonis, like Schroeder, was a strict follower of Schultens.[21] It seems probable that Pusey, as might be expected of one taught on the principles of Schultens, began Arabic with Dr Macbride[22] before his first visit to Germany, since he borrowed the Arabic Lexicon of Jacobus Golius on 2 June 1824, borrowing it again, after his first visit to Germany, on 22 November 1825. This lexicon dated from 1653, but was still at this time the standard work, being superseded only when Freytag's lexicon was published 1830–7.

Pusey's reading, as recorded in the Oriel Borrowers'

Register, was general until his first visit to Germany in June 1825, but with a marked interest in Old Testament and oriental studies. Other borrowings in this field included, for example, Lowth, *Isaiah*, and Stock, *Job* (5 November 1823), and Lardner, *Jewish and Heathen Testimonies*. Apart from this he read church history and the Fathers, e.g., Cotlerius, *Apostolic Fathers*, Chrysostom's *Works*, edited by Montfaucon, and Eusebius, *Ecclesiastical History*, edited by Reading. Other books borrowed include volume 1 of Clarendon's *History of the Rebellion*, Vincent's *Voyage of Nearchus* (twice), and Van Mildert's *Sermons*: the kind of reading that might be expected of a scholar with Pusey's interests at that time.

Pusey's first visit to Germany began on 5 June 1825 and continued until mid-October. His first aim was to improve his knowledge of the German language and German theology. While Pusey exaggerated when he told Liddon that only two persons in Oxford were said to know German at that time,[23] it was true that few scholars in England did know the language.[24] His visit enabled him to meet German orientalists, among whom were Eichhorn, Tholuck and Hengstenberg; it also made his name known among German scholars. It was during this visit that he determined that his growing interest in the Old Testament should become his main occupation. 'From that time I determined to devote myself more earnestly to the Old Testament, as the field in which Rationalism seemed to be most successful', Pusey said in 1878.[25] This remark, fifty years and more after the event, is no doubt coloured by the changes in his opinions after 1835; in the years immediately following his visits to Germany his interests were not so confined and negative.

On his return from this first visit to Germany, it is evident from the Oriel Borrowers' Register that he lost no time in setting to work on what Liddon describes as 'the duty of the hour . . . to make good the claims of Christianity against infidel opponents', quoting Pusey's own description of his occupations in the late autumn of 1825, 'I am at present employed in preparing to examine the evidence for the books of the Old Testament'.[26] On 1 November he borrowed Clerici, *Translatione Pentateuchus*, on 4 November Calasio, *Concordantiae Sacrorum Bibliorum Hebraicorum*, four volumes, and on 13

76

November three volumes of Michaelis, *Supplementa ad Lexica Hebraica*. Other borrowings followed, including Michaelis, *Commentaries on the Law of Moses*, volumes of Montfaucon's edition of Origen's *Hexapla*, and once again, the Arabic Lexicon of Jacobus Golius. As previously, his borrowings were not confined to his special subject, and included Eusebius, Josephus, Sleidan's *History of the Reformation* (1689) and Chandler's Bampton Lectures for 1825. His last borrowing before his departure for Germany on 17 June 1826 was Miller's Bampton Lectures for 1817, borrowed on 2 June. Miller's Bampton Lectures made a great impression at the time;[27] to-day they are remembered probably only by the footnote to the poem for St Bartholomew's Day in Keble's *Christian Year*.

There is a full account of Pusey's second visit to Germany in Liddon's *Life*, vol. 1. chapter 5, although Liddon does not go into any detail about Pusey's Semitic studies. There is also considerable doubt about the accuracy of Liddon's account of the relations of Pusey, Freytag and Ewald, especially the statement that Ewald was at the time Freytag's *famulus*.[28] The evidence is given in full, with quotations from letters by Wellhausen, Kamphausen and Nöldeke, in T. Witton Davies's *Heinrich Ewald*.[29]

Much information about Pusey's activities during this second visit can be gleaned from the manuscript letter to Dr Nicoll towards the end of his visit.[30] Pusey omits the address and date, but there is a postmark, Mar. 12–1827. In it he tells Nicoll about work on Arabic in Germany, including Freytag's edition of the Ḥamasa[31]:

I am very much obliged to you for ye subscribers wh. you have procured for Prof. F. . . . A 2nd part of this will soon appear. The whole of ye wk., I understand, will be occupied by ye elegies; forming ye 2nd book.[32] I look to this with great interest, as altho' in a civilised people, miserable wd. be ye results, wh. their sepulchral poetry wd. furnish as to their religious condition or hopes, we may here from ye rest of their poetry be certain that ye genuine feelings of ye Arabs will be expressed. The whole of ye 1st part will probably appear this year.

Pusey also gives news of the progress of Freytag's Arabic Lexicon:

> In $1\frac{1}{2}$ years we may hope to see Pr. Freytag's A. Lex. Without a very philosophical mind, he has still lived so long in this language and is a man of so much accuracy, that it will be an immense gain, & in Arabic probably less than in any other language from it's [*sic*] composite origin, w^{d}. a philosophical deduction of ye meanings of words be possible.

The letter from Bonn throws a great deal of light on Hebrew studies both in England and in Germany. Dr Nicoll had evidently asked Pusey about the progress of Winer's revision of the Simonis lexicon, and about the possibility in the meantime of obtaining further copies of the Eichhorn edition (1793). Pusey replied:

> I have again endeavoured in vain to ascertain something about Pr. Winer's Lex. It is hoped it will appear soon, but ye time does not seem fixed—you have probably seen ye Specimen. Prof. Freytag however thinks that by application to ye Waisenhaus at Halle copies of ye Simonis ed. Eichh. would still be to be obtained. I have a single copy in Oxford[33] to the use of wh. I need not say any of your class would be welcome.

There is news too of Gesenius's Lexicon:

> Dr Winer's is . . . expected soon to appear, Ges. tho' already begun to be printed not within 2 years. G. is also engaged in a new edit. of his smaller Lex. but I fear again in German. In some respects Prof. W's is expected to supply some defects in that of G.—His is considered as a more philosophical mind; and as in a language, wh. we know only as a religious language, very much must often depend on ye knowledge of the peculiarities of that religion, it is supposed that he will thus also often be enabled to present a truer view of ye connection of ye significations of ye same word than Ges. by his mere science can do.

Pusey brings Ewald's Grammar to Dr Nicoll's notice:

> As you differ in many points from Ges. views of Heb.

Grammar, you may be interested by the publication of a Critical Grammar which has just appeared. . . . The author (Ewald of Göttingen) . . . has for some time & I thought, philosophically, studied ye Semitic languages. He has too had ye assistance of Eichhorn. . . . Ew. is only a Repetent in Gött. I became acquainted with him this year in Berlin,[34] when I for some time in part read Syriac with him.

Winer's Lexicon was published the following year, 1828.[35] In the Preface he explains that the edition by Eichhorn was sold out, and the publisher had asked him to edit it afresh. He had been unwilling to do so because he was aware of Gesenius's intention to produce a third edition of his smaller Lexicon, and that he was beginning a Thesaurus in Latin. The publisher had urged him to undertake the work, believing that a Hebrew-Latin manual lexicon would have a ready sale in England and the Netherlands.

Winer's revision was thorough, as he himself states:

His ita institutis factum est, ut SIMONISII lexicon aliam plane formam induerit ac vix amplius SIMONISII dici recte possit.[36]

Winer frequently cites Gesenius in the text of his lexicon, and sometimes Ewald's Grammar.[37] The influence of the younger Hebraists was beginning to prevail.

2

'On the 24th of June Pusey left Bonn for England . . . [and] reached his father's house about the middle of July.' So Liddon reports the end of Pusey's second visit to Germany, which, he says, had made him a Semitic scholar and had largely familiarized him with the history of modern Protestant speculation on religious subjects.[38] It was his intention immediately on his return to begin a revision of the Authorised Version of the Old Testament. In this he had the encouragement of Bishop Lloyd. He wrote to his friend, R. W. Jelf, in Germany, to tell him of his plans, and received in reply a letter encouraging him in the undertaking, dated 26 September 1827.[39] It does not seem possible that Pusey had much opportunity to work at his revision of the AV text during the late summer of 1827. He returned to England in mid-July. He was in London on 20 August, whence he sent a letter to his mother, postmarked that date. In late September he went to Cheltenham and became engaged to Miss Barker, and returned to Oxford at the end of September or the very beginning of October, sending a letter to Miss Barker with the postmark, Oxford, Oct. 2. 1827. Letters from Miss Barker addressed to Pusey were sent on 3 October, addressed to Pusey House, and on 20, 22, 23, and 28 October, addressed to Oriel College.[40]

Pusey's name first appears again in the Oriel College borrowers' register on 11 October. The books he borrowed then would all be useful to someone making a revision of the AV text: Bochart, *Opera Omnia* . . . *Phaleg, Chanaan et Heirozoicon*, all four volumes of Calasio's *Concordance*, a Bible, described in the Handlist as 'Bible 1549', another Bible described in the Handlist as 'Geneva Bible 1577', one volume of Montfaucon's edition of Origen's *Hexapla*, containing Proverbs, Ecclesiastes, Canticles, and the Major and Minor Prophets, and a volume of Ainsworth's *Annotations on the Old Testament*, containing the whole of the Pentateuch. The day after, 12 October, he borrowed Buxtorf's *Lexicon Chaldaicum, Talmudicum et Rabbinicum*. His next borrowings were on 5 November; a volume of Jerome's *Commentaries*, containing Tom. 4, the four Major Prophets, Tom. 5, Ecclesiastes and the twelve Minor Prophets, Tom. 6, the Gospels and four Pauline Epistles, and Tom. 7, The Psalms. There was one further book borrowed on 11 October, and two on 11 November, marked 'missing' in the Handlist.

These borrowings suggest that Pusey was making plans for a very thorough revision; but not one to be put into effect immediately, since most of the books were returned before his departure for Brighton on 12 November. His immediate plans were for a preliminary revision, as he stated in his letter to Miss Barker on 28 November 1827,[41] 'My object is, not a new translation, but, retaining the old as far as is possible, to correct it . . .'. The larger interleaved Bible mentioned by Liddon[42] is now nowhere to be found. An interleaved Old Testament in four volumes was discovered in the cellar at Pusey House in February 1981, and is listed in the foolscap sheets at Pusey

House at a page 49, 'Biblia Hebraica ed. C. Doederlein, 4 vols. $4^{\text{to.}}\frac{1}{2}$ calf, Interleaved, Lipsiae, 1793'. This cannot, however, be the one mentioned by Liddon, since there are no corrections in Isaiah. The small Bible mentioned by Liddon[43] is preserved at Pusey House, and is the prime source of information about Pusey's proposed revision.

Liddon's description of the corrections as 'numerous and minute' is apt. In the books corrected in detail they are minute not only in their detail but also in their handwriting. The Book of Job is particularly difficult to decipher, since not only is the writing even worse than in the Psalms, but there are also many corrections in pencil, now much rubbed and impossible to read. The Psalms are done throughout in ink, and in even more detail than the Book of Job. The Psalms are very extensively corrected; only Psalms 113, 117 and 130 have no corrections. There are a few corrections in several books of the Old Testament, and even some in the New Testament, though these are confined to one correction in St Luke, fourteen in St John (but in chapters 14–17 only), nine in Acts, and seven in Romans, these being in chapter 1 only.

It is clear from Liddon's *Life* that the corrections in the small Bible were done over the period of a very few months, and must have been intended as a preliminary exercise before beginning more detailed work. The present writer has transcribed all the corrections in the Psalms, and compared Pusey's corrections with the Massoretic text. The corrections are of various kinds: a number of them alter the tense in the English, some are the omission of words not in the original, written in italics in the AV, others again are matters of style. There appears to be one possible conjectural emendation, in Psalm 119. 89, where Pusey alters, 'For ever, O LORD, thy word is settled in heaven' by deleting 'in' and substituting 'like the', reading perhaps *kaššāmayim* for *baššāmayim* in the Massoretic text.

There is another kind of correction which Pusey occasionally makes which is more in the nature of an exegetical note. One such example is at Psalm 134. 1., where Pusey puts brackets round 'Behold' instead of crossing it out, as he usually does when making corrections, and writes 'Up' above it. Pusey evidently understands this psalm in the same way as the

Targum, as a calling of the Temple Watch, as Gesenius appears to do in the *Thesaurus*, and as later commentators have understood this verse.[44] By taking this course, Pusey avoids giving the impression that he rejects 'Behold' as a less than satisfactory translation of *hinnēh*: probably, if he had continued with the work of revision, the substitution of 'up' for 'behold' would have been explained in a footnote or some other way.

The great majority of the corrections, however, are simple changes in translation. From the short time available to Pusey it seemed likely that the work had been done with a lexicon, seeing that the changes were chiefly lexicographical. The problem was to find out what lexicon he might have used. Gesenius's *Thesaurus* gave in Latin what might well be translated into English in the words of Pusey's corrections. The *Thesaurus*, however, was too late to have been used by Pusey in 1827; but the similarities suggested the influence of Gesenius. By great good fortune a copy of the 1832 English edition of the *Hebrew and English Lexicon* of Josiah W. Gibbs of Andover, Massachusetts (first published in America in 1824),[45] was available in Sheffield City Library. This lexicon is a translation of the 1815 *Handwörterbuch* of Gesenius, and was published in England in 1827 and 1832. It was used to compare Pusey's corrections with the translations of the Massoretic text given in Gibbs's Lexicon. In a large majority of cases throughout the Psalter the corrections made by Pusey correspond with the translation in Gibbs. Occasionally in the Psalms Pusey quotes Arabic words in the margin, e.g., Ps. 35. 5. 15; Ps. 135. 7. In all of these cases the Arabic quoted by Pusey is cited by Gibbs, and Pusey corrects the English to correspond with Gibbs's translation. It became clear on internal evidence that Pusey is dependent upon Gibbs; but there is no copy of his lexicon at Oriel or Christ Church, and the Bodleian Library had surprisingly not taken up its entitlement to a copy of the English edition; there are copies in the British Library and Cambridge University Library. A search of the foolscap pages at Pusey House, listing Pusey's books, revealed however that Pusey possessed his own copy of the original American edition. On a sheet marked '∮ 10' [*sic*] the first entry is, 'Gibbs Hebrew & English Lexicon 1 vol. 8vo. calf. Andover 1824'. The corrections to the Psalms are much too numerous to give here, and to make a selection might seem to be choosing evidence favourable to the writer's opinion: instead, the corrections to the Pentateuch, which are few, are set out below. They amply demonstrate Pusey's method, and his dependence upon Gibbs, including his quotations from Arabic.

Liddon states that Pusey began his new plan by correcting the Book of Job.[46] It is reasonable to assume that he continued with the corrections in the Psalms; but in what order he corrected the other books it is difficult even to guess at. It seems most unlikely that he would find as few corrections necessary in, say, the Pentateuch as in fact he made in the small Bible, after correcting Job and the Psalms so minutely. Perhaps his method was to make a preliminary survey, making very few corrections, and then to go over the books again. If that is so, Pusey got no further than the preliminary survey in the Pentateuch before the events of 1828 caused the work to be set aside, never in fact to be resumed.

The first correction in Genesis is at Gen. 3. 15., where on both occurrences of the word Pusey deletes 'bruise' and substitutes 'bite'. Gibbs at p. 593a, under *šūp* gives these meanings:

1. *to break*, or *smite in pieces*.   2. i.q. Lat. *ferio*, Greek πλήττω, *to smite, strike*; also spoken of the serpent, *to bite*. Gen. iii. 15. [Gibbs here quotes the MT, and then translates] *he (the seed of the woman) shall smite thee on the head, and thou shalt bite him on the heel.*

Pusey here adopts Gibbs's translation: the verse corrected is cited, and the words are quoted in Hebrew and English.

The next correction made by Pusey is at Gen. 4. 1. He deletes 'gotten' and substitutes 'obtained'; he also deletes 'from' and substitutes 'thro''.

Again Gibbs cites the verse at p. 526a under *qānāh*. As meaning (4) he gives, *to obtain for a possession, to obtain. Gen. iv. 1.* Pusey again follows Gibbs. For the second correction in this verse Gibbs at p. 62a under III *'ēṯ* writes: I *with, together with Gen. iv. 1.* [he again quotes the MT and translates] *with God*, i.e., with his aid, *Deo juvante.* The translation and interpretation of *'eṯ Yhwh* here is a perennial problem for commentators: Pusey dispenses with 'from' in the AV and attempts to find a word

83

giving the sense of the comment in Gibbs, 'with his aid, *Deo juvante*' and chooses 'thro''. This, perhaps, like the instance cited above from Ps. 134. 1., might have been explained in a marginal note or comment if the revision had ever been completed.

Chapter 14. 17, is an example of a stylistic correction by Pusey: to make the rather unwieldy sentence clearer he puts brackets round 'after his return from the slaughter of Chedorlaomer and of the kings that *were* with him': he suggests no change of words. Later in the same chapter, at 14. 19., he deletes 'possessor' and substitutes 'former', and makes the same correction at verse 22. Again he follows Gibbs: at p. 526a under *qānāh* he writes:

> 6. *to prepare, form, make*. (In Syr. *idem*. In Arab. [In Hebrew script] qyn, [In Arabic script] *q'n* med. Je *formavit, concinnavit*) . . . *Gen.* xix [*sic*: obviously a misprint for xiv], 19, 22.

The one correction by Pusey in chapter 18 is to delete 'because' in verse 20 on both occurrences. Pusey here follows a general principle set out by Gibbs. The word in the MT is *kī*. Gibbs writes at p. 270b:

> *kī* 8. It is often used at the beginning of a proposition, where it may be omitted in translating, like the German ja! *Zech.* iii. 8. 2 *Sam.* xix. 23. So before the direct address like the Greek ὅτι, *Ruth* i. 10., *Josh.* ii. 24., 1 *Sam.* x. 19., and after oaths, 1 *Sam.* xxvi. 16; xiv. 44; xxv. 54; 2 *Chr.* xviii. 13.

The same deletion of *kī* is made by Pusey at Gen. 22. 16. In chapter 27 there are two corrections, at verse 40 and at verse 42. In 27. 40. 'have the dominion' is deleted, and 'strive' substituted. The verse is again cited by Gibbs, and quoted in Hebrew, followed by a translation: Gibbs, p. 545a, under *rūd*:

> Hiphil 2. *To desire, seek, to strive to accomplish*. (Arab. *idem*.) *Gen.* xxvii 40 [Hebrew quoted] *when thou shalt seek to effect it*.

Pusey follows Gibbs, but not slavishly: he adopts the translation 'strive', but does not quote the suggested translation for the whole phrase: *ka'ᵃšer tārīd*. In verse 42 again Pusey deletes a whole phrase, 'as touching thee, doth comfort himself, *purposing* to kill thee', and substitutes 'will avenge himself upon thee'. Gibbs again quotes the whole phrase in Hebrew, and provides a translation. Gibbs, p. 384 a,b:

nāḥam in Kal not used.
Hithpa. 3. *to take revenge, Gen.* xxvii 42 [Hebrew quoted] *behold Esau thy brother will take revenge upon thee, by killing thee.*

Pusey follows Gibbs, using the synonym 'avenge': there is some question about the end of the phrase, Pusey's correction leaves out Esau's intention to kill Jacob. It is a matter of speculation whether the length of the deletion was literally a slip of the pen, or whether Pusey intended the correction to follow the lexicon. This was only a first draft, which could, if it had been revised, have been corrected or expanded, as the case may be.

In chapter 31. 1., Pusey deletes 'this glory' replacing the words by 'these riches'. This verse is not cited in Gibbs's Lexicon, but in the entry on *kābōd* on p. 264a, b, he gives as meaning (3) *abundance, riches,* which Pusey adopts.

The correction in chapter 32. 11. is of a different kind, which occurs also in the corrections to the Psalms. Pusey leaves the text of the AV 'with', but deletes the marginal note 'Heb. *upon*'. The word in the MT is *'al*, which is usually translated 'upon'. Gibbs however cites this verse in support of the rendering 'with', and gives a similar translation of *'al* at Exod. 35. 22. The AV text in both places is in accord with this translation, so it is not altered by Pusey. At verse 28 of the same chapter Pusey deletes 'as a prince' and 'power' and substitutes 'contended'. The verse as corrected would read, 'for thou hast contended with God.' Gibbs cites this verse under the first meaning in the entry for the verb *śārāh*, and does not derive *śārītā* from *śrr*, 'rule', as the compilers of the AV had done: Gibbs p. 576b:

I *śārāh* to *contend, struggle* with a person; construed with *'im*. *Gen.* xxxii. 28 . . . (Arab. *śr'* conj. III *idem*.).

Chapter 33. 18. gives an example (of which there are many in the Psalms) where Pusey changes the tense of a verb in the AV. At this verse he deletes 'when he came' and substitutes 'after he had come'. In the MT the word is *bᵉḇō'ō*, the Qal infinitive with the preposition *b*.

The final corrections in Genesis are in chapter 49. The first of these at verse 14 is of particular interest, since Pusey quotes Arabic words alongside his correction, and the Arabic words are quoted in the same way by Gibbs. At verse 14 Pusey puts a small cross above 'strong', and a note in the margin 'i.e. bone'. He writes in the margin also the words in Arabic script *ḥm'r frs jrm*. Gibbs writes at p. 121b:

> *gerem* 1. *bone. ḥᵃmōr gerem, an ass of bone,* i.e. a strong-built ass, *Gen.* xlix. 14. The Arabs say in like manner, *ḥm'r jrm frs, a strong horse, ass,* and *jrym strong-boned.*

Apart from the correction 'i.e. bone' there are three points to note here. Firstly, the other lexicon Pusey is known to have possessed, that of Simonis as edited by Eichhorn, has only the one Arabic word *jrm* quoted. Pusey could not have got the three Arabic words from there, and Simonis is an unlikely source for his corrections, since it is in Latin, and it would be remarkable if Pusey almost always translated Simonis's Latin into the precise words used by Gibbs in English. Secondly, while Pusey, newly-returned from his Arabic studies in Germany would not have needed a lexicon to see that *ḥm'r* in Arabic is from the same root as *ḥᵃmōr* in Hebrew, and *jrm* the same as *gerem*, there would be no purpose in quoting *frs* unless he were copying from Gibbs. As Gibbs states, *frs* in Arabic is a common word for horse, but the cognate word in Hebrew, *pārāš*, while it is occasionally used for 'horse', more often in Hebrew signifies 'horseman'.[47] Here in Genesis 49 there is no mention in the text of horse or horseman. Thirdly, the Arabic words as they appear in Gibbs are not a phrase, but rather a shorthand way of saying that the Arabs say either *frs jrm,* a strong horse, or *ḥm'r jrm,* a strong ass. Gesenius makes this clear in the *Thesaurus,* and there cites Schultens as his source.[48] The inevitable conclusion must be that these Arabic words are a simple quotation by Pusey from the lexicon in front of him. The last correction is at verse 26. Pusey deletes 'that was separate from' and substitutes 'who is a prince among.' This is another simple following of Gibbs. At p. 381b Gibbs enters:

> *nāẓīr,* m. verbal from *nāẓar.* 1. *separated from others, distinguished,* hence *a prince. Gen.* xlix. 26.

The corrections in Exodus follow the same pattern as those in Genesis, spread throughout the book, but in Exodus with seldom more than one verse altered in any chapter. The first correction is in chapter 6. 9., where Pusey deletes 'anguish' and substitutes 'impatience'. Again he follows Gibbs: the noun *qōṣer* from the root *qṣr* appears only here, in the phrase *qōṣer rūaḥ*, so the entry in the Lexicon is very short (p. 529a):

> *qōṣer*, verbal from *qāṣēr*, found only in the phrase *qōṣer rūaḥ* *impatience. Ex.* vi. 9.

In chapter 14. 3. Pusey deletes *'are* entangled' and substitutes 'wander perplexed', adding a marginal note 'cf. Joel 1.18', and in Arabic script, *b'k*. The correction once more comes directly from Gibbs, except that Pusey writes in the corresponding Arabic root in Arabic script. The part of the entry in Gibbs referring to this verse is as follows (p. 69a):

> *būk* found only in Niph.
> *Ex.* xiv. 3. [Hebrew text quoted] *they are entangled in the land,* i.e. they wander about in confusion. *Joel* i. 18. (spoken of herds of cattle). In Arab. *idem.*

Pusey makes his correction by using Gibbs's interpretation, changing only 'in confusion' to 'perplexed'. The reference to Joel 1. 18. and the reference to the Arabic parallel follow, and Pusey copies them. He does not cite the other reference given in the Lexicon, viz., Esther 3. 15. At verse 13 of the same chapter he deletes 'salvation' and substitutes 'help'. Once again, Gibbs cites this verse and quotes the phrase, *yᵉšūat Yhwh* in Hebrew (page 259a):

> 1. *help, deliverance, salvation.* [Hebrew quoted] *help obtained from God. Ex.* xiv. 13.

This correction, 'help' instead of 'salvation', is a favourite with Pusey: for example in the Psalms he makes the same correction at Ps. 74. 12 and at Ps. 78. 22.; by the time he reaches Ps. 96. 2 and Ps. 118. 15. he merely deletes 'salvation' without writing in any other word, as if he has rejected 'salvation' as a translation altogether in favour of 'help'. These verses in the Psalms are not cited in the Lexicon; the correction is Pusey's own. He may have been influenced by the remark in the Lexicon under the root verb *yāša'* (p. 260a):

> In Arab. *wasa'a* [*sic*], *to be wide, enlarged*; an idea which in the Shemitish languages often indicates *deliverance* or *happiness*.

The correction at Exodus 15. 2.; delete 'strength', substitute 'praise', is another adopted frequently by Pusey. Again, Gibbs cites this verse (p. 441b.):

> '*ōz* 4. *praise. Ps.* viii. 3.; xxix. 1.; lxviii. 35.; xcix. 4. *Ex.* xv. 2.

In the Psalms cited in the Lexicon Pusey makes the same correction at 8. 3., 29. 1.; at Ps. 68. 35. and 99. 4. he deletes 'strength', but substitutes 'glory' instead of 'praise'.

In chapter 21. 8., Pusey deletes 'dealt deceitfully with her', but underlines 'deceitfully', which is Pusey's usual method of retaining a word otherwise rejected. He enters the words 'deserted her', so the whole correction would read 'deserted her deceitfully'. At p. 65b in Gibbs the verse is cited:

> *bāgad* 1. *to act faithlessly, perfidiously* . . . Construed with *b to deal treacherously against* any one . . . with *b'iššāh, to forsake one's wife, Mal.* ii. 14, 15, 16.; *Ex.* xxi. 8.

The next three corrections are ones in which not only is the verse cited; but the exact correction made by Pusey is suggested. At chapter 23. 2. 'speak' is deleted, and 'pronounce sentence' is substituted. At page 457b. Gibbs has:

> I '*ānāh* 5. *to pass a sentence, responsum dare*; spoken of the judge. *Ex.* xxiii. 2.

Likewise, at chapter 24. 10., Pusey deletes 'the body of' and inserts 'itself' after 'heaven'. Gibbs writes (p. 462b):

> '*eṣem* f. verbal from '*āṣam.* 3. *the same, very, itself* . . . *Ex.* xxiv. 10. [Hebrew quoted] *as the heaven itself.*

The substitution of 'acacia' for 'shittim' at chapter 25. 5. can be supposed to refer to the other two occurrences in the same chapter at verses 10 and 13, and to 26. 26. and 27. 1, 6. As in the deletion of 'salvation' in the Psalms without correction mentioned above, it is probable that Pusey did not always correct every occurrence of the word corrected, as elsewhere in these three chapters. All occurrences are cited by Gibbs (p. 598b):

> *šiṭṭāh . . . the acacia, spina Ægyptia* of the ancients . . . Plur. *šiṭṭīm* 1. *acacia wood. Ex.* xxv. 5, 10, 13.; xxvi. 26.; xxvii. 1, 6.

The final correction in Exodus is another example of an apt alteration which gives a graphic interpretation with a minimum of change in the AV text. Once again, Pusey corrects in his Bible only one of the two occurrences. This is at 34. 22., where he changes 'ingathering' to 'fruitgathering'. Gibbs (p. 44b) renders *'āsīp* as '*harvest-time*', *Ex.* xxiii. 16., xxiv. 22. As the correction 'up' at the beginning of Psalm 134, mentioned above, relates the psalm to the calling of the Temple Watch, so here the choice of 'fruitgathering' for the name of the feast refers in one word to the vintage in September. It is likely that if the revision had gone further, Pusey would have added some explanatory note, as S. R. Driver did in his commentary nearly ninety years later:

> The *third* pilgrimage, the Feast of *Ingathering*, held at the end of the year, in September, when the threshing was finished, the vintage over, and the juice pressed out from the grapes and olives . . . It is called the 'Feast of Ingathering' also in Ex. xxxiv. 22.†[49]

In the Pentateuch Pusey has made comparatively few alterations, and they are not evenly distributed among the books: the greatest number are in Genesis and Deuteronomy, rather fewer in Exodus. In Numbers he makes four corrections, in Leviticus only one. The correction at Lev. 25. 20. is more complicated than usual: he deletes 'behold' and 'shall' two words later in the verse: over 'not' he writes a figure 2, and over 'sow' a figure 1. After 'behold' there is a mark, which is probably 'if' in worse handwriting than is usual even for Pusey. The result is that the verse as corrected would read, 'And if ye shall say, What shall we eat the seventh year? if we sow not nor gather in our increase'. Gibbs tends to confirm the reading of Pusey's mark as an ill-written 'if'. The MT reads *hēn lō' niẓrā'*. In the Lexicon at p. 159b we find:

> II *hēn* with Makkeph *hen* 2. *if. Lev.* xxv. 20. *what shall we eat in the seventh year hēn lō' niẓra'* [*sic*] *if we shall not sow.*

Pusey adopts the translation, with the stylistic change of 'sow not' instead of 'shall not sow'.

Pusey's next correction, in Numbers 11. 25, is a very full and clear example of straightforward copying from Gibbs's Lexicon. It is to bracket 'cease' at the end of the verse, and to enter in the margin 'not again (afterwards)'. This cryptic alteration becomes clear on looking up in the Lexicon at pp. 246b–7a the entry on *yāsap*:

> 3. Construed with the infin. of another verb, or with a finite verb, with and without a copula . . . it expresses the *repetition* or *continuance* of an action, and may be rendered in English by various adverbs; . . . The action itself, the repetition or continuance of which is intended, is often omitted, and must be supplied from the context . . . *Num.* xi. 25. *and when the spirit rested upon them they prophesied,* w'lō' yāsāpū, *namely* l'hitnabbē', *and (afterwards) never again.*

There are two corrections in chapter 14. At verse 8 'delight in' is deleted, and 'be well-pleased with' substituted. Here Pusey makes a correction in his own words, choosing from among the translations in the Lexicon which include 'take delight in' which he rejects. The entry in the Lexicon (p. 204b) on *ḥāpēṣ* includes:

> 2. intrans. and figuratively, *to be favourably inclined towards* any one, *to take delight in* him, *to love* him . . . Spoken of God, *Num.* xiv. 8.

The verse is cited by Gibbs: Pusey clearly attempts to find a word giving the sense of being favourably inclined and loving, and chooses a synonym, not found in Gibbs's entry, for the purpose. His second note in chapter 14 is a comment rather than a correction; at verse 11 he makes no deletion, but writes 'notwithstanding' in the margin. It is scarcely a lexicographical correction, even though at p. 64a Gibbs gives in the entry on *b'* a meaning 14, 'on account of'. This may more probably be a note by Pusey to give emphasis to the unbelief of Israel, in spite of, notwithstanding, the signs performed by God.

Finally in Numbers there is a correction at 21. 4.; Pusey deletes 'soul of' and 'was much discouraged' and substitutes 'were very impatient'. This he derives from the entry in the Lexicon (p. 529a):

qāṣar 2 ... intrans. ... *to be short.* Particularly (2) *qāṣrāh rūḥī, napšī I am impatient, grieved, vexed. Num.* xxi. 4, 5.

Pusey adopts the word 'impatient' from Gibbs; the deletion of 'soul of' is explained by the treatment in the Lexicon of *rūaḥ* and *nepeš* as synonyms for the person mentioned; 'the soul of the people' is in Hebrew a way of saying 'the people'.

The kinds of corrections made by Pusey in Deuteronomy follow the pattern of those in the other books of the Pentateuch, with a continuance of the tendency sometimes to recast the translations in Gibbs, and also with two references to the Psalms, connecting the corrections made here with the more thorough work done earlier on the Psalms.

The first alteration in the text is a deletion without any word being substituted: the crossing out in 7. 20. of 'destroyed'. The verse is cited by Gibbs in the entry on *'ābad* at p. 3a., and at section 3. The meanings are given, *to be destroyed, rooted out, Deut.* vii. 20. It is a matter for speculation whether Pusey intended to substitute 'rooted out', and merely failed to enter it, or intended to choose some other synonym. It seems likely that the omission of an alternative rendering is an oversight; indeed it is remarkable how infrequently omissions and obvious slips of the pen occur in the corrections in this small Bible.

At 8. 15. Pusey deletes 'drought' and substitutes 'a thirsty land'. The entry by Gibbs (p. 507b) on *ṣimmā'ōn* is very short:

m. verbal from *ṣāmē'* a *dry* or *thirsty land, Deut.* viii. 15. *Is.* xxxv. 7.

It may be that the American edition owned by Pusey gave the other occurrence, Ps. 107. 33.[50] All three occurrences are cited in Simonis, edited by Eichhorn,[51] which Pusey possessed. In any event, Pusey made a similar correction at Ps. 107, deleting 'dry' and substituting 'thirsty'.

At chapter 10. 21. Pusey deletes 'terrible' and substitutes 'aweful' [*sic*]. This verse is cited by Gibbs in the entry on *yārē'* pp. 253b, 254a.:

91

Niph. *nōrā'* *to be feared* . . . (3) *wonderful, great, noble* . . . Plur. *nōrā'ōt, wonderful deeds* . . . particularly of God, *Deut.* x. 21.

The word 'aweful' is an independent choice by Pusey, combining the ideas of fear, wonder and nobility, and expressing this combination rather better than 'terrible' in the AV.

In 13. 1, 2 (13. 2, 3 in the MT), Pusey replaces 'wonder' by 'token'. Gibbs cites these verses (p. 315a) under *mōp̄ēt̲*:

1. *a wonder, a wonderful occurrence, portentum prodigium* . . . Particularly *a sign, token, pledge, omen*, given by a prophet for the accomplishment of something future; comp. *'ōt̲* no. (4) . . . *Deut.* xiii. 2.3.

Verse 1 (MT2) is also cited by Gibbs under *'ōt̲* (p. 19a).

The deletion of the second '*it*' in 15. 2. is an example of the practice of Pusey which occurs constantly in the small Bible, viz., the omission of words which do not appear in the Hebrew, and which are not essential for the sense.

Verses 17 and 18 of Deut. 26 are extensively corrected. In verse 17 Pusey deletes 'avouched' and alters the verse so as to read. 'Thou hast caused the LORD to promise this day to be thy God . . .', and in verse 18 he also deletes 'avouched' and 'promised' and alters the verse to read, 'the LORD hath caused thee to promise this day to be his peculiar people, and he hath commanded thee, so that thou shouldest keep . . .'

Gibbs cites both verses at p. 41b, under *'āmar*:

Hiph. i.q. Kal, but intensively, *to declare solemnly, to promise* . . . *Deut.* xxvi. 17, 18.

Pusey follows, but expresses the Hiphil in the conventional manner, 'to cause to promise'. The first correction in verse 18 repeats the alteration in verse 17; the remaining correction in verse 18, changing 'promise' to 'command' is probably mainly for reasons of style. Gibbs does not cite verse 18 under *dibbēr*; the change is a natural one, since anything God speaks to Israel expresses his will, and can be called a command.

The remaining corrections in Deuteronomy are all in chapter 32. At verse 2 Pusey substitutes 'drops of rain' for 'showers'. Again the verse is cited by Gibbs at p. 541a:

rᵉḇīḇīm masc. plur. verbal from *rāḇaḇ, showers of rain,* so called from the *multitude* of drops. *Deut.* xxxii. 2. Arab. *rbb, aqua copiosa.*

Pusey chooses the rather more literal translation here, as he does sometimes in the Psalms.

In verse 5 he deletes 'perverse' and substitutes 'faithless'. Gibbs cites the verse, and gives the sense of falsity specifically to this verse (p. 464b):

'iqqēš, m. verbal adjective from *'āqaš, perverse, froward . . .* Without addition, *false, Deut.* xxxii. 5.

The correction in verse 6 involves the verb *qānāh,* as in Gen. 14. 19, where Pusey quotes the cognate verb in Arabic in the margin (see above). As in Gen. 14 he substitutes 'former', so here he substitutes 'formed'. Verse 22 gives another bold and graphic correction by Pusey. He deletes 'mine anger' and substitutes 'my nose'. This verse is not cited by Gibbs under *'ap;* the literal translation adopted by Pusey immediately attracts the attention of the reader.

The final two corrections give references to the corrections in the Psalms. Pusey deletes 'wrath' in verse 27, writing in the margin 'vexation from, see on Ps. 10.14.' Gibbs cites this verse, and quotes the words corrected by Pusey in Hebrew (p. 280b) under *kaʿas, 'Deut.* xxxii. 27. . . . *vexation from an enemy'.* In the correction to Ps. 10. 14. he deletes 'mischief and strife' and writes in the margin 'vexation and trouble'.

Likewise in verse 36, Pusey, having deleted 'repent himself for' in the text, writes in the margin, 'have compassion on, Ps. 135.14'. Both verses are cited by Gibbs in the entry on *nāḥam* (p. 384b):

Hithpa . . . 1. *to be grieved;* and so (1) *to have compassion,* construed with *'al, Deut.* xxxii. 36. *Ps.* cxxxv. 14.

At Ps. 135. 14. Pusey alters the AV text in the same sense, by deleting 'will repent himself concerning' and substituting 'have compassion upon'.

It seems clear that despite Pusey's doubts about Gesenius's rationalism, his support for the non-Esaian origin of the last chapters of Isaiah, and the defects he speaks of in Gesenius's lexicographical work in a letter to Nicoll,[52] in the preliminary work on his revision of the AV text he in fact follows Gesenius's renderings of Hebrew words in a great majority of cases. Pusey also, despite the great amount of time and effort he had himself given to the study of Arabic, had become doubtful of its value as an essential tool for the Old Testament scholar. Writing to Robert Wilberforce less than a month after the letter to Nicoll, Pusey dissuades him from learning Arabic, and advises him to turn his attention rather to Syriac and Chaldee.[53]

One of the most important of Gesenius's contributions to Hebrew lexicography was his moving away from the dependence upon Arabic of the school of Schultens, and his greater emphasis on Hebrew usage, and on Aramaic and Syriac.[54] Gibbs sums up the approach of Gesenius in the Preface to his Lexicon.

> The intrinsic value of a critical lexicon consists chiefly in the views of lexicography held by the author. The leading trait of Gesenius, in this respect, is judgement. He makes a sober and temperate use of the various means for determining the signification of a Hebrew word. His reasoning from grammatical analogy, from the usage of the Hebrew language, from the context, from the kindred dialects, and from the ancient versions spontaneously commends itself to the understanding. It is not sufficient to say that he rejects all mystical derivations. He has also avoided the error, nearly as dangerous, into which some modern lexicographers have run—I mean, their extravagant use of Arabic derivations, in disregard of the fact that the Hebrew is a distinct dialect, and as such has its peculiarities. But although Gesenius has restricted himself in this particular, yet his accurate knowledge of the Oriental languages, especially of their constructions and inflexions, sheds a constant and powerful light on Hebrew criticism.[55]

3

Dr Alexander Nicoll died on 25 September 1828 at the early age of 35. The Duke of Wellington wrote to Pusey on 13 November to inform him that the King had approved his appointment as

Regius Professor of Hebrew in succession to Dr Nicoll, and Pusey wrote to accept the day following.[56] This event changed everything. The doubts about the future, whether he would be able to continue to live in Oxford, whether perhaps he would have to teach in a German university, whether he might have to become a country parson, were all set at rest. Pusey and his wife moved from the Lodgings of the Regius Professor of Divinity in the south-east corner of Tom Quad, where they had been staying as Bishop Lloyd's guests, to the Lodgings of the Regius Professor of Hebrew in the south-west corner, where he remained until his death. There were other changes: Dr Nicoll had left uncompleted the Catalogues of the Arabic manuscripts in the Bodleian; these were to occupy much of Pusey's time until 1835. Apart from this, he had to organize the work of his Chair. During his second visit to Germany Pusey had been making plans for voluntary Hebrew lectures at Oriel on his return, and had written to Dr Hawkins (then Sub-Dean and Tutor) about it. He had written also on the same matter to Newman from Berlin on 25 November 1826:

> I rejoice that you are learning Hebrew, and that you already relish it. . . . I even think . . . of proposing a voluntary Hebrew Lecture, if approved of, within the College: as I think many might come to me who would be alarmed at going to Nicoll; but I must feel my way and my strength first.[57]

The opportunity now presented itself, and the lectures began on Tuesday, 3 February 1829; there were two sets of lectures, one of an elementary character, and one for more advanced students.[58] Liddon does not record that Pusey engaged the services of an assistant in giving these first lectures. But without mentioning his name, the writer of his obituary in *The Times* states:

> Dr. Pusey entered as little as he could into the controversies of the day, which could not but be painful for him, not to say embarrassing. He devoted himself to the work of his Chair. He had classes in Hebrew—senior and junior—taking the former himself, and engaging for the latter a gentleman of Hebrew extraction, who did his work well.[59]

No direct evidence has come to light concerning the identity of the gentleman of Hebrew extraction, but there is much circumstantial evidence to suggest that it might be C. W. H. Pauli, who worked closely with Pusey in the early years of his professorship.

Christian William Henry Pauli was born 'on August 11th in the first year of this present eventful century', as he wrote in later life, into a Jewish family long settled in Breslau, by name Hirsh-Prinz. He qualified as a Rabbi, and received the title of *Morenu*. He was influenced by the Reform movement in Hamburg and later was converted to Christianity, being baptized on 21 December 1823. His movements after his baptism are not known in detail, but it is known that he changed his name to Christian William Henry Pauli, moved to England and at some date before 1827 married an English wife, Ellen Gillman.[60] He had seven children, three of whom were later ordained; the eldest son, Henry Samuel Benoni, who took the degree of BA from Worcester College, Oxford in 1851, and died aged 27 in 1854;[61] Christian Abraham Manasseh, who graduated from Trinity College, Dublin in 1855, and was vicar of Bolton with Redmire, Yorks from 1856 to 1905, and died in 1906,[62] and the third son, John, who was trained at Lichfield Theological College, deacon 1861, priest 1862, and vicar of Audley, Newcastle-under-Lyme from 1874. His name appears in Crockford's *Clerical Directory* for 1917, but not in 1920, so he died between 1917 and 1920. Two other of his children became medical practitioners, the youngest having the Christian names Gillman Churton. The Christian name Churton has continued to be used in the Pauli family down the generations, and there is a family tradition that Christian William Henry was befriended by a Churton, presumably by Edward Churton, later Archdeacon of Cleveland, who was an undergraduate at Christ Church at the same time as Pusey, or possibly William Ralph, who was a Fellow of Oriel with Pusey, and who died in 1828. Christian William Henry Pauli himself was ordained deacon and priest in 1841, and spent the rest of his life as a missionary for the London Society for promoting Christianity among the Jews, first in Berlin, then at Amsterdam, and died on 4 May 1877. C. W. H. Pauli was never a member of Oxford or any other

university, but was given the status of Privilegiatus in 1841.[63]
Whether or not he was in fact the gentleman of Hebrew
extraction in *The Times* obituary, he worked closely with Pusey,
and his work throws much light on the teaching of Hebrew in
Oxford in the 1830s.

Before he began his Hebrew lectures Pusey wrote to
Newman about the form they should take, and answered
Newman's reply on 10 January 1829.[64] He mentions in the
letter the plan of using a Hebrew Grammar as a text-book,
either Lee's or Stuart's:

> I fear, however, that there will be some difficulty in putting
> this into practice [he wrote to Newman] because that which I
> have compiled is on too different a plan to be easily
> conformed to either: something however of this I hope to be
> able to do, at least to select the portions of Lee's Grammar
> which should be read previous to each lecture, and criticise
> this as far as I may venture, but without binding myself down
> to mere criticism or illustration.

Samuel Lee, the author of the Grammar, was in 1829 Sir
Thomas Adams's Professor of Arabic at Cambridge, becoming
Regius Professor of Hebrew there in 1831. His *Grammar of the
Hebrew Language* was first published in 1827, in an edition of
1500 copies. These sold well, and a second edition was needed
by 1832.[65] Lee had left school at the age of twelve, and been
apprenticed to a carpenter. While working at his trade he had
taught himself Latin, Greek, Hebrew and a number of other
oriental languages. At the age of 30, with the help of the Church
Missionary Society, he matriculated at Queens' College, Cambridge in 1813, took his BA in 1818, MA in 1819, and was
appointed to the Arabic Chair. Lee was a touchy and quarrel-
some man: he had written tracts against Dr Laurence's *Remarks
upon the Critical Principles*: his Grammar and that of Ewald
appeared in the same year, and a lively and long-lasting
controversy broke out between them.[66] The polemical tone of
Dr Lee's writing is well illustrated in the Preface to the second
edition of his *Hebrew Grammar* referred to above. In 1835 Ewald
wrote to Pusey to thank him for the gift of the completed Arabic
Catalogues, and to commend to Pusey a friend of his who was

about to visit Oxford. In this letter he writes, 'Quite out of his own impulse he resolved to translate the Hebrew Grammar, and as Lee's work does not seem to satisfy science, I willingly gave my consent . . .'.[67]

Moses Stuart, the author of the other Grammar, was three years older than Lee, was born on 26 March 1780 at Wilton, Connecticut, and had been trained as a lawyer, but never practised. He was ordained to the ministry, and became pastor of a Congregational church in New Haven in 1806. Less than four years later he was appointed Professor of Sacred Literature at Andover Theological Seminary, Massachusetts. Here he began to study Hebrew, and wrote a short grammar which he circulated among his students in manuscript. In 1821 he enlarged his Grammar and imported a fount of Hebrew type, which he set himself. He reprinted this Grammar with a praxis on portions of Genesis and the Psalms in 1823.[68] This Grammar was mainly a translation of Gesenius's work, and would be the edition Pusey intended to use.

Moses Stuart is an important figure in the history not only of American, but also of English work on Hebrew grammar and lexicography. Josiah Gibbs, the translator of the 1815 Gesenius *Handwörterbuch*, was a pupil of his, and gave some help in the preparation of the Grammar in 1821.[69]

This lexicon continued to be the standard Hebrew lexicon in the U.S.A. until the appearance in 1836 of Edward Robinson's translation of Gesenius's *Manual Lexicon* of 1833. Robinson, too, was a pupil of Moses Stuart, moving to Andover in 1821, and becoming an instructor in Hebrew at the Andover Theological Seminary in 1822.[70]

During this period books from America were not imported into Britain in any quantity, and were therefore difficult to obtain here. Pusey's possession of the 1824 American edition of Gibbs's *Lexicon* is consequently the more remarkable. The difficulty of obtaining copies of Gibbs's *Lexicon* was overcome by its publication in England (London 1827, price £1–5s, second English edition 1832).[71]

Bearing in mind the idiosyncracies of Samuel Lee, it is not surprising that there was a desire for Stuart's Grammar to be generally available for use in England, as can be seen from

Pusey's reference to Stuart's Grammar in the letter to Newman quoted above. The principles on which he compiled his Grammar are set out by Moses Stuart in his Preface to the 1828 Andover edition, signed THE AUTHOR and dated '*Andover Theological Seminary*, Sept. 10. 1828',[72] and in the Preface to his *Hebrew Chrestomathy*, Andover 1829.[73] In the Preface to the Grammar he writes:

> In regard to the copiousness of the present grammar, it does not exceed the number of pages in the abridged edition of Gesenius' Hebrew Grammar, which has now gone through nine editions. That it contains much more than these abridged editions is true; for these continually refer to the large *Thesaurus*[74] by the same author. Experienced teachers, who have a thorough knowledge of Hebrew, and who wish to communicate a radical knowledge of it to their pupils, will not employ a *skeleton* grammar. . . . Whoever uses a skeleton grammar merely, must either remain ignorant of more than one half of the grammatical phenomena of a language, or he must consume his time in filling up, by means of his teacher or of other Grammars, the skeleton which he uses.[75]

Later on in the Preface at p. vii, he refers to the notes on Part 1 and Part 2 of his *Chrestomathy*, where he sets out the method he recommends for the learning of Grammar and the reading of the Hebrew text in the *Chrestomathy*.[76]

> In the Preface to my Hebrew Grammar, p. vii, I have given general directions for the *first* reading or study of the same, recommending that the parts included in *brackets* should be omitted, and that when the student has advanced as far as *the declension of nouns*, he should begin to read and parse in the Chrestomathy.[77]

Stuart allows himself a justifiable boast in the Preface to the *Chrestomathy*:

> As the circle of *elementary* Hebrew books is now completed, and a Lexicon, Grammar, and Chrestomathy will not, all together, cost more than the former price of a Hebrew Lexicon, it is hoped that the progress of Hebrew study may

keep pace with the facility and cheapness of the means to aid it.[78]

The 11th edition of the *Encyclopaedia Britannica* gives the credit for the publication of Moses Stuart's Grammar in England to Pusey: '[the Grammar] was republished in England by Dr. Pusey in 1831.'[79] This is not strictly correct, and the truth of the matter is more interesting. In a publisher's announcement at the beginning of the Oxford edition of the *Chrestomathy* there appears the following:

A GRAMMAR OF THE HEBREW LANGUAGE. Republished under the care of Mr Pauli, professor of the Hebrew and Chaldaean languages; and the Rev. J. Jones, of Christ Church. Fourth edition; reprinted with the concurrence of the Author, 8vo. *bds.* 14s. Oxford, 1831.

This is enlarged upon by the Publisher in a prefatory note, The Publisher to the Reader:

The principal reasons that have induced me to reprint the following work, are the high encomiums which have been bestowed upon it by all acquainted with its usefulness; the difficulty of obtaining a sufficient supply from America to meet the demand; and the high price at which it must be sold when procured, in consequence of the expensiveness of importation.

Among those most conversant with the subject in this University, whom I may particularise as approving of this Grammar, are Dr Nicol [*sic*] the late Regius-professor of Hebrew, who regretted that he could not constantly recommend it to his pupils from the difficulty they found in obtaining it, and Dr Pusey, the present Regius-professor, who recommends its employment to beginners, and to those names I might add a host of others, if they were not in themselves quite sufficient. . . . This reprint is made with the full sanction and approbation of the learned Author; and . . . will shortly be followed by a reprint of his Chrestomathy, or a selection of easy lessons adapted to this Grammar.

The following pages, besides a more than common

diligence in the office reading, have been carefully superintended through the press by Mr Pauli, professor of the Hebrew and Chaldaean languages, and the Rev. J. Jones of Christ Church, who has lately earned himself so much credit by a new translation of Isaiah from the original Hebrew. From the scrupulous attention which these gentlemen have given to their task, I feel sure that I run no risk of contradiction in asserting that this Grammar will be found as correct as any yet published in the same language.[80]

It is not in itself surprising that Pusey should have introduced the grammar and lexicon of Gesenius to Oxford, despite his reservations about his theological and critical opinions. What is remarkable is that after his two visits to Germany, Pusey should have introduced Gesenius's work to Oxford not direct from Germany, but by way of the United States of America. No doubt one reason would be the fact that up to this date Gesenius had published his works in German, which was known by so few in early nineteenth-century Oxford. How the American Hebraists came to have so great an influence in early nineteenth century Oxford is an interesting matter for speculation; but there seems little doubt that Pusey was an important figure in furthering their influence. The error in the *Encyclopaedia Britannica* mentioned above shows that the author of the article there believed that Pusey's part in the reprinting in England of Stuart's Grammar was very important, even though he exaggerates in saying that Pusey himself republished the work.

It is possible that the connecting link between Pusey and the Andover Hebraists might have been Edward Robinson. After coming under the influence of Moses Stuart in 1821 and working at Andover until 1826, he went to Germany, where he stayed for four years, working in Göttingen, Halle and Bonn, and becoming a friend of Gesenius, Rödiger, Tholuck, Neander and Ritter, the great geographer, and married in 1828 Therese Albertine Louise, the daughter of Ludwig Heinrich von Jakob, a professor at Halle.[81] He is probably best remembered in this country for his *Hebrew and English Lexicon of the Old Testament* (1836).

No evidence has come to light that Pusey met Robinson

during his second visit to Germany, but it is not beyond the bounds of possibility that these two young English-speaking scholars, moving in the same circles in Germany might have become acquainted. If it were so, it would help to explain Pusey's possession of a copy of the American edition of Gibbs's lexicon, his furtherance of the publication of the works of Moses Stuart in England, and their use by his pupils. Whether they met then or not, credit can be given to Pusey for the fact that from the time that he became Regius Professor the influence of American scholars, particularly those at Andover, Massachusetts, had a leading place in the English-speaking world of Hebrew studies.

Pusey himself published no Hebrew Grammar or text-book. C. W. H. Pauli in 1839 published his *Analecta Hebraica*, with a key to the second and third sections.[82] The first edition was in two volumes: a second edition appeared in 1842, a reprint of the first, but with the two parts bound up together in one volume.[83] Despite the need for a second edition within three years, *Analecta Hebraica* does not appear to have been a work constantly in demand by students of Hebrew: the copy of the 1839 edition in two volumes in the Bodleian[84] had the pages of the work itself cut only to page 45 in September 1981. The present writer bought a copy in York in 1979 of the 1842 edition in one volume, with hardly any of the pages cut. Nevertheless, it is an important work for those interested in Hebrew scholarship in Oxford in the early years of Pusey's professorship, as illustrating practically the principles on which he wished the teaching of Hebrew to be based. These principles Pusey set out in his letter to Newman in 1829, and five years later in a letter to the Revd W. Dalby in February 1834.[85] He told Newman that he intended to use a Hebrew Grammar (Lee's or Stuart's) as a text-book, requiring his class to read portions of the grammar before each lecture, enlarging upon these in the course of the lecture.

'Unless one teaches . . . more than the common matter of fact which is to be found in grammars', he wrote to Newman, 'the lectures will be (as were, at first at least, those of poor N.'s in grammar) thought to be of little use.' In his letter to Dalby he

was able from experience to state his principles under
numbered headings: '(1) to read *at first* nothing of grammar
but what is absolutely necessary: . . . (2) In reading the Bible,
to become thoroughly acquainted with the meaning of the
words in each portion which is read, . . . (3) Read loud. (4)
For a long time read no criticisms or commentators—read
Hebrew and not about Hebrew. (5) Read the easiest
Hebrew . . . for a long time before attempting the more
difficult.'

This method, and these principles, were those adopted by
Pauli. He begins with the alphabet, vowels and pronunciation.
The section headed Pronunciation consists of the whole of the
first chapter of Jonah in Hebrew, followed by a Praxis of
pronunciation by his friend the Rev. W. T. Phillips, Fellow of
Magdalen. Thus the student is first of all, without any
instruction in grammar or vocabulary, introduced to the
Hebrew text. Every word is transliterated, every vowel sign and
accent is described. In the Preface Pauli recommends three
Grammars: 'By W. T. Phillips, BD, Fellow of Magalen College,
Oxford, Second Edition; the Rev. S. Lee, DD, Professor of
Hebrew in the University of Cambridge, &c., &c., Second
Edition; Moses Stuart, Associate Professor of Sacred Literature
at Andover, United States, Fifth Edition.' He adopts these as
being those in most common use.[86] Before going over the
praxis of reading, the pupil is required to read either Phillips
from §22 to §86, or Lee from Art. 58–69 or Stuart from §53 to
§104.[87] The explanation of the first word in Jonah I.1. amply
demonstrates Phillips's method:

JONAH I.1

Vā'-y'heé. The first consonant is *vaw* (*v*), under which is
Pathach (*ă*). The second consonant is *Yōd* (*y*), under which is
Sh'va simple, which indicates the absence of a vowel. The
third consonant is *Hay* (*h*), which has under it *Chirik*, and
when alone, is pronounced like the *i* in *pin*; but being
followed by *Yōd* (*y*), with which the preceding *Chirik*
quiesces, is thus made long, and expressed by the symbol (*ee*).
The sound of final *Yōd* being quiescent, is not heard, and is
therefore not expressed in Roman characters. The mark

103

affixed to *Pathach* is the euphonic accent, also called *Metheg*; it separates the *Pathach* from the following consonant *Yōd*, and gives it a long sound, expressed by the symbol (*ā*). The mark over the last *Yōd* is the tonic accent, which serves to elevate the syllable.[88]

Phillips deals with every word in the first three verses in as much detail. From verse 4 the detail is reduced, and after verse 5 there is little more than transliteration. This is Pusey's method applied rigorously: prepare first from a grammar, then immerse the pupil immediately in the text. The portions of grammar set in Lee consist of Lecture 2, On the Hebrew Accents, &c., which itself contains a transliteration at Art. 68 of 2 Kings 1.6., with commentary in section 69.[89] The transliteration of Jonah 1 concludes Section 1. Section 2 is on Nouns, Adjectives, the Construct State, and comparison of Adjectives. Section 3 is on Verbs, and Section 4 is again on Nouns, treated at a much more advanced level, with copious notes and references, particularly from mediaeval Jewish grammarians. There is also an appendix, seventy-two pages long, treating at a more advanced level points from the Lectures on Verbs in Section 3. Before each part of each lecture, in the first three sections, references are given to Phillips, Stuart, and Lee for grammatical preparation. The Praxes are all from Hebrew to English, with copious footnotes. The Key covers only the second and third sections of the work: Pauli gives no translation of the fourth section, because as he explains (*Key*, p. i), 'the student, having come thus far, will not only be tolerably expert in the use of his Lexicon, but will also possess some copia verborum'.

Pauli reflects Pusey's views on the Massoretic text, and on Gesenius, and holds very strongly to the AV text in English: by the time *Analecta Hebraica* was published, Pusey's views had become more conservative, and in November 1839 he wrote a note in the small Bible repudiating the alterations made in 1827.[90] Pauli states in the Preface to the *Analecta* (p. iv) that he places entire confidence in the Massoretic text. In the Preface to the *Key* (p. iii) he commends Van der Hooght's Bible, 'This is decidedly the best of all Hebrew Bibles ever printed'. Van der Hooght's Bible was the one used by Pusey throughout his life, and found open on a table by his bed when he died:[91] it is preserved at Pusey House. Pauli, like Pusey, recommended Gesenius's Lexicon, but with the same reservations:

> Beginners should use Gesenius' Hebrew and English Lexicon by Dr Robinson, and be on their guard, as it is, alas! not free from some dangerous doctrines. Simonis' Lexicon by Winer is, *as a Lexicon*, decidedly better than Gesenius'; but is, on account of his theory of deriving every word from a verb, too difficult to be used by beginners.[92]

Pauli was, it must be remembered, a Jewish Rabbi converted to Christianity, and this too is reflected in *Analecta Hebraica*. As a convert, he repudiates much Rabbinical work; but points out, too, its virtues:

> The writings of the Rabbies [*sic*] contain, doubtless, much useless and superstitious matter, but they are undeniably a rich storehouse of important truth, especially as it [*sic*] regards Grammar; a fact which Gesenius acknowledges in the Preface of his Lehrgebäude; although at the time he wrote that book, he could not have entered further than the threshold of this vast labyrinth.[93]

Particularly in Section 4 he frequently quotes the Targums and Jewish Grammarians and Commentators, for example D. Kimchi, Ibn Ezra, Rashi and Solomon ben Melech, with page references to Kimchi's *Michlol*. He takes opportunities to relate comments by Jewish writers to Christian belief: for example:

> Isa. xlv. 25. Jonathan paraphrases this verse with these, for the Christian, highly interesting words, . . . '*By* the WORD OF GOD (ὁ λόγος τοῦ θεοῦ) all the seed of Israel shall be justified and glorified'.[94]

Apart from this tendency to make use of his Rabbinic learning, often for apologetic purposes, Pauli's *Analecta Hebraica* is clearly a practical attempt to put in a permanent published form the principles adopted by Pusey; something not surprising in one who had worked with him in the publication in England of Stuart's Grammar, who may have acted as a deputy lecturer for Pusey, and one who shared his cautious and

conservative views. *Analecta Hebraica*, published when Pusey
had been Regius Professor for a decade, and not a work which
was to become a standard text-book, gives an insight into
Hebrew studies in Oxford in Pusey's early years as Professor.

4

No survey of Pusey's early Semitic work would be complete
without some account of his activities in increasing the
collections of Semitic manuscripts and printed books in the
Bodleian. His first opportunity came during his second visit to
Germany, when Dr Nicoll asked him to report on the condition
of the books in the Oppenheimer library. David ben Abraham
Oppenheimer (1664–1735) had made an outstanding collection,
estimated by J. C. Wolf at seven thousand items, including 1000
manuscripts.[95] After Oppenheimer's death the collection
passed to his son Joseph; after his death it came into the
possession of his son-in-law, and then passed to his widow, who
sought the opinion of Moses Mendelssohn and J. D. Michaelis,
who valued it at between 50,000 and 60,000 thalers in 1775. It
became the subject of a lawsuit between the heirs, and was not
released until 1826. A catalogue was made of it in 1764, and
another in 1782.[96] Finally, yet another catalogue was published
in 1826, in Hebrew and Latin, with a preface giving an account
of its valuation, expressing the hope that it might be sold as a
complete collection, but ending with the threat that 'if within a
year and a half the result does not match the hope we entertain,
beginning on 11 June 1827, the printed books and manuscripts
will be put separately to public auction in Hamburg.'[97]

   This was the position when Pusey wrote to Nicoll from Bonn
in March 1827:

   I trouble you thus soon with another [letter] from ye fear that
   in ye plan wh. ye Curators of ye Bodleian have adopted with
   reference to ye Oppenheimer collection, ye real Jews will
   out-Jew ye Judaising Straus. I hardly know whether the
   former wd. feel themselves in conscience bound to abide by
   any offer they had made if a prospect of a better presented
   itself, and indeed they are suspected to be only feeling ye
   pulse of ye difft. wd.-be purchasers, but ye present plan of
   offering a lower sum in ye 1st instance has already been tried

by ye Berlin Ministerium, & served at least as ye pretext for subsequently refusing ye sum (Near £1800, I believe) for which it was offered to them. Possibly, were their proposal at once acceded to, they might feel themselves not justified in retracting. £200 is not a sum, for wh. to lose ye opportunity of acquiring a collection, superior in its printed books to that at Parma of De Rossi, and wh. probably wd. never again be formed.[98]

Nicoll acted upon Pusey's advice immediately. He consulted his fellow Curators, and set off for Germany, ready to offer a price for the collection. When he arrived in Hamburg he found that the legal squabbles were still continuing, so he left Hamburg, and arrived in Göttingen just in time to attend the funeral of Eichhorn, who had died on Thursday, 14 June. He remained in Göttingen to visit the University, returning to Hamburg only to find that the legal battle still continued, and that no end of it was in sight. He therefore had to return to Oxford with his mission unaccomplished.[99] By the time the legal difficulties had been overcome, Dr Nicoll was dead, and Pusey was a Curator in his place.

Pusey's estimate in his letter to Nicoll was a remarkably accurate one: the great collection which had been valued at between 50,000 and 60,000 thalers was bought for the Bodleian Library for 9,000, a sum in sterling of £2,080. The Hebrew section of the Bodleian was not, until the purchase of the Oppenheimer collection, very large. To the nucleus there in Bodley's lifetime had been added some fifty manuscripts received from Archbishop Laud, and a collection of printed books from Selden; in 1693 the collections of Pococke and Huntington provided together about 325 manuscripts, and a further 110 were added in 1817 when the Canonici collection was acquired. With the Oppenheimer collection were acquired some 5,000 volumes, of which 780 were manuscripts.[100] W.D. Macray goes so far as to say that 'the great Hebrew collection, which at present forms so distinguished a feature in the contents of the Library, was virtually commenced in this year [1829] by the purchase at Hamburg, for £2,080 of the famous Oppenheimer library'.[101]

Pusey was in a very good position to exercise his skill and acumen in enlarging the Hebrew collections in Bodley. The constitution of the Library was regulated by a statute of Convocation made in 1813. Under it the general direction of the Library was left in the hands of eight ex-officio Curators, who were the Vice-Chancellor, the Proctors, and the Regius Professors of Divinity, Civil Law, Medicine, Hebrew and Greek.[102] Bodley's Librarian from 1813–60 was Dr Bulkeley Bandinel, Fellow of New College, son of the first Bampton Lecturer, Dr James Bandinel of Jesus. He had served as a naval chaplain in HMS *Victory*, and was a formidable character, who lashed his staff with his tongue in true quarter-deck manner. The Curators themselves found their Librarian alarming, apart from two of them: Max Müller says that there were only two men of whom Dr Bandinel was afraid, Dr Pusey and Benjamin Jowett.[103]

The composition of the body of Curators made Pusey's influence the greater: the Vice-Chancellor and Proctors were Curators only during their terms of office, and had little to do with the day-to-day control of the Library, and in Pusey's younger days three of the five Regius Professors, Dr Hampden, Dr Phillimore and Dr Kidd, did not take a very active part in the affairs of the Library. The result was that 'the control of the library, for which the whole body of Curators were nominally responsible, was in fact in the hands of Dr Pusey and Dr Gaisford. The latter in particular, with his enthusiasm for Greek manuscripts and his intimate knowledge of book values, was the real ruler'.[104]

If Dr Gaisford were the real ruler, Pusey ran him a close second. Of his early Semitic work, this eagerness for, and ability in, the purchase of books for the Semitic collections of the Bodleian was the only part that continued unchanged and unabated after he began to take a leading part in the Tractarian Movement from 1835 onwards. A notable feature of the later purchases was that many of them, like the Oppenheimer collection, were bought for very low prices. In 1843 the collection of Ethiopic manuscripts made by James Bruce, the explorer of the sources of the Nile (who had presented the manuscript of the Ethiopic Enoch, edited by Dr Laurence), together with some seventy important Arabic manuscripts collected by him, was bought for the Bodleian for £1000. Bruce had offered the collection to the British Museum nearly seventy years earlier for £25,000.[105]

In 1844 Pusey was instrumental in buying for the Library 483 volumes from the library of Gesenius, who had died in October 1842, and whose library was sold by auction at Halle in January 1844. The Curators secured this collection for £146 14s 6d.[106] Four years later, in 1848, the library of Heimann Joseph Michael, the Jewish collector (1792–1848) who had spent thirty years in building up his collection, was sold in Hamburg. The British Museum bought his printed books, but the manuscripts, in 862 volumes, comprising nearly 1300 works, were bought for the Bodleian for £1030. The collection included 110 vellum manuscripts, written between 1240 and 1450.[107] At this period additions were being made almost every year through the agency of Asher, a Jewish bookseller in Berlin, and others, apart from the great collections bought at auction. In 1853 seventy-two manuscripts from the Reggio collection were bought for £108, and other manuscripts appear year by year in the accounts.[108] Interest in the Samaritan dialect of Aramaic increased in the 1860s, and Dr Pusey in 1868 persuaded Convocation to vote £360 for the purchase of a collection of Samaritan manuscripts. In this purchase Pusey did not allow his enthusiasm to outrun his business acumen: the manuscripts were found on examination to be Arabic texts written in Samaritan characters, so the sale was not completed, and they were bought instead by Lord Crawford. In the following year, however, a fragment of a Samaritan Targum and two Hebrew manuscripts were bought for £200 from Dr Neubauer.[109]

It was in 1868 that Dr Neubauer began his catalogue of the Hebrew manuscripts, which occupied him until 1886.[110] It was due to the influence of Pusey that this great scholar settled in Oxford.[111] The credit for bringing the other great cataloguer, Moritz Steinschneider, to Oxford must go to Dr Bulkeley Bandinel, but Pusey was responsible also for starting Payne Smith in 1859 on a catalogue of all the Syriac manuscripts which the Library then possessed.[112]

It is a strange and interesting feature of Pusey's life and work that the only part of his early work as a Semitic scholar that came through the cataclysm of his adherence to the Tractarian Movement and continued unabated was this enthusiastic effort to build up the Semitic collections in Bodley: it could be seen, indeed, as one aspect of his scholarship being subordinated to what was really a curious sort of statesmanship, as Dr H. C. G. Matthew has so cogently argued.[113] To do so would, however, be unduly to simplify a very complex question. The keen prices at which the collections were bought are evidence of business acumen; but the discernment in making the purchases is that of a scholar, as is his encouragement of such men as Neubauer and Payne Smith to catalogue the collections. Pusey's activity as a Curator of the Bodleian provides an illustration of what might have been in other aspects of his work, if the course of his life had been different. His revision of the text of the Old Testament in the AV, if he had continued with it, might have anticipated the work of S. R. Driver in this field by half a century. As it is, on the scanty evidence provided by the corrections in the small Bible, it is remarkable how often Pusey anticipates the translation adopted by S. R. Driver in *The Parallel Psalter*.

In the exercise of his duties as Professor, Pusey's memory has been ill-served by his biographer: Liddon is presenting ὁ μέγας to succeeding generations, and his work comes nearer to being hagiography than biography. Robert Gandell, editor of Lightfoot's *Horae Hebraicae*, and Laudian Professor of Arabic 1861–87, who was Pusey's deputy lecturer from 1848 to 1882, gets no mention in Liddon's index.[114] Dr Neubauer is referred to only once in the index, i.e., when Liddon cites Pusey's request to Neubauer to edit the work on the Jewish interpreters of Isaiah 53, which Neubauer produced in collaboration with S. R. Driver, and with an Introduction by Pusey, in 1876.

The importance of Pusey's initiative in the production of these volumes is well brought out in R. Loewe's Prolegomenon to the reprint of the work in 1969.[115] In particular Loewe draws attention to Pusey's ability in dealing with Rabbinical literature:

In his introduction to the present corpus [Pusey] reveals an unsuspected familiarity with post-biblical Jewish literature; and although his access to much of it will have been, in the

110

first instance, through such secondary sources (or rather *collectanea* with translations) as Ugolini's *Thesaurus*, he could clearly read rabbinic texts in the original competently enough to control the available translations and to make responsible use of those not translated in print.[116]

Pusey's library also was kept up to date in the field of Hebrew and Old Testament Studies. On one sheet, numbered 34, of the lists at Pusey House there appear among other works, *The Jewish Interpreters on Isaiah LIII* (Driver and Neubauer) 2 vols. cloth. Parker 1877; *A Commentary upon the Books of Jeremiah and Ezekiel* (Driver) 1 vol. paper (Williams and Norgate, 1871);[117] *Use of the Tenses in Hebrew* (Driver) 1 vol. cloth (Clarendon, 1874); Ibn Ezra's *Commentary on the Canticles*, 1 vol. cloth (Trübner, 1874); *Samaritan Targum* (Nutt) 1 vol. cloth (Trübner, 1874). On other sheets A. B. Davidson's *Hebrew Grammar*, 1874, and *The Merchant Taylors' Hebrew Grammar* (Bagster 1877), appear.

Pusey's life was a sad one: his wife died in 1839, and he survived all but one of his children. This, however, is not enough to account for the extremes of asceticism he wished to practise, and his appalling desire not to smile except in the presence of children.[118] This aspect of his life merits investigation; but it must not be assumed that these aberrations are reasons in themselves for dismissing him out of hand as a scholar. The *Lectures on Daniel the Prophet* too have become almost a byword in some quarters for an unscholarly and unbudging conservatism.[119] But S. R. Driver, who was far from sharing Pusey's opinions, gave a very different verdict upon this work, describing it as 'extremely learned and thorough.'[120] Sir Steven Runciman's warning should always be borne in mind by those who investigate the work of scholars of former times, 'Scholarship should be judged by the standards of its age, not be the tastes of subsequent generations'.[121]

Nevertheless it must be admitted that G. Buchanan Gray's estimate of Pusey's later works is fair, that Pusey's commentaries on the Minor Prophets and Daniel 'were monuments of learning, but especially in the latter, of learning devoted to a dying, and now long-dead cause'.[122] Perhaps the most unfortunate feature of Pusey's ultra-conservative position was that it was not something that grew with advancing years, but was adopted by him in early middle age, as shown by the repudiation in 1839 of his corrections in the small Bible in 1827. His early promise as an innovator in Hebrew and biblical scholarship never came to fruition. It is surprising to find him writing in his mid-sixties or later in much the same way as he wrote to Newman and R. I. Wilberforce in the 1820s, and giving the impression that he saw Hebrew scholarship as mainly a means towards the end of making improvements in the English text. After his death a letter appeared in *The Guardian* from the Revd A. J. M'Gowan, enclosing a letter he had received from Dr Pusey in reply to an enquiry he had made about the critical study of Hebrew. The date of Pusey's letter is not given, but it must have been later than the date of Mr M'Gowan's ordination in 1863, perhaps some years later. In it Pusey dissuades his correspondent from learning Arabic, and then goes on to say,

> For devotional use—i.e. for the vivid perception of the force of the words, in which men, taught by the Holy Ghost, wrote—a moderate knowledge of Hebrew suffices, which may be obtained without great difficulty. But for a critical knowledge of Hebrew by which a person would be fitted to improve on the Eng. Vers., years of continual study would be required.[123]

Buchanan Gray points out one way in which Pusey's influence continued:

> By the part he took in establishing university scholarships for Hebrew he secured a succession of students aiming at an exact and comprehensive study of the language, and thus prepared good ground for his successor.[124]

Pusey's achievement in completing the Arabic Catalogues is everywhere acknowledged. He was the prime mover, at the age of 27, in acquiring the Oppenheimer collection, the greatest of the Hebrew collections in the Bodleian.

Over and above all these, perhaps his greatest memorial as a Hebrew scholar is the first paragraph of the Preface to the *Oxford Hebrew Lexicon*. His name is not mentioned there, but those of Josiah Willard Gibbs and Edward Robinson are. It was

Pusey who introduced to Oxford the works of Gesenius, not direct from Germany but by way of the work of the American Hebraists, Moses Stuart and his pupils Gibbs and Robinson. In doing this he set the course for British students of Hebrew for more than a century. This bore further fruit in Anglo-American co-operation when Robinson's Lexicon was revised by the collaboration of his successor with two American scholars to produce the *Oxford Hebrew Lexicon,* known to all English-speaking Hebraists by their names, 'Brown, Driver and Briggs.'

So many people have helped me in writing this essay that it is impossible to name them all here: I hope they will accept this general acknowledgement. I must, however, mention particularly Professor James Barr, Professor E.W.Nicholson, and my former Tutor, Professor T.W.Thacker, who all read this essay at all its stages, and made many valuable suggestions; also Canon Cheslyn Jones, who first encouraged me to work on Pusey's Bible. To them, as to others not named, I am deeply grateful.

NOTES

1 *The Times,* Monday, 18 September 1882, p. 5.

2 A. S. Herbert, *Historical Catalogue of Printed Editions of the English Bible, 1525–1961* (London, BFBS, 1968), p. 283.

3 See B. M. Metzger, *The Early Versions of the New Testament.* (Oxford 1977), pp. 72–73.

4 Liddon, vol. 1, p. 23.

5 Bodleian Library, Oxford, MS. Montagu d. 11 (135b.).

6 See *On a New Translation of the Bible,* Bodleian shelfmark 8° N 43 BS, containing five such pamphlets, including Laurence's *Remarks upon the Critical Principles.* . . .

7 Bodleian shelfmark 8° V 176 Th.

8 R. Laurence, *Reply to 'Some Strictures'* . . . pp. 12–13.

9 J. A. Emerton, *Obituary of G. R. Driver. Proceedings of the British Academy,* vol. 63 (1977), pp. 345–62, especially pp. 360–1.

10 Ibid., p. 360.

11 Liddon, vol. 1, pp. 54–5.

12 For details of Nicoll's life and work see J. L. Speller, *Alexander Nicoll and the Study of German Biblical Criticism in Early Nineteenth Century Oxford, JEH* 30 (1979), pp. 451–9.

13   I wish to thank the Provost and Fellows of Oriel College for allowing me to copy from the Borrowers' Register the books borrowed by E. B. Pusey, and to see many of the books borrowed by him, and to thank the staff of the Library for their help and patience with me.

14   Bodleian Library MS. Top. Oxon. c.326, fos. 50–51. I am grateful to the Revd P. F. Johnson for drawing my attention to Dr Speller's article, whence I obtained the reference to this letter.

15   I wish to thank the Principal and Librarians of Pusey House for allowing me to copy Pusey's corrections in this Bible, and to work in the Pamphlet Room at Pusey House.

16   I am obliged to the Dean of Durham, Dr Peter Baelz, who described to me the lay-out of his (and Dr Pusey's) former lodgings in Christ Church.

17   Liddon, vol. 1, p. 62.

18   J. Parsons, *Some Particulars of the Life of Alexander Nicoll, D.C.L., etc.*, in A. Nicoll, *Sermons*, (Oxford, Baxter, 1830), p. xxxvii.

19   See Pusey's letter to Nicoll, 1827, MS. Top. Oxon. c.326, fo. 51.

20   M. M. Kalisch, *A Hebrew Grammar* (London, Longmans, Green, and Co., 1862–3), pt 2, p. 38.

21   Ibid., p. 39.

22   Liddon, vol. 1, p. 96.

23   Liddon, vol. 1, p. 72.

24   See Speller, pp. 451–452.

25   Liddon, vol. 1, p. 77.

26   See Liddon, vol. 1, p. 89.

27   See, for example, J. W. Burgon, *Lives of Twelve Good Men* (London, John Murray, 1882), vol. 2, p. 82.

28   Liddon, vol. 1, p. 105.

29   T. Witton Davies, *Heinrich Ewald* (London, T. Fisher Unwin, 1903), pp. 7–9.

30   Bod. Lib. MS. Top. Oxon. c.326, fos. 50–51.

31   Liddon, I. p. 105.

32   An account of the *Hamasa* is given in Reynold A. Nicholson, *A Literary History of the Arabs* (London, T. Fisher Unwin, 1907). Book 2 is the Chapter of Dirges (Babu 'l-Marathi).

33   This copy appears on the foolscap sheets of Pusey's books at Pusey House.

34   Not Bonn, as stated by Liddon (vol. 1, p. 105): see T. Witton Davies, pp. 7–9.

35   *Lexicon Manuale Hebraicum et Chaldaicum in Veteris Testamenti Libros,* . . . edidit Dr Georg Benedict Winer (Lipsiae 1828).

36   Ibid. Preface, p. 3.

37   A few examples of the citing of Gesenius in Winer's Lexicon, picked at

random, can be seen at pp. 428, 461, 505, 585, 644. An example of the citing of Ewald's Grammar by Winer can be seen at p. 120.

38 Liddon, vol. 1, p. 114.

39 Liddon, vol. 1, pp. 117–118.

40 The dates shown by postmarks are from letters preserved at Pusey House, Oxford.

41 Liddon, vol. 1, p. 118.

42 Liddon, vol. 1, p. 120.

43 Liddon, vol. 1, p. 120.

44 See Gesenius, *Thesaurus*, tom. 1. fasc. posterior (Lipsiae 1835), p. 386b. where he translates, *agite! celebrate Dominum*. Cf. also Delitzsch, *Biblical Commentary on the Psalms*, trans. D. Eaton (London 1889), vol. 3, p. 319; Perowne, *The Book of Psalms* (1871), vol. 2, p. 405; Kirkpatrick, *The Book of Psalms* (Cambridge 1903), p. 772, and Kittel's translation, *Wohlan* (*Die Psalmen*, Leipzig 1922, p. 408).

45 *A Hebrew and English Lexicon to the Old Testament, including the Biblical Chaldee.* Edited with improvements, from the German works of Gesenius, by Josiah W. Gibbs, AM, of the Theological Seminary, Andover, U.S. (London, James Duncan, and Whittaker, Treacher, and Co., 1832). (Henceforward cited as 'Gibbs': page references are to the 1832 English edition.)

46 Liddon, vol. 1, p. 120.

47 Cf. *Oxford Hebrew Lexicon*, ed. Brown, Driver and Briggs (1906), p. 832a.

48 See Gesenius, *Thesaurus*, tom. 1. fasc. prior (Lipsiae 1829), p. 303a.

49 S. R. Driver, *The Book of Exodus* (Cambridge, 1911), p. 244.

50 Cf. *Oxford Hebrew Lexicon*, p. 855a.

51 Cf. J. Simonis, *Lexicon Manuale Hebraicum et Chaldaicum*, ed. J. G. Eichhorn (Halle 1793), p. 1370.

52 Bodleian shelf-mark MS. Top. Oxon. c.326, fo. 50, 51.

53 See Kensington MSS. B.2. 16 April 1827, cited by David Newsome, *The Parting of Friends* (London, John Murray, 1966), pp. 78–9.

54 For a full survey of the development of Gesenius's views on Hebrew Lexicography, see E. F. Miller, *The Influence of Gesenius on Hebrew Lexicography (Contributions to Oriental History and Philology no. 11)* (New York, Columbia University Press, 1927).

55 Gibbs, preface, pp. iii, iv.

56 Liddon, vol. 1, pp. 186–7.

57 'E.B.P. to Newman', vol. 1, p. 53 (Pusey House).

58 Liddon, vol. 1, pp. 194–7.

59 *The Times*, Monday, 18 September 1882, p. 5.

60 I am grateful to Mr H. C. Pauli of Northallerton, grandson of Christian

Abraham Manasseh Pauli, for information about the history of his family, and to Mrs P. Pauli of Ross-on-Wye for preparing for me a copy of the family tree, and for extracts from C. W. H. Pauli's manuscript autobiographical notes.

61   Foster, *Alumni Oxonienses, 1715–1886*, vol. 3, p. 1080a.

62   Crockford's *Clerical Directory* (1906), p. 1080a.

63   See W. T. Gidney, *The History of the London Society for Promoting Christianity among the Jews from 1809 to 1908*, pp. 220, 221, 226, 284, 315, 329, 346. Crockford's *Clerical Directory* (1877), Foster, *Alumni Oxonienses 1715–1886*, p. 1080b. M. Steinschneider, *Bibliographisches Handbuch über die theoretische und praktische Literatur für hebräische Sprachkunde* (Jerusalem 1937), p. 109.

64   Liddon, vol. 1, pp. 194–5.

65   S. Lee, *A Grammar of the Hebrew Language*, 2nd ed. (London 1832), p. v.

66   There is a full account of this controversy in T. Witton-Davies, *Heinrich Ewald*, T. Fisher Unwin, 1903, pp. 48ff.

67   'German Correspondence of E.B.P.', p. 113 (15 Dec. 1835). (Pusey House).

68   W. F. Albright, in *Dictionary of American Biography* (London, O.U.P., 1936), vol. 18, pp. 174b–175a; M. Steinschneider, p. 138.

69   C. C. Torrey in *Dictionary of American Biography*, vol. 7, p. 247.

70   W. F. Albright, vol. 16, pp. 39–40.

71   Steinschneider, p. 53.

72   This Preface is reprinted in the edition published in Oxford by D. A. Talboys in 1831. (Bodleian shelf-mark 31. 736.) See also Steinschneider, p. 138.

73   This Preface is reprinted in the edition published in Oxford by D. A. Talboys in 1834.

74   By *Thesaurus* Stuart means of course the *Handwörterbuch* of 1810–12: the *Thesaurus* was published 1829–53.

75   Preface to the *Grammar* (Oxford, Talboys, 1831), pp. vi–vii.

76   *Hebrew Chrestomathy* (Oxford, Talboys, 1834), pp. 66ff, 73ff.

77   Ibid., p. 73.

78   Ibid., pp. x, xi.

79   *Encyclopaedia Britannica*, 11th ed., vol. 25, p. 1048.

80   *A Grammar of the Hebrew Language*, by Moses Stuart, Associate Professor of Sacred Literature in the Institution at Andover, Fourth Edition, reprinted with the concurrence of the Author (Oxford, Talboys, 1831), pp. iii–iv.

81   W. F. Albright in *Dictionary of American Biography*, vol. 16, pp. 39b. ff.

82   Steinschneider, p. 109.

83   C. W. H. Pauli, *Analecta Hebraica, with critical notes and tables of*

paradigms . . . for the use of students in schools and universities, 2nd ed. with a key (Oxford, Parker, 1842).

84   Shelfmarks 39. 1188–9.

85   Liddon, vol. 1, pp. 194–6.

86   Pauli, *Analecta Hebraica*, 2nd ed., p. iv.

87   Ibid., pp. 3–4.

88   Ibid., p. 6.

89   Lee, *Grammar*, 2nd ed., pp. 24–32.

90   Liddon, vol. 1, p. 122.

91   Liddon, vol. 4, pp. 385–6.

92   Pauli, *Key*: Preface, p. i, note b.

93   Pauli, Preface to the *Analecta*, p. iv.

94   Pauli, *Analecta*, p. 172, 12n; cf. also other similar remarks, e.g., p. 192, 1 n, p. 204, note *.

95   *Encyclopaedia Judaica* (Jerusalem 1971), vol. 12, p. 1419.

96   There is a copy of the 1782 catalogue in the Bodleian (shelfmark 259.a.45).

97   *Collectio Davidis* (1826), (Bodleian shelfmark 2590.e. Oxf.1d.1.) For a full account of this history of the Oppenheimer collection, see A. Marx, *Some Notes on the History of David Oppenheimer's Library*, in *Révue des études juives*, tome 82; *Mélanges offertes à M. Israel Lévi par ses élèves et ses amis* (Paris 1926).

98   Bodleian Library: MS. Top. Oxon. c.326, fo. 50.

99   See J. Parsons, *Memoir*, in Nicoll, *Sermons*, ed. Parsons (Oxford, Baxter, 1830). (Bod. Lib. shelfmark 100.r.136. Durham Univ. Lib., Bibl. Routhiana, shelfmark R.xi.E3.).

100 Edmund Craster, *History of the Bodleian Library, 1845–1945* (Oxford 1952), p. 105.

101 W. D. Macray, *Annals of the Bodleian Library, Oxford*, 2nd ed. (Oxford, 1890), p. 319.

102 Craster, p. 38.

103 Craster, pp. 29–30.

104 Craster, p. 38.

105 Craster, p. 107.

106 Macray, p. 348; Craster, p. 105.

107 Macray, p. 350; Craster, p. 105. For details of the Michael collection, see *Encyclopaedia Judaica*, vol. 11, p. 1436.

108 Macray, pp. 353, 358.

109 Craster, p. 106.

110 A. Neubauer, *Catalogue of the Hebrew Manuscripts in the Bodleian Library and in the College Libraries of Oxford* (Oxford 1886).

117

111 A. E. Cowley, *Obituary of S. R. Driver. Proceedings of the British Academy, 1915–1916*, p. 541.

112 Craster, p. 107.

113 *JTS*. n.s. (1981), pp. 101–124.

114 See J. W. Burgon, *Lives of Twelve Good Men*, vol. 1, pp. xxii–xxiv; D. S. Margoliouth in *D.N.B.*, vol. 20, p. 400a; J. S. Reynolds, *The Evangelicals in Oxford 1735–1871* (Marcham Manor Press 1975) Additional Chapters: Chapter 1, pp. 1–2; Biographical Appendix, p. 105.

115 *The Fifty-Third Chapter of Isaiah according to the Jewish Interpreters* (Driver and Neubauer), New York, Ktav, 1969, vol. 2, pp. 31–4.

116 R. Loewe, p. 31.

117 This is S. R. Driver's first published work: *A Commentary on Jeremiah and Ezekiel by Mosheh ben Shesheth, edited from a Bodleian MS., with a Translation and Notes*. See *The Ideals of the Prophets, Sermons by the late S. R. Driver* (ed. G. A. Cooke) (Edinburgh, T. & T. Clark, 1915), Appendix A, p. 213.

118 See Liddon, vol. 3, ch. 4 *passim*.

119 See e.g. B. M. G. Reardon, *Coleridge to Gore* (London, Longmans, 1971), p. 357.

120 S. R. Driver, *The Book of Daniel* (Cambridge 1912), pp. ciii–civ.

121 S. Runciman, *The Last Byzantine Renaissance* (Cambridge), 1970, p. vii.

122 G. Buchanan Gray, *Obituary of S. R. Driver. The Contemporary Review*, vol. 105 (1914), pp. 484–90, at p. 486.

123 *The Guardian*, 27 September 1882, pp. 1325–6.

124 G. Buchanan Gray, p. 486.

5

Dr Pusey's Marriage*

DAVID W. F. FORRESTER

The story of the Anglican Revival or Oxford Movement of the years 1833–45, which aimed at the restoration of High Church ideals of the seventeenth century within the Church of England through the propagation of *Tracts for the Times*, is well known. Similarly the causes which gave rise to the movement, such as the progressive decline in church life, the spread of 'liberalism' in theology, the impact of Romanticism, and the fear of Erastianism, have been thoroughly investigated. The remarkable thing, however, is that interest in the characters and activities of many of its principal participants has continued apace; witness for example Miss Meriol Trevor's full scale biography of John Henry Newman, Miss Battiscombe's study of John Keble, and persistent curiosity concerning Hurrell Froude. Equally significant, on the other hand, is the reluctance so far of anyone to come forward and take a fresh look at the person whom Dean Church at least thought of as occupying the chief place in the movement, namely Dr E. B. Pusey, Regius Professor of Hebrew and Canon of Christ Church. Why is it that present day historians and biographers alike have fought shy of investigating the outlook and achievements of the one man who, during the period of the movement, was regarded by Church as 'the most venerated in Oxford'[1] and by Newman as 'the mighty one'?[2]

It seemed probable to me that the answer to this question could be found in the official four-volume biography of Pusey, written by H. P. Liddon and published in the years 1893–7. In this *Life of E. B. Pusey* Liddon traces Edward Pusey's activities from his birth in 1800, through his early years at Eton and

* First published in *The Ampleforth Journal* 78 (1973), pp. 33–47.

Oxford, and as a young don at Oriel; as a student in Germany under Eichhorn and Schleiermacher, to his appointment as Professor of Hebrew and Canon of Christ Church at the age of 28; right through the eventful period of the Oxford Movement to his founding of Anglican sisterhoods and building of St Saviour's Church, Leeds; amidst the endless ecclesiastical battles and university affairs of the Victorian age to his death in 1882. Like his cousin Lord Shaftesbury, but for very different reasons, Pusey saw his name become a household word in the nineteenth century. And Dean Church would seem to have been right when he remarked that Pusey knew the meaning of real learning, and that in controversy it was his sledge-hammer and battle mace. It is not without a sigh of relief that one closes the fourth volume, so heavily documented and painstakingly detailed, so impressive and monumental is the work.

Although Liddon was undoubtedly living so close to the events he describes that he thereby lacked historical perspective, and though he may occasionally have adopted too reverential a tone when describing the work of his master, one cannot help wondering if he did not do the job too well. Hasn't everything about Pusey by now been said? Is this the reason why no one tackles him these days? Or could it be that the overall picture of Pusey which emerges from Liddon's pen is so off-putting? After all, wasn't Christopher Dawson merely following Liddon's lead, but nevertheless correct, in suggesting that 'all Pusey's characteristic qualities—his learning, his orthodoxy, his gravity, his solidity—were *heavy* qualities'?[3]

With these questions in mind, it came as something of a shock then to discover that a second perusal of Liddon's work suggested that he was not telling the whole truth; at least, that is, in regard to relations between Pusey and his father and to the courtship and marriage of the young Pusey and a woman called Maria Barker.

If one carefully examines chapter six of Liddon's biography, for example, it is evident that almost the whole of it is based on the letters which Pusey exchanged with his fiancée in the years 1827–8. The remarkable thing about this, however, is the bias with which Liddon selected the excerpts for quotation; none are from the letters of Maria. (This is in striking contrast with

Liddon's usual procedure of quoting copiously from Pusey's correspondents.) Indeed, not until Liddon is referring to events which occurred late in 1835 (by which time Pusey and Maria had been married seven years), and not until he has reached page 86 of his second volume, does Liddon venture to include a single excerpt from any letter of Maria's.

Was Liddon's veil of silence deliberate, I wondered? Why does he tell us so very little indeed about Maria; the one human being who entered into the young Pusey's life and thoughts the most, and whose death in 1839 threw him into such uncontroll-able grief? Was I mistaken in finding Liddon's sole description of Maria cleverly contrived?

> Besides the attraction of her good looks [Liddon tells us] Maria was undoubtedly accomplished; while her character although as yet very unformed, combined with elements of impulsiveness and self-will, qualities of very rare beauty, which Pusey believed himself to have discerned from the first and instinctively.[4]

Armed with these questions, I decided to go behind Liddon and to examine the manuscript letters themselves.

Before doing this, however, I discovered at Pusey House, Oxford, an unpublished 'Narrative of Events', composed by Pusey's niece Clara Fletcher, and, from internal evidence, it had clearly been written for and extensively used by Liddon in writing his biography of Pusey, though he nowhere acknow-ledges the fact. In this document Clara Fletcher had written:

> I cannot touch on so sacred a subject as the peculiarities of Pusey's wife on paper—though I feel you ought to know them (if indeed you do not already) because they illustrate some phases of his perfect character and some otherwise rather inexplicable events connected with the past.

And in another notebook, containing the record of a conversa-tion Liddon had with Newman in 1883, I learned that the octogenarian Cardinal also remembered Maria's eccentricities.

> She was a tall, handsome person. Before her marriage she had no interest in religion, but she must always have had qualities

of goodness . . . which only required to be drawn out by Grace. She was however at first, after their marriage, very odd, and I did not like to go to the house. Her oddities were the talk of Oxford: Whately [former Fellow of Oriel and later Archbishop of Dublin], who was a rough, noisy talker, was open-mouthed about it. She underwent a great change: and I loved her exceedingly in later life.

By this time I was extremely anxious to dispel the apparent mystery concerning Maria and to see the nature of her relationship with Pusey. Were Maria's 'peculiarities' and 'oddities' the cause of Liddon's extreme reticence? It was in a spirit of research then, that I read the surviving 81 letters from Maria to Pusey and 113 letters from Pusey to Maria on which the following generally unknown story is largely based. It transpired that the contents of these hitherto unpublished documents, together with other discovered material, went far towards explaining why Liddon preferred to suppress such a tale; more than anywhere else they reveal the root causes of Pusey's depressive nature.

Pusey in bondage

After leaving Eton and shortly before going up to Oxford at 18, Pusey met and fell deeply in love with a girl a year younger than himself called Maria Barker, the youngest child of John Raymond Barker of Fairford Park in Gloucestershire. Little is known about the physical appearance of Maria, beyond the fact that she was reputed to be tall and beautiful, but from her letters of 1827–8 she was clearly extremely vivacious, uninhibited in the expression of her opinions, subject to powerful moods and the possessor of a strong personality. A friend of hers once remarked that, had she herself been blind, she would have pictured Maria as 'a large, strong, masculine looking, ruddy and athletic person',[5] and a cousin of Maria spoke of her as 'better fitted to attack the oppressor than comfort the oppressed'.[6] By way of contrast Pusey in early manhood was of slight build and timid disposition and according to his niece possessed in his make-up all 'the gentleness of a woman'.

Throughout his childhood and adolescence Pusey had led an extraordinarily austere and disciplined life. He had been born in 1800 of aristocratic parentage at Pusey House in Berkshire, and subsequently educated at preparatory school and Eton during a critical moment in the nation's history. Not only was England then facing the problems caused by the agrarian and industrial revolutions, but she was also actively engaged in war with revolutionary and Napoleonic France. Pusey's character training, however, was less influenced by these events than by the impressions he received from his parents at home. Both his mother and father were firm upholders of the traditions, privileges and responsibilities associated with the landed ruling classes of the eighteenth century, and both of them were noted for the narrowness and rigidity of their outlook which occasionally bordered on the eccentric.

Pusey's mother, a practical and unsentimental woman, reinforced or silently adopted the precision required in everything by her husband.

> Her time was laid out by rule: a certain portion was always given to reading the Bible; and another to some book of established literary merit — generally an historical author. She would read this book with a watch at her side; and as soon as the self-prescribed time for such reading had elapsed, she eagerly turned to the more congenial task of needlework for charitable purposes. On Sundays, the time before, between, and after the Church services, was regularly spent in taking short walks or in reading sermons.[7]

As late as 1850 and whenever resident in London, Lady Lucy Pusey had herself carried by sedan chair to church twice on Sundays and in winter she was invariably preceded by footmen bearing lighted flambeaux. Throughout her life she was never known to lean back in a chair, always considering such a practice a sign of laxity.

Pusey's father, who was 52 by the time he married, utterly set in his ways, and an ultra-Tory of deeply ingrained prejudices, can only be described as an autocratic though benevolent martinet. As Pusey was later to complain gently to Maria: 'From the early habit of ruling everyone, as he did first his own and my

Mother, he seems to think it necessary that he should act for everyone'.[8] Certainly Pusey stood in awe of his father; a man whose behaviour and attitudes seemed governed by an almost pathological need for strict routine, punctuality and blind obedience on the part of others.[9] His obsession with formality meant that at Pusey House meals, daily activities, visits to neighbouring gentry families and attention to the estate followed an ordered pattern with an almost military exactness.

Later, Pusey was to recognize the particularly debilitating influence which his father's dominance had exercised on his development.

> I feel myself now [Pusey was to tell Maria in 1828] as a branch which has been so long bowed down, that even when the weight which depressed it has been removed, though it can partly, cannot wholly recover its original direction.[10]

On occasion Pusey was also inclined to think of his father's will as like a 'citadel' which needed sometimes to be 'shaken', 'sapped' and forced to 'yield'.[11] Because he felt like this, however, when his father died Pusey was to be stricken with guilt feelings; shutting himself away for several days, he refused to attend his father's funeral, was unwilling to receive visitors and would describe his mood as 'more an involuntary undefined depression, an internal burning, than actual grief'.[12]

At 18 though, and having previously always been compelled to repress any views and feelings of his own, Pusey's first encounter with Maria came as a revelation. Clearly he had never met anyone like her before. 'I was no free agent (unless principle bade me stop)', he later told her, 'after I had seen you. . . . Everything has been the necessary consequence of that.'[13] Pusey was indeed utterly distracted.

When Pusey's father inevitably issued his son with an ultimatum and forbade him to see and communicate any further with Maria, the effect on Pusey's outlook was disastrous. By now an undergraduate, Pusey considered leaving Oxford without taking his degree. Naturally shy and retiring, he now and ever after became a depressive; he genuinely feared he would go mad.

Pusey's closest friend at this time was Richard Jelf, the future

Principal of King's College, London. When Jelf heard of the ban imposed by Pusey's father on relations between Edward and Maria, he was outraged.

> Can I believe [he wrote] that any human being can form a determination (relative to the happiness of a child) which is to yield in no circumstances, which is to take its course though it break the heart or poisons the future existence of the wretched victim and that victim too a child? No, No—. . . .[14]

Jelf, however, was reckoning without intractability such as was to be found in Pusey's father; a person who was to remain inflexible for another six years.

Under the circumstances, then, and because he was temperamentally incapable of open defiance of his father, it is not surprising that during these years Pusey alternately surrendered himself to grief and to reading avidly the works of poets such as Byron, 'the prophet of the disappointed'. Indeed the Romantic Movement, with its emphasis on subjectivity and in its revolt against previously accepted views, might have been a movement tailored uniquely for the young Pusey, hamstrung by the outmoded eighteenth-century dictates of his parents. It is probable also that Byron's personal dilemmas woke subconscious echoes in Pusey. Byron's physical deformity, which the poet himself described as 'a discouraging weight upon me like a mountain',[15] and which he spoke of as the bane of his life, remind one of Pusey's thoughts concerning the oppressive nature of his father. The private journal Pusey kept of a Swiss tour he made in 1822 is similarly redolent of Byronic overtones of despair.[16] Was it accidental then, that Pusey now began ardently embracing Liberal views in politics, whilst his father persisted in his inexorable Tory opinions, equating Whigs with atheists and forbidding the marriage for two years of Pusey's brother with the daughter of a Whig peer?

Pusey's personal misfortune was to lead to further regrettable results. Unlike so many of his contemporaries, for example, who found the 1820s at Oxford a time of buoyancy and optimism,[17] Pusey seemed almost unaffected by the renaissance of culture and sense of exuberance in the ethos of the university, following the ending of the wars with France. Instead, it was during this period that he first began deliberately overworking himself in semi-seclusion in order to take his mind off his situation; a state of affairs which eventually became a way of life for him. After taking a First in Greats and obtaining a Fellowship at Oriel, he spent the next six years studying theology and the formidable German 'Higher Critics', as well as acquiring a proficiency in Hebrew, Arabic, Syriac and Chaldee.

> I have lived so retired [he later informed Maria] that of me is known less than the little which it (the world) ordinarily knows of any one; it has only known that I have been at times, intensely employed: it has given me the credit for being so always, and not knowing any of the mixed motives, anything of the distress of mind, which this study was partly intended to cure or at least stupify. . . .[18]

Not until September 1827, nine years after the first meeting between Pusey and Maria, did Pusey's father finally agree to their engagement. Pusey, now aged twenty-seven, set off immediately for Cheltenham where Maria was staying to secure her consent; he later described this visit as 'the melting of the ice after a Northern winter'.[19]

Pusey in Love

After so long an interval, Pusey was understandably nervous of the outcome of this renewed encounter.

> I scarce ventured [he confessed to Maria] to form a hope, believing myself to be to you an entire stranger. . . . Every word, silence, look, action was then of too anxious importance ever to be forgotten. I suppose never was mind so tortured to discover a meaning in what perhaps had none, or heart so racked till the first dawn of real hope beamed upon me. . . .[20]

Indeed, so anxious was Pusey, that shortly afterwards he suffered a complete breakdown in health and was compelled to spend the next four months recuperating at Brighton.

Unlike Liddon, who was later to be so ambivalent in his views concerning the character of Maria, Pusey's friend Jelf had no doubts about the good effect that her strong personality would have on his colleague. 'I rejoice to hear of the commencement of your Despotism,' Jelf was to write to Maria: 'The truth is Pusey is a child, quite unfit to be trusted with the management of his own health'. Nevertheless, it is clear that Jelf hoped the powerfully-willed Maria would deal kindly with the gentle Pusey: 'Let the rod, with which you rule him,' he advised her, 'be invisible or clad in velvet.'[21]

Pusey, however, was under no illusions about the differences in temperament and outlook between himself and Maria, and in so far as she was able to dominate him in all but religious matters, it became apparent that he revelled in her doing so. Pusey was equally taken with Maria's passionate enthusiasms and ungovernable emotions. He compared her to Kate in *The Taming of the Shrew* and he described his efforts to withstand her as a 'Falstaff-like shew of resistance'.[22] Very quickly he became accustomed to her outbursts of rage, and to such occasions as when she remarked that her fingers had a strong tendency to turn into 'tiger's claws'.[23]

Relations between Maria and her mother especially were frequently strained, owing to what Maria termed her mother's plausible nature and her knowledge of how to 'administer small doses of flattery where they will be acceptable'.[24] Pusey spilt a great deal of ink reminding his fiancée of the need to honour parents, but it is doubtful whether his words had much effect. Certainly Maria's behaviour in society remained unchecked; she continued to be remarkably outspoken, critical of her mother's friends, and indifferent to the impression she gave. 'Not being . . . at all solicitous,' she said, 'for the favourable opinion of persons I never care to see again, I can always talk nonsense to anyone, and moreover can always lead people to talk of that most interesting person *themselves*.'[25] After reading this, one begins to understand why Newman and other Oxford dons would have found Maria's behaviour strange, and one can appreciate why Liddon was anxious to conceal such conduct, so unbecoming in the future wife of a Professor and Canon of Christ Church.

Not all of Maria's criticisms were directed at those immediately around her; even Pusey himself, recuperating at Brighton, was soon to come under fire for being 'formidable' and 'gloomy'.

> For my formidableness [Pusey responded] I will not say that I expect to have the same fate of the King, whom Jupiter is said to have sent to certain inhabitants of the marshes (on their requesting a Viceroy) which much awed them by the splash it made in descending amongst them, but when they recovered from their first amazement they found to be a log; but I expect that I am a very log in comparison to what you think me.[26]

After this Maria altered her adjectives and instead accused Pusey of being 'grave' and 'stuffy'. (To be honest she would seem to have a point.) Only once, however, in these letters passing between Brighton and Cheltenham did Pusey come close to losing his patience; in itself this very imperturbability must have been something of a trial to Maria.

Happily, Pusey and Maria at least shared a common political outlook, both despising the ultra-Tories, applauding the Greek War of Independence, favouring the repeal of the Test and Corporations Act, and eagerly following the efforts to introduce Catholic Emancipation.[27] On the one hand Maria declared her detestation of Wellington, then Prime Minister, suggesting that 'so accustomed as he is to the arbitrariness of military discipline his every feeling and idea must be in favour of despotism';[28] and on the other hand, Pusey poured scorn on the Duke's party:

> The country is [he said] except in a time of excitation or distress naturally Tory, and it is perhaps as well that persons who cannot think for themselves should acquiesce in others thinking for them, if our Tories did but think! or rather if one were but not quite certain beforehand that the result at which they arrive by thinking, is the very same with which they set out.[29]

Allied to Maria's robust opinions was her Romantic interest in heroes. After reading J. F. Cooper's three-volumed novel *Red Rover*, she turned to accounts of sea-battles and developed an infatuation for all things to do with the navy, describing it as a profession, 'which as an English woman I have a right to glory in', and delighting in 'the coolness in the hour of danger which is so general among our naval heroes'.[30]

Skill in fighting won Maria's particular admiration; she was keenly interested in the activities of George Washington, Körner, and Joan of Arc. On her honeymoon she was later to express delight at seeing and handling the two-edged sword of Bruce, at visiting the battlefields of Culloden and Falkirk, and at spending a whole day reading an account of the 1745 Rebellion.

Pusey tried desperately hard to show a similar enthusiasm for Maria's hobbies. He made the gallant effort of reading *Red Rover*, insisted that he shared her preference for the naval way of life over all others save his own, reported that he had enjoyed Southey's *Life of Nelson*, and sent her descriptions of ships to be seen off Brighton. Whatever Whately might have thought of Maria and of her unusual interests and outspoken behaviour, it is certain that Pusey found her fascinating.

This was especially so when he recalled how for many years he had been merely 'a reading automaton' and how previously he had been so depressed that 'from the autumn of 1822 till September 1827, I never ventured to open a book of poetry or to enter any scenery in which there was any chance of excitement'.[31] Instead, Pusey now found it difficult to express the depth of his feelings for Maria; he told her that if only he had a window in his breast, she might read 'what else you can never know, how deeply, fervently grateful and obliged is your Edward'.[32] After seeing her briefly in London in January 1828 he was similarly overcome:

> My mind is so full at a return to this place [Brighton] and to solitude, that I know not wherewith to begin, what to say or what not to say . . . but that write I must, and can write about nothing else.

> My visit to London [Pusey informed Maria] has been to me . . . one long, or rather short day; you were the centre round which every part of it (as indeed of so much of my existence) turned, and every interval was but as the divisions of a many sided figure in rapid motion, in which all the distractions of the several parts are lost in the whirl. Now that the motion has somewhat relaxed. . . . It leaves me convinced

that whatever defects one so softly, beautifully, gently kind may discover in me, she will still look as favourably upon them, and that we shall go on hand in hand, alternately perhaps assisting, reminding, comforting each other until the time come, when both shall be translated to the presence of a pure and holy God. Everything shews me more and more how great a treasure God has given me in you. . . .[33]

Even after the death of his father shortly afterwards, a traumatic experience for Pusey, he quickly recovered his ardour. In face of Maria's concern for him, he also began believing for perhaps the first time in his life, that he not only loved but could be an object of love:

Though my heart [he told Maria] is full almost to choking, of a thousand different feelings, I still can rest upon the thought of that love, as a bright cheerful spot among all present sorrows. . . . Yet I had for years thought it so impossible that any one, much more such an one as she I loved, could do more than give me her esteem. I had thought it so little possible that I should have any opportunity of obtaining even that, and what has been given me is so exceeding great a blessing, that I have been throughout inclined to understand every kind expression, in the lowest sense it could convey. I have not dared to attach to them their full meaning, or to believe to how great a degree I had a right to be happy.[34]

Not only were there occasions when 'everything appears so inadequate and one's heart often swells so much as to choke utterance',[35] but Pusey also had a premonition of what would be his reaction should he lose Maria:

I cannot picture to myself [he said] what would be my condition without you: it seems as if it would be a long, long time before I could then so sanctify memory as to dwell solely, as I do generally in the present case—I will not go on, for you will think it, as it indeed is, horrible; but kind as you are, beyond all human kindness to me, and deeply as I love you, we must not become so necessary to each other, as to 'sorrow without hope' were the other taken . . . I fear I shall be plunging deeper and deeper, if I continue.[36]

It is not surprising then that, confronted with this devotion, and so much misunderstood by her friends and relatives, that Maria should eventually become convinced that Pusey was the only person who really understood her. 'You were the first person,' she told him, 'I ever knew, to whom I fancied myself not incomprehensible.'[37] And faced with Pusey's deep need of her and so full of pent-up emotions herself, it was but a short step for Maria to discover how attached she had become to him in the meantime. By April 1828 Maria was emphatic in her assertion to Pusey that, 'You *are* more to me than all the world besides; and to be as one in feeling and in affection in spite of separation is to me a happy and a hallowed feeling. Ever dearest and best of beings'.

How is it one may ask that, given Maria's influence, Pusey a few years later had become the severe and forbidding figure depicted by historians? Why was it that Maria was unable to persuade Pusey permanently away from the paths of self-depreciation, guilt and gloom?

In the first place it would seem that the damage to Pusey's character inflicted by his father was of too long standing by the time Maria and Pusey finally came together. In the second place, it is probable that, because Maria needed and enjoyed Pusey's tremendous love, she permitted him in time to indoctrinate her with his religious views; and religion was the one sphere in which Pusey could be as obstinate by nature as his father, and in later life obsessional.

Maria's unbelief

In what was probably her first letter to Pusey, Maria Barker made it clear that she was of those who, in the early nineteenth century, were experiencing difficulties in religion; in her case the problem centred on contradictions in Scripture, but did not cease there.

> Religion [she told Pusey] has certainly never been to me the source of comfort and serenity which it has to others. I could not but admire the beauty of its precepts and the sublimity of its views, and as far as a trust in a Supreme Being in temporal concerns goes, so far, I have felt its use in calming my mind;

131

but there does appear to me so much uncertainty, if not of contradiction in Scripture itself, so much more of that contradiction in the opinions of men . . . that I could frequently only find peace of mind, in banishing the subject from my thoughts. . . .[38]

Maria was particularly puzzled why revelation was not 'a clear and distinct annunciation' of God's will, and why, if the Holy Spirit enlightened the minds of everyone who applied for his aid, 'some are apparently misled, and many, unable to obtain fixed opinions, are in danger of running on in endless mazes'.[39]

Having previously met with unbelief in his elder brother and in an old Etonian friend Julian Hibbert,[40] Pusey clearly regarded Maria's outlook on religion as a challenge. The encounter with Hibbert indeed had left an indelible impression on Pusey; he later described it as 'my first real experience of the deadly breath of infidel thought upon my soul'. And now here was his fiancée doubting the truths of Christianity!

It is fearful [Pusey replied] to think how near you were to the borders of entire unbelief: your heart (which is the main thing) was a better believer than your intellect, but there is probably scarcely any male mind, which had got as far as you did, and to some of the principles in which you seem to have almost acquiesced, which would have stopped short of abandoning Christianity. Do not distress yourself about this; I mention it as proof of God's mercy to you, and in part to shew the danger of the principles, not to blame; I should not *necessarily* by any means think any man the worse for having been not only on the verge, but within the prison of unbelief. . . . The unbeliever is to me the object of compassion not of censure.[41]

For some time, however, Maria was able to withstand Pusey's relentless pressure on her to conform and was not averse to challenging his opinions. After reading a few verses of the Epistle to the Romans, she informed Pusey that 'had that Epistle been given to me to read as a mere human production, I should have thought its author was . . . either a fool or an hypocrite, either ignorant of what he was about, or willing to deceive with a shew of understanding what no one else could'.[42]

It is equally clear from Maria's correspondence with Pusey, that her frequent mention of the well-known Evangelical preacher Francis Close, who exercised great influence on the public life at Cheltenham by his opposition to the theatre, horse racing and Sabbath breaking, was not chiefly out of an interest in religion; much more Maria was angry at the ill-effect of Close's views on a friend of hers. 'How comes it,' she asked, 'that he is permitted to disseminate doctrines capable of doing so much harm?' Maria lamented the fact that her friend ate nothing but the coarsest food, described herself as a great sinner, spent hours on her knees in apparent distress and preferred not to speak to anyone.[43]

Marriage

The exchange of letters between Brighton and Cheltenham finally ended when Pusey and Maria were married on 12 June 1828, in a ceremony performed by Pusey's friend Richard Jelf. Despite the evidence this early correspondence gives in the years 1827–8 of the oppressive influence of Pusey's father, and of potentially solemn qualities in Pusey himself, the overall picture it conveys is one of steadily increasing joy and abundant human happiness; as yet there was little to indicate that Pusey would eventually become the grim figure handed down to us in history. And on his honeymoon at least, a holiday which lasted three months, Pusey's thoughts were far from gloomy.

Touring Derbyshire, Scotland (for part of the time the guest of Sir Walter Scott), the Lake District and Shropshire with Maria, Pusey was able to write to a relative that, 'my happiness is at present too recent, too unaccustomed, too like a dream from its strange contrasts with years of misery to allow me to think of it without shuddering'. And for her part Maria was similarly moved, though as yet she was still capable of recounting loudly any material discomforts she might be experiencing. In her diary for 13 July for example she wrote: 'Unwilling to sleep a second night on hay covered with blankets, and annoyed by insects, sharing our room with fowls, we returned to T——

which was delightful after all we had endured'. They arrived in Oxford in September and just over a month later Pusey was appointed Regius Professor of Hebrew, with which went a Canonry of Christ Church. It is ironical, incidentally, that Pusey and Maria owed this promotion in their fortunes to Wellington, the Prime Minister, about whom they had not so long past been so critical.

For the first few years of their life together the halcyon quality of their early days of courtship persisted into married life, despite what the gossips of Oxford may have thought of Maria. And though heavily engaged in teaching Hebrew, writing a history of the theology of Germany and cataloguing Arabic manuscripts at the Bodleian library, Pusey joined with Maria in maintaining an arduous social routine of entertaining and exchanging hospitality. In addition they became the parents of four children called Philip, Katherine, Lucy and Mary.

By 1835, however, a series of events national and domestic had gradually blighted the precarious seeds of optimism in Pusey's outlook, which the engagement and marriage with Maria had initially fostered.

Austerity in the family

It has been suggested that it was the death of Maria in 1839 which left Pusey a changed man,[44] and this is the natural conclusion one draws from reading Liddon's biography, but Maria's death in fact only speeded up a process already established. 1835 much more truly represents the watershed in the life of Pusey. By then not only had he been seriously disturbed by the death of his father and of his spiritual mentor Charles Lloyd (Bishop of Oxford 1827–9), but he had been subjected to severe personal attacks, on account of the broad-minded views expressed in his books on Germany. Political revolutions on the continent, fear of government attacks on Church property and the issue of admitting non-Anglicans to Oxford and Cambridge had also caused Pusey to experience a change of heart concerning liberalism. In 1828 he had been able to write to Maria in jest that 'the love of liberty, whether displayed in Whiggism, Radicalism, Liberalism etc.,

etc., you *know* means for the most part nothing more than the love of being one's self free, perhaps with the additional privilege of tyrannizing others',[45] but in 1835 he had come seriously to believe it.

Until Pusey awoke to the Liberal threat to the Church, he retained his earlier sympathies, his gentle optimism and even an interest in things not technically religious. In 1835, however, he deliberately narrowed his outlook and, with the appearance of his *Tract on Baptism* emphasizing the gravity of post-baptismal sin, publicly threw in his lot with the Tractarians. Thereafter, alongside Newman and Keble, Pusey was of the number who openly set themselves to oppose the Liberalism of the 1830s, which bore the aspect of a philosophy of material enlightenment; its adherents believing firmly in material progress and abhorring the otherworldly features of Christian teaching[46].

The tragedy in this volte-face on Pusey's part lay in the effect that it had on Maria and the children; in a sense they became the victims of his personal revolution. From now onwards one can trace the beginning of Pusey's insistence on seeing everything from a religious standpoint, his rigorous concern for moralism, his increasing antipathy to frequenting society, and the introduction of fasting and the foregoing of luxuries in his domestic life. In order to raise money in 1835 for the building of new churches in London, for example, he not only donated £5,000 himself, but persuaded Maria to sell her jewellery, reduced the number of his household servants and sold the family carriage. Whereas for Pusey these austerities were introduced either through inclination or with the highest of motives, they gradually reaped havoc for Maria; now suffering the first onslaughts of tuberculosis, she felt compelled to bow before her husband's stern conviction, example and determination. The Pusey known to history was now coming to the fore.

It was at this time that Pusey also became convinced of his own utter depravity and believed that the death of his daughter Katherine in 1832 had occurred as a chastisement for his sins. Such thoughts did little to console Maria, who was not only approaching death herself, but having to nurse her children through a wide variety of illnesses and at the same time ensure that they adhered to the strict regime initiated and approved of by her husband. At first Maria was able to regard this with amusement, but her letters of the last three years of her life are totally devoid of humour. And on one occasion at least, when the oldest of the children was only nine, and when Lucy was suffering from an inflammation of the eyes, Philip was thought to be dying and able to move only on crutches, and Mary was having leeches applied to a swollen foot, their restriction in diet to 'plain food' caused a heated argument between Maria (following Pusey's rules as to fasting) and the doctor attending them. Even when strongly criticized by his elder brother, Philip, for the excessive discipline which he meted out to his offspring (in his will Philip forbade his own children to be entrusted to the care of Pusey), Pusey remained adamant. 'Our system', he told Maria, 'if it is worth anything must be contrary to the world's system'.[47]

The ultimate result of Pusey's insistence on or at least strong encouragement of Maria to follow his highly idealistic path from 1835 onwards, was the reduction of her life to a state of intolerable suffering from religious scruples and that of their children to that of a veritable nightmare. In his personal relations Pusey was gradually becoming like his father before him; and when Maria died in 1839 the revolution had come full cycle. It is small wonder that Liddon preferred to say as little as possible about the hidden life of young Dr Pusey, revealed here for the first time.

NOTES

1   R. W. Church, *The Oxford Movement: Twelve Years 1833–45* (1891).

2   J. H. Newman, *Apologia pro Vita Sua* (1864).

3   C. Dawson, *The Spirit of the Oxford Movement* (1933).

4   Liddon, vol. 1, p. 23.

5   MS copy of letter from M. Barker to Pusey, 18 November 1835.

6   Ibid., 28 October 1827.

7   Clara Fletcher, 'Narrative of Events' (Pusey House).

8   MS copy of letter from Pusey to M. Barker, 1 February 1828.

9   This behaviour of Pusey's father was later gently satirized in a novel by his daughter-in-law, Emily Pusey, wife of Pusey's elder brother. See *Waldegrave*, published anonymously in 3 vols. in 1829.

10   MS coppy of letter from Pusey to M. Barker, 16 May 1828.

11 Ibid., 27 October 1827 and 5 November 1827.

12 Ibid., 19 April 1828.

13 Ibid., 27 December 1827.

14 MS copy of letter from R. Jelf to Pusey, August 1821.

15 *The Deformed Transformed*, pt 1, sc. 1, 11, pp. 331–2.

16 This unpublished document is at Pusey House, Oxford.

17 See D. H. Newsome, *The Parting of Friends* (London 1966).

18 MS copy of letter from Pusey to M. Barker, 28 November 1827.

19 Liddon, vol. 1, p. 116.

20 MS copy of letter from Pusey to M. Barker, 18 January 1828.

21 MS copy of letter from R. Jelf to M. Barker, 21 June 1828.

22 MS copy of letter from Pusey to M. Barker, 15 January 1828.

23 MS copy of letter from M. Barker to Pusey, May 1828.

24 Ibid., 7 November 1827.

25 Ibid., 1 March 1828.

26 MS copy of letter from Pusey to M. Barker, 11 December 1827.

27 In the Oxford election of 1829, which revolved around the question of Peel's advocacy of Catholic Emancipation, Pusey, an avowed Peelite, was viewed as an opponent of Newman, Keble, H. Froude and R. Wilberforce.

28 MS copy of letter from M. Barker to Pusey, 11 January 1828.

29 MS copy of letter from Pusey to M. Barker, 3 June 1828.

30 See MS copies of letters from M. Barker to Pusey, 2 February 1828 and 14 February 1828.

31 See MS copies of letters from Pusey to M. Barker, end of 1827 and 3 November 1827.

32 Ibid., 7 February 1828.

33 Ibid., 1 February 1828.

34 Ibid., 13 May 1828.

35 Ibid., 1 February 1828.

36 Ibid., 8 May 1828.

37 MS copy of letter from M. Barker to Pusey, 2 February 1828.

38 Ibid., 3 October 1827.

39 Ibid., Liddon's sole acknowledgement of Maria's unbelief occurs in one sentence of his biography and then he did not refer to her by name. See Liddon, vol. 1, p. 122.

40 Liddon's account of Hibbert is inadequate and misleading. He concealed Hibbert's identity under the letter 'Z', gave the false impression that Hibbert was resident in France and referred to Pusey's brother's loss of faith as having occurred to 'an intimate friend' of Pusey. See Liddon, vol. 1, pp. 44–9.

41   MS copy of letter from Pusey to M. Barker, 16 October 1827.

42   MS copy of letter from M. Barker to Pusey, 18 October 1827.

43   Ibid.

44   See Owen Chadwick, *The Victorian Church*, vol. 1 (1966), p. 198.

45   MS copy of letter from Pusey to M. Barker, 12 February 1828.

46   See H. ScottHolland, *Personal Studies* (1905), pp. 76–7.

47   MS copy of letter from Pusey to M. Pusey, 25 October 1836.

6

'Nurseries of a learned clergy' Pusey and the Defence of Cathedrals

ROGER JUPP

It seems to have become an established tradition amongst writers on nineteenth-century church history to introduce at some point in their work an extract or two from the goings-on in and around the Cathedral Close at Barchester. There is a popular view to which this may contribute that Anthony Trollope presents a virtually complete portrait of clerical life at the time. What he does show is a knowledge of the professional life of the clergy and of ecclesiasticism, that is, of the prevailing church system, warts and all. His novels reveal his own liberal view that the Church of England needed some reform particularly where the disparity between poor and lucrative livings went unchallenged. With all this in mind, he erected Barchester and its cathedral, and this was in an age when cathedrals were unpopular and thought by many to be overstaffed, absurdly rich and largely useless. The popular press and pamphleteers regularly attacked the abuses of a Church still hampered by a medieval framework that supported the rich and well placed, but neglected the less fortunate clergy who struggled on poor stipends, often under difficult conditions. One pamphleteer[1] faithfully summarized the accusations brought against the Church: the iniquity of the tithe as a means of clerical payment; the inequality in the value of benefices; the system of pluralities and commendams; the maintenance of cathedral chapters; and the privileges of bishops as peers in Parliament. All of these in some measure exercised the thoughts of those who worked for the reform of the Church, and some were in time the subject of redress by Parliament.

Of the many publications on church reform in the first decades of the nineteenth century, three were to be of note in that they attracted the special attention of the public. The first was Lord Henley's *Plan of Church Reform*, produced in 1832. He was an Evangelical and a brother-in-law of Peel, and so was of sufficient influence and reputation to command a wide audience. His was undoubtedly the most influential of all pamphlets at this time, because it led the attack on the cathedrals and their immense wealth vested in property. Henley promoted the idea of a redistribution of church property and revenues, so that endowments could be properly used to make the Church's task of evangelization more effective. It was the cathedrals that were to bear the major burden in this shareout of wealth.

The second notable publication was Thomas Arnold's *Principles of Church Reform* which appeared in 1833. He was driven into print by Henley's proposals, which he considered not only insufficient but of the wrong kind.[2] It was written he said 'on the supposition—not implied but expressed repeatedly —that the Church Establishment was in extreme danger'.[3] The alarm of the situation called for far-reaching remedies: the commutation of tithes; the remodelling of the episcopate to obtain efficient church government; the division of dioceses to extend the influence of the Church in every town; the annexation of prebends to unpaid livings; and the enforcement of residence. New parishes should be created in large towns and populous districts, especially in the manufacturing areas. All of this would be strengthened and aided by the inclusion of Dissenters in a comprehensive national Church on the basis of union in a common task, not of conformity of belief. The failure of the Church lay in its inability to get to grips with its task in a changing society. Arnold therefore attacked the establishment because it was far from being the Church of the nation. It was failing in its mission to an industrial society, in its separation from Dissenters, in its internal life, its ministry, theological opinions and doctrines. 'The most general complaint against the Church turns upon the excessive amount, and the unequal distribution of its property, and especially upon the burdensome and impolitic nature of the tithe system'.[4]

The third pamphlet was Pusey's *Remarks on the Prospective and*

Past Benefits of Cathedral Institutions, and, like Arnold's pamphlet, was occasioned by Henley's proposals. But Pusey came forward as the defender of cathedrals, giving evidence of their past work as centres of theological learning from which sprang the best of English theology, and suggesting the means by which they could be preserved and their educational task continued and extended. The work had been written late in 1832 and the manuscript sent to Newman as he prepared to embark with Hurrell Froude and his father for the Mediterranean. Newman's comments were cogent enough to persuade Pusey not to publish it as an open letter to Henley, for its merit, he observed, lay in its form as a 'reference book of arguments' or a 'digest', whose remarks and suggestions went beyond what was needed to refute Henley. This would leave Pusey the freedom to say what he wanted, and this was what was required from one of undoubted learning, who could speak authoritatively from within a cathedral environment. 'After all, even if things are so bad, yet it is true, we ought to tell men what is right, that the fault may not lie with us, if they yield where they should resist', urged Newman.[5] With this in mind Pusey published in 1833 and under a title that was almost Newman's.

A response to the call for Church reform was the context in which these pamphlets were produced. Although Henley's proposals were much admired and some prepared the way for future legislation, Pusey's pamphlet (at least in Liddon's opinion) contributed to their discredit. More especially it advanced Pusey's reputation as a scholar and weighty controversialist and prepared him for his contributions to the *Tracts*. Arnold, too much an idealist for his time, was widely misunderstood, but his far-reaching ideas high-lighted an urgent situation, that the Church needed to awaken to its task with renewed vigour and set about redressing the manifold inequalities in the system. A large amount of money was needed not only to build new churches but to augment poor livings. From where was it to come? The government had provided some money since 1820 but it was not enough. It did not take long for reformers to cast their eyes over the quiet precincts of cathedral closes where, comments Hammond, they 'saw the rich indolence of numerous dignitaries ... noted poor priests

141

labouring in vast parishes in great towns and observed that it might be possible to alter such a situation'.[6] Lord Henley made the point with Evangelical zeal.

That the Church was in need of reform was evident, and, as the partner of the State, it could not continue without its own inequalities and distortions being subjected to the same process of reform which Parliament had itself recently undergone. Within Parliament there now sat Roman Catholics, Nonconformists, and radical elements, all of whom had some reason to despise the privileged position of a Church that was not their own. In an age when privilege and position were resented, the Church of England represented another face of exclusiveness with its large endowments, its property and patronage. To the critic there were abundant abuses, which caused the Church to fall short in its mission to all classes of men in society, as Arnold put it. The system of tithes was a source of bitterness and embarrassment and seemed like a form of unfair taxation, especially to those who were not Anglicans; the inequality of clerical stipends, pluralism, and non-residence led to a widespread break-down in pastoral relationships and made a nonsense of the parochial system; and preferment openly admitted of favouritism and corruption. But the greatest failure was the lack of places of worship in the new industrial areas.

> It was estimated that there were no places of worship for about 6,364,000 of the population, and that most of the neglected lived in the new towns and manufacturing areas. In the metropolis alone 1,425,000 people were left unprovided with spiritual aid. The parishes which attempted to assist the poor of the manufacturing areas were often worth only £150, and did not attract the clergy in the same manner as a rich country living worth £400 with a population of only a hundred souls.[7]

But the wealth of the cathedral chapters provided an obvious source of income that could be redistributed to those clergy who, said one reformer, 'did all the work'.

Bishop Blomfield of London, the architect of ecclesiastical reform during this period, recognized the expediency of diverting this money to a fund to increase the endowments of poor parishes and provide clergy in neglected areas. His speech in the Lords is often quoted. As he walked the streets of London the great Cathedral Church dominated the metropolis, yet, he asked, to what degree does it answer the object to which it is consecrated, the glory of God? Its dean and three residentiaries received an income which together amounted to nearly £12,000 a year, and twenty-nine other clergy with connected duties that were all but sinecures received a similar amount.

> I proceed a mile or two to the east and north-east and find myself in the midst of an immense population, in the most wretched state of destitution and neglect. . . . I find there, upon an average, about one church and one clergyman for every 8,000 or 10,000 souls . . . in one parish, for instance, only one church and one clergyman for 40,000 people. . . . No, I am told, you may not touch St Paul's. It is an ancient corporation which must be maintained in its integrity. Not a stall can be spared. The duties performed there are too important to admit of any diminution in the number of those who perform them. . . . Not a farthing must be taken from those splendid endowments, for which so little duty is performed, to furnish spiritual food to some of the thousands of miserable, destitute souls, that are perishing of famine in the neighbourhood of this abundance. Is it then asserted, at this time of day, that there can be no such thing as a lawful redistribution of Church property?[8]

This assertion had, however, been continually made by conservative churchmen, who did not see it as the salvation of an endowed Church, whose survival was threatened. It had been made at the start of the Oxford Movement when the government of Lord Grey, pledged to reform as it was, introduced a measure to suppress ten bishoprics of the Irish Church and redistribute their revenues. It seemed to many churchmen that their worst fears were being realized, that the State would be the instrument whereby a reform in the Church was to be effected. To men like Blomfield it was a practical measure, seeking to alleviate a situation in which the Irish clergy were losing their income, because Roman Catholics were refusing to pay the tithes. To men in Oxford, to Keble and Newman particularly, it was an act of the grossest sacrilege. Keble's Assize Sermon in July 1833 enunciated the guiding principle of the inviolability of church property and its spiritual independence. Newman's first *Tract* directly appealed to the clergy to petition the bishops since the whole matter of the Church's temporal possessions rested on the question of wherein lay the basis of the Church's authority.

The adherence to such a principle was as much Pusey's, but his contribution to the vexed question of the redistribution of ecclesiastical revenues was begun in his pamphlet on cathedral institutions before the birth of the Movement with which he later allied himself. He made his position on the Irish Church question known to the young Gladstone early in 1833. He wrote:

> a priori, one should be very sorry to see the Irish Church destroyed. . . . If there be any way . . . by which the advantage of equable distribution among the successive holders, can be secured to the Church without the sacrifice of this portion of its property, then this surplus ought unquestionably—not to be confiscated to the State, but—to revert to the purposes for which it was originally given, God's service through the promotion and extension of Christianity . . . since our ancestors (and those frequently individuals) gave certain lands for the maintenance of Christian Ministers, I see not what right the State has to offer *our* property for sale.[9]

By 1836 much had changed but the principle remained the same, and Pusey's attitude was the more vehement. His feeling is demonstrated to his brother Philip, a Tory MP, but a supporter of the Government's policy on church property. The principle of reform that had been adopted, he wrote, would lead to the destruction of the Church. His brother had seemed to say that the Church 'should not be allowed to maintain our own spiritual rights unless we gave up to the State our temporal subsistence, or, still more, the patrimony which we have received in trust to use ourselves to the service of Almighty God, and to hand down to our successors to be so used'. This he considered to be sacrilege, 'taking away money which has been consecrated to the service of Almighty God'. He concluded, 'If what we give for the endowment of a Church may be resumed and secularized, so may the ornaments of the Church itself'.[10]

Pusey held a high view of the Church and so the integrity of her property was a principle to be defended at all times, whether it were to be sold off (as in the Irish Church question) or redistributed elsewhere by such a scheme as Lord Henley's. If this went through without a fight who could tell what other assaults would be made on the Church? Once the position was yielded, that the State had the right to interfere with Church property, its ancient endowments and revenues, who could doubt that it also had the right to determine its doctrine and liturgy? Newman expressed this fear when writing to Pusey from Rome, suggesting that only good could come from Pusey's pamphlet, whereas he feared that Arnold's was 'opening the door to alterations in doctrine some day to come'.[11] But Arnold in fact was expressing what many thought, that church property was 'trust property' with the King and parliament, whom he named 'the sovereign power in the Church', as the divinely appointed trustee.[12] This agreed with contemporary Radicalism, and churchmen went in fear. So when the idea of the inviolability of church property was defended, men like Arnold were forced to disagree:

> the Industrial Revolution had brought social change and a large scale increase and redistribution of population. Radical efforts were needed by the Church in this situation. To become self-conscious of the Church as a separate institution possessed of its own rights, privileges, and constitution—all held to be sacred—was not to be intellectually wrong, but [Arnold thought] morally powerless.[13]

It is in Pusey's pamphlet that the question of right as a matter of principle is eloquently stated. This was before the main thrust of the *Tracts*, and his opinions were no doubt influential in those formative years. Pusey was not unaware of the problems facing parishes nor did he deny the need for reform. The furnishing of the needs of neglected populations and the assistance of poor parishes was urgent and a task the Church had to face, but to do it at the expense of ancient endowments settled by benefactors for a different purpose, particularly the cathedral establishments, was for him a holy cause advanced by unholy means. So he wrote at the beginning of his pamphlet:

> It is said, and truly, that our Church has been a learned Church, or, more truly, that it has been adorned by individuals, who to deep piety have added the profoundest learning; but persons have not inquired by what institutions this learning was fostered, or whether we now, actually as well as in name, possess the same advantages. Still less does any one seem to inquire, whether there be any right to make the alterations proposed. On the one hand, they set forth the neglected state of our large towns, or our mining districts, or our scattered agricultural population; on the other, insulated, or at all events incidental, abuses in the appointments to our large Cathedral establishments; and without further inquiry into the justice of the case, it is thought that a double benefit would be conferred upon the Church, by providing for the one, through the extinction of the other.[14]

Of the many plans for church reform at this time[15] Lord Henley's attracted most attention and went through eight editions after it appeared in the summer of 1832. It was he who was the spokesman of those who proposed the radical alterations that moved Pusey to take up his pen, setting down clearly and directly those things to which his Christian duty bade him direct his readers. His *Plan of Church Reform* was a comprehensive document that stated plainly what many drew back from admitting, that the Church was in urgent need of reform and that there was much that could be reformed. In the broadest terms he demanded a radical redistribution of wealth largely held by cathedral chapters, the resurrection of Convocation (suppressed since 1717) to give the Church an effective body of government, the creation of new sees, and the withdrawal of bishops from Parliament. The Plan's central feature was an improved management of the Church by a permanent board of commissioners by which the sphere of State action would be extended into the administration as well as the redistribution of church property. This, comments Brose, 'came closest to later legislation, for he proposed to redistribute episcopal and cathedral property by vesting all such estates in the hands of a corporation for its exclusive management',[16] that is, a body of commissioners who would oversee its handling and superintend its application.

The *Plan* largely centred around the reduction of cathedral and collegiate establishments and the re-allocation of the major part of their revenues to the poorer clergy. Looking at populous cities he saw only an 'unchristianized land'. Where could money be found to reverse this? When he looked he found a fund yielding nearly £300,000 a year that was (in his opinion) 'devoted almost entirely to Sinecures: the ostensible purpose for which it is paid being that of providing Divine Service in about thirty Cathedral and Collegiate Churches'. This was an obvious misapplication of money, and his Plan was to 'apply the superfluity on the one side of this melancholy account, to the deficiencies on the other'. This distribution of the temporalities of the Church, he believed, 'is a matter of civil regulation, and may not only without impropriety be treated by the Laity, but is expressly within their peculiar and appropriate province'.[17] Although he argued that the State had no right to confiscate the Church's endowments, that is, what had been donated in order that the Church could perform its spiritual functions, Henley asked if the Church was in fact carrying out the donor's intentions. It was up to the State to intervene to ensure that this was so, and if necessary it could alter the original contract so that the purpose was fulfilled. In the widest sense he saw the Church as a corporation with the State redistributing her endowments for the increase in the effect of her mission.

Henley realized that the Church was unjustly accused of being wealthy; if there was an equitable division of its revenues no clergyman would receive more than £185 annually, and if all the Church's property, including that of deans and chapters, were put into a common fund, each clergyman would only receive a stipend of £350 per annum. Even so, Parliament should act to place a minister in every parish with an adequate income and to support one in towns for every four thousand souls. Augmentations to poor livings could not be made by reducing the already unequal revenues of the parochial clergy or the revenues of bishops, but turning to the deans and chapters he found an estimated £300,000 per annum, more than

147

one-sixth of the estimated income of parochial clergy. Thus 'it becomes material . . . to inquire, what the services are, in return for which so large an amount is paid'.[18] On inquiry he found those offices to be virtual sinecures requiring little or no residence and few sermons but with an excessive financial reward. The resulting indictment was that 'the existence of Sinecures, can only be defended, as a maintenance for that very small portion of the theological world, which consists of retired Students, fitted neither for Episcopal nor for Parochial duties'.[19] His conclusion was that 'the augmentation of small Livings and the Endowment of Churches in poor and populous places, can only be effected by the application of some portion of Cathedral property: the other Endowments of the Church being in one case insufficient, and in the other barely adequate, to the present demands upon them'.[20] In his *Plan* Henley therefore provided for the maintenance of cathedral services only by the dean, assisted as necessary by chaplains, and the abolition of prebendaries if they were supernumeraries or sinecurists, together with the annexation of cathedral town livings in the gift of the chapter to existing stalls or prebends. If all this were successfully achieved an estimated annual sum of £150,000 could be devoted to augmenting livings and church extension.

Henley wrote in a spirit friendly to the Church and out of pious concern, but many were disturbed and aggrieved. He wrote, said Liddon, with 'less knowledge than zeal. His remarks on non-residence, sinecures, and pluralities would not now be challenged in any quarter; his insistence on the claims of the dense populations in the manufacturing districts was well-timed and not unnecessary. But if there was little room for controversy as to the disease, controversy could not but begin with the projected remedy'.[21] His *Plan* evoked letters of dismay and regret in the popular journals and from individuals.[22] On the whole, 'it made the blood of many churchmen boil', comments Best, and not only because Henley had welcomed Dissenters as an excellent and influential group within the community, but because his 'material proposals were as open to serious objection as his theological and political ones. It cannot be denied that he made a dead set at the cathedrals. They semed to him . . . entirely to lack merit, therefore he was prepared to reform them altogether, and put their endowments to a more useful purpose. The present uselessness and waste of the cathedrals were not seriously contestable in 1832, but it was not as self-evident as Henley assumed it to be that they were incapable of better service in the future'.[23]

No better person could come to the defence of the cathedrals and of the rights of the Church to manage her own property than Pusey. He was from the sheltered theological world, but no man could call him a student in retirement fit for little else. Pusey answered Henley not by denying the abuses or inequalities but by producing a wealth of evidence as to their past and present utility. He suggested how this could be extended to raise the level of clerical education so as to better fit the clergy for their ministry. This in itself would be of benefit to the Church at large and better equip the parishes. He believed that the two universities did not offer a full professional and theological instruction for the clergy, but it was in other established institutions, in fact in the cathedral establishments lately under attack, where the study of theology by the clergy had been anciently pursued and from which centre the sound religious instruction of the people had been promoted. So Pusey determined in his pamphlet to defend the cathedrals by weighing 'their advantages or capabilities solely as means of promoting the theological learning necessary for any Church'.[24] He felt that reformers had begun at the wrong end:

Our first object ought not to be, to ascertain how much one might by any possibility curtail, but how much one ought to retain; what offices the good estate of the Church demands, if not in their present, at least in some kindred form; what duties, in fact, besides those of the parochial Clergy and of Episcopal superintendance, are required for the healthful condition of the Church.

The neglect of clerical education was Pusey's first consideration. He saw at Oxford and Cambridge an education that was general and preparatory to all, but it was not professional. It gave a basic religious education for all students, but those intended for holy orders suffered in that no specific training was

149

given to them. Those intended for the law or medicine received further practical guidance but

> in the case of the Christian minister, the case is more urgent . . . because, by the present system at least, he does not engage in his duties under the direction of another . . . he is, very frequently, at once entrusted with an office as important as any which may be committed to him during his whole life; and for the right discharge of this, he is left, as far as man is concerned, unaided and uninstructed, and his errors un-remedied.[25]

All students were required to study the evidences for Christian religion, the Old and New Testaments and their histories, and the doctrines of the Thirty-nine Articles as proved out of Scripture. All that the candidate for ordination needed to add to this was to attend a short course of twelve lectures from the Regius Professor Divinity on a general survey of theology, with his recommendations for further but private reading. 'One fortnight now comprises the beginning and the end of all the public instruction which any candidate for holy orders is required to attend previously to entering upon his profession'.[26] Other lectures were available, but few attended, and the assistance of other clergymen was not often engaged. The majority Pusey observed 'confine their preparation to the private and unaided study of such books as the Bishop or the Professor, or some older clerical friend, may recommend'. This resulted in a general lowering of standards so that 'something more is needed for the momentous office to which God has called us, than what the ordinary routine even of a Christian education can supply.[27] He pointed to the obvious impracticality of learning and training whilst in office, even if the young minister was blessed with the guidance of a more experienced man. Bishop Lloyd of Oxford gave to Pusey himself and to many of his contemporaries a paternal guidance that was of lasting value, and this in itself led him to make these observations on the meagreness of clerical training, having received himself only the most rudimentary instruction before his ordination.

These results of our neglected education would be a sore evil to the Church at all times, and under all circumstances: it would at all times be very pernicious to her, that her ministers should have to learn their duties empirically, while endeavouring to perform them, when the subject of their experiments is the souls of men: it would be very hurtful at all times, that many should enter upon their office, having very little ground on which to rest their trust.[28]

And he felt that a deeper knowledge of theology by its ministers would promote the unity of the Church and the co-operation of its two parties—'a more catholic study of Christian doctrine must needs further a more catholic spirit'.[29]

Admitting such a situation, Pusey turned for comparison to the system of clerical education in Germany and suggested a union of what was best in England with the best of the German system. Pusey had trodden some of this ground already in a letter to Tholuck in May 1830.[30] Pusey had a direct knowledge of the subject. He had witnessed the work of the universities in his visits to Germany in 1825 and 1826 when, at the suggestion of Lloyd, he took time to investigate current biblical criticism. He had visited Göttingen, Berlin, and Bonn during his tours, and made the acquaintance of the great names of German scholarship: Pott, Eichhorn, Tholuck (whom he had met in Oxford before), and Schleiermacher. Having heard them lecture, he was well able to comment on German professors and the learning they imparted to their students. He had already defended the trends of German scholarship in 1828 when he produced his first work in answer to Hugh James Rose's criticism of its rationalist character. Now his work took on a more balanced approach, for when speaking of this German system, he spoke equally of its defects as well as its advantages, commenting that the Germans 'have sacrificed the preparatory branch of University education, we, the professional; they have a complete scheme of theological instruction for students unprepared to receive it: we have an admirable preparatory education, but no suitable system engrafted upon it'.[31]

Pusey thought that in Germany there was no adequate

preparation for the student's studies: at a young age he was introduced ill-equipped to a strenuous theological diet, whilst lacking guidance and discipline of mind. Pusey expected that clergy in training should have guidance as to their Christian and moral life. Moreover the oral system of teaching produced only slavish imitators who were content to listen to their present mentors rather than consult past witnesses. As a result, the scholarship of the past was soon forgotten. To this the English catechetical system was infinitely preferable with its full employment of the mind and promotion of independence of thought. On the other hand German education had the advantage in its completeness. Pusey found there to be 'no portion of theological knowledge requisite or desirable for the discharge of the pastoral office, or for the more scientific portion of the clerical duties, for the study of which provision is not made . . . in the main, the studies there pursued are such as would be every where acknowledged to be valuable and necessary for the well-instructed Christian minister'.[32] There was continued instruction in the Old and New Testaments in the original, the history of the early Church and of the German churches, Christian doctrine and practice, together with the application of all this to the purpose of the ministry and the instruction of believers. Pusey naturally commended the study of the biblical languages, and particularly his own discipline, Hebrew. This, together with church history, he lamented had only lately been thought necessary to be part of clerical education in England. Other points of commendation included the position given to the professor, with a clear division of labour that allowed him to devote his energies to one department of study and gave him time for theological composition. In contrast, the duties of an English professor were too diverse, and this led to a division of energies or neglect in some portion of instruction. The compulsory nature of the German system with the added spur of a final examination was also preferable to the individualism that predominated in England.

Despite the disadvantages he saw in Germany, Pusey felt that the educational system there did obtain its object, the promotion of extensive learning. He could state that the clergy there were a learned clergy, and that in itself was enough to earn his approbation. In Germany he counted no less than twenty-three theological seminaries with an array of teachers, whereas England boasted only two institutions slenderly provided with divinity professors—seven in all, in fact, at both Oxford and Cambridge. When he surveyed the scene here, he saw 'a wide field open for future exertion', already founded upon the scholarship of men with an existing and profound reputation: Nicholl, Lee, Burton, and Chalmers. The future Church should boast a learned clergy, an influential body of divines, and a supply of theological literature no longer deficient because of the neglect of the past. All this could be attained by a single process in which the existing cathedral establishments were advantageously placed to play their part.

> Germany, then, in Pusey's opinion, furnished the model of a practical system of instruction, the application of which to Cathedral institutions would make the latter useful to the Church. If Cathedrals were to survive, he felt that they must be centres of learning and of clerical education.[33]

Here was Pusey's main consideration, that the cathedrals stood with many advantages for this task. Distributed throughout the country, each had some sort of library. Candidates would benefit from the society of the bishop and senior clergy, and their qualifications would be more readily supervised. Pusey did not set out any plan, but made suggestions. The length of course might be two years after a university education. The numbers he estimated might be 450, giving a number of 900 candidates training at a given time. He saw that this number had to be increased if effective measures were to be adopted to provide clergy for the large towns. Although some dioceses might be too small or inconveniently placed, Pusey suggested that a portion of twelve cathedrals each with its own provision for education could be selected with seventy or eighty students at each seminary. Five professors would be sufficient from a cathedral staff to give instruction in every subject of theology, a parish in the town with an experienced minister giving instruction in pastoral work.

Pusey felt his suggestion was in no way new and gave many

153

examples of its earlier supporters, beginning with Cranmer. Then, by comparison with the forgotten names of German theology, he listed the great men of English theology, who flourished within the precincts of a cathedral, whose memory remained alive. The cathedrals, he argued, 'were the nurseries of most of our chief Divines, who were the glory of our English name; in them these great men consolidated the strength which has been beneficial to the Church'.[34] Learned studies are not the work of industrious parish clergy: by abolishing cathedral establishments, should the English Church content itself with a half-learned clergy? Should it lose a source from which the ablest scholars have been raised to the episcopate or to responsible office within the Church? Pusey admitted, however, the abuses of advancement through family connection or party interest, but blamed the system of patronage which should be given up for a better means of appointment. He favoured not the abolition of trusts which have been profaned, but rather their rededication to the service for which they were first established.

It was here that Pusey directly challenged Henley on the lawful disposal of cathedral property and endowments. The gifts of private piety were made with a special intention which the law should uphold. The will of the donor was often the maintenance and promotion of religious learning. Now Henley had maintained that the inviolability of corporate rights should no longer be upheld when public necessity or expediency demanded otherwise. Pusey objected to this principle:

> Is it now esteemed that the public have a right to take what they never gave? and because private individuals, instead of aggrandizing their own families, bestowed portions of their property in promoting the public good, in a way in which they thought most beneficial, does it follow that it so becomes public property, that it may be converted, against the will of the founder, to a different class of objects, merely because those objects are of undoubted importance?[35]

If a reformation were demanded, it should be:

> not an outward change in the disposition of property, but an

154

abandonment of the corrupt principles upon which patronage has been exercised ... that those to whom this high trust is committed, should execute it as faithful stewards. When the will of the founder shall again be executed, there will be no further question, whether that will was wise or no. .... The first object must be to ascertain in each case what the intentions of the founder were; the next to apply the funds carefully and faithfully according to those intentions. Such a reformation were a wholesome, were a righteous change. Any other application of any portion of church property is but a national robbery of what the nation never gave, for purposes which the nation ought to supply, but to which our own has hitherto been unhappily indifferent.[36]

Pusey ends on this note of principle, that the maintenance of cathedrals and their property was a sacred trust, yet the promotion of this did not make him insensitive to the abuses to which Henley had referred nor to the need for initiatives in Church extension in the large towns and manufacturing districts. Pusey concluded:

The condition of our large towns must indeed be a painful and oppressive subject of thought to every Christian mind. ... It is, then, an advantage in our present evils, that when once brought forward, we cannot escape observing them; we cannot pass through, or hear of, a single manufacturing or commercial town, or a single mining district, without its being forced upon our minds, that a large portion of that population, the sinews of our national strength, is left ungratefully in a state of Heathenism.

When the full extent was known a solution would surely be found to meet the need, 'without purchasing one gain by another loss, and lopping off an useful limb, in order to throw additional circulation, for the time, into the rest of the body'.[37] He looked to those in authority to find the remedy and trusted that it would be the clergy who executed it and thereby sacrificed most. Meanwhile he was content to commit the Church to Divine Providence to succour and preserve her.

Pusey's pamphlet with its extensive research and painstaking argument was generally well received, but the attack on the cathedrals was under way and Pusey saw much in later years to disappoint him. Lord Grey's Commission of Inquiry into Church affairs had been set up in 1832 and it was renewed in subsequent years. Its Second Report came in March 1836 and resulted in three Bills: Pluralities and Residence, Dean and Chapter, and the Established Church Bill. The first was not passed until 1838 and the second continued to distress the Cathedral bodies and perturbed the Commons until 1840. Pusey contributed in some measure to this second Bill's erratic progress by drawing up a petition in which he repeated his reasons for the utility of preserving the cathedral bodies in much the same terms as in his pamphlet.[38] But the Bill tried to get to grips with the urgent want of churches and clergy, and it was out of necessity that the Commissioners urged the use of surplus cathedral and collegiate revenues. The die was cast and when it was enacted nearly 360 non-resident prebends were suppressed and the number of canonries was limited. The bishop acquired the patronage that once belonged to individual members of chapters, whilst he was also to appoint to twenty-four non-stipendiary stalls such deserving clergy as he wished to honour. Only the Established Church Bill was passed in 1836 which incorporated the various proposals for episcopal redistribution as set out in the Commission's Third Report. This had momentous results, for by it a permanent body was established, the Ecclesiastical Commissioners. All the money eventually accumulated by the 1840 Act was transferred to the administration of this agency as a fund to supplement poor livings and assist new parishes. A sum nearing £360,000 was to be the result of this legislation.

Pusey always feared the work of the Commissioners, but the cathedral bodies proved strong enough to resist excessive spoliation. They argued that they could not bear the full burden of reform in the Church. In April 1838 Pusey continued his attack in an article in the *British Critic* and prophesied that 'we shall live under the supremacy of the Commission, it will be our legislative, executive, the ultimate appeal of our bishops; it will absorb our Episcopate; the Prime Minister will be our

Protestant Pope'.[39] Best judges this to be 'the most comprehensive and amazing' of indictments against the Commissioner's work, 'which presents the melancholy spectacle of a high-principled clerical mind almost unhinged by excitement and morbidity'.[40] Newman congratulated him,[41] but Blomfield considered his criticisms 'invidiously and even unfairly put'.[42] When the time came for the redistribution of property to have its day, Pusey put much of the blame on the silence of the cathedral clergy.[43] He later explained what was his real vision:

> I should have liked much better [he wrote to Keble] that the property of each Cathedral should have been kept entire, and that non-residentiary prebends should have been multiplied
> . . . instead of giving money to a parish to find a Minister, I should have liked to have sent them one from the Cathedrals, and so to have enlarged their efficiency, and made *them*, (as the Commission saw) not their money, the means of benefitting the country, and made them again the Evangelizers of the Country.[44]

But if Pusey had failed in this, there was achievement in other ways. Although he was perhaps not alone in his idea of the formation of theological houses alongside the cathedrals, his pamphlet set this idea clearly before the public. An attempt to save the income of the stalls of Durham by annexing an educational institution to the Cathedral had already been made in 1832 by Bishop Van Mildert and this led to the foundation of Durham University. No wonder the next bishop, Maltby, wrote to Pusey subscribing to the idea of cathedral association with clerical education.[45] Various institutions were already in existence (St Bees was founded in 1816 for candidates for holy orders who were not graduates), but the first diocesan theological college was founded in 1838 under the shadow of Chichester Cathedral by the bishop, William Otter and Dean Chandler. Wells followed in 1840, and others were established later. From its inception Chichester bore the imprint of Pusey's outline, and through Manning, a contributor to its founding, and Charles Marriott, its first principal, it bore the hallmark of Tractarian influence. Marriott was appointed through Newman's suggestion, and this was at a time when Newman and Pusey were collaborating on their house for theological study (the *coenobi-tium* Newman called it) in St Aldates, a house open to graduates contemplating ordination who wished to read further and live a common life. Marriott and his first students lived this life in the College's first home in the Cathedral close. Any further link with Pusey has yet to be established.[46]

Educationally there was another achievement. Pusey had regretted the lack of teachers in theology and had suggested the appointment of two additional professors at Oxford, one of Ecclesiastical History, and one of Practical Theology, to be provided with canonries at Christ Church.[47] Pusey further promoted this idea in his contribution to the memorials sent by deans and chapters to the Commission of Inquiry repeating the assertions of his pamphlet and comparing the German system. Pusey noted that no provision was made for teaching ecclesiastical history or pastoral theology, the latter including instruction in sermons, catechizing, and the cure of souls generally.[48] The Commissioners' Fifth Report and then the 1840 Act brought such proposals into being. A canonry at Christ Church was annexed to the Lady Margaret Professor and two new canonries were annexed to two new professorships. Eventually the chair of Pastoral Theology, of immense value to candidates for ordination, was founded in 1842. Edward King, principal of Cuddesdon Theological College, was elected to the chair in 1873, and here was the perfect marriage of Pusey's ideas. Liddon is entirely sure of his foresight: 'If of late Theological Colleges have been attached to Cathedrals, and if the study of theology has been promoted at such centres and elsewhere by a division of labour, these results are originally due to Pusey's pamphlet'.[49]

Pusey's pamphlet was an immense work, but it bore little fruit. His attitude to the preservation of cathedrals was idealistic and essentially archaic. He saw a cathedral:

> some times an additional church in a large town, with a succession of well-appointed ministers who may usefully influence its society; sometimes a church in which Divine worship may be conducted with more attention to beauty and order than elsewhere; sometimes an institution in which

clerical merit may be appropriately rewarded, and in which, after periods of exhausting labour, its own clergy may find religious refreshment in more tranquil duties, and 'the pure and holy harmony of the choral service'.[50]

But Pusey's appreciation of their worth did not provide the funds needed to equip the Church for its task in a rapidly changing society, and the superfluous endowments of cathedral bodies provided a ready-made source. When many were going in want of a place of worship and a minister, who would deny the remedy in favour of maintaining a sinecure prebend in office because he was the trustee of an ancient endowment? But the value of Pusey's work lies in its place within what was to become 'the context of Oxford Movement orthodoxy',[51] the fight for principle, but written as it was before the Movement had begun. Pusey wrote at a stage of definition: he wrote to underpin the Catholic ideal of a Church that preserved its heritage and continued the work of its forefathers in an unbroken tradition. The assault upon the cathedrals provided him with an early opportunity to promote this doctrine: they were for him a sacred trust bestowed on the Church by which sound learning and theology could be extended to all parts of society and by a useful and learned clergy. To desert this trust because of expediency in awkward times was an abandonment of the principle of the inviolability of sacred things. It was 'national robbery of what the nation never gave'. Not much later Keble ascended to the pulpit at St Mary's and warned his hearers that 'the Robbery Bill' (the Irish Bishoprics' Bill) was but the beginning of National Apostasy. And the Oxford Movement was begun.

NOTES

1 The Revd G. R. Gleig, 'A Letter to the Lord Bishop of London on the subject of Church Reform' (London 1833), p. 1f. (Pusey House).
2 A. P. Stanley, *The Life and Correspondence of Dr Arnold*, 2 vols (London 1844), p. 297.
3 Ibid., p. 278.
4 Arnold, *Miscellaneous Works*, ed. A. P. Stanley (London 1845), p. 219.
5 Newman to E.B.P., 15 December 1832 (Pusey House).

6   P. C. Hammond, *The Parson and the Victorian Parish* (London 1977), p. 33.

7   D. Bowen, *The Idea of the Victorian Church* (Montreal 1968), p. 14.

8   Hansard, 3rd Series, 55 (30 July, 1840).

9   E.B.P. to Gladstone, 15 February, 1833 (Pusey House).

10   H. P. Liddon, vol. 1, 392f. Also Pusey House, letter of 15 February, 1833.

11   Quoted in Liddon, vol. 1, p. 249.

12   Stanley, p. 222.

13   Arnold, *Principles of Church Reform*, with an introductory essay by M. J. Jackson and J. Rogan (1962), p. 51.

14   E. B. Pusey, *Remarks on the Prospective and Past Benefits of Cathedral Institutions in the Promotion of Sound Religious Knowledge and of Clerical Education*, 2nd ed. (London 1833), p. 4. This second edition of the pamphlet was published very soon. It is an expansion of the first edition by Pusey and is best consulted. All references are from this edition. See Liddon, vol. 1, p. 235.

15   See G. F. A. Best, *Temporal Pillars* (Cambridge 1963), pp. 278ff.

16   O. J. Brose, *Church and Parliament* (London 1959), p. 123.

17   Lord Henley, *A Plan of Church Reform*, 7th ed. (London 1832), pp. vi–viii.

18   Ibid., pp. 23f.

19   Ibid., p. 29.

20   Ibid., p. 31.

21   Liddon, vol. 1, p. 226.

22   See Liddon, vol. 1, p. 227; Best, pp. 286f.

23   Ibid., p. 286f.

24   Pusey, *Cathedral Institutions*, p. 12.

25   Ibid., p. 21. For a full treatment of this see M. A. Crowther, *Church Embattled* (Newton Abbot 1970), ch. 9.

26   Ibid., p. 25.

27   Ibid., p. 27.

28   Ibid., p. 31.

29   Ibid., p. 40.

30   Liddon, vol. 1, pp. 238ff.

31   Pusey, *Cathedral Institutions*, p. 42.

32   Ibid., p. 50.

33   Liddon, vol. 1, pp. 230f.

34   Pusey, *Cathedral Institutions*, p. 103.

35   Ibid., pp. 146f.

36   Ibid., pp. 151ff. Pusey later wrote on this issue that 'the only case in which it has ever been thought right to alter the regulations of the founder is when the purposes he contemplated have ceased to exist'. See Liddon,

vol. 1, p. 397. See also a letter to H.E.Manning, 28 September, 1837, (Pusey House) on the reform of patronage and the violation of a founder's gifts by diverting them to a different purpose.

37 Pusey, *Cathedral Institutions*, pp. 159f.

38 See Liddon, vol. 1, pp. 96f.

39 *The British Critic*, 23 (1838), p. 526. Pusey's article was separately published as 'The Royal and Parliamentary Ecclesiastical Commissioners', and is attributed to Pusey in Liddon, vol. 4, Appendix A. See also a letter from Manning to Newman asking him to encourage E.B.P. to produce his article as a pamphlet rather than in *The British Critic*. Manning himself wrote 'The Principle of the Ecclesiastical Commissioners Examined: a Letter to the Lord Bishop of Chichester' (1838) and 'The Preservation of Unendowed Canonries: A Letter to William, Lord Bishop of Chichester' (1840). These clearly emulate Pusey. Manning had previously sent an 'Address' by the clergy of Chichester to the Archbishop of Canterbury in 1837. Pusey wrote (28 September, 1837, Pusey House) commending it, but drawing attention to Manning's omission, 'in speaking of Cathedrals, and their most sacred uses, as places of intercessory prayer, and especially N(ewman) adds for the celebration of the Holy Eucharist. Soon after the Reformation until the unhappy second book of Edward VI, the Communion was daily'.

40 Best, p. 314.

41 J.H.Newman to J.W.Bowden, quoted in G.Faber, *Oxford Apostles* (London 1974), p. 253.

42 Blomfield to Pusey, 7 April 1838 (Pusey House).

43 Pusey to Keble, 13 October, 1836 (Pusey House) and quoted in Liddon, vol. 1, pp. 398f.

44 Pusey to Keble, 11 February, 1840 (Pusey House). Pusey even suggested the self-taxation of the clergy to benefit destitute places. See letter to Manning 28 September, 1837 (Pusey House).

45 Anon. [M. Trench], *The Story of Dr Pusey's Life* (London 1900), p. 71.

46 For a full study of this subject see F. W. B. Bullock, *A History of Training for the Ministry of the Church of England and Wales from 1800 to 1874* (St Leonards-on-Sea 1955).

47 Pusey, *Cathedral Institutions*, p. 92.

48 Church Commissioners' Papers (1835), *Memorials from Deans and Chapters*, 112.02, p. 37.

49 Liddon, vol. 1, p. 235. Liddon also comments on Pusey's opposition in the pamphlet to what was eventually to become the Final Honours School of Theology in 1868. In this he took a leading part after changing his opinion. See Liddon, vol. 1, p. 231.

50 Ibid., vol. 1, p. 232.

51 Matthew, p. 113.

7

'Such a Friend to the Pope'[1]

ROBERT HARVIE GREENFIELD SSJE

When Dr Pusey's *Tracts on Baptism* appeared in 1836, the *Christian Observer*, an organ of the Evangelicals, suggested that he ought to teach at Maynooth or the Vatican rather than at an institution of the Church of England. Throughout the remainder of his long life, he continued to be accused of being a 'Romanizer' and of importing Roman Catholic doctrines into the Church of England.

Nearly a century and a half has gone by, and relationships among Christian churches have changed dramatically. Seeing the Christian faith as a whole attacked by various forms of atheism and agnosticism, Christians have become aware not only of their need to stand together, but also of the large areas of agreement which they share. Major changes in Roman Catholicism, made by the Second Vatican Council, have opened a new era of good will and friendliness. Except by a small number of extreme Fundamentalists, the Roman Catholic Church is no longer viewed with horror and suspicion. A climate of opinion now exists which makes it possible to re-examine the evidence for the charges of 'Romanizing' made against Dr Pusey. If true, they will inevitably be seen in a different context; if not true, an analysis of his position may clarify the first principles of Anglicanism in general and the Anglo-Catholic Movement in particular.

The issue which dominated Pusey's mind throughout most of his life was the nature and content of the Catholic Faith. In the Oxford University Statutes of his day, it was stated that none *directe vel indirecte doceat, vel dogmatice asserat quod fidei Catholicae vel bonis moribus ulla ex parte adversatur.*[2] In order to understand what he meant by the 'Catholic Faith' and the related question of his attitude towards the Roman Catholic Church, it is necessary

162

to examine the doctrinal presuppositions which underlie his writings. The relative claims of Antiquity, the Reformation, and Doctrinal Development will give us a framework for understanding why he held certain doctrines, and show us the foundations of his ecclesiology.

In later years, it seemed to Pusey that he had learned doctrines like that of the Real Presence from his mother, and the impression has persisted that he was a hereditary High Churchman; this is not so. His views before the beginning of the Oxford Movement may be seen clearly in the two volumes which he wrote in reply to a study of German theology by H. J. Rose. One of the somewhat rare High Churchmen of his day, Rose believed that a decline into rationalism had taken place in Germany, which was due, in part, to the Lutheran insistence on *sola scriptura*, and from the absence of episcopal authority.

Pusey, who had studied in Germany and knew German theology better than any Englishman of his day, corrected what he thought was an inaccurate and misleading picture of German theology, and dismissed Rose's notion that Scripture needs to be interpreted in the light of Tradition.

The Scripture did need no such adscititious means to preserve its healthful truths from such corruption as would neutralize their efficacy, appeared to result from the history of the early church, in which for above two centuries no symbols were at all received, and even when heretical speculation did render such safe-guards in individual cases, they were extended no further than the emergency of such cases required; the rest of the body of Christian doctrine was committed to the keeping of unauthoritative tradition: that a recurrence to Scripture is sufficient to regenerate the system where corrupted, independent of, or in opposition to, existing symbols, resulted from the various portions of the history of the Reformation.[3]

In teaching that 'Scripture is the only authoritative source of Christian knowledge'[4] and that 'Scripture is its own interpreter',[5] Pusey set himself apart from the High Church tradition. A further rejection of traditional High Church

163

teaching may be seen in his response to Rose's assertion that episcopal authority would have prevented the growth of rationalism: he pointed to the failure of the bishops of Denmark to stem the tide of rationalism, and went on to argue that the Church of Scotland, without bishops, had been more successful in arresting infidelity than the Church of Denmark with its bishops.[6] The doctrine of Apostolic Succession does not seem to have entered his mind.

When we turn from his views about tradition and episcopacy to his sacramental beliefs, it is apparent that he cannot have learned the doctrine of the Real Presence, as he held it later, from his mother. Since most English people were unfamiliar with German terminology, he clarified it for them:

> It may perhaps be necessary to state, in order to avoid misconception, that the term Evangelical is used in the following sheets according to the phraseology of the German Church, to designate the Lutheran body, that of 'Reformed' or 'Calvinist' for such as agree in the doctrine of the Lord's Supper with ourselves.[7]

His matter-of-fact rejection of the eucharistic realism of Lutheranism is all the more striking when seen against his admiration of Martin Luther. In reply to Rose, he declared that the German Reformer possessed a special charism which made it possible for him to discern the essentials of the Christian Faith, a gift which 'raised him . . . above the assumed authority of the Church, and above the might of tradition . . .'.[8] That he continued to venerate the continental Reformers can be seen from the fact that Newman chided him, in the year before the beginning of the Oxford Movement, for calling Calvin a saint.[9]

In his replies to Rose, Pusey made much of the sterile 'orthodoxism' which he believed had paved the way for dangerous trends in German theology. In his descriptions of 'orthodoxism', it is apparent that he had in mind the 'High and Dry' churchmen of his own day in England, with whom he did not identify himself. If not a High Churchman, neither was he an Evangelical. While greatly influenced by pietists like Spener, he was less than enthusiastic about their successors; in his descriptions of their shortcomings, we can see him writing with one eye on the English Evangelicals who shared their defects. Pusey's theological position, before the beginning of the Oxford Movement, was neither High nor Evangelical; it seems to have been a central position, with distinct tendencies towards what later became the Broad Church position.

Since he did not believe in the Real Presence or Apostolic Succession, and found no need for Tradition to interpret the Scripture properly, it is not surprising that he felt no particular attraction for the Roman Catholic Church, in which all of these were crucial doctrines; had he been a High Churchman he might well have felt some sympathy for a Church which shared these elements of the Catholic Faith. Certainly, he did not, like many Evangelicals, believe that Rome was *the* Antichrist: already, he distinguished between basic trinitarian and christological dogmas and the popular religion which he had seen on the Continent.

> The Romish Church holds the essential doctrines of Christianity, but the addition of a corrupt human system has a grievous tendency to oppress them and impede their influence.[10]

Because he made this distinction, he was able to affirm that 'there are very many even in the Romish Church, at whose feet it would be presumptuous for men who are conscious only of ordinary advances in holiness to sit in the kingdom'.[11] As for the religion of the people, he wrote after visiting Einsiedeln that it was 'founded on abject and mercenary superstition'.[12] Saint Catherine of Siena appeared to him to be moved by a 'half-distracted fanaticism'.[13] He saw no contradiction between Reformers and Antiquity, and judged the Roman Catholic Church by the standards of the Reformation. He took it for granted that the commonly accepted teachings of the Church of England were the Catholic Faith, and consequently the Roman Catholic Church was, in his eyes, less than Catholic.

In the years which followed his return from Germany and his appointment as Regius Professor of Hebrew, Pusey moved in a High Church direction. At first, this was probably due to the

165

influence of his friend and patron, Bishop Lloyd of Oxford, but later it was through the influence of Keble, either directly or as mediated by Newman. Even before the Oxford Movement began, Keble's theology was causing an intellectual and spiritual ferment among his friends. His High Church position was different from that of the 'High and Dry' Churchmen; he was strongly influenced by the Nonjuring Divines, many of whose teachings were commonly thought to be outside the pale of the Church of England.

Once free of their connection with the State, the Nonjurors found themselves in two camps. The more conservative was content to continue the teachings of the mainstream of the Caroline Divines; its followers appealed to Antiquity in a somewhat selective way, and used it to buttress the results of the Reformation. Those who were more radical saw their break with the Establishment as an opportunity for change: they saw that they could not just use the appeal to the primitive Church to defend the Anglican *status quo*: the English Reformers and their work also stood under the judgement of Antiquity. Where the Reformation Settlement differed from the doctrines and practices of the Fathers, the radical Nonjurors believed it was their opportunity and their duty to remodel the English Church in accordance with the pattern of primitive Christianity. Keble's sympathy for the more radical Nonjurors gave him a vantage point from which to criticize the establishment, and his outlook proved to be a heady stimulant for the circle of people around him. No mild and bland country parson, Keble was not certain that he could function within the established Church, even before the Tractarian Movement began.[14]

With the appointment of Dr Hampden as Regius Professor of Divinity in 1836, Pusey threw himself wholeheartedly into the Tractarian camp.[15] Until that time, he had merely been sympathetic with the Tractarian Movement in a general sort of way, but he saw in the appointment the influence of the same anti-dogmatic stance which he had known and deplored in Germany. He was now aware of the value of Tradition as a restraint on the doctrinal vagaries of liberalism; at the same time, he began to defend the usages of the primitive Church which had been preserved by the Nonjurors. While not advocating changes in the Liturgy, he admitted that he thought the First Prayer Book was preferable to the later books,[16] and defended the Invocation of the Holy Spirit in the Eucharist, the Eucharistic Oblation, and Prayers for the Departed.[17] In the following year, he preached a sermon, dedicated to Keble, in which he strongly defended the Nonjurors in their opposition to the dethroning of James II, and blamed the ills of the Church on its moving away from the teachings of the Caroline Divines.[18]

By 1838, his criterion for defining the Catholic Faith was the often-quoted dictum of Vincent of Lérins in the *Commonitorium*: 'the faith which has been believed everywhere, always, and by all, for that is truly and in the strictest sense Catholic...'. Scripture was, of course, the primary source of revelation, but it was to be interpreted by the consensus of the 'Catholic Fathers and Ancient Bishops'.[19] Their teaching, he believed, was maintained by the Caroline Divines and their successors among the Nonjurors. He wrote that the 'doctrine of the Eucharistic Sacrifice mostly found refuge among the Non-Jurors and our brethren of the Scotch Church',[20] and his catena on this subject in Tract 81 draws on writers like Brett, Hickes, and Leslie.[21]

As yet, he saw no discrepancy between this position and that of the Reformers; he wrote of 'Cranmer committing himself to Antiquity',[22] and pointed to the 'Primitive Church, after whose model our own was reformed, and which, amid the entanglement of the modern deviations of Rome, our reformers wished, I believe, to trace out'.[23] Against this background, it is not surprising that he initially saw no difficulty in a plan to build a memorial to the Reformers at Oxford.[24] Later, when the proposal was brought forward to establish a bishopric in Jerusalem under the joint sponsorship of the Churches of England and Prussia, it caused great anguish to Newman and to other participants in the Catholic Revival, but once again, Pusey initially saw no problem. He wrote 'the King of Prussia... is at heart an Episcopalian... I should not be inclined to oppose it'.[25] It is clear that when he appealed to the consensus of the Fathers to interpret Scripture and saw this principle carried out by the Caroline Divines and the Nonjurors, he believed that he was only following the basic principles of the English Reformers.

As a loyal son of the Reformation, Pusey continued to speak out against the practices of the Roman Catholic Church. In his sermon on the Nonjurors, he wrote:

> From the time that the Church of Rome began to forsake the principles of the Church Catholic and grasp after human means, she began also to take evil means to good ends, and . . . at last took evil means for evil ends. She shewed herself rather the descendant of them that slew the Apostles. . . . There is not an enormity which has been practised against people or kings by miscreants in the name of God, but the divines of that unhappy Church have abetted or justified.[26]

In the lengthy *Letter to Dr Jelf*, vindicating Newman's Tract 90, Pusey again condemned the corruptions of popular Roman Catholicism, and what he thought were its doctrinal excesses.

> . . . in all [countries] over which she has dominion she will tolerate and profit by what she dares not approve; will sit by in silence while men tell falsehood or use violence in her behalf; will suffer visions and miracles which she does not believe to be believed by her people, and to bring gain to her clergy, and even in her own guarded province of the faith will permit unauthorized doctrines (such as that of the Immaculate Conception) to creep in and take the public honors of truth. . . .[27]

Pusey condemned official Roman Catholic doctrine as well as the corruptions of popular religion and the practices of the Roman Church; he singled out transubstantiation and the invocation of saints for criticism.

> . . . the error of Transubstantiation has modified other true doctrine, so as to cast into the shade the one oblation once offered upon the Cross; . . . the addition of the single practice of 'soliciting the saints to pray for men' has in the Romish Church obscured the primary articles of Justification and of the Intercession of our Blessed Lord.[28]

168

That he did not just mean popular religion can be seen by his
reference to the 'unhappy and fatal canons of the Council of
Trent'.[29] Years later, in 1843, he was still insisting 'I
have . . . often and decidedly expressed my rejection of the
doctrine of Transubstantiation, and the Canon of Trent upon
it. . .'.[30] Thus, throughout the entire period of the publication
of the *Tracts for the Times* Pusey remained under the impression
that the Reformers accurately reflected the beliefs of the early
Church, and consequently continued to attack both popular
Roman Catholicism and the official teachings of Rome. Far
from being a Romanizer, he was only concerned to introduce
the full scope of patristic theology into the Church of England;
the fact that Rome shared some of the same teachings was
unimportant.

As rumours of Newman's unsettlement as an Anglican and
the Romeward direction of his thought began to spread, we
begin to see a change of attitude in Dr Pusey. His old friend, Dr
Hook of Leeds, wrote to him late in 1844 expressing a reaction
to the rumours about Newman which was far from uncommon.

> . . . may he be preserved from the fangs of Satan . . . any
> person going from light to darkness would endanger his
> salvation. I should fear that it would be scarcely possible for
> anyone who should apostasize from the only true Church of
> God in this country to the popish sect, to escape perdi-
> tion . . . [Newman's] eyes have been blinded so that he
> cannot see the soul-destroying errors of the Romish sect.[31]

Pusey replied to Hook's tirade, which went on to identify
Rome as the Antichrist and expressed a much more benevolent
attitude to Rome than he had ever shown before.

> I am frightened by your calling Rome Antichrist, or a
> forerunner of it. I believe Antichrist will be infidel and arise
> out of what calls itself Protestantism, and then Rome and
> England will be united in one then to oppose it. . . . The
> ground seems clearing and people taking sides for the last
> conflict, and we shall then see, I hope, that all which hold 'the
> deposit of the Faith' (the Creeds, as an authority without [i.e.,

outside] them) will be on one side, 'the Eastern, the Western, our own', and those who lean on their own understanding on the other. I wish you would not let yourself be drawn off by your fears of 'Popery'. While people are drawn off to this, the enemy (heresy of all sorts, misbelief, unbelief) is taking possession of our citadel. Our real battle is with infidelity, and from this Satan is luring us off.[32]

The contrast between the sympathy which Pusey expressed for Rome in this letter and the position, which he had until recently held, may be accounted for, in part, by the results of accepting the primitive Church as the norm for doctrine and practice. His disciple and biographer, Liddon, notes that 'the revival of true Anglican principles, with its appeal to the Primitive Church, really involved logical consequences far beyond what had been contemplated by the old High Churchism with which they had originally identified it'.[33] He was now less sympathetic with changes made at the Reformation, particularly in the doctrine of the eucharistic sacrifice.[34] Writing to one of the more conservative Tractarians, he also declared, 'I can see things in Antiquity which I did not (especially I cannot deny some purifying system in the Intermediate State, nor the lawfulness of some Invocation of Saints). . . .'.[35]

Already in 1841, he had written to a friend about the unnatural isolation of the Church of England from the rest of Catholic Christendom, East and West, and observed that this feeling was stronger than it had been in the time of Andrewes and Ken.[36] In 1845, just before the secession of Newman, he wrote:

> It is only by identifying itself with some stronger authority that it (our Church) can have any hold of peoples' minds. If we throw ourselves in entire faith upon the early undivided Church, and say dogmatically. . . . 'This is the voice of the whole Church, and, in it, of God, to you,' this will tell. But in proportion as we do this, I am sure that our protest against Rome will be weakened, and that we shall see that she is Catholic in some points, where we have been thought to consider her uncatholic.[37]

The result of appealing with consistency to the life and teachings of the primitive Church was that he could not 'anymore take the negative ground against Rome'.[38] As it finally became apparent to Pusey that Newman would secede from the English Church, his attitude underwent further changes. In attempting to rationalize his friend's secession, he came to look upon it as a 'mysterious dispensation, as though . . . Almighty God was drawing him, as a chosen instrument, for some office in the Roman Church. . .'.[39]

For Newman himself, one can well imagine that He Who formed him as so special an instrument, may will to employ him as a restorer of the Roman Church. It too is quite powerless to meet its difficulties, and some in it look to Newman to give some new impulse to it, like that of the Jesuits.[40]

Because of his conviction that Newman was being called to play a unique role in the Roman Catholic Church, Pusey gradually came to look upon the reunion of the two Churches as part of this special dispensation and saw it as his responsibility to help prepare the Church of England for the reunion to come. In the course of adapting French devotional manuals, he had always avoided any invocation of saints as not tolerable in the English Church. Now he was willing to go a little farther, and wrote to Keble about the problem as it was raised by his forthcoming edition of the *Paradisus Animae*.

The feeling you speak of, of those who prefer the mention of 'the prayers of the whole Church, visible and invisible' to the specific mention of S. Mary is one I had; but facts seem to testify that she has a power of intercession greater than other Saints, and then one seemed to be holding back what might be a privilege to know, as well as a means of breaking down the wall between the two Churches. For if there is any doctrine as to S. Mary which should be acknowledged, then our not holding any, or the contrary, must be an injury to ourselves, and a barrier to union, like the extreme popular system among them.[41]

To Newman, Pusey admitted that he had violated their

agreement to avoid any doctrinal innovations; he acknowledged that he was going beyond the teaching previously allowed in the Church of England: while prayers for the departed had been recognized as lawful, any sort of invocation of saints was something new.

> This about the special mention of S. Mary is a different question, because in the prayers for the departed one is following the direction of our Church which guides us to the early ages, whereas the special mention of S. Mary is later.
>
> I should not say anything about either subject, however, in preaching, in which I am the direct organ of the Church, but, if it is right, I do not feel the difficulty, acting as an individual, in editing books.[42]

By the summer of 1845, the adaptations of the Roman Catholic devotional books, which had originally been conceived as a measure to prevent secessions and thought to be in line with Antiquity, had now received another purpose: to promote reunion. Because of the differing styles of piety in the two Churches Pusey thought it desirable to draw English piety closer to the Roman in the hope of bringing the churches closer together. His purpose, he admitted in another letter, was 'to form a certain $\eta\theta$os in the confidence that if that were formed, all beside would by His Grace follow . . .'.[43]

Pusey explained his new policy and his change in theology to Manning in an effort to win the anti-papal archdeacon to 'more love for Rome'.[44] In the midst of all the difficulties caused by Newman's impending secession and the unsettlement which it was creating, Pusey could see only one thing clearly: his duty to remain in the Church of England and work for her as God enabled him. Negatively, however, he admitted 'I can say nothing against the formal decrees of Rome, i.e., the Council of Trent'.[45]

> So then all I can do is within certain limits. Our Church directs us to the Ancient Church; when I take her as my $\kappa\acute{\alpha}\nu\omega\nu$, I am following the line of my own Church and that to which God, by his Providence directs me. This I have desired to do, teaching in my public ministrations, with still more

reason holding in reserve what seems in contradiction to her teaching and about which if any thing were said, it must be said very fully, e.g., as to some purgatorial process; and holding myself in abeyance as to what I do not see, but denying nothing.[46]

He now held that 'we have the consensus of the whole Church, although not formally expressed, against our popular theology and the traditional interpretation of our Articles.'[47] He viewed the current state of the English Church as provisional, and his reading of Thorndike had put a doubt in his mind, 'that a particular Church had a right to reform itself'.[48]

And all that I have since seen of the temper of those engaged in the Reformation makes me feel that there was very much human in it, that it was not done as it ought. Our subsequent history makes me feel that we thus brought in a wrong element into our Church, which has been struggling with Catholicity ever since, and that one or the other must in time be ejected. I feel too that if we had not allied ourselves to so much that was wrong, we must not be in the condition in which we are.[49]

The Catholic Faith, which he had once seen as the consensus of the Fathers of Antiquity, and later as the consensus of the undivided Church, was now seen to be *all that was held in common by the Roman Catholic and Eastern Orthodox Churches*, even after their centuries of separation. It was the duty of the Church of England to bring itself into agreement with the rest of the Catholic Church 'on the basis of what is now [*sic*] held alike by the East and the West'.[50] Replying to Manning's charge that he preferred Rome and ignored the Eastern Church, Pusey admitted that there was a sense in which this was true. The Faith, held in common by the East and the West, would be more naturally expressed by the English in Western terms and with a Western spirituality; England's first duty was with Rome, to which she owed so much in the past. A reunited West could then approach the East to settle differences which were not the same as those separating England from the rest of the Western Patriarchate.[51] Pusey was optimistic in thinking that Manning would agree with him; his conclusion was that if he were in authority and intercommunion were offered 'on the terms of the reception of the Council of Trent, leaving us . . . all matters of discipline, including the cup, our Liturgy in our own tongue, I should do, I believe, what in me lay to induce people to accept it'.[52]

Pusey recognized the validity of Newman's theory of Doctrinal Development as it applied to the early Church, but could not accept Newman's premise that the locus of infallibility was the Roman Church; the existence of a truly Catholic Church in the East, separated from Rome, meant that infallible decisions could not be made by either the Eastern or the Western Church in isolation from the other. It seemed to him that the ability to define developments might be 'part of the fulness of the illumination through the indwelling Spirit, while the Church was one, which was forfeited, when her unity was impaired'.[53]

Conscious that this position left unclear his appeal for reunion on the basis the Council of Trent, he wrote to Manning:

> . . . I can not but hope that it may prove that the Council of Trent may become the basis of union, that those assembled there, were kept providentially free from error . . . again, the Council of Trent might, by subsequent reception, become a General Council, and it might be so now virtually, although unrecognized as such by the whole Church, but in a state of suspense; so a person might be right in receiving it, and yet the doctrine of Roman supremacy, which is, I think, not contained in it, not obligatory.[54]

Although Pusey embraced a Western, Roman version of the faith shared by the Roman Catholics and the Eastern Orthodox, and saw Trent as potentially ecumenical and binding, he did not accept Newman's use of the theory of doctrinal development to defend the papal system or popular Catholicism.[55] Unconvinced by it, Pusey had no intention of becoming a Roman Catholic. Newman, after his own secession, expected Pusey to join him shortly and was puzzled and annoyed when this did not happen.[56] He wrote to Pusey, 'I think that the year can hardly be named which you ended with the same view of the Roman

Catholic religion as you began with. And every change has been an approximation to that religion'.[57] Others were puzzled too, and Pusey explained some of his reasons in an extended letter 'to a lady'.

> That there are very serious things in the Roman Communion which ought to keep us where we are. I would instance chiefly the system as to the Blessed Virgin as the Mediatrix and Dispenser of all present blessings to mankind. (I think nothing short of a fresh revelation could justify this). Then the sale of Masses as applicable to the departed, the system of indulgences as applied to the departed, the denial of the Cup to the laity. . . . I find myself (with our divines) as far off as ever from being able to use the prayers to the Blessed Virgin they use, and repelled by the language of their devotional books—'have recourse to Jesus and Mary', 'by the aid of Jesus and Mary'. . . . It goes far beyond the Council of Trent.[58]

Writing to another correspondent, he declared:

> Mysterious as it all is, I cannot think that such good men as J.H.N. and your brother will be thrown away there, sorely disappointing as to me dear N.'s extreme line is and unconvincing. It seems to throw me further back; I had hoped that things which go so far beyond their own formularies would have disappeared. I could not imagine dear N. writing, as the French R.C. writers do. . . . It would be entirely different from his sermons. . . . But his defense in his essay is as disappointing to me as it is unsatisfactory. If the French language is to come in, I do not see . . . of what use the Epistle to the Hebrews is to be to us. . . .[59]

Pusey rejected the more extravagant forms of the Marian cultus and the extreme claims made for the Papacy; they were not only untenable in the Church of England, but unacceptable in themselves. Nevertheless, he distinguished these aberrations from the faith held in common by the East and West, from the formal decrees of Trent, and even from the Catholic pietism of the devotional books.

Newman complained about the position taken by Pusey:

175

he has indeed *no business* where he is; he cannot name the individual for 1800 years who has ever held his circle of doctrines. . . . Who before him ever joined the circle of Roman doctrine to Anglican ritual and polity?[60]

Aware that such charges were being made, Pusey made the bold experiment of building a church in Leeds, where his position could be held and vindicated. The results were a fiasco; the doctrines taught and the customs practised brought the wrath of Dr Hook, vicar of Leeds, and there were a number of secessions to the Roman Catholic Church. Hook accused Pusey of propagating 'Romish Methodism',[61] and wrote, 'I am ready for war, if it should be the Lord's will that I should maintain the cause of his Church here against you'.[62] Pusey was deeply distressed by the events in Leeds, but was inflexible about his programme.

Another part of his plan to make good his understanding of the Catholic Faith involved the establishment of religious orders, since monasticism clearly had played a major role in the life of the ancient Church, as well as in both Eastern and Western Christendom in later times. Those living in religious communities require a richer spiritual fare than was offered by the usual piety of the English Church, so Pusey introduced an expurgated breviary and pietistic devotions similar to those used in Roman Catholic convents.

Once again, he got his fingers burned. One of his allies in establishing the first sisterhood had been the Revd William Dodsworth, but Dodsworth had become alienated from the Church of England by the Gorham Judgement, in which the State seemed to undermine sacramental doctrine. In a widely read pamphlet,[63] he painted a picture of Pusey's doctrinal stand and his devotional practices which was calculated to inflame opposition to Pusey and, perhaps, drive him out of the Church of England. It did not succeed in weakening Pusey's ties to the Church of his baptism; it merely served to inflame public opinion even more. Pusey was a marked man; few people could see any legitimate place in the English Church for men of his views. Liddon writes of the general attitude towards him:

During this time, he was an object of widespread, deep, and

fierce suspicion. Some of the Heads of Houses would not speak to him when they met him in the street. The post brought him, day by day, from all parts of the country, various forms of insults, by letters signed and anonymous, reflecting on his honesty and his intelligence . . . acquaintance with him was regarded by the governing authorities in the university as a reason for viewing with suspicion those who enjoyed it.[64]

The new wave of secessions, which included Manning, and the establishment of a Roman Catholic hierarchy in England further enflamed opinion against the Roman Catholic Church and against Pusey, who was regarded as a Trojan horse within the walls of Anglicanism. The more conservative Tractarians and their friends decided that Pusey must be removed from the place of leadership which he held, and urged a manifesto against Rome, which they knew Pusey would not sign.[65] Liddon describes the situation throughout this period:

> Pusey might have lessened the suspicion with which he was regarded, if he would have consented publicly to join in those vague popular declarations against the Church of Rome which are the stock in trade of Protestant oratory.[66]

The battle lines were drawn, and the war was fought in the nascent Church Unions. Pusey would not endorse the Reformation, and he would not attack the Roman Catholic Church; he was willing only to sign a statement affirming his loyalty to the Church of England. In the end, he won, and from that time on, his doctrinal stand was to dominate the English Church Union. One of the old High Church party wrote bitterly, 'It will be a matter of convenience to the public to have it clearly understood that the London Union is Dr Pusey's body, and Dr Pusey the mind of the London Union'.[67]

Fourteen years and many controversies later, Manning wrote an attack on the Church of England, which Pusey felt that he must answer; in the course of preparing it, the idea came to him of turning it into the *Eirenikon* which was published in 1865. He had always distinguished between the official teachings of the

177

Roman Catholic Church and popular piety; his hope was that it might be possible to have a declaration of what was *de fide* and what was not *de fide*. Newman was quite naturally offended by the catena of outrageous quotations which Pusey wanted repudiated, and he pointed out the logical impossibility of defining what was not *de fide*: 'It is to determine the work of all Councils till the end of time'.[68] He also noted in a letter to a disciple:

> Pusey's move is remarkable—he is at once trying to get into communion with the Greeks and with us. . . . He has changed his basis, and says that, provided *he* is not obliged to use the Italian devotions to our Lady, etc., he will let what he calls popular corruptions take their course in Italy, etc., and is willing to unite the Anglican to the Catholic Church on the basis of the Council of Trent. You recollect that at the beginning of the Tracts for the Times the Council of Trent was considered to be an act of Apostasy;—so that it is a very great move on his part.[69]

Pusey had indeed moved a long way from the position which he held when the *Tracts* were appearing. In the second *Eirenikon* in 1869, he made a further concession; the defining of the dogma of the Immaculate Conception in 1854 had left him in silent sorrow, but Newman's explanation of the dogma after the first *Eirenikon* had opened 'a gleam of hope where the clouds seemed thickest before'.[70] What Pusey wanted was an authoritative explanation of the dogma and of the more difficult articles of the Council of Trent, since it was not realistic to rely only on the opinions of individual theologians. Because of the controversies caused by the *Eirenika*, Pusey explained in *The Weekly Register* why these authoritative statements were needed.

> We readily recognize the Primacy of the Bishop of Rome; the bearings of that Primacy upon other local Churches, we believe to be a matter of ecclesiastical not Divine law; neither is there anything in the Supremacy itself to which we should object. Our only fear is that it should, through the appointment of our Bishops, involve the reception of that practical *quasi-authoritative* system, which is, I believe, alike the cause,

and (forgive me) the justification in our eyes of remaining apart.[71]

In the third *Eirenikon*, published in 1870, he stressed again the need to separate defined dogma from the excesses of popular piety and the extreme interpretations of the Ultramontanes. Recognizing that it was being said that the forthcoming Vatican Council would define the dogma of Papal Infallibility, he thought it necessary to express his beliefs about that issue and about the Infallibility of the Church as a whole.

> I do indeed hope on different grounds, that the Roman Church will not define . . . that the Pope speaking ex cathedra is infallible. . . . But if the whole Church, including the Greek and Anglican Communions, were to define these or any other points to be 'de fide', I should hold all further inquiry to be at an end. In whatever way they should rule any question, however contrary to my previous impressions, I should submit to it and hold it as being, by universal consent of the whole Church, proved to be a part of the Apostles' faith. I have ever submitted my credenda to a power beyond myself. We have differed then and must differ, upon a point of fact—what are the component parts of that Church, whose reception of any doctrine saves . . . further inquiry, and rules that doctrine for us; not as to the principle, whether any such power exists.[72]

Pusey stressed that the Infallibility of the Church did not extend to the possibility of defining new beliefs, in contrast to the assertions of some of the Ultramontanes; it could only declare that a particular belief, now challenged, had always been part of the faith held in Antiquity. The role of Tradition, he had written years before and still believed, is 'not a supplementary, not an independent, source of truth, but a concurrent, interpretative, definitive, and harmonizing witness of one and the same truth'.[73] Now, in the third *Eirenikon*, he reaffirmed his belief, in contrast to the idea that the Pope could define dogmas unilaterally, which rumour said would be decreed by the Vatican Council.

This is our security in submitting at once to the Creed of the

179

Church or to the Ecumenical councils, in which the whole Church, East and West, were united, that we know that we are submitting to an infallible authority. This is our safety in taking as our rule of faith the *quod semper, quod ubique quod ab omnibus*, that we know that 'the gates of hell shall not prevail against the Church'.[74]

The infallible teaching to which he appealed was expressed through the organ of Ecumenical Councils representing both Eastern and Western Catholicism. Papal Infallibility did not fit this pattern. When it was defined, he wrote to Newman, 'The last Eirenikon has sunk unnoticed to its grave. . . . I have done what I could, and now have done with controversy and Eirenika'.[75] In fact, he did engage in several more controversies, one of which involved the Old Catholics, who seceded after the Vatican Council. In spite of his desire for reunion with the East, he intervened at the Bonn Conference of 1875 to oppose any omission of the *Filioque*, on the grounds that it was a traditional part of Western Catholic doctrine and piety. Its omission would be damaging within the context of Trinitarian thought in the West.[76]

Although he gave up further attempts to bring about a reunion with Rome, his friendship for Newman did not cease. They continued to exchange letters until Pusey's death in 1882. Ten years after the ill-fated Vatican Council, he wrote, 'You may assure your friends that nothing has or can come between [sic] my deep love for John Henry Newman'.[77] If his hopes for reunion had died, his benevolent attitude toward the Roman Catholic Church, and the friendships which were so much a part of it did not die, but survived to inspire later generations.

During the course of his long life, Pusey understood 'the Catholic Faith' in different ways. Before his association with the Tractarians, he identified it with the commonly received teaching of the Church of England; where Rome differed from this standard, it was less than Catholic. When he joined the Oxford Movement, he saw 'the Catholic Faith' as the whole life and doctrine of the primitive, undivided Church, and believed that it was necessary to make patristic teaching the norm of the English Church. For some time, he thought that he was merely following the path of the English Reformers, but the facts of the Reformation forced him to abandon this theory and to reassess the role of the Roman Church as a witness to the Catholic Faith.

When Newman left the English Church, Pusey believed that his friend had received a special dispensation of the Holy Spirit for some work in the Roman Catholic Church; his actions show that he believed that his own role in the English Church was linked with this. He was to do all in his power to bring about the reunion of Catholic Christendom, especially the reunion of the English and the Roman Churches. Since the Catholic Faith could hardly be that which was held by any Church by itself, he wanted a more adequate definition of 'the Catholic Faith', which the Church of England claimed to hold; he came to the conclusion that this Faith was that which had been held in *Antiquity*, and which the Roman and Eastern Church *both* held in spite of their separation. What they held in common was truly Catholic, and capable of being defined as *de fide* by a fully ecumenical council; what either church held in isolation was an open question. With this in mind, he saw it as the duty of the Church of England, if it claimed to be Catholic, to move away from the doctrinal separateness caused by the Reformation, and to adopt the doctrine and practice common to the rest of Catholic Christendom. Since he declined to hold or teach those doctrines and practices which were uniquely Roman Catholic, he claimed that he was not in fact a Romanizer. However, his insistence upon a Western expression of the common faith gave his work the appearance of being exclusively Roman in its orientation.

Pusey's hopes for reunion were destroyed by the promulgation of Papal Infallibility. His achievement was to broaden the comprehensiveness of the Church of England by making good his claim to hold the Catholic Faith maintained in common by Roman Catholicism and Eastern Orthodoxy. By defining 'the Catholic Faith' in this way and by importing this teaching into the English Church, he increased the areas of agreement between it and the rest of Catholic Christendom. His own scheme for reunion failed, but his ecumenical vision has continued, because, as he wrote, 'The longing for Reunion is supernatural. It is the fruit of the Divine love shed abroad in

various hearts. . . . Absence of love and prayer and holiness are
alone the real hindrances to Reunion'.[78]

NOTES

1 Liddon, vol. 3, p. 140, 'Who be that that preached?' said one young rustic
maiden to another as we left the church; 'a monstrous nice man, but
dreadful long.' 'Don't you know?' replied the other; 'it is that Mr
Pewdsey, who is such a friend to the Pope . . .'.

2 Ibid., vol. 4, p. 21.

3 Pusey, E.B., *An Historical Enquiry into the Probable Causes of the Rationalist
Character Lately Predominant in the Theology of Germany*, 2 vols (London,
Rivington, 1828–30) vol. 1, pp. x–xi.

4 Ibid., p. 26.

5 Ibid., vol. 2, pp. 15–16.

6 Ibid., vol. 2, p. 15.

7 Ibid., vol. 1, p. xiv.

8 Ibid., vol. 1, p. 8.

9 Liddon, vol. 1, p. 234.

10 Pusey, *An Historical Enquiry*, vol. 2, p. 91.

11 Ibid., p. 92.

12 Liddon, vol. 1, p. 40.

13 Ibid., p. 131.

14 *Letters and Diaries of John Henry Newman*, ed. C. S. Dessain (Oxford
University Press, 1975) vol. 28, p. 358.

15 Ibid., vol. 25, p. 375.

16 Pusey, *An Earnest Remonstrance to the Author of the 'Pope's Pastoral Letter
to Certain Members of the University of Oxford'* (London, Rivington, 1836),
p. 28.

17 Liddon, vol. 2, p. 20.

18 Pusey, *Patience and Confidence the Strength of the Church* (Sermon preached
on 5 November 1837) 2nd ed. (Oxford, Parker, 1838).

19 Liddon, vol. 1, p. 418.

20 Pusey, *Tract 81* (1838) *Tracts for the Times*, vol. 4, (London, Rivington,
1840), p. 41.

21 Ibid., p. 51.

22 Pusey, *A Letter to the Right Rev. Father in God Richard Lord Bishop of
Oxford on the Tendency to Romanism* (Oxford, Parker) p. 36.

23 Ibid., p. 22.

24 Liddon, pp. 249–50.

25 Ibid., p. 251.

26 Pusey, *Patience and Confidence*, p. 29.
27 Liddon, vol. 2, p. 215.
28 Pusey, *Tract 67, Tracts for the Times*, vol. 2, p. 6.
29 Pusey, *Letter to the Bishop of Oxford*, Appendix, p. 13.
30 Liddon, vol. 2, p. 313.
31 Ibid., vol. 2, p. 447.
32 Ibid.
33 Ibid., vol. 2, p. 362.
34 Pusey, *Tract* 81, p. 3.
35 Liddon, vol. 2, p. 457.
36 Ibid., vol. 2, p. 271.
37 Ibid., vol. 2, p. 489.
38 Ibid., vol. 2, p. 456.
39 Ibid., vol. 2, p. 453.
40 Pusey to Keble, 28 March, 1845 (Pusey House).
41 Pusey to Keble, 24 July, 1845 (Pusey House).
42 Pusey to Keble, 23 July, 1845 (Pusey House).
43 Pusey to Keble, 19 July, 1845 (Pusey House).
44 Liddon, vol. 2, p. 454.
45 Pusey to H. E. Manning, 12 August, 1845 (Pusey House).
46 Ibid.
47 Ibid.
48 Ibid.
49 Ibid.
50 Ibid.
51 Ibid.
52 Ibid.
53 Pusey to H.E. Manning, Autumn 1845 (Pusey House).
54 Pusey to H.E. Manning, 20–22 July, 1845 (Pusey House).
55 Liddon, vol. 2, p. 504.
56 J.H. Newman, *Letters and Diaries*, ed. C.S. Dessain (London, Nelson), vol. 11, p. 171.
57 Ibid., vol. 11, p. 127.
58 Liddon, vol. 2, p. 505.
59 Ibid., vol. 2, p. 504.
60 Newman, *Letters and Diaries*, vol. 12, p. 273.
61 Liddon, vol. 2, p. 431.
62 W.F. Hook to E.B.P., 3 August, 1847 (Pusey House).
63 W. Dodsworth, *A Letter to the rev. E.B. Pusey* (London, Pickering).

64 Liddon, vol. 3, p. 137.

65 Pusey to Keble, 17 September, 1850 (Pusey House).

66 Liddon, vol. 3, p. 141.

67 *The Guardian*, London, 30 November, 1850, p. 766.

68 Liddon, vol. 4, p. 99.

69 Newman, *Letters and Diaries*, vol. 22, p. 143.

70 Pusey, *First Letter to the Very Rev. J.H.Newman D.D.* (London, Rivingtons, 1869). (*Eirenikon* 2), p. 50.

71 Pusey, *Letter to the Editor of the Weekly Register*, November 1865.

72 Pusey, *Is Healthful Reunion Impossible?* (London, Rivingtons, 1870). (*Eirenikon* 3) pp. 3–4.

73 Pusey, *The Rule of Faith* (Oxford, Parker, 1851), p. 15.

74 Pusey, *Eirenikon* 3, p. 310.

75 Newman, *Letters and Diaries*, vol. 25, p. 197.

76 Liddon, vol. 4, pp. 293ff.

77 Newman, *Letters and Diaries*, vol. 29, p. 144.

78 Pusey, E.B. Introductory Essay in *Essays on Reunion*, ed. F.G.Lee (London, Gilbert and Rivington, 1867), p. xxvi.

8

Dr Pusey and the Church Overseas

RUTH TEALE

Guide and prosper, we pray thee, those who are labouring for the spread of the gospel among the nations, and enlighten with thy spirit all places of education and learning; that the whole world may be filled with the knowledge of thy truth.

This passage from the Prayer for the Church Militant in the 1928 prayer book, brings together the two aspects of Pusey's interest in the Church overseas. The first is the question of augmenting the colonial episcopate and the manner of appointing such bishops, a question touching the relations of Church and State and the supremacy of the Crown; the second involves the education and training of the clergy.

Both issues were of concern to the Church of England at home as well as overseas. The function and duties of bishops, the rationalization of the size and incomes of sees, the episcopal patronage of the Crown and the appointment of suffragans were all issues of the 1830s and thereafter, issues born as much of the political and social changes of the period as of the Oxford Movement's tenderness for the Apostolic Succession. At the same time it was argued that the appointment of pastoral, non-political bishops, both at home and in the colonies, would augment the supply of clergy and promote better standards of learning and piety in those on whom they laid hands. This interest in the training of the clergy reflected not only the tendency inherent in the Oxford Movement to exalt the priestly office, but also the professionalization of the clergy in the nineteenth century.[1]

The classic *Life* of Pusey, published posthumously in 1893–97 by his disciple, Canon H. P. Liddon, does not mention

Pusey's interest in the Church overseas. In a recent thesis deserving of wider recognition, D. W. F. Forrester[2] explains this and other shortcomings of Liddon's biography as the result of his seeing Pusey in one light only: as the central figure of the Oxford Movement, the arch-priest of the Anglo-Catholic revival. Georgina Battiscombe in her biography of John Keble imputes to Pusey the same insularity, for she sees *her* hero as the one who carried the Oxford Movement to the world outside the University after Newman's secession.[3] Neither Liddon nor Battiscombe does justice to Pusey's political awareness and connections; nor do they take account of his commitment to the extension of the Church catholic and apostolic and of episcopal church government. For in the 1830s and 40s, the initiative in extending the colonial episcopate lay at home, in the hands of the Colonial Bishoprics' Fund and men like Charles Blomfield, bishop of London (1828), Samuel Wilberforce, bishop of Oxford (1845), Edward Coleridge of Eton and Benjamin Harrison, chaplain to the archbishop of Canterbury, and over all these men Pusey had a considerable and direct personal influence, which historians of the colonial Church have so far failed to recognize.[4] It is true that by the 1850s and 60s, the initiative had been assumed by the colonial bishops themselves, in particular William Grant Broughton, bishop of Australia (1836) and subsequently bishop of Sydney and metropolitan of Australasia (1847), George Augustus Selwyn, bishop of New Zealand (1842) and Robert Gray, bishop of Cape Town and metropolitan of Africa (1847). In the struggle over the Royal Supremacy, they came to repudiate the Erastianism and timidity of the English bench. But they too, sought Pusey's counsel and made use of his opinion; while Pusey, for his part, looked upon them as defenders of the faith at a time when the English episcopate was divided and (in his view) doctrinally suspect.

1

Pusey's first public commitment to the Church overseas was made in September 1838, when he preached two sermons at St Mary's, Melcombe Regis, in aid of the Society for the Propagation of the Gospel (founded in 1701).[5] The first, entitled 'The Church the Converter of the Heathen', was both an exposition of what he considered the apostolic method of evangelization and an indictment of the methods of recently formed missionary societies controlled by mixed (i.e., partly lay) committees representative of their contributors.[6] The apostolic or 'church' method was that employed by the apostles and the bishops they consecrated, who personally established churches 'from this then benighted isle to India', before even the whole of the New Testament had been written. By the blood of these saints were the heathen converted, not by 'the mere circulation of the printed Bible . . . the easy unsacrificing multiplication of copies of the written Word'.[7] The other 'defective' missionary theory of the day, said Pusey, was to regard 'the qualities of the *individual* Missionary, his zeal . . . his readiness to spend and be spent' as all that was necessary to convert the heathen.[8]

> No! For the wants of mankind an institution is needed, unvarying in its main character, independent of man . . . supported by God . . . and having His permanency imparted to it. Such an institution He has given us in His Church, against which 'the gates of Hell shall not prevail'. The Church is, in prophecy as in history and fact, *the* preacher of the Gospel and the converter of the heathen. . . . Societies, in themselves, would change and have changed essentially; the Church has the principle of perpetuity imparted to it through His promise, who is her Head and Lord; her succession of Bishops mount up, by a golden chain, link by link, to the apostles. . . .[9]

In the second sermon, Pusey elaborated upon this 'church' system of evangelization as it should be applied contemporaneously. He believed that missionaries should not go out on their own initiative or that of some society, but only with episcopal ordination together with a commission from the bishops or the Church collectively; that the Apostolic Succession was necessary to avoid error, to nourish the Body of Christ and to preserve the connection with the Head.[10] He then surveyed the history of the SPG, 'the accredited organ of the whole Episcopacy of our branch of the Church Catholic . . . it has ever gladly submitted itself to our Bishops abroad, and placed its missionaries at their disposal'.[11] His history

concluded by deploring the withdrawal of the state grant to the
SPG missionaries in Canada and the neglect of the Colonial
Office in appointing too few convict chaplains in the Australian
colonies.[12]

Pusey's exposition of the Church and her bishops as the one
missionary agency accredited by Christ, became the standard
High Churchman's theory of missionary enterprise. Around it
in the 1850s and 60s, a whole literature of missionary method
evolved, and central to it was the notion of the so-called
'missionary bishop'.[13] Pusey in the second of these sermons,
cited numerous examples from the early Church, and declared
that modern efforts could not compare to those of St Boniface,
who founded eight bishoprics and received the crown of
martyrdom.[14] The undoubted hero of contemporary literature,
however, was George Augustus Selwyn, the pioneering bishop
of New Zealand and founder of the Melanesian Mission. Selwyn
himself expounded the theory in 1854 in a letter to Edward
Coleridge: first a bishop should be sent, with perhaps one or two
friends to support and succeed him, and several schoolmasters;
they were to 'raise up' a ministry of 'native disciples', supported
from the beginning by the contributions of the people;[15] and 'If
people wish to have a Bishop of their own, and men can be
found willing to hold the office upon such income as is offered, I
cannot see what right any one has to object',[16] especially not the
Colonial Office. Selwyn's somewhat fanciful remarks in a speech
at the Mansion House—that given the £500,000 raised annually
by the missionary societies, *he* would found 500 new sees at £500
per annum each[17]—set imaginations to work. Five years later,
when the subject of missionary bishoprics reached the Upper
House of Convocation, the impression had been circulated that
some 'scheme' was 'about to be launched on the Colonial
Church . . . without any competent authority', whereby
bishops and suffragans would be consecrated wholesale, 'at the
head of merely inchoate Churches'.[18] Bishops, bishops and yet
more bishops became the simplistic catchcry for converting the
whole world and as a corollary, a structured classification was
evolved, with missionary bishops and their suffragans in a
distinctly special (and by implication, lower) category.[19]

The optimism of this period of missionary expansion is best

seen in the initial success of the Colonial Bishoprics' Fund. This fund grew out of a public appeal to the Church launched at Whitsuntide 1841 by Bishop Blomfield of London, for means to establish bishoprics in colonies where the state no longer offered endowments. By 1853 it had fully or partially endowed eleven of the fifteen new sees erected in those twelve years; of the thirteen places designated in 1841, only three had not yet been made bishoprics, while others were already being sub-divided. At the public consecration of four colonial bishops in Westminster Abbey in June 1847, there were a record 760 communicants and an offertory of £550 and it was confidently asserted that 'Surely there has not been such a Communion seen in this our day, nor, as we believe, for ages in the Church here in England'.[20] Expectations abounded of a second era of St Augustine.

2

Pusey had been among those High Churchmen who had welcomed this missionary revival, and who had elucidated those traditions and 'primitive' examples by which, allegedly, it was inspired. But he himself remained aloof from the extravagant hopes to which it gave rise; for several reasons, quite unrelated to his image as the hermit of Tom Quad. In the first place, his regard for bishops was never one of unmixed adulation; in the second, he disapproved of Blomfield's pragmatic acceptance of Crown nominations to colonial sees; thirdly, he and his fellow Tractarians were early disappointed in attempts to remould the SPG and the Society for Promoting Christian Knowledge (the SPCK); and lastly, while his views on the Church's need for state financial support altered considerably in the 1840s, he never subscribed to the position adopted by colonial bishops regarding lay participation in church government. The thought of laymen, however well schooled, pronouncing in a synod upon faith and doctrine, horrified him.

Pusey's regard for bishops was equivocal, sustained in his own mind by nice distinctions between the man and the office. In the 1820s he suspected many of rationalism. Though on Blomfield's insistence he rewrote certain passages in the second volume of *An Historical Enquiry* . . . , to express 'my sense of the

189

superiority of episcopal government more strongly', yet he remained convinced that while episcopal appointments were made by the Crown and not by the bench itself, bishops would never be 'free from the general infection [rationalism]. Even in this country we have had Prelates, of whom it were little to say that they were very lax', naming three eighteenth-century examples.[21]

Pamphleteers of the day were less restrained. They named contemporary examples, who stuffed their heads into mitres in the reign of George IV, and made themselves 'mighty men with dowagers at little Sunday dinners'. Their manner of appointment, by the sovereign on the advice of his chief minister, gave rise to the description of 'those reverend guardians of the morals of court and nation' as 'a snivelling, snuffling, truckling set of rogues' who followed the ministers of the Crown 'like well-trained pointers'.[22] Such was the odium in which the bishops were held for their affluence, pluralism and nepotism, that in 1833 Parliament moved to secularize a portion of the revenues of Irish bishoprics and two years later appointed a commission to report upon the English sees. The first measure occasioned John Keble's sermon on 'national apostasy', usually taken as the beginning of the Oxford Movement; the second, Pusey's decision to join it, out of fear for the Church at the hands of parliament and its ecclesiastical commission.

Pusey never disguised his distaste for parliamentary interference in the Church's affairs and for Crown appointments to the bench in particular. His article on 'The Royal and Parliamentary Ecclesiastical Commissions' appeared in *The British Critic* in April 1838, while as early as August 1836, Samuel Wilberforce (not yet in lawn sleeves) was consulting him as to how far he might impugn the present 'unchristian' manner of electing bishops.[23] In a letter of April 1837 to Henry Manning, Pusey expressed at length his concern at the 'tyranny' of having Irish Romanists in the commons legislating for the Church of England; to him it was a 'grievance' most 'gross', that the Church should have 'thrust upon her' bishops who were vehement party-men, 'unrestrained in society', one of whom he described as a 'rattle'.[24]

Even before the Oxford Movement, the reform of episcopal

nomination had been a common theme, the aftermath of 'those Boeotian ages' of the Hanoverians.[25] In 1828 an anonymous pamphleteer had argued for the vesting of the rights of election and translation in the hands of the bishops themselves, 'according to apostolic institution and the canons of the primitive Church, so as to add to the respectability and dignity of Bishops'; he also advocated the reward of merit in the Church.[26] In 1834 both Pusey and Newman advised against the publication by the Revd the Hon. A. P. Perceval, a royal chaplain and a Tractarian disciple, of a pamphlet proposing that the bishops of the province should make three nominations to the king, of whom he should select one. Though sympathetic, Pusey considered the time not yet ripe for such a suggestion.[27] A few years later, however, after the establishment by Parliament of the Ecclesiastical Commission, Pusey found the prospect of filling a considerable number of new colonial sees established by the Colonial Bishoprics' Fund, to be a most opportune occasion. Scholars writing on the colonial Church[28] have hitherto failed to point out that it was Pusey who in mid 1840 proposed to Blomfield a plan whereby the archbishop of Canterbury (or perhaps a committee of English bishops) should submit two or three names to the Crown of whom one was to be chosen. Pusey argued that since the Crown was not providing the endowment and thus could not claim any *ius fundatorium*, such a method might be adopted without infringing the royal prerogative. That this was the justification for the bench appropriating the nomination became clear when Blomfield referred to Pusey the one case in which he was doubtful: where a colonial legislature provided portion of the endowment.[29] The Secretary of State for the Colonies and the Law Officers of the Crown resolutely rejected this plan, for fear of establishing a precedent which might thereafter be applied at home. Lord John Russell did agree, for himself, to take the Archbishop's advice, but he declined to bind any future government thus 'to limit the prerogative of the Crown'.[30] Blomfield succumbed. He considered the 'necessity of additional Colonial Bishoprics . . . so clear' as to override reservations about the mode of appointment, though he greatly lamented 'the want of your [Pusey's] countenance and of that of many excellent persons who will follow your example'.[31] Howley, the archbishop of Canterbury, also acceded. But Pusey, believing it timely to limit 'this system of giving Bishops authority from the State', tried to rescue his plan. He proposed that one or two bishoprics be reserved from state nomination and thus 'save the principle, and establish a precedent of sufficient value to counterbalance the mischief of the others'. But when even Keble gave in, Pusey retired, disappointed.[32]

In the 1840s, the principle was established whereby the missionary society endowing a new colonial see should nominate to the Colonial Secretary: in practice, the secretaries of these societies and Canterbury's chaplain supplied the names.[33] The Revd Benjamin Harrison, who from 1843 to 1848 was Archbishop Howley's chaplain, had been Pusey's distinguished Hebrew student and prizeman in Christ Church in 1828–33, and in the 1840s was in close consultation with him, not only on colonial church matters but also as regards the founding of nursing sisterhoods, for Harrison's father was treasurer of Guy's Hospital;[34] the Revd Ernest Hawkins, secretary of the SPG in 1843–64 and of the Colonial Bishoprics' Fund, had been at Balliol in Pusey's student days and sub-librarian of the Bodleian in the 1830s; while the Revd Edward Coleridge, a most able organizer on both committees and a housemaster at Eton, had been Pusey's schoolfellow there. And so, informally, Pusey did offer suggestions. One particular nomination for which he was responsible was that of the Revd John Medley, translator of St Chrysostom in the *Library of the Fathers*, to the bishopric of Fredericton, New Brunswick in Canada in 1845.[35] Because the missionary initiative in the 1840s lay with the High Church party, with the SPG and the Colonial Bishoprics' Fund, whom he regarded more favourably than the Church Missionary Society, Pusey remained content.

But the situation was a delicate one. On the one hand, the Colonial Secretary still safeguarded the Crown's prerogative of nomination.[36] On the other, colonial bishops in the field were questioning the Erastian restraints imposed upon them by English ecclesiastical law, which was still thought to run in the colonies and which was embodied in their letters patent.[37] The two notable South African cases were but amplifications of difficulties earlier encountered by Broughton in the see of Australia and Francis Nixon in Tasmania.[38]

Pusey took special interest in the South African schism. He knew Robert Gray personally, having met him first before his elevation to the bench, at the consecration of St Saviour's, Leeds, in 1845;[39] and on principle, he regarded the right of appeal to the Judicial Committee of the Privy Council (that is, to the lay Law Lords), to which both litigants had recourse, as a manifestation of the royal supremacy in ecclesiastical matters, a usurpation of episcopal authority in the Church.

The issue in both cases was the jurisdiction of a colonial bishop over his fellow clergy, which had allegedly been defined in his letters patent: in the first, his jurisdiction as ordinary over a beneficed clergyman (the Revd William Long, incumbent of a Cape Town suburb) holding his licence; in the second, as metropolitan over a suffragan of his province (the Rt Revd William Colenso, bishop of Natal). In the Long case, the Supreme Court of South Africa had ruled in Gray's favour but on appeal, the Privy Council in June 1863 ruled that his letters patent had no validity in a colony possessing its own legislature: which meant that the jurisdiction of an ordinary in the colonies extended only to those clergy who agreed to abide by it.[40] In the Colenso case, Gray cited the bishop of Natal for heresy before his consistorial court (composed of the suffragans of the province) and therein deposed him; Colenso appealed not to an ecclesiastical authority, such as the archbishop of Canterbury, but to the Privy Council, which in March 1865 ruled in his favour. Gray refused to recognize its jurisdiction; he excommunicated Colenso and took measures to fill the vacant see. But his attempts were for a long time frustrated: English bishops who thought that defying the Privy Council endangered the royal supremacy, refused to consecrate, while Colenso took action in the chancery courts to retain the church property in Natal and the stipend of the see (provided by the Colonial Bishoprics' Fund).

Of his many supporters at home, Gray was bound by ties of intimacy and affection to Samuel Wilberforce and John Keble, as their correspondence reveals.[41] His relations with Pusey were more formal, though he called on him in Christ Church (but not to stay) on his several visits to England in the 1850s and 60s, and in his letters continually sought Pusey's counsel to reinforce his own determination to defy the Privy Council and uphold his metropolitical jurisdiction.[42] Pusey for his part, though sympathetic to Gray's immediate difficulties, saw the South African crisis as a further justification for freeing the Church from the State and placing her under the control of her bishops, rather than 'that infidel Privy Council'. He even consulted Keble on the possibility of their coming out 'severally with strong views on the absolute necessity of a change in the law of Appeals, if schism is to be averted'.[43] In a letter to *The Churchman* following the 1865 privy council judgement, he wrote:

> The Church in South Africa, then, is free, and this freedom is far better than a temporal jurisdiction created by the State . . . The South African Church will have to organize itself as the Scotch Church and the Church in the United States had to do before it; and as the Church in the United States rose from the dust in which it had been trampled, and flourished as it did not when under the patronage of the State, so by God's help will the African. . . .
>
> The organization of the South African Church is . . . complete. . . . Had the Bishops been (as we are told by the Judicial Committee) 'creatures of [human] law' they would have expired with the law. But since . . . the Episcopate has a Divine right, and is a Divine institution, the withdrawing of human props will only show that it endures through a Divine strength lodged in it.[44]

The question of metropolitical jurisdiction, which became the most divisive issue of the first Lambeth Conference of 1867, was the other issue of primary importance which Pusey saw at stake in the South African difficulties. He went so far as to advise Gray that as metropolitan, he should not countenance *any* appeal from his jurisdiction even to the archbishop of Canterbury, for he (Pusey) knew that Canterbury (J. B. Sumner) would only take advice from laymen, namely his chancellor and the Law Lords. Instead, he was foremost in urging Gray to fill up the see immediately, in South Africa itself, in order to 'embarrass' the Privy Council 'exceedingly'.[45] On Pusey's very strong recommendation, Gray had the Natal synod elect as the new bishop William Butler, vicar of Wantage, though no one in Natal had so much as heard of him.[46] No small part of Pusey's recommendation was Butler's interest in forming sisterhoods in South Africa. When Butler had second thoughts about his legal position, Pusey urged Gray to consecrate him immediately as suffragan to himself, who for all intents and purposes should be bishop *in* Natal, and who need place no reliance upon election by a synod.[47] And when Butler finally withdrew, Pusey nominated a clergyman from Norwich. He, too, 'failed Dr Pusey', who thereupon put forward, hopefully, a clergyman from a distant colony (the Revd F. H. Cox of Hobart Town) while at the same time writing to friends asking them to name other possible candidates.[48] Gray meantime had found his man at home; but he encountered insurmountable difficulties arranging the consecration in England, and the delay drew from Pusey a 'very strong, almost reproachful letter' pointing out the danger to souls and to the Church therefrom.[49] Gray was quite determined in his own mind upon his course, but he was equally determined to be seen to take it with the acquiescence of his suffragans. Pusey, on the other hand, was urging the colonial metropolitans forward, including Selwyn[50] who chaired the Lambeth sub-committee on the Colenso trouble, in order that the timidity and '*utter weakness*'[51] of Erastian members of the English bench might be put to shame. He saw the Colenso schism in English terms. It was for young Oxford men that he gave conferences in his rooms for upwards of seventy, to defend episcopal authority, in the same way as two Cambridge dons simultaneously defended Colenso's 'scriptural' opinions.[52] If the colonial Church could bring forth such confessors of the faith as Gray, said Pusey, should not the Church at home unite against Erastianism and the Privy Council? If the metropolitan of Africa could deliver himself of a 'really noble' charge, 'like a piece out of the fourth century',[53] why alas! did the rulers of the Church at home, whenever they were faced with a 'great spiritual responsibility', contrive to appear 'inevitably ridiculous'?[54]

195

Pusey's views on the 'divine right' of bishops were reflected in two other issues: his attempts to reform the SPG and the SPCK in the 1830s and 40s and his opposition to the revival of synodical church government in the 1850s. High Churchmen of the old school had long dominated the SPG. W. F. Hook and his father (the archdeacon of Huntingdon) were active supporters of both societies in the 1820s, and it was probably Hook, Pusey's contemporary in Christ Church, who first interested him in their missions. Certainly it was Hook who in 1840 exhorted a disappointed Pusey not to desert the archbishop and leave the societies in the hands of 'our enemies', the Low Churchmen.[55] By 1834 Newman was the not uncritical secretary of the Oxford committee of the SPCK, with Pusey, Manning and William Palmer (of Worcester) as members. Pusey's concern was that episcopal influence be re-asserted, particularly in the SPG, from which it had been displaced by the 'unruly tongues' of its members.[56]

> ... The great evil in its practice has been the excluding the Bishops from its meetings and deliberations generally, by the conduct of Mr R ... Clarke and his friends; how are the Bishops now to be secured from the like disrespectful treatment either of their personal presence or of their recommendations? How shall the Society bind itself to more dutiful conduct towards them?[57]

As Professor of Hebrew, Pusey had been active in the 1830s upon the translation committee of the SPCK and he was anxious that nominations thereto should be freed from lay influence and placed solely in episcopal hands.[58] In June 1840 the 'sudden termination' of Perceval's motion reasserting episcopal influence in the SPCK 'sickened many of our friends' who hastily left the society; Pusey, Manning and Keble remained however, and Harrison assured Pusey that although he was known to be behind the defeated measure, his continued membership would be welcomed, for it was 'altogether best for you to have the opportunity of testifying to the principle of deference to episcopal authority'.[59] However by February 1844 Keble admitted to Pusey that he too was at his 'wits' end' over the

society and seemed resigned to its being relegated to a mere
Bible and Prayer Book society, so as to avoid its constant
squabbles and the responsibility for contradictory tracts.[60]

The case of the SPG was more critical, for Pusey always
regarded it as 'the accredited organ' of the Church in missionary
matters. In preparing his two sermons in its aid, he had
consulted Harrison in an attempt to find material to illustrate its
'church character', for he believed that 'now the Church
Societies countenance in a degree the un-church or anti-
church'.[61] In a letter of October 1839 to Harrison, he supposed
that

> the object for the SPG is . . . to get rid of sending out
> Missionaries altogether, and send grants of money, as the
> French Missionary Society does, to the respective bishops.
> The plan of sending out Missionaries comes from a defective
> time, when it was a case of necessity, since Bishops were
> forbidden . . . the Missionaries should not be called the
> Society's Missionaries—they are the Bishop's, whom the
> Society enables [him] to support. . . .[62]

Pusey wanted the monthly meetings confined to the voting of
moneys, so as to restrain 'all the jarring and strife' therein
'which are the great evil of the Society'.[63] By this means he
expected it

> to be put upon a less republican basis, to have *future* members
> of the Committees nominated by the Bishops, and the
> functions of the Board, i.e., such of the 14,000 subscribers, as
> can attend, limited.[64]

Pusey's other concern was for the selection of candidates: as
far as possible he wanted the colonial bishops to find the men;
but where the choice had to be exercised at home, he wanted it
placed 'in official hands' (i.e., supervised by the bishops), and
not 'left to a mixed body of laymen and Clergy'. He noted with
distaste that small groups like the Canada Society, had hived
themselves off from the SPG in the manner of sects, 'on the
modern principle of keeping the selection and control of
missionaries in the hands of the Society'.[65]

Pusey's notions for reforming the SPG were somewhat

academic. As Harrison pointed out, the society dealt in practicalities: emigration was rapidly increasing, the colonies of themselves could not provide the men, and it therefore chose from among those offering at home. In any case he assured Pusey that by 1840 laymen no longer exercised influence upon the candidates' committee, and even though that committee was obliged to accept Low Church and Irish men, it now declined the class, who predominated in the past, those 'under some difficulties at home'.[66] Nevertheless, what Pusey had feared yet half expected proved true: the bishops were reluctant to take a greater part in the society's affairs, lest they be saddled with blame for past deficiencies.[67] He welcomed the formation of the Colonial Bishoprics' Fund as an episcopal initiative; but with the notable exceptions of Blomfield and Howley, and later Wilberforce at Oxford, the English bishops remained dormant members. By the mid 1840s, his interest in the societies was limited to annual subscriptions; he no longer attended meetings and appears not to have contributed to the 1847 appeal for the new colonial bishoprics.[68]

To some extent, therefore, he welcomed the episcopal initiative assumed by the colonial bishops in the 1850s. In May 1860 he told Keble that he was 'out of heart' because of 'recent evident party nominations' to the home bench, but felt the results of extending the colonial episcopate to be 'very encouraging. . . . They seem as centres of new life'.[69] Yet on some points he found himself out of step with them, so that Selwyn, at home for the first Lambeth Conference, found need to assure him: 'Do not suppose that I have been far off: and that I have no sympathy with you and yours. If you think so you wrong your loving friend and brother G. A. New Zealand'.[70]

The main issue between Pusey and the colonial bishops was that of reviving synods. The first held since the suppression of Convocation in 1717, were summoned by colonial bishops to discuss matters pertaining to their episcopal jurisdiction: Selwyn summoned his clergy in Waimate in September 1844 and again in Auckland in 1847; Broughton as metropolitan convened his suffragans in Sydney in October 1850. These synods had been assemblies of clergy only; but with the withdrawal of state aid and the 'disestablishment' (if ever it had been established) of the Church in the colonies, the bishops saw need to invite laymen to these deliberations. In Australia, for example, diocesan synods grew naturally out of the diocesan church societies, voluntary fund-raising bodies with considerable lay influence upon their management committees.[71]

The example of the revival of synods in the colonies was of value to the movement at home, led by Wilberforce, to revive Convocation. But whereas in the colonies the initial stimulus was the need to define a bishop's jurisdiction vis-à-vis his clergy, after instances of scandal or defiance by individual clergymen, at home the stimulus owed much more to the need to define the position of laymen within the Church, i.e., to redefine the royal supremacy as exemplified by the jurisdiction of the Privy Council in matters of faith (such as the Gorham case) and by Crown appointments to the bench. Now the two distinctive features of colonial synods as they developed in the 1860s were the participation of laymen with an equal vote not necessarily exercised by orders, and the powers to elect bishops. When convocation was revived at home, these features were not there incorporated. And for two reasons: because the financial necessities which obliged colonial bishops to invite their laity did not pertain, and even more importantly, because High Churchmen strongly opposed replacing an Erastian settlement by a lay domination of the Church. In a letter to Gladstone in January 1852, Pusey spoke of the 'exceeding risk' of such an 'untried plan' as to introduce laymen to convocation and permit them a veto on episcopal nominations; the Church's one experience of such a mixed body, he noted with horror, was the American church, which had since laid aside the Athanasian Creed![72] And while Keble seemed not unwilling to countenance further lay participation while retaining episcopal influence over 'doctrine and discipline' and exhorted Pusey to consider Selwyn's views thereon, Pusey remained adamant.

> ... The power of the laity is a growing power. To admit them into Synods, and then exclude them from what is to both parties of most real interest, will ... never hold ... I look with terror on any admission of laity into *Synods*. It at once invests them with an ecclesiastical office, which will

develop itself sooner or later, I believe, to the destruction of the Faith.[73]

On this point the colonial example did not bear fruit till after the first World War.

4

The question of the training of the clergy was one in which Pusey took a particular interest, since upon that depended a right understanding of the priestly office. For while he believed that there could be no substitute for an English collegiate education and that there was a '*religio loci* about this beautiful place [Oxford] and in the memory of the past' to act upon young men, he well knew that Oxford colleges of the day were wanting in 'moral influence' over them. The idea of founding a missionary institute made him envisage a new type of college, with 'a set of good strict rules', where the principal ate with his students and was not given to 'the relaxed, easy, dining-out ways of our Heads . . . talking about high duty and only doing easy ones', 'entertaining each other with Fish, Soup, Turkeys, Claret, perhaps Champagne'; and he envisaged its products as men noted for their 'discipline, simplicity, self-denial', 'content to be pious and leave all for Christ's sake', and not calculating upon their £300 a year. In other words, he saw the proposed missionary college very much in English terms, as a means to reform the universities, to show that their present habits were 'not invincible' and to teach piety among the clergy.[74]

Pusey's interest in clerical education was first enunciated in 1833 in his work on *Cathedral Institutions*,[75] wherein he advocated a reform of cathedral chapters to provide post-graduate diocesan training for ordinands; none such was then offered or expected. The original suggestion for a college specifically for missionaries may well have been made by the bishops of Australia and Tasmania, as Pusey's disciple Charles Marriott claimed,[76] though the Colonial Bishoprics' Fund had in 1842 attempted an expensive and fruitless scheme grafted onto King's College, London. But from the beginning it was Pusey who was behind the plan to establish a missionary college in Oxford, with Marriott as principal, and it was he who in December 1842 wrote the letter of proposal to his diocesan.[77]

Dr Pusey and the Church Overseas

Bishop Bagot's answer was not encouraging. He pointed out very gently that Pusey and Marriott's sponsorship would arouse 'a jealousy and suspicion wh: would render it [the college] useless, and perhaps thus be the means of defeating any consideration of a more general scheme' in the future.[78] Marriott was in a quandary. He had sought the bishop's sanction as 'unavoidable with our principles' of acknowledging episcopal authority; but since the 'responsibility is OURS', he felt that that sanction should not have been withheld unless the plan were deemed 'positively wrong'. He was prepared to undertake it 'under the stigma of mere suffrance' rather than abandon it altogether, for it was his only present opening 'beyond a mere literary life'; he considered a house for rental in Pembroke street opposite Pusey's windows, which he thought to furnish 'in Littlemore style'; he said he would reject the breviary and 'put up with Bishop Cosin's book *de tempore*'. For he considered he was only expanding upon what Pusey himself had done for years: taking in one or two unmatriculated men to improve their Greek, Latin, Old Testament, 'polish' or whatever, with a view to their seeking orders, most often in the colonies—and Pusey had never sought his diocesan's approval for so doing in his own house.[79]

The real problem was not however in finding a principal, but a site: Oxford or elsewhere. There were practical as well as party difficulties at Oxford: 'the dangers, to which such an institution would be exposed by immediate or near vicinity to a great body of students of a somewhat higher grade, and living at a much greater expense'. The site of the former archiepiscopal palace at Southwell was suggested as giving 'a more emphatic character' to the institution;[80] another possibility was the ruined monastery of St Augustine at Canterbury, where a close connection with 'the fat chapter' might be anticipated. But Pusey stood out for Oxford. He argued that there tutors were to be found, as 'devoted as they wish the taught to be', and their services secured without endowments and 'comfortable' incomes; that libraries were at hand; that his favourite *religio loci* might be brought to bear. He urged upon those daunted by Bagot's frown that the bishop of London was not afraid of Oxford, only of the fears of others over Oxford, and that these 'fears of fears

201

are continually crippling us'.[81] Even if the bishops feared the tide of suspicion, he asked, 'is not rather our passage to the promised land through it?'[82] At all costs he wanted the college at Oxford, to serve domestic rather than missionary ends.

Meantime Edward Coleridge at Eton had taken up the scheme, at Broughton's suggestion. He was its fund-raiser; and understanding the practical difficulties, thought it 'foolish and wrong to stand hopelessly for Oxford'.[83] Besides, as early as November 1842 he believed he had sufficient funds in hand and had secured his cousin, the retired bishop of Barbados, as honorary first principal; and by the end of 1844, he had from Alexander Beresford Hope the promise of means to restore the Canterbury site. He thought of Pusey's role as advisory: as an apologist for the college, but not its patron. He suggested that Pusey draw up a 'subtraction' of the college statutes, 'as a man does of his will, before he goes to the lawyers', and he explained that he wanted 'realities . . . without the use of obnoxious words' and certainly not a prospectus for a monastery. Pusey's role was to explain to the public 'the real inward meaning of the Institution . . . and the probable effects of it on the Ministry and Public at large'.[84]

St Augustine's College, Canterbury was consecrated in June 1848. It never flourished. Englishmen contemplating orders wanted a secure benefice and a social position not offered in the colonies; and in any case, colonial bishops had since determined to train men locally. Pusey took little interest in it after 1846. But he still envisaged a college at Oxford 'on really catholic principles', offering inexpensive education to those willing 'to bear hardness as soldiers of Christ', where voluntary poverty should be respectable. In time, he thought, it would raise the tone of the whole university; and meanwhile it might serve as the first of a series of 'diocesan colleges' to train missionaries to the industrial cities of England.[85] He even asked Gladstone whether the government would charter it.[86] Marriott was still to be principal. But he was a dreamer: he wanted to buy land 'out Headington way', and when lay financial support did not materialize, thought of beginning a monastery in the clergy house of St Saviour's Leeds (1847) and later of reviving Reading abbey as a monastery.[87] The opening of diocesan theological colleges in the 1850s, colleges like Cuddesdon and Wells, under episcopal patronage and outside the universities, quashed Pusey's schemes; the colonies learned to look locally; and Pusey turned his attention to the formation of sisterhoods.

5

In conclusion, two questions remain: from Pusey's point of view, how far did his knowledge of the Church's missionary endeavours contribute to his overall view of the Church and of her bishops; and how far did he succeed in using colonial examples to reform the Church at home? And secondly, from the point of view of the colonial Church, how much did her independence of the state, so hardly won in the 1860s by the province of Africa, owe to the principles derided by Low Churchmen as 'Puseyism'?

It is no accident that the great missionary expansion of the 1830s and 40s, exemplified by the success of the Colonial Bishoprics' Fund, was contemporaneous with the Oxford revival. The Catholic definition of the Church as the Body of Christ, militant here in earth, helped inspire that sense of duty, of responsibility of empire, which was so often used to justify attempts to convert the heathen. Editorials in *The Colonial Church Chronicle* continually enunciated this theme. Pusey saw church extension—what in contemporary jargon we call 'outreach', 'on-going mission' and such—whether it be in the colonies, among the heathen or at home in the populous industrial cities of the Midlands or in the East End of London, as a reawakening of the Church, a renewal of her apostolic mission. In this sense, he did not distinguish between Leeds and Liverpool, Cape Town and Calcutta; he saw the revival of Anglican religious communities, such as the monastery proposed for St Saviour's, Leeds, or the sisterhood of St George at Cape Town, as a means of furthering this mission; and he gave of his prayers, his time and his purse to their encouragement. He interested himself in the Church of England worldwide—from penal conditions in Tasmania to the clergy reserves question in Canada. Not only did he preach her catholicity; he understood her diversity.

His acquaintance with the colonial Church also made plain

his view of the episcopate. For Pusey, more so than many nineteenth-century churchmen, entertained a very real appreciation of the distinction between the man and the office. He believed in the 'divine right' of bishops and he saw the colonial Church as a field where they might assert their Apostolic Succession and secure their independence of the State: hence his distaste for Crown appointments in the colonies and his championing of men like Gray and Selwyn, who perforce had learned to assert that independence. At the same time, he did not hesitate to admonish individual members of the bench, his own diocesans included. At the height of the Hampden controversy, he asked for God's mercy 'for our poor Church', blighted by one bishop whose faith was under 'grave suspicion' and a second who took 'ether and other things, which affected his head'.[88]

But Pusey's success in applying colonial examples at home was limited. The stigma imposed by the Colonial Clergy Acts on overseas ordinations and the failure to recruit to the missionary college both underlined the fact that Englishmen drew a clear distinction between the Church at home and abroad. The missionary college did not succeed, as Pusey had hoped, in establishing its 'direct usefulness as regards the spread of Christianity by a ministry trained on a uniform and that a primitive system' and in exerting its influence 'in many ways on many classes of persons not immediately interested in it'.[89] And he certainly did not want to see colonial church government introduced at home. On the other hand, the example of bishops in the colonies 'on a shoestring' so to speak, who devoted themselves to their duties, added weight to the demands made at home for more 'pastoral' bishops.[90] For while the colonial clergy were ostracized, a number of colonial prelates accepted translation home, notably Selwyn to Lichfield in 1867, James Moorhouse of Melbourne to Manchester in 1886, and G.W. Kennion of Adelaide to Bath and Wells in 1894, while there were others like William Tyrrell of Newcastle (New South Wales) who declined offers.

The answer to the second question, how much did the colonial Church in its turn owe to 'Puseyism', is just as equivocal. Did the independence of the colonial Church, the revival of synods, the definition of metropolitical authority, owe more to High Church principles than to necessity, when the State cast off the Church overseas? Colonial laymen would never themselves have asserted independence of the state or of the church at home; many were known to be in love with letters patent, and Gray once complained to Pusey of the 'drag' of the laymen of Durban, who were much more afraid of a Puseyite than of Colenso.[91] But the leadership of the colonial Church was not in lay hands; it was with her bishops. And insofar as they believed that they derived their authority from the apostolic succession and not from the state and that they privately sought Pusey's counsel when trying to establish this principle, the colonial Church can be said to owe much to 'Puseyism'. Again, insofar as in the century since Pusey's death the colonial Church has derived much of her strength from the vitality of her religious communities, her sisterhoods, her bush brotherhoods and monastic orders, she owes Pusey a debt she has never repaid.[92]

NOTES

1 Anthony Russell, *The Clerical Profession* (London 1980).

2 'The Intellectual Development of E. B. Pusey', 1800–50 (unpublished thesis, Oxford 1967).

3 *John Keble: a Study in Limitations* (London and New York 1964), preface, p. xviii.

4 Much recent work in colonial church history has been biographies of the founders of sees, wherein 'Puseyism' has featured rather than Pusey himself, a result, doubtless, of reliance upon colonial sources. Perhaps this study may redress the balance. As examples, see G. P. Shaw, *Patriarch and Patriot: William Grant Broughton* (Melbourne 1978); Judith Brown, *Augustus Short* (Adelaide 1974): A. de Q. Robin, *Matthew Blagden Hale* (Melbourne 1976); Sylvia Boorman, *John Toronto* (Toronto 1969); J. H. Evans, *Churchman Militant: George Augustus Selwyn* (London and Wellington, 1964).

5 E. B. Pusey, *Parochial Sermons preached and printed on Various Occasions* (Oxford and London 1865), nos. 11, 12.

6 Ibid., no. 11, pp. 4–5.

7 Ibid., no. 11, pp. 6–8.

8 Ibid., pp. 9–10.

9   Ibid., pp. 10–11.

10 Ibid., pp. 36, 33.

11 Ibid., p. 47. This point is open to question.

12 Ibid., pp. 51–4.

13 A typical example was the anonymous *The Duty of the Church in respect of Christian Missions* (London 1866). The best collection of this literature is in the *Colonial Church Chronicle*, first published in July 1847 under the aegis of the SPG. Hans Cnattingius in his *Bishops and Societies: a study of Anglican Colonial and Missionary Expansion, 1698–1850* (London 1952), p. 202, attributes the notion of 'missionary bishops' to the American Episcopalian, Bishop G. W. Doane and Bishop Heber of Calcutta and claims that it was introduced to the English public in 1837 by Samuel Wilberforce and J. H. Newman.

14 Pusey, *Parochial Sermons*, p. 39.

15 Selwyn to Coleridge, 14 August 1854, Wilberforce MSS (Bodleian Library), c 19, ff. 191–2.

16 Selwyn to Wilberforce, 18 July 1854, ibid., f. 224.

17 July 1854; reported in edit., *Colonial Church Chronicle*, February 1855, p. 288.

18 *CCC*, July 1859, pp. 263–5.

19 Edit., *CCC*, May 1856, pp. 407–10.

20 Report of the Council for Colonial Bishoprics, 20 Apr 1853, pp. 1–2 in *Documents relative to the erection and endowment of additional bishoprics in the colonies, 1841–55*, with an historical preface by the Revd Ernest Hawkins 4th ed. (London 1855); *CCC*, August 1847, p. 44.

21 Pusey to Blomfield, undated draft [January 1830], Bishop Blomfield to Pusey, 1830–5 (Pusey House); *An Historical Enquiry into the Probable Causes of the Rationalist Character lately predominant in the Theology of Germany* 2 vols (London, 1828, 1830). Pusey later tried to suppress the work.

22 James Crow, *How to Rise in the Church* 4th ed. (London, 1837), pp. 18–19.

23 Wilberforce to Pusey, 20 August 1836, Wilberforce to Pusey, 1836–65 (Pusey House).

24 28 April 1837, Pusey to Manning, 1837–50 (Pusey House).

25 Anon., *Church Patronage. A Letter to the Right Hon. Robert Peel, M.P.* (London 1828), p. 43.

26 Ibid., pp. 37, 59–60, 82.

27 Letters of 14 December, 29 December 1834, Keble and Newman to Perceval, 1821–44 (Pusey House). Perceval nevertheless published the work anonymously as *A Claim for Relief on behalf of the Church of England, at the Hands of His Majesty's Ministers in the Appointment of her Bishops* (London 1836).

28 Forrester's thesis (p. 300) is the only study to make this point.

29 Blomfield to Pusey, 2 June, 7 November 1840, Blomfield to Pusey, 1830–55 (Pusey House).

30 Blomfield to Pusey, 4 November 1840, 21 April 1841, ibid.

31 Blomfield to Pusey, 4 November, 7 November 1840, ibid.

32 Pusey to Keble, 12 November 1840, Pusey to Keble, 1 (1823–45); Keble to Pusey, 15 November 1840, Keble to Pusey, 1 (1823–45) (Pusey House).

33 Colonial Bishoprics' Fund Papers (Church House, Westminster): e.g., Australia—Adelaide, contains unsuccessful applications to Hawkins for appointment to the sees of Adelaide and Cape Town; Hawkins to Robert Gray (mentioning Harrison's opinion), 8 March 1847, in C. N. Gray, *Life of Robert Gray, Bishop of Cape Town and Metropolitan of Africa* (London 1876), vol. 1, pp. 112–13.

34 Pusey to Harrison, September, October 1840, *et passim*, Pusey to Harrison, 2 (1839–80) (Pusey House).

35 Packet of letters, Medley to Pusey, uncat. MSS, Pusey House.

36 Henry Labouchere to Wilberforce, 4 August 1856 over the see of Grahamstown, Wilberforce MSS, c 19, ff. 42–43.

37 E. D. Daw, *Church and State in the Empire: the Evolution of Imperial Policy, 1846–56* (Canberra 1977), pp. 4–5.

38 R. Border, *Church and State in Australia, 1788–1872* (London 1962), chs. 9–11.

39 C. N. Gray, vol. 1, pp. 86–7.

40 P. Hinchliff, *The Anglican Church in South Africa* (London 1963), pp. 51–3, 91.

41 Wilberforce laid hands upon his own son and Gray's eldest together, in December 1864; while one of Keble's last acts was to send Gray £1,000 toward his legal expenses. Gray's correspondence with Keble is published in C. N. Gray, op. cit; the correspondence of Gray and Wilberforce is at d 39 in the Wilberforce MSS.

42 Gray to Pusey, 14 January, 14 April 1864, 24 May 1865, uncat. packet, 'Bishop Gray and other colonial bishops to Pusey' (Pusey House); C. N. Gray, vol. 2, pp. 125, 137, 204.

43 Pusey's opinion, quoted in Keble to Gray, 29 February 1864, Gray, 2, p. 121; Keble to Gray, 4 August 1864, ibid., 2, p. 134.

44 Ibid., 2, pp. 196–7.

45 Cited in Keble to Gray, 29 February 1864, loc. cit.

46 Gray to Pusey, 24 May 1865; Gray to Butler, 12 April 1865 in Gray, vol. 2, p. 297.

47 Gray to Butler, 13 November 1867, ibid., vol. 2, pp. 365–6.

48 Undated scrap [1865] in Copies of letters of Pusey and Wilberforce, Wilberforce MSS, e 3, f. 87; Pusey to Wilberforce, 1 November 1865,

ibid., ff. 85–6; Gray to Pusey, 12 December 1865, uncat. packet 'Bishop Gray . . .'.

49   Gray's diary entry, 5 May 1868, cited in Gray, vol. 2, p. 416.

50   Selwyn to Pusey, 17 September, 21 September 1867, uncat. packet, 'Bishop Gray . . .'.

51   The phrase is Liddon's, whom Keble described at the time as 'a second edition' of Pusey (Gray, vol. 2, p. 123). Liddon to Wilberforce, 7 May 1866, Wilberforce MSS, d 41, f. 78.

52   Keble to Gray, 29 February 1864, Gray, vol. 2, p. 123.

53   Keble's description, cited in Wilberforce to Gray, 3 September 1864, Gray, vol. 2, p. 167.

54   Liddon to Wilberforce, 7 May 1866, loc. cit., f. 80.

55   Hook to Pusey, 31 December 1823, 9 June 1840, Hook to Pusey, 1822–47 (Pusey House).

56   Harrison to Pusey, 30 May 1840, Archdeacon Harrison to Pusey, 1831–82 (Pusey House).

57   Harrison to Pusey, 21 May 1840, ibid.

58   Pusey to Manning, 29 April 1838, Pusey to Manning 1837–50 (Pusey House).

59   Pusey to Manning, Whitsunday 1840, ibid.; Harrison to Pusey, 4 June 1840.

60   Keble to Pusey, 12 February 1844, Keble to Pusey, vol. 1 (1823–45).

61   Pusey to Harrison, 6 July 1838 [18 October 1839], Pusey to Harrison, vol. 1 (1831–7) (Pusey House).

62   Pusey to Harrison [18 October 1839], ibid.

63   Pusey to Manning, 1 June 1840.

64   Pusey to Harrison, 5 June 1840.

65   Pusey to Harrison, 6 September, 3 September 1839.

66   Harrison to Pusey, 18 September, 26 October 1839, 22 October 1840, loc. cit.

67   Pusey to Harrington, [24 May] 1840, loc. cit.

68   Printed papers relating to the University of Oxford 1846–47 (Bodleian, Oxf. c. 63), pp. 153–5: 'Oxford Commemoration. New Colonial Bishops', with list of subscribers.

69   Pusey to Keble, 5 May 1860, Pusey to Keble, vol. 5 (1857–60), loc. cit.

70   Selwyn to Pusey, 21 September 1867, 'Bishop Gray and other colonial Bishops . . .'. loc. cit.

71   A. P. Elkin, *The Diocese of Newcastle* (Sydney 1955), ch. 14.

72   Pusey to Gladstone, 19 January 1852, Pusey to Gladstone, vol. 1 (1833–56) (Pusey House). Cf. Gray's account of his conversations with Pusey in 1852 on the same point, Gray, op. cit., vol. 1, p. 358.

73 Keble to Pusey, 12 June 1854, Keble to Pusey, vol. 3 (1850–6) H. P. Liddon, undated, 1852, vol. 3, p. 346.

74 Pusey to Coleridge, 17 November [1842], undated letter postmarked 25 November 1842, undated letter [?1843], 'Sundry notes and letters by Dr Pusey to the Rev. E. Coleridge' (Pusey House); Pusey to Keble, 21 April 1846, Pusey to Keble, vol. 3 (1846–8).

75 *Remarks on the Prospective and Past Benefits of Cathedral Institutions, in the Promotion of Sound Religious Knowledge and of Clerical Education*, 2nd ed. London 1833).

76 Pusey to Bagot, [8] January 1843, Pusey to Bagot, vol. 2 (1841–4) (Pusey House). Fitzherbert Adams Marriott, archdeacon of Van Diemen's Land was Charles' cousin.

77 Pusey to Bagot, 18 December 1842, ibid.

78 Bagot to Pusey, 4 January 1843, Bagot to Pusey (1838–44) (Pusey House); Marriott to Pusey, January 1843 in Pusey to Bagot, vol. 2.

79 Charles Marriott to Pusey, 7 January 1843, Pusey to Bagot, [8] January, 15 February 1843 in Pusey to Bagot, vol. 2; Marriott to Pusey, 9 January [13 January] 1843, Uncat. letters of Marriott to Pusey, 1840–51 (Pusey House).

80 Coleridge to Pusey, 11 November 1842, Coleridge to Pusey (1839–76).

81 Pusey to Coleridge, undated, 'Sundry notes and letters . . . to Coleridge'.

82 Pusey to Coleridge, 3rd Sunday in Lent 1844, ibid.

83 Coleridge to Pusey, 11 November 1842.

84 Coleridge to Pusey, [3 April] 1844, 22 January, 27 January 1845.

85 Coleridge to Pusey, 11 October 1845; Pusey to Gladstone, 23 August 1845, Pusey to Gladstone, vol. 1 (1833–56) (Pusey House); Pusey to Keble, 21 April 1846, Pusey to Keble, vol. 3.

86 Pusey to Gladstone, 9 April, 15 April 1845.

87 Marriott to Pusey, 4 October, 12 October 1846; 8 January 1847; 31 July 1848.

88 Pusey to Harrison, 15 November 1847, vol. 2 (1839–80). He referred to two recent appointments, Renn Dickson Hampden to Hereford and James Prince Lee to Manchester.

89 Coleridge to Pusey, [3 April] 1844.

90 Edit., *CCC*, July 1855.

91 Gray to Pusey, 14 April 1864, 3 February 1866, 'Bishop Gray and other colonial bishops . . .'

92 It is interesting to note that the new Australian prayer book of 1978, whose calendar recognizes many more recent and local saints, mentions Keble and Newman, Selwyn, Broughton and the martyred bishop of Melanesia, Coleridge Patteson, but not Pusey.

9

Dr Pusey as Confessor and Spiritual Director

KEITH DENISON

Introduction

In his first sermon, preached on 7 September 1828, Dr Pusey took as his text Hebrews 12. 14: 'Follow peace with all men, and holiness without which no man shall see the Lord'. The themes of holiness and perfection permeate the whole, because 'this world is but a preparation for the next'. The preacher exhorted his congregation to strive after perfection:

> Certain preparations must indeed be made, certain habits of mind must indeed be commenced to enable us to enjoy heaven; the kingdoms of grace and of glory differ in degree, not in kind . . . a certain preparation of holiness, a certain commencement of that frame of mind, which is to be perfected in heaven is necessary here.[1]

But, having exhorted his hearers to moral excellence, Pusey left them without any indication of how they were to cultivate the desired 'habits of mind', nor where they could seek guidance in their preparations for heaven.

During the following decade, although he became more and more insistent about the need for people to cultivate a much greater earnestness in their spiritual life, Pusey also became gradually convinced of the absolute necessity to search out and to publicize remedies for sin and aids to perfection. Much later, in 1878, he was to write:

> Somewhat more than forty years ago, there was taught a strict doctrine of the great offensiveness and ingratitude of a Christian's sins, and of the minute searching accuracy of God's judgment in the Day of account, and a somewhat strict

210

doctrine of repentance. Men asked, what should they do against that great Day? The Prayer-book gave the answer.[2]

The answer given by the Book of Common Prayer, in one of the Exhortations in the Order for Holy Communion, was that if people could not find peace of mind through the private confession of their sins to Almighty God, then they should go to their parish priest 'or to some other discreet and learned Minister of God's Word' to make their confession and receive counsel and absolution. However, this was a part of the Prayer Book's teaching which had long been neglected, and which was viewed with grave suspicion as 'Romanist', even though a formidable catena of Anglican divines could be quoted in support of both the teaching and the practice of confession to a priest.

The Pre-Tractarian Practice of Confession and Spiritual Direction

Richard Hooker, the most scholarly theologian of the Anglican settlement in the sixteenth century, died before he had completed *The Laws of Ecclesiastical Polity*, but there is no good reason for doubting that the uncompleted books, published posthumously, represent his beliefs. In Book 6 he denied Roman Catholic views on the necessity of secret confession to a priest on the ground that 'antiquity knew them not'[3] and that current Roman Catholic practice was a handicap to spiritual maturity, whereas in the Church of England 'we labour to instruct men in such sort, that every soul which is wounded with sin may learn the way how to cure itself'.[4] Hooker defended the general confession in the Anglican rite on the ground that 'the difference between general and particular forms of confession and absolution is not so material, that any man's safety or ghostly good should depend upon it', but insisted that in the Church of England 'the priest's power to absolve is publicly taught and professed.[5] In his *Life of Mr Richard Hooker*, Izaak Walton wrote that shortly before Hooker's death:

Dr Saravia, who knew the very secrets of his soul,—for they

were supposed to be confessors to each other,—came to him, and, after a conference of the benefit, the necessity, and safety of the Church's absolution, it was resolved the Doctor should give him both that and the sacrament the following day.[6]

The evidence for the seventeenth century is considerable. Archbishop Ussher, in his *Answer to a Jesuit* (1625), showed that the Anglican Church exhorts the people 'to confess their sins unto their ghostly fathers' and testified to 'the due execution of that power of the keys, which Christ bestowed upon his Church'.[7] Archbishop Bramhall wrote of the 'dependent ministerial power of loosing from sin' but complained that confessions were generally 'a little too careless, as if we were telling a story of a third person that concerned us not'.[8] Bishop Jeremy Taylor lamented the dearth of books of conscience in the Reformed Churches, and laboured hard to remedy the lack in his *Holy Dying* (1651), *Unum necessarium or Doctrine of Repentance* (1655), *Ductor Dubitantium* (1660) and *Dissuasive from Popery* (1664–67). Henry Dodwell, in his *Two Letters of Advice* (1673), exhorted candidates for ordination to study 'Casuistical Divinity', and John Kettlewell's *Companion for the Penitent and for Persons Troubled in Mind* combined devotion with spiritual counsel. Bishop Wilson's *Instructions for the Clergy* (1708) and *Sermons* offered many suggestions for the confessor, and among the Nonjurors, George Hickes (d. 1715) and Jeremy Collier (d. 1726) wrote about the 'power of the keys'.

However, by the beginning of the nineteenth century the practice of confession had all but disappeared, even among High Churchmen. Archdeacon Palmer was probably representative of the old 'High and Dry' school in the 1830s, when the Oxford Movement was gathering momentum. William had asked his father to be his confessor, and received the reply that he would do so, even though the penitent were his own son, if, but only if, William was in the position of those referred to in the first Exhortation in the Communion Office, who could not 'quiet his own conscience' by the means there generally recommended. If, on the other hand, the request were made—'as in reality it was' in his father's opinion—under the influence of other views as to the necessity or propriety of confession, he could not encourage it consistently with his sense of duty. He told his son, 'In the exercise of our functions, we are restrained by the order and discipline of the Church whose servants we are. That Church discourages the use of private confession, as practised in some other Churches. . . . In two cases only, as it appears to me, has the Church provided for the exercise of the 'Priest's function in private'—in sickness, and before 'participation of that holy rite which she considers generally necessary to salvation'. In both cases, he stressed, it was provided as an exceptional ministration.[9]

This attitude to the Prayer Book's teaching on confession and absolution even among avowed 'High Churchmen' shows that there was no immediate and obvious remedy available for those whom the new teaching about sin and judgment stirred to repentance and contrition.

Pusey's teaching on the gravity of post-baptismal sin

It was Pusey particularly who stressed the gravity of sin in the baptized, in the early days of the Oxford Movement. In his *Tract on Fasting* in 1833, he had declared:

> It would not be too broad or invidious a statement to say, that for real insight into the recesses of our nature, or for deep aspirations after God, we must for the most part turn to holy men of other days: our own furnish us chiefly with that which they have mainly cherished, a *general* abhorrence of sin, they guide us not to trace it out in the lurking corners of our own hearts.[10]

Three years later, 'real insight into the recesses of our nature' had led Pusey to believe that the effects of baptismal grace were cancelled out by post-baptismal sins. He feared that 'every deadly sin after Baptism is not only a step towards final impenitence, but weakens Baptismal grace, and tends to deprive the individual of the ordinary means of restoration'.[11] Those among whom the *Tracts for the Times* circulated had hitherto been content with a much more easy-going attitude to sin, which they attributed, rightly or wrongly, to the prevailing Protestant orthodoxy. They were now jolted out of their complacency, and felt an urgent need to discover an antidote to sin. Looking back on the early years of the Movement, Pusey was later to write:

> No wonder then that an unqualified teaching of the gravity of postbaptismal sin fell on people's hearts like a thunder-clap. It fell, doubtless, sometimes on tender consciences, whom God had not made sad. Some accused it of Novatianism, which of course could not have been, had there been any ordinary mention of confession or Absolution. Any how, I did not hear any mention of it, or make any.
>
> The practice spread from conscience to conscience, before there was any oral teaching as to the remedy. Living men, whose minds were stirred, taught the nature of the disease; the Prayer-book, which the Church of England puts into the hands of all her children in their own language, taught the remedy.[12]

Pusey here reflects accurately the consternation caused by his *Tracts on Baptism*. Like so many others, H. J. Rose protested against the doctrine of 'no Remission' of sins 'but in Baptism'.[13] Pusey's reply, however, shows that he was well aware of the inadequacy of that doctrine; he admitted that it was 'in itself *incomplete*, and that it ought to be followed by a fuller examination of "Absolution" and the "Holy Eucharist", as far as they are means, or tend to assure us, of the forgiveness of sins. And this I hope to do hereafter, if God permit'.[14]

The revival of the practice of Confession

The Prayer Book might have 'taught the remedy', but confession was not a generally accepted part of the life of the Church of England. The subject aroused considerable suspicion and unease. There were a few advocates of the benefits of confession and absolution, such as William Sewell in 1835,[15] but since these dwelt primarily on its use in the Roman Catholic context they tended to reinforce the popular prejudice against confession as a 'Popish' practice. Nevertheless, the matter was being publicly debated; for example, in the number of *The British*

Magazine for 1 September 1837 appeared a letter headed 'Disclosures in Confession' from a Cambridge correspondent, on the need to keep the secrecy of the confessional.[16]

Once the consciences of readers of the *Tracts* had been stirred, the desire to repent and to make a general confession before a priest quickly followed. Pusey began to hear confessions in 1838,[17] though he did not make his own first confession until 1 December 1846. He did not seek out penitents; they came to him to demand the rights offered by the Prayer Book.[18] He claimed, indeed, that even when opportunity presented itself he was 'scrupulous at that time not to suggest confession to those who individually consulted me'. He did not seek to give undue prominence to confession; his sole concern was 'to bring whom I could to repentance for sin, for the love of Him Who has so loved us, our Lord Jesus Christ'.[19]

But, when people came to him, he could not in conscience refuse to hear their confessions, and to give counsel and absolution, recognizing that the requests arose out of a deepening awareness of sin. 'It is,' Pusey maintained in a sermon delivered in 1846, 'part of the humility of penitence to feel one's self unable to guide one's self'.[20] The difficulty was, however, that the guides themselves needed guidance, and there were few sources to draw on. By the summer of 1845, Pusey was acutely conscious of this lack. Experience alone was not enough.

> I am very anxious [he wrote to Copeland] to bring out a translation of the *Manuel des Confesseurs*, by the abbé Gaume. I feel more and more that we need a system of confession, and that there is no remedy to our great practical evils, or any adequate guidance, without it. One must urge it somehow upon people in general, tho' not on individuals and prepare guides for the clergy in it.[21]

The controversy over 'habitual' confession

After they had made a first confession, penitents found that they needed to return to their confessor. A general confession made them keenly aware of their true spiritual condition, and of their continuing need both to unburden their consciences and to receive the benefit of the grace of absolution. It was this tendency towards 'habitual' confession which the bishops especially opposed, on the grounds that the Prayer Book allowed for confession only in serious sickness or after the committing of grave sins, that 'habitual' confession gave too much power to individual clergy and so was open to abuse, and that it would lead the Church of England to approximate to the system of the Roman Catholic Church.

Pusey believed that these were spurious objections, and that the Church of England would be much more gravely damaged by refusing to meet the real needs of its members than by offering them the ministry of absolution. In another sermon of 1846, he spoke of his own experience in this field:

> It is well known that one who has once tasted 'the benefits of absolution' for heavier sins, and found good for his soul in the special counsels of God's ministers, longs mostly to continue to 'open his grief'. . . . Is he to be told that the remedy he seeks for is only for those more deeply wounded, or bid go into other folds, if he still would have it?[22]

In addition to the general objections to 'habitual' confession, Pusey had to face opposition to his ministry as a confessor because of the alleged 'minuteness and detail' of his spiritual counsel. It was this which led Bishop Samuel Wilberforce in 1850 to inhibit Pusey from officiating in the diocese of Oxford: 'You seem to me to be habitually assuming the place and doing the work of a Roman confessor, and not that of an English clergyman'.[23] Pusey's defence was that 'minuteness and detail' were often a vital part of the exercise of this ministry. Faced with the same accusation from another quarter, he asserted that 'those who confess are anxious to be asked such questions as shall help them to make their confession more complete. They themselves ask the priest to ask them, or are distressed often, if on any ground he do not ask them'.[24] He denied vehemently that he had ever 'enjoined' confession on anyone,[25] although there is abundant evidence that members of the Park Village Sisterhood were strongly urged to use confession: for example, in 1846 Pusey wrote to Marian Hughes, the future foundress of the Society of the Holy and Undivided Trinity, lamenting that a prospective sister was reluctant to enter the Park Village Sisterhood 'out of dislike to confession. . . . While she remains in this state of mind, it would be manifestly wrong to admit her into the sisterhood'.[26]

Where people were urged to make a confession, it was because, as Pusey saw it, they stood little chance of making progress in the spiritual life otherwise. But he repeatedly warned his penitents against over-reliance on their spiritual guide. In a letter of 1853, he wrote:

> Our business is to teach people to walk, not to be crutches to them. But if they want a crutch, we must be that crutch, until they can walk. There is, I fear, an inclination among some to talk too much about their 'not doing anything without their spiritual guide', whereas I suppose those who so talk please themselves the most.[27]

Indeed, it could be said that Pusey's failing was not that he exercised too close a control over those who sought his guidance, but that he did not exercise sufficient control. For example, in the climate of the time the use of a rosary was almost calculated to arouse accusations of 'Romanism'. In his public letter to the Bishop of London in 1851, Pusey admitted that he had been 'asked by some five or six persons, who had them, whether there was any harm in using them?' And his answer was, 'Surely a priest would not be entitled to interfere with a form of devotion in itself indifferent, but through which the soul of the individual was more fixed upon God'.[28]

It seemed that Pusey could not win. On the one hand, his critics accused him of 'minuteness and detail'; on the other hand, they attacked him for not interfering with the private devotions of his penitents. As to the charge that he was leading people inexorably, even if unwittingly, towards the Roman Catholic Church, there is clear evidence that Pusey's ministry had restrained some who felt drawn Romewards. A former student of Cuddesdon College, Oxford, J. A. Vincent Maude, wrote to Henry Parry Liddon, vice-principal of the college, late in 1858 to explain why he had left the Church of England. After stating that he had made 'a general confession to Dr Pusey' but had been unable 'to get grace' in the Anglican Church, he added:

'Such men as *you*, my dear Vice Principal, and Dr Pusey and a very few others, are the monuments of Anglicanism, who prevent many men from doing what their conscience tells them is the right thing, viz., to join the Catholic Church'.[29]

Dr Pusey as a Guide to the Young

After six years' experience of hearing confessions, Pusey told Newman in 1844 that he had 'never had a confession from any except younger persons'.[30] A letter to Benjamin Harrison, archdeacon of Maidstone, in 1846 shows how many young penitents there were:

> People object to all confession as applied to the young, because their minds, they say, are poisoned. I know how the young suffer from want of confession. Every case of penitence I know of (and it is borne out by others) began in early sin from which confession would have been the remedy. I must know of some 1000, I believe I may say 1000s (for one hears indirectly of so much more, without hearing names) of deadly early sin, which confession might, by God's blessing, have saved.[31]

Very many of these penitents, of course, were young men from the university. His dealings with them made him especially aware of, and concerned about, their sins against purity. His experience in hearing confessions taught him that

> in cases where there has been sin against the 7th Commandment, it has been the exception, where sin, which has, perhaps, desolated or blighted the subsequent life, has not been first fully known, either at 8 or 12 years old, their first or their second school, or the date of their free intercourse with other boys. And what has been specially miserable has been, that almost uniformly sin was not known to be sin, until it had a hold upon the sufferer. All this might be prevented by the simplest, most modest questions, if parents were not afraid of the whole subject.[32]

The sin to which Pusey alludes is, he continues,

> the besetting trial of our boys; it is sapping the constitutions

218

and injuring in many the fineness of intellect. 'If I had but known confession then', (it has often been said to me, and now is written to me), 'I should not have had all this misery'. And I know that confession became a remedy against this evil, when its victim had long struggled in vain.[33]

These words were not written until 1866. But long before that, in 1843, Pusey had endeavoured to persuade E. D. Coleridge, then a tutor at Eton College, to encourage the practice of confession among the boys there. He warned his friend of the existence of 'a terrible mass of corruption, infecting and burrowing in most of our schools (more frequently perhaps private), leaving the outward surface skin-deep, unbroken, yet consuming the more within. No discipline can reach it. . . . I believe that there is nothing but the habit of private confession, of some sort, which can set a dam against all these miseries'. These 'miseries' included 'lying, swearing, passion, uncleanness, shame of God, neglect of prayer, even overt acts against the 7th Commandment, some gambling, cruelty to animals'. Coleridge had expressed doubts about the propriety of his hearing confessions, because he was answerable to the Headmaster and was in duty bound to report breaches of discipline. Pusey assured him that there was no conflict:

> Discipline has to do with discovered faults, confession with undiscovered and mostly undiscoverable. What is found out, or in the way to be found out, is not to be made subject of confession, for the value of confession is gone; but if a boy brings his secret grief to his tutor, as a Clergyman, I should say he ought not to discover them, (unless there be something, for the boy's own sake, which should make it desirable, which must be very rare, and then I would make it the boy's act rather than my own).

Pusey insisted that a clergyman on the staff of a school should act as a priest, not just as a 'confidant and friend', nor even as having a 'parental office' towards the boys—'they should look upon you, as having the office to treat their souls'. Starting in a small way 'with promising boys', it might be possible 'to introduce it as a system' later on.[34]

It was not just young men who looked to Pusey for counsel and absolution. Many young women also became his penitents, 'the tenderest, the most scrupulous, most conscientious,— whom, both from age and sex . . . forms of society interfere with free consultation of spiritual guides, even where it might be had'.[35] This reference to their 'age and sex' indicates that Pusey was aware of the dangers of too close a relationship with his female penitents, but even then, his friends had to warn him to be on his guard against possible misinterpretations of his conduct. Keble upbraided him for letting one young woman, Helen Richards, address him as 'my very very own dearest father', and pointed out that her natural father's angry reactions were quite understandable.[36] Helen Richards, like so many other female penitents, was a potential candidate for the religious life, and was being schooled by Pusey for eventual admission into one of the infant communities under his guidance. Pusey's personal ministry had a transforming influence on large numbers of young people, such as a fourteen-year-old girl, 'who has been almost miraculously changed . . . all who knew her *before*, ask 'What magic has been practised with her?'.[37]

Pusey on mortification

The personal ministry of Pusey ensured not only that the 'tendency to Romanism' could be checked, but also that watch could be kept on the temptation to excess in spiritual disciplines and mortification. The absence of such personal ministry in the early days of the Movement contributed directly to the death of Emily, sister of Frederic Rogers (the future Lord Blachford). Rogers wrote to Newman, 'Indeed I am afraid Pusey's tracts have something (among many other things) to do with her illness. I cannot help now thinking she has abridged herself more than she ought to have done in eating and drinking while most of the family only thought she had a small appetite. . . . And even now I think she is half afraid of getting habits of self-indulgence'.[38] Pusey's response to this news was a significant pointer to the future:

So it is in this miserable state of the Church . . . that people

220

have no individual advisers, and one has to resort to this quackery of printing, which sends out a medicine into the world without being able to say how, or in what proportions, or by what individuals it is to be used.[39]

Much later, looking back on those early days of the Oxford Movement, Pusey regretted that the stern teachings of the times, without the benefit of spiritual advisers equipped to guide people who followed those teachings, had led to many serious mistakes. Writing in 1879, he told members of the second generation of the Movement,

They were strict times. One said of himself, 'sackcloth hath my girdle been'; even women tried it, though they had to give it up. Fasting was often prolonged, as in the ancient Church. An eminent physician expressed surprise at there being so much indisposition in Eastertide. I do not name these as things to be imitated, but as illustrative of the times. Of course blunders were made; some about health, grave.[40]

Some of these 'blunders' arose from Pusey's own direct advice. Clarissa Powell, the future Sister Clara of the Park Village Sisterhood, was engaged by Pusey to translate Avrillon's *Guide for Passing Lent Holily*. In translating this book she was uncertain what the word *cilice* meant, and asked Pusey. He replied, '*Cilice* is hair-cloth; it is very penitential; and hardly to be used by a person at their own discretion'.[41] She requested a sample, which he forwarded,[42] and he gave her directions for its use.[43] By June 1846 she was wearing herself out through fasting and the constant irritation of the nervous system caused by wearing sackcloth. Pusey did not discourage her austerities, though he did suggest, 'If then the serge in this hot weather has any such bodily effects, e.g., opening of the pores, as would naturally tend to weaken, you must defer it until you are, by God's blessing, stronger'.[44] Not until Advent 1846 did he adopt a firmer tone: hair-cloth was not to be worn 'at present', and 'rule of the speech' must replace 'hard clothes'.[45]

Pusey introduced his penitents not only to rigorous fasting and the use of sackcloth but also to the 'discipline'. He asked Clarissa Powell in September 1844, 'Have I mentioned a very solemn act of penance, the "Discipline"? It may be [used] in memory of the Scourging of our Lord'. It was made of thin whipcord, with five knots, and should be used to strike the back of the shoulders—'it should rather pain the skin, than bruise or wound'. He wrote in like vein to another future Sister, Mary Bruce, in the Advent Ember Week; and on 9 September 1844 he asked the layman Hope-Scott, who was travelling on the Continent, to purchase a sample 'discipline' and obtain directions for its use.[46] The object of these mortifications was to lead his penitents away from self and closer to God, and Pusey was aware of the need for caution here. Chapter 11 of the Sisters' Rule at the Park Village Sisterhood, entitled 'Of Mortification and Fasting', warned:

> The body is not to be immoderately mortified nor indiscreetly to be fatigued with watching, abstinence or other outward acts, so as to hinder the performance of greater good. Therefore it is fit that every one should make known to her spiritual father whatever she does of this kind.[47]

Pusey on Spiritual Direction

That chapter of the Rule of the first Anglican sisterhood illustrates Pusey's attitude to spiritual direction. He did not require obedience to precise rules; his aim was to guide people to guide themselves. He acted always as a confessor and counsellor rather than as a 'director', insisting that 'the subject of "direction" is altogether distinct, and is at most only incidentally connected with confession'.[48] By that he meant that in dealing with souls he had not sought to impose on them his own will, but only and always to help them to see what God wanted of them.

Pusey dealt with this distinction at length in his Preface to Gaume's *Manual for Confessors*:

> The office of 'confessor' and 'director' being thus distinct, I have myself never undertaken what is technically called the office of 'director'. Naturally, I have given such spiritual advice as I could, and have answered questions, whenever I have been asked them, to the best of the ability, which God

may have given me. . . . When I say that I never undertook the office of director, I did not, and could not, when it was laid upon me, in the Providence of God, decline that of guiding in what way I could, by His help, souls which came to me, and did not willingly fail those who came to ask my help, in any respect in which I could help them. But from the first moment, in which people entrusted me in any degree with the care of their souls, I remember that my object was to see, how God was leading them, not to lead them myself.[49]

Plainly any who should use confession for advice rather than for absolution, should be sent back to learn what all sin is, an offence against the infinite love of the All-good God.[50]

Pusey as a director of Religious

As the 'Founder' and 'Spiritual Superintendent'[51] of the first Anglican sisterhood, Pusey had to proceed—he could only proceed—by trial and error. There were no models, no precedents, to draw from other than those in the Roman Catholic Church, learned for the most part at second or third hand. It is not surprising, therefore, that errors were made in the early days of the Park Village Sisterhood. Mrs Welland, sister of Jane Ellacombe, one of the first members of that community, later testified that her sister 'was a bright, healthy creature naturally, but she died (1854) at the age of 35, without any particular disease, worn out, I believe, by the cramped mental life, and the bodily austerities of those nine years. I think many mistakes were made in that first sisterhood'.[52]

It is impossible to apportion blame, for the earnestness of the sisters was the very reason for their joining the sisterhood. Only time could tell how far they might safely go with their physical mortifications. Pusey did not set out with a fully-fledged programme of austerities. His sole concern was to ensure that those who felt called by God to a more dedicated life would be able to answer that call within the Church of England. The Tractarian zeal for holiness as a mark of the Church needed some definite manifestation such as a sisterhood could give.[53] Writing to Isaac Williams in 1842, Pusey expressed his conviction of the need to show that God is in us of a truth. . . . [Sisterhoods] open a higher standard of life, which, beside its positive gain for those who embrace it, and for our Church which shall contain them, it will be a token the more in our favour, and will tend to make people more hopeful.[54]

Without a *mone* or sisterhood, the Church of England would, Pusey feared, lose more ardent young members like Isabella Young, a penitent whom Pusey had considered a prospective candidate for a projected sisterhood in Isaac's parish of Bisley. Her departure for a Roman Catholic convent in 1842 'was evidently regarded too, by Dr Wiseman, as a remarkable failure on the part of our Church, as though I must have taught her all which could be taught, and yet it had no hold'.[55] When, therefore, plans were maturing early in 1844 to found a sisterhood of mercy in London, under a committee of laymen (including A. J. B. Hope, Sir T. D. Acland, Lord John Manners, the future Duke of Rutland, and W. E. Gladstone), Pusey threw himself enthusiastically into the project. He chose as Superior Miss Emma Langston, who protested her inadequacy,[56] for 'I shall rather need training myself than be able to guide and watch over others'.[57]

It fell to Pusey, therefore, to provide that guidance. The daily timetable, and the devotions of the sisters, were under his control.[58] In the absence of English models to draw upon, Pusey felt that he had no option to do other than follow Roman Catholic practices. Among the sisterhood's supporters this became a great bone of contention. A leading layman of the committee, A. J. Beresford Hope, objected strongly to Pusey's assurance that 'the length of the devotions was the same as that of the R.C. Sisterhoods in Ireland. To be candid the knowledge of this has not allayed my fears (nor if the Bishop were to make the same objection would it satisfy him—rather I should think the contrary, he would say—Then you go out of your way to make your sisterhood like the R.C. ones)'.[59]

The Committee of Laymen accepted that the interior conduct of the sisterhood was Pusey's special sphere. But the Bishop of London, and the general public, to whom appeals were made for financial support for the work, believed that the committee was entirely responsible for its management. Since the committee was kept in ignorance of the sisterhood's devotional practices, it resented being put in the invidious position of having to justify them to the Bishop. The use of the breviary (an adaptation of the Roman, not the Sarum, Breviary) constituted a major difficulty. Pusey argued that there were no alternative daily devotions which would meet the need; and on this he had the general support of William Dodsworth and Upton Richards, two London clergymen, who assisted Pusey in the sisterhood's spiritual management.[60] Whether or not the Bishop approved, Pusey was adamant that the sisters required for their spiritual formation the daily liturgical diet which the breviary alone could give; and that this liturgical diet should be supplemented by devotional books which were mostly of continental provenance, 'adapted' to the use of the Church of England.

The use of 'adapted' devotional books

The publication of English translations, edited by Pusey, of devotional books from the counter-reformation period was opposed by many of Pusey's close friends, who were convinced that these 'adapted' books fostered an 'unfilial spirit'.[61] Dodsworth pointed out to Pusey, 'It is strongly avowed in our printed circular that our Sisterhood is a Church of England Institution. We obtain toleration from the Bishop and contributions from others on that express understanding. It does not seem honourable then to put into the hands of Sisters Roman books'.[62] Dodsworth refused to accept the defence that such books were private, for, after all, 'a Community necessarily abridges individual liberty'.[63] These adapted books were not only allowed by Pusey, but had been translated at his instigation. He justified his work as editor of numerous English translations of devotional books on the ground that 'people were using R.C. books extensively already, and this was unAnglicanising them'.[64] He denied, therefore, that he was actually creating an appetite for such books; rather, he was performing a service to the Church of England in ensuring that

225

editions of Liguori, Rodriguez, Scupoli and Avrillon were 'suitably adapted for English use'.[65]

This was not altogether an adequate answer, for Pusey was instrumental in introducing people to such books. In 1844, he recommended a penitent to read Rodriguez on *Christian Perfection*, St Peter of Alcantara's *Meditations*, and St Ignatius Loyola's *Spiritual Exercises*, adding, significantly, 'only I do not know what these last are in, besides Latin'.[66] Three years prior to this, when visiting Roman Catholic convents in Dublin, he had written to Isaac Williams:

> I learnt of several additional French spiritual books and books of devotion from the Nuns, which I hope may be of use if you can find any one to read and examine them. There is employment for many hands.[67]

The interest in, and circulation of, English translations of spiritual classics from the Continent was not spontaneous, despite Pusey's protestations. The fact that Pusey had himself given Mother Emma Langston a copy of one of Liguori's works moved Dodsworth to protest that such actions had a 'Romanizing' effect. Pusey's sanction for the use of such books led him to believe that 'the interior conduct' of the sisterhood 'is not honestly of a Church-of-England character', and that 'when you are gone, *your* sisters will go to Rome, not because they will not find others willing to guide them, but because no others will allow what you allow'.[68] Bishop Wilberforce, one of the few bishops who were sympathetic to the restoration of the religious life, and for whom Pusey had a high regard, publicly attacked 'Dr Pusey's "Adaptations"', alleging that they 'wean the mind from the earnest sobriety of our own Prayer Book',[69] and appealing to him not to 'circulate devotions which . . . prepare the way for secessions which he so deeply mourns'.[70]

Conclusion

The controversy engendered by the publication and use of adapted devotional books caused Pusey great pain. His intention was simply to provide the spiritual resources for which he saw a genuine and growing need. There was a rich supply of devotional helps to hand, and he saw no compelling argument against using these helps. He refused to believe that a Romeward tendency was implied by his 'adaptations', any more than it was by the practice of 'habitual' confession, or by the use of other spiritual disciplines. The fact that these things were to be found in the Roman Catholic Church was to him irrelevant, and he was deeply saddened by the isolationist tendencies of his Church which were a practical denial of its claims to catholicity. In 1844, Pusey issued a protest against this isolationism: 'it was never meant that any portion of the Christian Church should be thus insulated . . . whatever [God] has any where given to the Church, He has given to the whole Church'.[71]

What mattered to Pusey—what alone mattered—was that souls were led closer to God, and advanced along the path of perfection. By facing misunderstandings, protests, calumnies, and episcopal inhibitions, and by standing firm against all opposition, often at great personal cost, Pusey restored an ascetic theology, and the religious life, to the Church of England, and helped many to grow in the knowledge and love of God.

NOTES

1 Pusey House Papers (hereafter 'P.H.P.'), MS. sermon, p. 10.

2 *Advice for Those who exercise the Ministry of Reconciliation through Confession and Absolution, being the Abbé Gaume's Manual for Confessors* (1878), Preface, pp. iiif.

3 *The Laws of Ecclesiastical Polity*, 6. 4. 13.

4 Ibid., 6. 6. 4.

5 Ibid., 6. 4. 15.

6 *Izaak Walton's Lives* (London, Thomas Nelson, n.d.), p. 202.

7 *Works*, vol. 3, pp. 90f.

8 *Works*, vol. 5, p. 190; ibid., p. 160.

9 Roundell Palmer, Earl of Selborne, *Memorials, pt 1, Family and Personal (1766–1865)*, vol. 1 (1896), pp. 268–9.

10 *Tracts for the Times*, 18, 21 December 1833, *Thoughts on the Benefits of the System of Fasting enjoined by our Church*, p. 12.

11 *Scriptural Views of Holy Baptism, Tracts* 67, 68, 69 (1836), p. 49.

12 *Gaume's Manual for Confessors* (1878), Preface, p. vi.

13 P.H.P., MS. letter, March 16 1836.

14 J. W. Burgon, *Lives of Twelve Good Men* (1888), vol. 1, p. 205.

15 *Sermons addressed to young men, preached chiefly in the Chapel of Exeter College, Oxford* (1835), pp. 374f.: 'Those who have been in Catholic countries must have often been struck with the sight, and longed to share in it, when they have beheld a penitent in tears, kneeling at the feet of one who professes to be above all taint . . . and there pour out to a fellow mortal the review of a burdened conscience'.

16 *The British Magazine*, vol. 12, p. 295.

17 Liddon, vol. 3, pp. 269, 335.

18 Ibid., vol. 3, p. 95; and *Gaume's Manual for Confessors*, Preface, p. clxviii.

19 *Gaume's Manual for Confessors*, Preface, p. viii.

20 *Entire Absolution of the Penitent* (1846), p. xix.

21 P.H.P., W. J. Copeland Papers, MS. letter, 20 July 1845.

22 *Entire Absolution of the Penitent. Sermon 2* (1846), p. 7.

23 R. G. Wilberforce, *Life of the Right Reverend Samuel Wilberforce, D.D. With selections from his diaries and correspondence*, vol. 2 (1881), p. 90.

24 *Renewed Explanation in consequence of Rev. W. Dodsworth's Comments on Dr Pusey's Letter to the Bishop of London* (1851), p. 17.

25 *A Letter to the Right Hon. and Right Rev. the Lord Bishop of London, in Explanation of some statements contained in a Letter by the Rev. W. Dodsworth* (1851), p. 3.

26 P.H.P. MS. letter, 'Mo. aft. 2 s. in L. 1846'; cf. W. Dodsworth, *A Few Comments on Dr Pusey's Letter to the Bishop of London* (1851), p. 6.

27 *The Story of Dr Pusey's Life, By the Author of 'Charles Lowder'* (i.e., Maria Trench) (1900), pp. 359f.

28 *A Letter to . . . The Lord Bishop of London*, p. 100.

29 MS. letter in the College archives, dated 'The Oratory, Brompton, London S.W., November 7th. 1858'.

30 P.H.P. MS. letter, 2 April 1844.

31 P.H.P. MS. letter, 2 March 1846.

32 *Gaume's Manual for Confessors, Preface*, p. xxi, quoting Pusey's letter to *The Times*, 12 December 1866.

33 Ibid., p. xxii, quoting his further letter to *The Times*, 14 December 1866.

34 P.H.P. MS. letter, '1st Wk. in Adv. 1843'.

35 *Avrillon's Guide for Passing Lent Holily* (1844), *Preface*, p. vii.

36 P.H.P. MS. letter, 14 June 1849.

37 P.H.P. Transcript of a letter to H. E. Manning, July 1845.

38 Newman Papers, Birmingham Oratory, vol. 10, no. 23 (compare No. 31), MS. letter, 31 May 1837.

39 [Maria Trench] *The Story of Dr Pusey's Life*, pp. 114f., letter dated 4 June 1837.

40 P.H.P., Pamphlet 74188, privately printed letter 'To the Members and Associates of the English Church Union', November 1879, p. 4.

41 Lambeth Palace Library. Transcripts. 'Monday after Sex(agesima) 1844'.

42 Ibid., 'Wed. aft. 2nd. S. in Lent 1844'.

43 Ibid., 'Fr. aft. 3rd. S. in Lent 1844'.

44 Ibid., 'Feast of S. Barnabas 1846' [11 June].

45 Ibid., Advent 1846.

46 *Memoirs of James Robert Hope-Scott* (1884), vol. 2, p. 52.

47 Rule as in 1847–8. P.H.P. Transcripts, 'Dr Pusey to Mr Beresford-Hope, 1848–74'.

48 *Gaume's Manual for Confessors*, Preface, p. cxlii.

49 Ibid., p. clviii.

50 Ibid., p. clxiv.

51 Lambeth Palace Library, 7.3, 'Dr Pusey to Sister Clara, 3. Miscellaneous. Sister Clara's Reminiscences'.

52 Lambeth Palace Library, MS. letter to the Revd A. Barff of St Paul's Choir School, 18 January 1885; and there is evidence to support this complaint in the volume of letters, 'The Revd W. Dodsworth to Dr Pusey, 1836–50', P.H.P., particularly a letter to Pusey from the sisterhood's physician, Dr Mervyn Crawford, 24 May 1845. On the austerities of Sister Katherine Ogilvie, who died 27 June 1850, see T. J. Williams and A. W. Campbell, *The Park Village Sisterhood* (1965), pp. 67–70.

53 See *The British Magazine*, 1 June 1835, p. 662: J. H. Newman, *Letters on the Church of the Fathers, No. XII*: 'Whether or not monasticism is right, we at least are wrong, as differing in mind and spirit from the first ages of Christianity'.

54 Lambeth Palace Library. Letters from Dr Pusey to Isaac Williams. 'Feb. 7' (? 1842).

55 Ibid., 'Oct. 28. 1842'. See also Newman Papers at the Birmingham Oratory, vol. 52, 'Movement towards Rome 1833–40', No. 40, Newman to Tom Mozley, December 12 1839: 'I should not be surprised to see conversions to Romanism some where or other. I think the women will be going, unless nunneries are soon held out to them *in* our Church'.

56 P.H.P. MS. letter, 9 October 1844.

57 Ibid., MS. letter, 23 April 1845.

58 Ibid., 'Corresp. about "the Home" in 1848'.

59 Ibid., MS. letter, 16 March 1848.

60 Ibid., MS. volume 'Rev. W. Upton Richards to E.B.P. 1840–57', n.d.

61 Ibid., MS. letter, Canon W. K. Hamilton to Dr Pusey, December 1844.

62 Ibid., MS. volume 'Rev. W. Dodsworth to E.B.P. 1836–50', n.d. (1848).

63 Ibid. (1848).

64 Ibid. Transcripts, Dr Pusey to Bp (Hamilton) of Salisbury 1840–68, 'F. of S. Thomas 1844' (December 21).

65 *A Letter to . . . the Lord Bishop of London* (1851), 57.

66 J. O. Johnston and W. C. E. Newbolt, ed., *Spiritual Letters of E. B. Pusey*, n. ed. (1901), p. 48.

67 Lambeth Palace Library. MS. letter, Pusey to Isaac Williams, 8 September 1841.

68 P.H.P. MS. letter in volume 'Rev. W. Dodsworth to E.B.P. 1836–50', 24 October 1848.

69 *A Charge to the Clergy of the Diocese of Oxford, at his Second Visitation, November, 1851. By Samuel, Lord Bishop of Oxford* (1851), pp. 59f.

70 Ibid., *Appendix*, 25.

71 *Avrillon, A Guide for Passing Lent Holily* (London 1844), Preface, p. x.

10
The Spirituality of E. B. Pusey

GABRIEL O'DONNELL OP

Introduction

Edward Bouverie Pusey was an extraordinary man possessed of a complex personality. His intellectual acumen and the amount of work he accomplished attest to his extraordinary stamina and insight; his deep religious spirit and his constant adherence to prayer and the sacraments, indicate the sincerity of his personal spirituality. He was a man close to God. Pusey's complexity, however, is exhibited in the number of contradictions one finds in his personality, his theological positions and his spirituality. It is at once this extraordinariness, coupled with his personal complexity, which make a clear statement of Pusey's spirituality difficult, if not impossible. The following pages attempt a brief description of the main 'line' of Pusey's spirituality, as reflected in his sermons and letters, as well as the spiritual writers from whom he drew as he developed his own ideas of the interior life and its discipline.

1 Pusey's Spiritual Formation

The development of Pusey's spirituality can conveniently be considered by dividing his life into three periods. The first, from 1800 to 1835, is perhaps the most important because of its formative and permanent effects and is marked by Pusey's relationship to his father, to Bishop Lloyd, to Maria Barker, and finally to his spiritual father, John Keble. The second period runs from 1836 to 1846 and is marked not only by what has been called Pusey's second intellectual 'revolution', but also his serious study of French spiritual literature and his own spiritual testing or crisis, as evidenced in his correspondence with John Keble in 1843–6.[1] The third period, from 1847 until his death in

231

1882 is marked by Pusey's enormous pastoral and intellectual undertakings, which were the fruit of the struggles experienced in his earlier years, and his untiring efforts to form others in the spiritual principles and ideals he had himself earlier developed.

The focus of this brief descriptive study is to trace from the end of the first period (1834–5) and the beginning of the second (1836–46), the experiences which formed the bases of Pusey's spiritual principles and to come thereby to some conclusions about the nature of his spirituality.

Pusey was from the earliest age an over-serious young man. His relationship with his father, the source of both great strength and conflict, caused him to deepen his serious attitudes and become what can only be called somewhat depressive of nature. He was so wounded by his father's death that he was unable to attend the funeral. It is thus no surprise that as the years went on and he applied his serious and sombre mind to the spiritual life as well as his academic studies, he made sometimes dramatic decisions for himself and his family.

The years 1834 and 1835, which saw Pusey's deliberate abandonment of his liberal opinions and broad churchmanship, mark also his admission of a strong desire for a less 'worldly' and more austere way of life, a style which he sought to impose upon his whole family. He proposed to his wife that a part of their fortune be given to build a church for the poor, a decision which would necessitate a simplification of domestic arrangements and comforts. In November of 1835 he writes of his first serious attempts to fast:

> . . . I have twice tried a little degree of fasting; once on the morning when I administered the Lord's Supper . . . and once today. On either occasion, I drank a cup of tea in the morning and had a meat-meal at $\frac{1}{2}$ past 1 or $\frac{1}{2}$ past 2: and this I should like to continue on Fridays, and I think it would do my body rather good. I will deal very honestly about it.[2]

Earlier in the same year he began to express his dislike at frequenting society: 'I am going to dine today with Barton . . . tomorrow Gaudy—Monday week Bodley dinner. Eheu! fugaces labuntur anni in dinnering. . . .'[3] In the same letter one encounters, and not for the first time, what may be termed Dr

Pusey's overly severe attitude towards his children, with a determination to impose upon them a standard of behaviour and sense of responsibility far beyond their years, even in this serious Victorian era.

Pusey measured the 'virtues' and 'vices' of his infant children with a seriousness which suggests a certain strain on both children and parents, which was to prove a characteristic of all Pusey's spiritual relationships. The constant waging of the battle against the world and sin tended to obscure the meaning of the simplest human situations.

a. Pusey's Spiritual Revolution

On another level, and in light of the complete correspondence between Pusey and his wife, the sombreness of Pusey's spirit and his stringent demands upon his family, all in the name of religious devotion, suggest that at heart it was perhaps less his demands upon others and more the severity of judgement upon himself, which he tended to project upon them. In a letter dated 6 November 1835 Pusey discusses the question of repentance for the sins of one's past life:

> One way in which persons commonly and sadly injure their repentance is—not of course by referring lightly to the sin itself, but—by taking pleasure in some circumstances more or less connected with it, or with what was sinful, and speaking of them: they forget the sin in the excitement of what is connected perhaps distantly with it.[4]

Then after a few sentences about the sadness of a period spent in 'forgetfulness of God', he speaks of himself:

> . . . with regard to myself, had the ten years during which I loved you before we were one, been years which I had patiently waited God's Will, then I might have had a right to refer to them with joy: as it is, shame ought to mix itself with the joy and thankfulness that God did, notwithstanding, bestow you on me; and so though one may refer to it with gratitude . . . yet I could not, without doing harm to myself, refer to it without the solemn memory of past sinfulness.[5]

These sentiments are only a preparation for what Pusey states later in the same letter concerning the death of his daughter Katherine, who lived for only ten months after her birth in January of 1832:

> The impression has come gradually upon me, and so the more irresistibly, that the loss of our dear Katherine was not merely a trial of my cheerful surrender of her, as I at first thought, but a chastisement to me . . . and so I pray God, and you will pray also, dearest, that this day, and all memory of our dear little sainted one may produce its fruit of humiliation and humbler walking in me. . . . God has been abundantly merciful, in what He has done for our others; and therefore we may feel that in this also He took her not away in displeasure to us, but as a merciful correction, although still as a correction.[6]

Not only is it probable that these sentiments were at the root of his later conviction of his utter depravity, but here again Pusey interprets a family death as a chastisement of his personal sins, an attitude which, in the event of his wife's death in 1839, reached its climax and had disastrous effects on his life. Pusey's austerities, begun in 1835, were only intensified in 1839 at the time of Maria's death, as was the accompanying gloom of his nature. He permanently retired from society and between 1839 and 1846, continued to mourn the death of his wife and to assume such a burden of personal guilt for her death that by the end of the six years he thought it wrong to express delight in nature or extend the simple greeting of a smile to others.[7]

b. Pusey's Personal Crisis

The extent and intensity of Pusey's crisis can be seen in his correspondence during these years, particularly with John Keble, for in that relationship Pusey began to find the one person to whom he could completely open his heart, confess his sins, and on whom he could depend for guidance in matters great and small. Their intimacy and a certain interdependence gradually increased between 1840 and 1843. By September of 1844 they were mutually confiding to one another not only their sense of personal sinfulness, but also their actual experiences of sin and infidelity to grace. It is just such an exchange, without yet the mention of sacramental confession and absolution, which Keble refers to in his letter to Pusey of 22 September:

> I cannot bear well to think of the pain I have been causing you: and yet I do not feel I have done wrong in it. Though you do not and cannot know the worst, you will think of me and pray for me differently from what you have done. . . .[8]

Pusey's response was, not surprisingly, an expression of his awareness that whatever the nature of Keble's confidence, his own burden was far more serious:

> My dear wife's illness first brought to me, what has since been deepened by the review of my past life, how, amid special mercies and guardianship of God, I am scarred all over and seamed with sin, so that I am a monster to myself: I loathe myself, I can feel of myself only like one covered with leprosy from head to foot; guarded as I have been there is no one with whom I do not compare myself, and find myself worse than they.[9]

It is in this letter, one of the most important in understanding Pusey's spirituality, that Pusey first raises the issue of confession for himself:

> I am so shocked at myself, that I dare not lay my wounds bare to anyone: since I have seen the benefit of Confession to others, I have looked round whether I could unburden myself to anyone, but there is a reason against everyone. I dare not so shock people . . . I must guide myself as best I can, because, as things are, I dare not seek it elsewhere.[10]

This letter contains many other significant passages, none of them written in haste for Pusey waited two days before finishing and posting the letter. For example, Pusey admits his confusion at being called to the ministry of confessor and spiritual director while as yet not seeking such for himself; he speaks of his deep attachment to Newman yet admits a definite reserve in sharing personal matters; he reveals his tendency to 'spiritualize' the consistent traits of dependence and mistrust of his own judgment.[11] Further, this letter precisely corresponds to the period of his work of editing the translations of various Roman

Catholic spiritual books and of his preoccupation with the establishment of the first religious sisterhood in the Church of England, factors which would have to be considered in greater depth than possible in this short article to understand or appreciate their effect upon Pusey.

The first Sunday of Advent in 1846 was a new beginning for Pusey in light of his recent first confession and the 'Rules' which he drew up and submitted to Keble for approval in his letter of 7 December. This document is of special interest because it betrays in Pusey's attempts to achieve self-forgetfulness a definite preoccupation with self, but also because it is evidence of that style of 'self-discipline', which Pusey later admitted that he borrowed from Roman Catholic writers.[12] Pusey has correctly titled these pages, 'Rules sanctioned for me', for they are a series of rules centred upon corporal penance, self-abnegation and voluntary humiliations rather than a 'rule of life', which might have led Pusey somewhat away from his extraordinary self-consciousness. His own natural temperament, confirmed by the spiritual books he was reading, led him to make such severe rules, which challenged his already weak health and deepened his already grave demeanour.

This same Sunday in 1846 marked the setting of his relationship with his spiritual 'Father', Keble, on surer ground; it also marked a new freedom in prayer. While one cannot overlook the ever present intensity of Pusey's despising of himself, the years 1844–6 are a watershed in his search for God's forgiveness and love and correspond to what has been termed the second 'drastic intellectual revolution', which was either caused or accompanied by a significant spiritual revolution. It is likely that Pusey himself would not have been able to untangle the causal relationship between his intellectual and spiritual development, for in the light of his self-disclosure to Keble he writes, '. . . I found my late Sermon [Entire Absolution of the Penitent] printed. Alas! what a key you have to it. I hardly know how I could have got through it now'.[13] He was influenced by the ideas of others, particularly Keble and Newman, but he was also a man who depended upon the 'rightness' of an idea, as it sounded in his own inner experience, a policy which has been described as Pusey's 'drastic limitation', but which also enabled him to be somewhat independent of the other Tractarians.[14] The interplay between spiritual dependence and intellectual independence was a major reason for Pusey's enigmatic role in church life of Victorian England.

2 *Some Roman Catholic Influences*

During the years which followed his wife's death, Pusey was occupied with a project which was to greatly influence his spirituality, i.e., the editing of various translations of Roman Catholic spiritual and devotional books. It is no great surprise to discover that Pusey, intent upon the interior life himself and determined to share that concern with others, began in the early 1840s to read and organize translations and adaptations of 'books on the spiritual life, on self-examination, and on mental prayer'.[15] Many authors interpret this project as resulting from the need of early Anglican religious sisters for spiritual reading and devotional material, but in the light of Pusey's own spiritual development and the initiation of the project in the early 1840s, it seems more accurate to see it as a result of his own hunger for spiritual nourishment and his need for guidance in his already developing ministry of spiritual direction.[16] Pusey was not the first person in the Church of England with such an idea, for already in 1842 Charles Marriott was writing to his friend Bishop Selwyn in New Zealand about adapting the *Exercises of Saint Ignatius* for retreats, and one may see here the origin of the later adaptations of Pusey and Oakeley.[17] Such facts suggest that it was a much broader group of people looking for some forms of devotional literature which the Church of England could not supply, rather than a small band of Anglican sisters. 'There is in the present life a craving after a higher life, . . . mental prayer, meditation upon God, . . . Yet in all, people feel that they lack instruction.'[18]

The majority of books which Pusey was reading and adapting for Anglican use were products of post-Reformation Roman Catholicism. This bears considerably on the quality of Pusey's spirituality, for these works represent the development of a detailed systematization of the spiritual life and a definite movement towards practical spirituality, best exemplified by the *devotio moderna* of the fifteenth century. Pusey was a man enamoured of caring for details and always saw the spiritual life as an essentially hidden and interior struggle to combat evil and seek after good. Thus, he was predisposed to the type of spirituality represented there. Further, the influence of these works upon Pusey suggests a certain kind of eclecticism on his part, for while he looked to antiquity for validation of his Catholic principles and sought in the Fathers of the Church the measure of orthodoxy, yet in terms of the spiritual life he looked to a tradition not only in contrast to patristic movements and tendencies, but one quite alien to the sources of the Book of Common Prayer which represented medieval English spirituality and the spirituality of the period just prior to the Reformation. This tendency to view the spiritual life as primarily a private affair was not inconsistent with his resistance to external expressions of piety and devotion even in liturgical worship.

One great attraction for Pusey in these spiritual writers was their direct treatment, at least to some degree, of methods of mental prayer. Pusey's letters of spiritual direction are remarkably silent as to detailed questions of prayer, while uncomfortably specific in such matters as forms of corporal penance and asceticism. Even his correspondence with Keble lacks a clear discussion of prayer, either vocal or mental. Is it that Pusey's notions of prayer are contained in these 'manuals' of prayer? Certainly one must concede that he was dependent upon Roman Catholic sources for such information and it is this fact which, perhaps above all others, indicates the centrality of these works in forming Pusey's ideas about prayer and the spiritual life.[19]

Already by 1846 Pusey had read most of the works which were eventually published, and so his introduction and first study of them coincided with the very years in which he experienced his personal spiritual and intellectual 'revolution' between 1839 and 1846.[20] Pusey gained much information about the life of prayer, the practice of meditation and Roman Catholic devotional practices from the spiritual and devotional books he read and adapted. He was even schooled in the way of spiritual direction and the hearing of confessions through them.

238

But the flaw in his taking over of these authors and their spirituality was precisely the fact that there was no proper setting for such an approach to the spiritual life in the Church of England at that time. The post-Reformation developments in the Roman Catholic Church were completely unknown to members of the Church of England and were often looked upon as alien and strange. Pusey's dependence upon this 'foreign' tradition and his insistence on it for others was to have long-range effects upon individuals and the religious communities that he was to influence so strongly.

It is quite probable that the intensity of his nature drew him all the more strongly to the paradoxical fusion of the high ideal of perfect love and submission, with a serious pessimism as regards human nature which he found among the French Ignatian writers, most notably Jean-Joseph Surin. His notions of detachment, self-abnegation, humility, and a call to a life of deep interior communion with God in Christ were drawn out and made explicit according to Roman Catholic models. As early as 1844 he wrote, 'I hope there will be an adapted translation of St Ignatius' *Spiritual Exercises*'.[21] There are clear indications that these influences in his personal prayer and spiritual life spilled over into other areas of ministry. In 1845 he admits to Keble that, 'The course of sermons was taken from St Ignatius' *Exercises*, and so "judgment" ought to have been "The (General) Final Judgment"'.[22]

a. Surin[23]

In 1844 Pusey published Surin's *Foundations of the Spiritual Life*, the single most discussed volume of the adapted series in his correspondence. His work at translating and editing Surin coincided almost exactly with the appearance of his expressions of self-disgust and personal agony in his letters to Keble of 1843–6.

On the first page of his Preface, seventy pages in all, Pusey insists that true conversion requires 'a vivid, penetrating, pervading sense of our own corruption, with the participation of the Cross of Christ',[24] and in the next twenty-five pages attempts to show the necessity and catholicity of these two principles of the spiritual life in what may well be his most complete and ordered exposition of such principles. He manifests here a wide knowledge of Roman Catholic authors and expresses an enthusiasm for Surin and his teaching, which is not typical of his caution and reserve. In referring to the details of Surin's assignment as exorcist at the Ursuline convent of Loudun in 1635 and his ensuing personal struggles, Pusey reveals himself as sensitive and perceptive to Surin's experience and doctrine, using extensive selections from the *Lettres spirituelles* to explain and support certain points. This indicates that Pusey's interest in Surin was more than cursory. It is perhaps too much to suggest that Pusey saw certain parallels between his life and that of Surin, but one may at least state that he identified himself with his spirituality and that the prominent part of the spirit of evil and devils in the life and ministry of Surin made a lasting impression on him.[25] It is always to these two principles, man's nothingness and God's goodness in Christ, that Pusey returns again and again in his Preface:

> What have we already but . . . the Evangelic precepts of fasting . . . of almsgiving . . . of discipline of the body, of detailed vigilance over the senses, of one continuous warfare with our whole selves, of 'bearing hardness, like good soldiers of Jesus Christ,' of living the hidden life in Him?[26]

In the preface Pusey exhorts Christians to frequent meditation on the Passion of Christ, and to devotions flowing therefrom such as that of the Five Wounds, the Precious Blood, the Holy Cross and the Sacred Heart. Pusey's faithfulness to the original text of Surin and the inclusion of a letter, which Surin wrote to another priest, describing the torments of the devils at Loudun, would have given rise to questions among Anglicans, perhaps even among Roman Catholics. Surin's doctrine is generally regarded as orthodox, but the extraordinary events of his life and the religious climate of France in the seventeenth century might have suggested to Pusey's prudence a more truly 'adapted' version. In the event, Pusey provided more of a translation of the *Foundations* than an adaptation, and since this is consistently so of most of the books produced in this series, one must move toward the conclusion that Pusey envisioned his prefaces and introductions as the chief means of adaptation.

Through careful introduction, explanation and acceptance on the part of one like himself, who never seriously questioned at this time his membership in the established Church, he hoped to convince others that these works were not only acceptable, but desirable for the sincere Christian.

b. Pusey's Prayer and Self-examination

One must in fairness observe that Pusey gained much from the interiority of those works more in the tradition of the French School. This appealed to his spiritual discretion and his own love of scriptural scenes as subjects for meditation, especially the Passion of Christ. In later years he was to emphasize the theme of adoration of the Trinity a great deal, but he never really borrowed the emphasis of these writers on the positive virtues involved, except as a prelude to a heavy concentration on his own lack thereof. Nor did he adopt the more positive form of examen which Tronson in particular advocated.

In the Pamphlet Room of Pusey House Library there is still preserved a copy book in Pusey's own handwriting, which contains a number of his personal devotional prayers and some questions for self-examination. There are no dates in the book though it seems to have been compiled over a period of several years. Here we find evidence of Pusey's Trinitarian devotion and his style of self-examen. One such examen deals with his personal prayer; it reveals Pusey's regularity in mental prayer and his seriousness in carrying out the instructions given in the various manuals that he read and adapted. 'Have I been careless about preparing for prayer,' he asks himself, 'making no great effort to ask God to gather my soul to Him?' He is equally concerned about extending the fruits of his meditation to the work of the day. 'Have I risen from prayer without . . . commending myself to God, for what I am to do?' This self-examination on the subject of prayer further reveals his personal agony over his 'gloomy thought about God's mercy' and his 'hopelessness'. In the attempt to achieve self-forgetfulness Pusey lapses into a preoccupation with self which gives his examination an overly negative spirit.

Other entries in the same copy book indicate how thoroughly Pusey organized his prayer life in the spirit of the French spiritual writers whom he read. In addition, Pusey was fond of using devotional prayers to fill the 'chinks of time' between various occupations. He particularly liked the Roman Catholic anthology of prayers and devotions entitled *The Paradise of the Christian Soul*. In his own prayers there is a deep yearning for the grace of true prayer and a sincere desire for the unity of the Church.

c. Pusey and the interior life

Over all the characteristics which typify Pusey's spirituality, there are two theological themes, mysteries of faith really, which form the outline of Pusey's experience and conception of the interior life. The one, pertinent to the whole of Tractarian spirituality, is the incarnation. The other, so prevalent in his letters and sermons, is what has been described as 'Pusey's mysticism of the cross'.[27] Pusey loved to dwell on the 'glory' of the Passion of Christ.

> Your infirmities will not hinder the grace of the Sacraments; only in this Easter time as well as in Passion-tide, recall yourself daily that our Lord's Human Nature was glorified in consequence of the depth of his humiliation.[28]

He encouraged others to unite themselves with the crucified Christ in every kind of suffering:

> Try habitually to unite your sufferings with those of our dear Lord. The bones of His Sacred Back must so have been torn, dislocated, severed, . . . the one from the other: and everything must have been so aggravated by the superhuman sensibility of His Frame. Pray to Him to sanctify yours by this.[29]

The imitation of the crucified Christ and the efficacy of his precious blood were themes which Pusey drew from the Fathers and from Roman Catholic sources; they were inserted into his letters of direction and were amplified in his many sermons which discussed almost every aspect of Christian holiness. For Pusey the incarnation and the cross were two aspects of the same divine reality. Thus Pusey's stress on the cross of Christ was no mere pietistic slogan, but a serious theological stance based upon what he learned from his study of Catholic tradition and ratified by his own experience. His efforts to inculcate the fundamentals of humility and self-forgetfulness in those under his spiritual care were intended to bring each person to a deeper understanding of the love of God and an increased sense of awe and reverence before God's presence in the human soul. In a sermon preached sometime before 1850 entitled 'The Incarnation, a Lesson of Humility', Pusey wrote:

> One had not dared so to speak of His Ineffable Humility, lest we, so little humble, should not be able with reverence to think on His Humility had they not of old, in more reverent days, so spoken.[30]

Baptized on Holy Cross day in 1800, Pusey ever observed that anniversary and was devoted to the cross of Christ as the symbol of God's victory over all our sins and weakness:

> I have sent you the Benediction, which I hope your Guardian Angel will convey to you: and once more
>   'The Cross of Christ
>   Seal thee as his own for ever!'
>   'For ever!' Without a word! Unintermitting, unending, ever enlarging.[31]

It was undoubtedly his own immersion in the things of God which drew so many to Pusey for guidance. Ever conscious of the power of God at work in us, Pusey could display great sensitivity in offering encouragement:

> And this mind may be formed in you now safely. There are penitential times and there are times of joy. If God makes joy most abound, then you need not fear to give yourself to that joy; and if you are sorrowful, he will give you joy in your sorrow, in the sense of his forgiveness.[32]

He could also beautifully express the mystery of union with God which grows out of ordinary human suffering:

> . . . But He will teach you through loneliness . . . to be alone with Him: and you will have felt already, how blest it is to be alone with Him, and how true His sympathy, and that His

comfort is with power, and you will by his grace, know it yet more and more.[33]

Thus for Pusey all begins and ends in God: '. . . it is your inmost self which must be changed, and no one ever changes but God, and He will, if you pray for it'.[34]

3   Characteristics of Pusey's spirituality

The assessment of any religious movement is difficult because of the hidden, interior principles and elements involved in any authentic religious experience or phenomenon. The Oxford Movement, primarily concerned as it was with a renewal of the spirit of holiness within the Church of England, is thus difficult to evaluate or criticize. This 'genuine revival of the spirit' did not appear in a vacuum; it had been prepared for by political, social and theological factors, chief among them the Evangelical Movement of eighteenth- and nineteenth-century Britain. For Keble, Newman and Pusey there was an intimate connection between the two 'Movements' for 'the Oxford Movement was a completion of the earlier revival of religion known as Evangelical'.[35] They, through the fusion of Evangelical fervour and sound Catholic doctrine created a spirit, an atmosphere, a movement which had a 'deeper significance' than any revival which might be simply doctrinal on the one hand or merely enthusiastic piety on the other.

The Bible

Pusey's affection for theEvangelicals came out of his love for all things biblical. From an early age he was interested in the study of ancient and biblical languages, which would unlock the meaning of the sacred text for him, and his studies only increased his reverence and awe for the word of God in Scripture. Only one so devoted and accomplished could undertake a revision of the Authorised Version of the Old Testament, as he did in 1827. It was a project never completed, but when beginning it he thought it would take him 'about nine years'. Pusey, however, feared the 'lack of doctrinal platform', which made the Evangelicals vulnerable to the menace of

liberalism in religious teaching, whereby the Bible would be
exposed to critical examination and a sense of its inspiration
diminished. Pusey's study, thought and prayer were steeped in
the Old and New Testaments. His sermons and theological
monographs displayed the breadth and depth of his scriptural
expertise. Although in some of his early letters to his fiancée
there are some explicit scriptural references, this is not generally
true of his letters, even those of spiritual direction.

> If one compares one's own petty sufferings with His
> sufferings, one feels ready to sink with shame into the earth
> for having given them a moment's thought. The fifty-third
> chapter of Isaiah or the history of the Crucifixion is an
> antidote to the bitterness of any sorrow.[36]

In another letter to Miss Barker young Pusey explains the value
in the study of Scripture, though Liddon believes that in later
years Pusey would have expressed himself with greater reservations.

> The sole object of Scripture being to provide what is
> 'profitable for doctrine, for reproof, for correction, for
> instruction in righteousness, that we may be perfected,
> thoroughly furnished unto all good works', all that is
> necessary . . . is willing study with a teachable heart.[37]

The aftermath of his father's death he spent reading St John's
Gospel which he found 'permanently tranquillizing to his
mind'.[38] Throughout his life he loved to meditate upon gospel
scenes, particularly the Passion of Christ:

> Surely when our Lord's Sufferings are so set before us, both
> in the Psalm and in the Gospels, it must be meant that we
> should dwell upon each portion of them, upon every pang
> which entered with them.[39]

Presuming that Pusey employed some form of mental prayer
suggested by the spiritual authors whom he studied and adapted
for the use of Anglicans, we can be sure that scriptural scenes
were the basis for his daily meditation and that he recommended
to others this biblical orientation.

Pusey's prayer and spirituality were certainly biblical in the sense that daily reading and study of the Scripture were part of his personal regime; in that he was devoted to the daily celebration of the Communion Service and the hours of the Prayer Book plus the complementary hours of the breviary; all of which brought before him the word of God for his consideration and inspiration each day and many times throughout the day. It was this personal experience of God's guidance through the Scripture, which was his mainstay and which made it possible for him to stand against the tide of public opinion and the advice of intimate friends, when he felt convinced that he should take some action or remain passive in a particular crisis. As he himself explained it, '. . . a spiritual mind, however limited, will see truth for itself, but it is only by having in the first faithfully followed guidance to that truth'.[40] Pusey was convinced to the end of this deeply interior principle. The biblical orientation of the Anglican Church and the liturgical emphasis, with which Pusey imbued them, assured that his love and reverence for the sacred texts would become part of the lives of his followers and become enshrined in their practice of meditation based upon scriptural passages, especially scenes from the Gospels.

The Fathers

There was a measure for the authenticity of the 'direct apprehension of personal experience', which Pusey, Keble and Newman discovered through their study of the Fathers of the Church: the rule of orthodoxy, the safeguard against error, was Catholic tradition: that lived experience of faith set forth in Scripture and preserved and interpreted in the Church. Continuity with the Church of the Fathers very naturally became a preoccupation of the Tractarians. Their concern was to restore the sacramental and ecclesiological vision of the patristic era to the nineteenth-century Anglican Church. Pusey was particularly familiar with the works of the Fathers, especially St Augustine.

Liddon insists that the real 'attraction to the School was ethical and spiritual rather than doctrinal', and yet because the Movement was set within the context of a patristic revival, the concern for the spiritual of necessity involved the doctrinal. In patristic thought there was no clear distinction between the study of Scripture, theology and spirituality. For the Fathers the Scripture was not only the starting point, but the summation of all that was necessary for the life of faith.

> Scripture was at once a source of knowledge and a key to salvation. Thus the Fathers attribute to it effects in the spiritual life which we would usually ascribe to grace. . . . They speak of Scripture as if it achieved the whole reconstitution of man in the image of God, the whole of the spiritual life from the initial purifications to the divine union.[41]

Knowledge and understanding of the scriptural text and its meaning can only be assured within the Church where the scripture is authentically read, proclaimed and celebrated. From the time of the Fathers through the Middle Ages the Bible was *the* textbook of theological thought and teaching. Thus, theology generally took the form of an 'exposition' of the sacred text. Further, the integrity of their outlook, linking together revelation, theological reflection and personal experience, produced a theology which was at once doctrinal and spiritual. For Pusey, Keble and Newman this unity of vision was most appealing, and Pusey's academic orientation to biblical studies and classical languages disposed him well to read and absorb the teaching of the Fathers of both East and West. Pusey's spirituality must be described as patristic as well as scriptural in its sources and fundamental inspiration. His theological tracts and argumentation are filled with direct quotations and cross references from the writings of the Fathers. His own spiritual journey however, as recorded in his correspondence, and his formation of others, seem set in the context of post-Reformation Roman Catholic spirituality. Thus, Pusey's instruction seems to have been more concerned with the methods and themes of a later age than that of the Fathers. His chief use of the Fathers was as a source of theological orthodoxy. It has been suggested that Pusey in his devotional life became 'absorbed in meditation on the Passion which was as unpatristic as possible'.[42] It is true that Pusey transmitted to others his own practice of using the Passion of Christ as a subject of mental prayer and this always in the terminology more reminiscent of Roman Catholic spiritual writers. Perhaps a more 'patristic' orientation might have supplied some of the needed balance.

Tradition

Viewed within this ambient, it is less difficult to understand what we have termed Pusey's eclecticism in developing his personal spirituality. Filled with the information he took from the Fathers and enthusiastic about the ideals which he found expressed there, Pusey became convinced that to live in the Catholic tradition, it was necessary to view the Anglican Church in a broader context, the Catholic context, and to be open to receive any authentic teaching within that broad outline. Thus his enthusiasm for and dependence upon the teaching of the Fathers were matched by his trust of the devotional and spiritual literature of post-Reformation continental Roman Catholicism. All spirituality as part of a living tradition must be based upon the one gospel of Jesus Christ. In this Pusey was no exception. However, to understand a tradition and to become part of it, to be able to distinguish between mere convention and authentic tradition, there must be continuity with the past and with previous interpretations and developments of that tradition. It is this note of continuity, which Pusey was lacking and for this reason his spirituality appears to be eclectic. Tractarian negligence of the medieval theological synthesis and their inexperience of the Catholic counter-Reformation created a lacuna in their understanding of what post-Tridentine Catholicism and its spirituality really meant. This was so in spite of the romantic idealization of the Middle Ages, which typified Tractarian revivals in ritual and architecture. Pusey's ignorance of the English mystical tradition, particularly that of fourteenth century writers such as Walter Hilton, Julian of Norwich and Richard Rolle is striking in this regard. More to the point, the rupture between the Church of England and the Church of Rome, based as it was on a rejection of church life as it had developed from the patristic era through the Middle Ages, signified a long and serious break with the Catholic tradition, affecting as it ultimately did both doctrine and spirituality.

Patristic spirituality, if one may use that term, is in marked contrast to the systematized programmes of the French Jesuits and other spiritual writers of the seventeenth century. The primitive Christian ascetical life and monastic observance, which was known to the Fathers, was different in every way from the religious life of the modern religious congregation. Yet Pusey, believing both to be expressions of the same basic realities of faith and therefore belonging to the Catholic tradition, borrowed from each as he saw fit, failing to distinguish what might be mere cultural accretions from unchanging principles, and unable to understand the process of development which often gave traditional realities new emphases or dimensions.

More importantly, the spirituality of Pusey centred upon the mystery of the incarnation and the cross of Christ as understood and celebrated by the Church:

> ... And as the two Mysteries to which God gives most power to draw and melt the soul, are the Incarnation and the Cross, and by them He pours into it a superhuman, a Divine love, Advent may ... work by His mercy a reverent love for His Divine Infancy, as Lent should nail us to His Cross.[43]

These same mysteries, so particularly emphasized in both patristic and post-Reformation spirituality drew Pusey by instinct to both periods. Doubtless Pusey recognized the roots of the themes of *adoration*, *imitation*, *union* and *prayer*, which he found among seventeenth century authors, in the theology of the Fathers, but there these themes would have had a broader, more biblical and liturgical orientation. The incarnation itself, a subject of critical theological discussion and clarification among the Fathers, signified Christ in his person as God-man; he is the revelation of the nature of God; for later spiritual writers and for Pusey the incarnation suggested the image of the divine infancy. The cross, understood originally in the Johannine sense of the throne of glory and the symbol of God's absolute triumph over sin and death in Christ, came to mean primarily the Passion of Christ, its satisfaction for our sins and its application to our daily lives in suffering, sickness and death. The later distinction between liturgical and private prayer and the organized programmes of discursive meditation would have been foreign and artificial among the early Christians, and while the Fathers demanded a strict accounting of the spiritual and moral lives of the faithful under their care, a structure of self-examination such as Pusey learned from Tronson and the French Jesuits would have been distasteful to them and unnecessary. The same realities of faith, the same mysteries, are approached from various points of view in different ages. Christian ascetical life stresses at one time the dangers of the world and the need to withdraw from it; at another time the goodness of the world as God's creation and the need to enter into it and bring to it the light of the gospel of Christ is emphasized. Thus, Pusey, familiar with two aspects of the tradition was very likely unable to sort out what he thought wisest to include or omit from his own ideas and practice and those of the early sisters. The lack of continuity in his experience of church tradition and his own complex personality were the chief reasons for this.

4   Conclusions

Edward Bouverie Pusey was an extraordinary man. There can be no doubt of this fact. But through some peculiarities of his background and personality his depressive nature caused him to develop a spirituality, which stressed the weakness and sinfulness of human nature, and he became convinced of the need for humility, humiliations and self-detachment in the extreme. There was much 'darkness' in his religious sentiments. There were, further, certain inconsistencies in his personality which clouded his judgement even on serious issues and caused him to transgress the bounds of prudence in directing others in the spiritual life. There is no question of his orthodoxy, but rather a certain imbalance which made it difficult for him to borrow from the Roman Catholic tradition as freely as he thought he could. The division created by the Reformation between the Anglican and Roman Churches could not be so easily healed. Pusey imparted to his followers a high doctrine of prayer and religious observance. He offered them ideals of generous love, perfect humility and abandonment to God's will. But he was unable to cast this high doctrine in a balanced mode and, in the case of the religious sisterhoods, the lack of any existing Anglican tradition of the religious life made it impossible for them to develop the healthy flexibility and joy which might have attracted new recruits. His teaching continued to the end to be overly serious and somewhat grim.

While we cannot fault the orthodoxy of Pusey's teaching, it is perhaps his overriding concern for orthodoxy, which is the most significant criticism which can be levelled against him. He was not by nature a creative man, but his taking of Roman Catholic sources *en masse* and transplanting them into the Church of England without any serious alteration and adaptation was indeed questionable. His fear of 'going wrong' with even the best of intentions and his concern that his foundation be truly Catholic and orthodox, were the source of much of the problem. It is this lack of creativity and originality, which perhaps marked the great flaw in his leadership of the first generation of the Oxford Movement and his lack of insight in borrowing a system of spiritual methods from a church situation so completely foreign to his own both in national temperament and historical development. The degree of pressure under which Pusey laboured during the 1840s was considerable. The aftermath of his wife's death and his personal spiritual crisis; his intellectual 'revolutions' and the opposition which he encountered from the two priests who were originally his associates in the spiritual direction of the first sisterhood, were sources of the great strain from which Pusey suffered and doubtless made him cling all the more to a literal interpretation of the Roman Catholic structures which he helped to introduce into the Anglican Church. If it was a mistake, it was an honest one. Only a more creative and original thinker, free from the harassment of his own troubled spirit might have managed a more palatable blending of the various traditions involved.

He was, for all that, part of the Catholic movement which fought for the reintegration of sound doctrine with authentic religious experience. He gave his life to the Church of England and was not unsuccessful in creating a spirit of reverence and prayer:

Men are moved by ritual symbols, hallowed associations of

251

custom. Whether these symbols are simple or elaborate, they are valued as they are inhabited, vessels for aspiration of conscience and yearning of soul. The Reformation pushed the focus of worship from altar towards pulpit; and the rational divines of the 18th century pushed it still farther from the chancel, into a pulpit which sometimes resounded like a rostrum, as preacher lectured or lecturer preached on moral duty and historic evidence. But now they peered into temple clouds and made obeisance before throne invisible.[44]

Pusey was among those who wrought this revolution in Anglican life, perhaps foremost among them, and his spiritual life and teaching were his pledge to the Church's holiness which was the centre of his existence.

NOTES

1   Cf. David W. F. Forrester, 'The Intellectual Development of E. B. Pusey, 1800–1850,' (unpublished thesis, Oxford, 1967), Preface.
2   Pusey to Maria Pusey, 13 November 1835.
3   Pusey to Maria Pusey, 1 November 1836.
4   Pusey to Maria Pusey, 6 November 1835.
5   Ibid.
6   Ibid.
7   Pusey to John Keble, 9 December 1846.
8   Keble to Pusey, 22 September 1844.
9   Pusey to Keble, 26 September 1844.
10 Ibid.
11 'You will almost be surprised that . . . I should attempt to guide any. I cannot help it. Those whom I in any way guide were brought me, and by experience, or reading or watching God's guidance of them, I do what I can, and God who loves them has blessed them through me . . . N. only knows that there were sins heavily on my mind when the anniversary of my wife's death impressed on me why I was so chastened. I wish nothing to be said for fear of disquieting him specially. . . . But I am trying to learn to wish to influence nothing on any great scale, to prefer, I mean, everyone's judgment to my own, and only to act for myself as best I may.' Ibid.
12 Pusey to Manning, 12 August 1845.
13 '. . . now, through God's mercy and your love, I can write freely, whereas for years past I believe, I have inwardly writhed in every letter I wrote, all

my relation to you seemed one lie . . . I can pray to Him as I never did before. This, of course, I could only say to you, as my Father in Christ. . . . I seem to hate myself more thoroughly. . . . However, things seem with me other than they were before . . . my prayers . . . have a love and hope I never knew before.' E.B.P. to Keble, 7 December 1846. cf. E. B. Pusey, *Entire Absolution of the Penitent*, p. 29, November 1846.

14 Edward R. Williams, 'Tractarian Moral Theology' (unpublished thesis, Oxford, 1951), p. 51.

15 Pusey to Miss Ellacombe, 18 September 1844.

16 O. Chadwick, *The Victorian Church*, 2 vols. (London 1971–2), I, 510.

17 Marriott to Bishop Selwyn, 13–15 September 1842.

18 Pusey to John Keble, 21 October 1844.

19 Ibid.

20 Ibid.

21 Pusey to Sister Clara, Feast of St Mark, 1844.

22 Pusey to John Keble, Feast of St James, 1845.

23 Jean Joseph Surin (1600–65): born at Bordeaux, he entered the Jesuit novitiate in 1616. His principal work was preaching and the direction of souls in the spiritual life. He is perhaps best known for his role of exorcist at the Ursuline Convent at Loudun.

24 J. J. Surin, *Foundations of the Spiritual Life*, ed. E. B. Pusey (London 1844), Preface, p. iii.

25 Pusey to Keble, 9 July 1848. In discussing a young woman he was directing Pusey says: 'I have had decided reason for being quite satisfied before this, that Satan had been allowed personally to try her, i.e., some of his devils. The fiercer than the rest had on a former occasion been seen by her; she has indeed *seen* devils, supernaturally, more than once . . . In such things I go by books, for what should I, wretched sinner, know about them?'

26 Ibid., p. ix.

27 Horton Davies, *Worship and Theology in England*, 4 vols. (Princeton 1962), vol. 4, p. 250.

28 Pusey, *Spiritual Letters*, ed. I. O. Johnston and W. C. E. Newbolt (London 1828–30), p. 125.

29 Ibid.

30 Pusey, 'The Incarnation a Lesson of Humility', in *Parochial Sermons*, vol. 1, p. 61.

31 Pusey, *Spiritual Letters*, p. 127.

32 Pusey to the Dowager Duchess of Argyll, August 1854.

33 Ibid., 11 July 1853.

34 Pusey to Sister Clara, 14 August 1845.

35 Liddon, vol. 1, p. 254.

36 Pusey to Miss Barker, 5 January 1828.
37 Ibid.
38 Liddon, vol. 1, p. 142.
39 Pusey, *A Letter to the Lord Bishop of London* (Oxford 1851), p. 152.
40 Pusey, *Tract* 67, p. iv.
41 Yves M. J. Congar, *Tradition and Traditions* (London 1966), p. 380.
42 Louis Bouyer, *A History of Christian Spirituality*, vol. 3 (New York 1963), p. 209.
43 Avrillon, *A Guide for Passing Advent Holily*, ed. E. B. Pusey (London 1847), p. vii.
44 Chadwick, *The Victorian Church*, vol. 1, p. 495–6.

11

Pusey and the Question of Church and State

PETER NOCKLES

I am not at all at home on church and state questions. Nor have I good historical knowledge of any sort.[1]

Thus wrote Pusey to Newman, after being asked by the Vice-Chancellor of Oxford University, Dr Gilbert, to preach the annual 5 November sermon in 1837, commemorating the deliverance from Guy Fawkes's Gunpowder Plot in 1605 and also the landing of William of Orange in 1688.

Certainly, the relative paucity of Pusey's sermons and published writings on questions of ecclesiastical politics rather than dogmatic theology, ecclesiology and spirituality, is significant. This apparent reluctance to dwell on what might loosely be called 'political' topics, has fitted in with a long-established tendency among historians to view the Oxford Movement as a whole as always antagonistic to and in conflict with questions of constitutional and political principle, state concerns or policy. For instance, the two greatest historical authorities on the Movement, Dean Church and Pusey's own biographer, Liddon, both revealed a remarkable reluctance to recognize any real political background to the Movement and almost entirely ignored the burning constitutional questions that so preoccupied the minds of churchmen at the time of its dawn. As Geoffrey Best has rightly observed:

The movement's political origins in the counter-revolutionary side of the quasi-revolution of 1828–32 have to be sought elsewhere. Church understood these well but chose to pass lightly over them. To historians who must measure the social

255

and political dimensions of ostensibly religious movements, Church's inattention to such critical events as Roman Catholic emancipation and the Reform Bill will seem almost misleadingly inadequate.[2]

The Tractarians, Pusey included, had done much to foster this impression. For instance, when the church historian, the Revd William Nassau Molesworth, wrote to Pusey in 1864 asking him for information on the political background of the Oxford Movement, the latter's reply reflected dismay that such a question should even be posed. For by this time, Pusey took the view, as expressed by his Tractarian friend, William Copeland, 'that the political element, the Reform Bill, had not any effect in producing the *Tracts for the Times*'.[3] Copeland not only insisted that the Movement had not been a response to the political and constitutional turmoil of the day, but could not even 'imagine how the two subjects could be brought into any intelligible relation to each other'.[4]

One purpose of this essay is to seek to show how those such as Copeland and Church, Liddon and many others in later years, chose to overlook or ignore an important dimension of early Tractarianism, and one which long continued to colour Pusey's own brand of it: a just sense of the mutual interconnection of politics and religion, of the duties and responsibilities of the State as well as the purity and independence of the Church. The terms 'Erastian' and 'Tory' in a pejorative sense, implying a worldly, political 'High and Dry' churchmanship, have been employed much too loosely[5] to categorize an attitude and approach towards the question of Church and State, which all Tractarians are credited with repudiating with disdain. What our essay will show is just how much of it Pusey retained. W. R. Ward's and Owen Chadwick's portrayal of a Tractarian abandonment of Toryism for 'Liberal Catholicism',[6] while applicable to many followers of the Oxford Movement, is a less than adequate representation of the history of Pusey's ecclesiastical politics. For in that deeper, more religious facet of Toryism as integral to a political tradition in High Anglicanism, which he inherited from John Keble, Pusey was as firm an adherent in the 1850s as the 1830s.

The primary preoccupation of Pusey and the Tractarians as a whole with matters spiritual and doctrinal, should not be allowed to disguise the fact that the occasion of the origin and rise of the Oxford Movement was eminently practical and political. As Chadwick, Brose, Norman[7] and other historians who have done much to rectify the earlier neglect of the constitutional background, have made clear, this occasion was a crisis and revolution in the old basis of the Church and State relationship. In short, the Movement's birth, symbolized by John Keble's famous Assize sermon on 'National Apostasy' on 14 July 1833, was a direct response to an immediate, practical emergency. The constitutional changes of the years 1828–33 had effectively placed the Church in an entirely new position vis-à-vis the State.

The old Church-State relationship, as expressed most clearly and fully in Richard Hooker's *Laws of Ecclesiastical Polity*, had depended on the assumption that the established religion was the religion of the state and nation as a whole. Moreover, John Kenyon has shown that perhaps the most important aspect of the High Church propaganda in the 1690s and 1700s 'was a passionate reaffirmation of the concept that the church was the state, and the state the church'.[8] Nevertheless, long before the constitutional changes of the period 1828–33, the ideal of an absolute unity of Church and State envisaged by Hooker and the Caroline Divines had suffered several damaging blows that undermined it as a practical reality. The formal recognition of the Presbyterian church as the established Church of Scotland in 1707, under the terms of the Act of Union, the suspension of Convocation which had acted as the ecclesiastical counterpart to Parliament in 1717, and the promotion of numerous latitudinarian and erastian, if not heterodox, Whig churchmen, such as Samuel Clarke and Benjamin Hoadly, all made it harder to maintain that the Church-State union was continuing to be operated in the real interests of the Church of England. Moreover, there was a subtle but marked shift in the grounds on which that union and the principle of establishment itself, were commonly defended and justified by Anglican churchmen in the Hanoverian as opposed to the Caroline era. In their theoretical rationale for establishment, the Caroline Divines, following

257

Hooker, stressed that it was religious truth and the welfare of the Church that was the only paramount consideration. As such, the spiritual independence of the Church was by no means sacrificed. On the contrary, it was deemed to be but better safeguarded under the protecting hand of a sympathetic State that could be regarded as a sort of temporal counterpart to the Church. There was at least the possible implication—followed out by the later Nonjurors in the wake of the Williamite and Hanoverian succession—that when the old balance broke down in favour of a less sympathetic State, establishment and the union might be deemed not to be worth preserving at any price after all.

The trend towards an unreservedly anti-establishment attitude among later Nonjurors such as Thomas Deacon, founder of the 'Orthodox British Church', and William Cartwright, who had himself consecrated as Nonjuring bishop of Shrewsbury, was encouraged by the increasingly utilitarian and erastian basis on which not only extreme Erastians such as Benjamin Hoadly, but more moderate Whig latitudinarian divines such as William Warburton and William Paley, defended and extolled the Church-State union. Hoadly's position was crudely erastian in the literal sense of the term: the Church was deemed to have no inherent spiritual rights or independence apart from the civil power. Warburton and Paley were more moderate, but nonetheless based their case for establishment and Test-laws not so much on religious truth but on the utilitarian interests of the State and mere political convenience.[9] Moreover, in practice, especially in the case of the Church of Ireland, Whig politicians in the Hanoverian era shamelessly exploited ecclesiastical patronage for overtly political ends. Furthermore, even many of the so-called 'High and Dry' or 'orthodox' Tory churchmen of the pre-Tractarian era, became infected by the more temporal considerations of establishment and neglected or forgot the fact that the Church was a divine society and constitution which for the first three centuries of its life had had no formal connection with any state. As Nancy Murray has put it, they 'considered themselves primarily as servants of the establishment and were concerned above all with the church as an established institution'.[10] Typical of such churchmen was the ultra-Tory statesman and Lord Chancellor, Lord Eldon, who as his biographer admitted:

> opposed the Dissenters and the Roman Catholics, not because he looked at them through any jaundice of theological dislike, but simply because he believed that the Church Establishment would be undermined by their admission to the functions of the state.[11]

Yet, it would be mistaken to regard such an attitude as representative of the pre-Tractarian High Church party as a whole, as some have implied: a point which Murray has made clear, by distinguishing the genuinely 'High Church' from the 'orthodox' in this period. Among the former, the old Caroline ideal, with establishment defended on *iure divino* rather than utilitarian grounds, lived on. This traditional High Church approach, abandoned by the later Nonjurors, was most effectively reasserted by the so-called 'Hutchinsonians', a group of Oxford High Churchmen, who followed the esoteric anti-Newtonian scientific theories of the eccentric Hebraist, John Hutchinson. Another example of its restatement was provided by American Loyalists such as Jonathan Boucher, himself a Hutchinsonian, at the time of the American War for Independence.[12] Moreover, as Murray has shown, the conservative reaction in England to the French Revolution strengthened the case for the traditional High Church rather than Erastian variant of the Church and State theory. Significantly, the herald and mouthpiece of that conservative reaction, Edmund Burke, threw his weight behind a vindication of religious establishment based not on the Warburtonian or Paleyite notion of an alliance of separate powers for mere mutual convenience, but on the strict Caroline view of a divinely-ordained inseparable union of two mutually interrelated ones. Furthermore, from then on until the dawn of the Oxford Movement, the so-called 'Hackney Phalanx' group of High Churchmen led by Joshua Watson and Henry Handley Norris, rector of Hackney, continued not only to uphold the theory but to put it into practice. Certainly, in the years immediately prior to 1828, with the 'Phalanx' in the ascendancy and in effective control of ecclesiastical patronage, the union of Church and State appeared to be working more in the Church's interests and in accordance with the ideal of Hooker, than at any time since the reign of Charles II. It was the constitutional revolution beginning with the repeal of the Test and Corporation Acts against Protestant Dissenters in 1828 and culminating in the Irish Temporalities Act in 1833, that rudely shattered this working harmony and introduced a new era.

In practice, the constitutional revolution of these years relegated the Church of England to the position of 'one sect among many'. Catholic Emancipation had broken down an important hedge-work of establishment. This and the Reform Act of 1832 had effectively opened up a hitherto exclusively Anglican parliament to the Church's enemies, both Dissenters and Romanists, thus making the fact that Convocation was in semi-permanent suspension all the more oppressive for the Church. Above all, the measure that prompted Keble's famous Assize Sermon, the spoliation of the Irish Church by the parliamentary suppression of ten bishoprics and two archbishoprics, seemed to signify a nakedly utilitarian and erastian approach to the church's internal well-being by the government of the day. As William Palmer, the Irish High Church Fellow of Worcester College, put it, the Irish Temporalities Act of 1833:

> appeared, in fact, to mutilate, to destroy the Church, by affording a demonstration of the truth of the unceasing charge against that church that it was a mere slave of the state, devoid of faith, and capable of being moulded into any form at the State's pleasure.[13]

Then, subsequent to this, the formal creation of an Ecclesiastical Commission, composed of laymen as well as bishops, to investigate and reform the Church's internal administrative and financial structure, appeared to be further evidence of the State's unwillingness to allow the Church to manage her own affairs. In short, the Church's union with the State suddenly seemed to be operating against her. The various schemes of would-be church reformers, many of whom such as Lord Henley and Dr Arnold, headmaster of Rugby, were pious churchmen, appeared to be yet another symptom of the erastian spirit coming from within. Both Lord Henley and Arnold in his notorious *Principles of Church Reform*, went so far as to press for doctrinal and liturgical changes in a latitudinarian direction, as part of a plan to widen the bounds of the national Church.[14] In short, Hooker's reality having become untenable, it was to be recaptured by diluting the Church's distinctive points of doctrine and discipline so as to comprehend the bulk of Protestant Dissenters. Nothing could have been greater anathema to High Churchmen, and their reaction was not slow in coming.

Yet, the main rearguard action among all conservative churchmen in 1833 contained within it different strands and facets that became wider as the years passed. The so-called 'Oxford Movement' was only the most important strand of this reaction. From the start, there were conservative High Church and even 'Eldonite' opponents of the Whig church campaign, for whom the new Movement was an object of suspicion. The fact was that for the Tractarians, the new Movement in defence of the Church was much more than a last-ditch attempt to save vested interests, and certainly where this entailed judicious compromise on deeper points of doctrine and discipline, as some conservative churchmen advocated. It was far more than just the old Tory church party cry of 'the Church in danger'. As William Copeland later argued:

> it is extremely important to keep the movement, which was from within, as clear as possible from the external circumstances, with which it came into contact, and this notwithstanding Keble's protest against Erastianism in his sermon on National Apostasy, and Hurrell Froude's strong denunciation of Whig politics.[15]

Like Newman, Hurrell Froude and John Keble, Pusey was clearly part of this 'movement from within', even if it was some while before he formally identified himself with what Palmer dubbed 'the movement party'. The clear line of distinction between this party, which Froude labelled the 'Ys' or 'Apostolicals', and the old High Churchmen, whom he designated the 'Zs',[16] largely centred on a divergence of approach on the question of Church and State. The former evinced a new readiness to face up to the logic of changed constitutional circumstances, by pressing for complete spiritual autonomy for the Church, even at the price of disestablishment if necessary. In his 'Remarks on State interference in matters spiritual' in *The British Magazine*, Froude trenchantly exposed the apparent anomalies and compromises he detected in the continued clinging to the status quo of many Tory old High Churchmen. In essence, Froude's argument was that it was idle now to rest content with a merely negative attitude of resistance to external threats to the establishment from without, when even the old apparent friends and supporters of establishment within had turned enemy and were corrupting and undermining the Church. Turning the tables on the conservative High Churchmen, he exhorted them to 'open your eyes to the fearful change which has been so noiselessly effected; and acknowledge that BY STANDING STILL YOU BECOME A PARTY TO REVOLU-TION'.[17] Froude purported to be but remaining true to the real principles of Hooker: principles, which had to be re-applied to meet conditions and circumstances which were new. Neverthe-less, implicitly, he went much further. He sought to take the opportunity to propagate notions on the Church–State relation-ship that were quite alien to the high Anglican tradition bequeathed by Hooker and the Caroline Divines. In place of theirs, the ideal he looked for now, was that not only of St Ambrose and St Athanasius and the early Church, but also of Hildebrand, Becket, Stephen Langton and the early medieval Church, wielding power over and inflicting censures on princes. Significantly, when Froude did point up elements of corruption in the late medieval Church, it was from a standard diametrically opposed to that of the 'Zs'. For instance, he argued that the usurpations of Roman Pontiffs as they existed by the end of the fourteenth-century, 'were usurpations, not on the rights of Kings and Governors, but on the rights of the Church itself, of the congregations of Christ's little ones, the poor, the halt, the lame and the blind'.[18] Froude's differences from traditional High Churchmen on this subject were also illustrated by his sympathy for the anti-church and state views of the early Puritans in their conflicts with the Elizabethan episcopate. In fact, Froude did not even except Laud from his verdict that 'all our divines since the Reformation had been very dark about church independence'.[19]

Both Newman and Keble and several other of the Tractarians

were much influenced by Froude's radical views on Church and State. For instance, Newman's assertion as a Roman Catholic in his *Difficulties of Anglicans* of 1850, 'that the established religion was set up in Erastianism, that Erastianism was its essence',[20] owed much to the working through of this influence. In fact, Newman's argument in that work had been prefigured as early as 1836, when he had insisted, 'that the English church subsists in the state, and has no internal consistency . . . to keep it together'.[21] Moreover, even Keble was ready to envisage the possibility of disestablishment rather than let the Church remain a slave to a State that tied its hands. As he asserted to Newman in 1833, 'Take every pound, shilling, and penny and the case of sacrilege along with it, only let us make our own Bishops and be governed by our own laws'. The contrast between these sentiments of a new High Churchmanship from the old was recognized instinctively by Keble, when he informed Newman in this same letter, that in the manner of Burke, he was planning 'an Appeal from the New to the Old Churchmen, or some such thing'.[22] The so-called 'Zs' were less inclined to interpret the changes of 1828–33 as the signal for a new start in Church–State thinking. As Copeland later recalled, 'Froude certainly as much dreaded the calm in the Church, as Palmer was frightened at the storm raised against it'.[23] Like the older generation in the 'Hackney Phalanx', William Palmer adopted a rigidly conservative stance. His continued traditional commitment to the old ideal of the Church's duty to consecrate the State and nation as a whole, found expression in the very words of Joshua Watson's loyal lay address to the Primate in 1834, 'We believe that the consecration of the state by the public maintenance of the christian religion is the first and paramount duty of a christian people'. As Palmer later remarked, these were 'words which were anathema to Froude, for all his idolisation of the "Martyr King"'.[24]

Significantly, there were a number of 'Zs' of the younger generation, such as Palmer, who were much more closely linked to the new Movement than their older counterparts in the 'Hackney Phalanx', but who retained a greater attachment to the establishment ideal and took issue with their Tractarian friends accordingly. The young William Ewart Gladstone, elected to parliament as Tory MP for Newark in 1832, was one of this group. It was Gladstone, who put up one of the most coherent and convincing defences of the Church–State relationship, even in the changed situation following 1833. It was all very well for idealistic 'Apostolicals' to complain that the purity of the Church was being corrupted by its union with the State, but what mattered to Gladstone, was simply whether the nation was more or less religious and inclined to Anglicanism as a result of the existence of a national Church. For Gladstone, the answer had to be in the affirmative, but the very fact that he even considered this question marks a significant shift in priorities from those of the 'Apostolicals'. It can be said of Froude and Newman, and to some extent, even Keble, that they were almost prepared to alienate the nation, as long as they could induce the Church of the day to become the Church of their dreams. Their viewpoint was primarily intrinsic to the Church. They often appeared unwilling to consider the Church's wider role or mission in the nation at large.[25] However, Gladstone viewed the relations of Church and State, primarily on the grounds of moral necessity and religious obligation. Precisely for this reason, he was able to meet both the challenge of radical Dissenting anti-establishmentarians and that of the liberal comprehensionist schemes of Arnold, on their own ground, and thus the more effectively. For instance, in repudiating his friend Henry Manning's fears about the corruption of the Church by its uniting with the State, he told him in a letter of 1835, 'What, however, are the interests of the church, which are supposed to be thus injured and corrupted? An institution can scarcely be said to be capable of an interest, distinct from that attaching to its members'.[26] In his correspondence with Manning in the 1830s and above all, in his great work of 1838 on the subject, *The State in its relations with the Church*, Gladstone hammered home this practical emphasis. He set forth the vision of a renewed Church of England taking its stand on the broader principles that had first inspired the Oxford Movement, but looking outwards and aiming to draw into its fold as many separatists as possible.[27] In short, catholicity and the principle of a national Church were complementary. Froude was deemed to be as mistaken in posing a dichotomy between them, as Arnold was

264

in seeking a more comprehensive national Church by means of abandoning some of the Church's distinctive doctrinal and ecclesial principles. The Tractarians certainly admired Gladstone's work on Church and State, and recognized the much higher tone and principle compared to that characteristic of the 'Eldonite' school of Tory churchmen. Nevertheless, Keble summed up the whole difference in approach when he remarked that it 'wants a little reconciling with Froude's theory'.[28]

It is against this background of divisions not only between all conservative churchmen and Whig-erastian church reformers, but within the former itself, between 'Zs' and 'Apostolicals', that one must set any consideration of Pusey's views on the relation of Church and State. Initially, from Pusey's early history, it is easy to understand his humble expression of ignorance of and unease about the whole question, in his letter to Newman in 1837 when called to preach on 5 November. For if Froude was to sing 'farewell to Toryism' and Newman was to move on from what he called 'High establishmentism', there would seem to have been no need for Pusey to modify his earlier views, when he formally threw in his lot with the Oxford Movement in 1834. Always shy, retiring and something of an academic recluse, Pusey was, if anything, even less at ease than Newman was in that London world of bureaucratic endeavour on behalf of the Church that characterized the 'Hackney Phalanx'. Above all, Pusey had no obvious point of contact or sympathy with the old Tory High Churchmanship that resisted the constitutional upheaval in the period 1828–33. Indeed, at the the very time that Newman, Froude and Keble were identifying themselves with that cause, in their battle against Peel at Oxford in 1829 for his having been a party to Catholic Emancipation, Pusey was on the opposite side. At this time, he was a political Liberal and Whig supporter of Catholic Emancipation, on abstract Whiggish grounds of liberty and religious toleration. He was an implacable enemy of the old constitutional framework in Church and State. Newman's Spanish friend, Blanco White, later to drift into unbelief, actually described Pusey as 'at that time one of the most Liberal members of the University'. Not surprisingly, Liddon was anxious to question this claim. He sought to play down Pusey's early Liberalism as a mere youthful reaction to his father's 'unbending Toryism',[29] and to explain his support for Catholic Emancipation and Peel to the influence of his friend and adviser, the High Church but eirenic Charles Lloyd, bishop of Oxford. Yet, Pusey's attitude, unlike Lloyd's, was as yet little dictated by sympathy for that in the Church of Rome that could be deemed 'primitive'. Still less, was his impatience with the Church's constitutional framework as yet dictated by a desire to assert her spiritual independence from an erastian State. Again this conviction only came later. For it was those who opposed Peel and Emancipation, who tended to take a much higher view of the independent spiritual rights and apostolical authority of the established Church. On the other hand, his controversy with the old High Churchman, Hugh James Rose, over the origins and causes of rationalism in Lutheran Germany, revealed that, in the words of Liddon:

> Pusey had not quite realised, as Rose had . . . that the Episcopate is an organic feature of the Church of Christ, the absence of which could not but be attended by spiritual disorder.[30]

In short, Pusey's political Liberalism and theological latitudinarianism were linked. For the very tone of his objections to exclusive Test-laws again reveals that it was abstract political Liberalism rather than ultra-High Church notions of spiritual authority that did not need any civil sanction, that governed his attitude. Thus, he could write to his fiancée, Maria Barker, at this time:

> I am very anxious about the Test and Corporation Acts. I think them both in their means and end, a disgrace and deterrent to religion. They, more than anything else, keep alive the bitterness of party spirit among Christians, agreeing in the same essentials of faith, in England.[31]

Clearly, it seemed that Pusey had not as yet the faintest conception of that deeper, moral and religious principle that animated Keble's, Froude's and Newman's espousal of the ultra-Tory cause: a resistance to 'the dangerous laxity of modern politics', as inseparably connected with a dangerous laxity of modern religion.

Pusey's shift from moderate political and religious Liberalism over to the High Church camp was comparatively sudden. Given the tenor of his writings on German theology in his dispute with Rose, Pusey might have been expected to have had some sympathy for the views of church reformers such as Lord Henley, if not those of Arnold himself. However, Pusey's much earlier friendship with the future Tract leaders matured into a drawing together in their respective views on church questions. At first, Pusey held aloof when the Tractarian party was formed in 1833, but he began openly to identify with the anti-Liberal cause with the publication of an answer to Lord Henley's scheme for church reform, *Remarks on the Prospective and Past Benefits of Cathedral Institutions* at the end of 1832. Significantly, old High Churchmen who had been uneasy with his earlier writings on German theology, warmly welcomed the work. Newman did likewise, apart from pointing out a few blemishes which prevented it from quite fully reaching the new High Church mark.[32]

It was certainly not the apparently political side of the High Church tradition that first attracted Pusey. It was the theological and above all, spiritual emphasis of the Movement that captured him. Significantly, what can be taken as his formal adhesion to the Tract party—his contribution of a *Tract for the Times* on fasting—illustrated this. His major contributions to the series were all on explicitly religious themes: fasting, baptism, the Eucharist, the rule of faith. His part in the creation of the *Library of the Fathers* again symbolized his chief priorities. Indeed, had the new Movement really only been another aspect of Tory High Churchmanship designed to defend the status quo in Church and State, he would never have joined it. However, he soon felt the fatuity of the charges of Liberals such as Arnold, that the Tractarians were but the Jacobites and 'Church Tories' resurrected.[33] As Pusey told his brother Philip, after reading an early criticism of the Tractarians in the evangelical *Christian Observer* based on these charges:

It has wholly mistaken the object of the so-called Oxford Tracts, which are directed wholly to things spiritual, and concern themselves not at all with anything which can be called the temporals of the church.[34]

Not surprisingly, to Newman, Froude and Keble, Pusey appeared clearly to be an 'Apostolical' rather than a 'Z' in his view of the establishment. Like them, he could see the crisis of 1833 not as one of unrelieved gloom and foreboding as it appeared to Palmer of Worcester, but rather, as a blessing in disguise, the opportunity 'to set the Church free'. Thus, Pusey was most anxious in his work on cathedral institutions, not to appear as the mere Tory apologist for all the real ecclesiastical abuses of establishment, the mere shallow defender of every entrenched privilege and vested interest.[35] Appointments to cathedral stalls, he insisted, had to be made on very different criteria from those which had guided advisers to the Crown in the earlier Hanoverian era. Citing even the latitudinarian Bishop Warburton's disapproval of damaging political influence on the Church, Pusey maintained that 'the time past has been long enough to degrade the service of God, and make offices appointed for His honour subservient only to the momentary and often selfish strife of worldly politics'.[36]

In his private correspondence as well as published writings, Pusey often referred to ministerial interference in spiritual affairs as the single greatest threat to the Church. Like Froude, he was prepared to envisage a repeal of the old statute of *praemunire* against the clergy, as a possible remedy. It was in this uncompromising spirit that he wrote to Manning in 1837:

> What think you of a petition to repeal the 'praemunire'? It is well when a party is pushed and the game going hard, to get the attack if you can. It is too, abominable law: its repeal could not be refused, and it would increase the sense of responsibility of the clergy much.[37]

Moreover, there was a thread of continuity here with his earlier attitude to the Test and Corporation Acts, in Pusey's horror of any apparent 'profanation' of religious offices for secular ends. For just as he had resented the way in which the sacrament of the Eucharist had been, in effect, made a test for civil office, so he now set out to oppose the whole system of ecclesiastical advisers making political views a test of religious office as 'a prostitution of the holy office of a bishop'.[38] For the active part which Pusey played in the Oxford campaign to remove Dr Hampden from the chair of Regius Professor of Divinity to which he was appointed by Lord Melbourne in 1836, on the grounds of religious heterodoxy contained in his *Bampton Lectures* of four years earlier, reflected this burning resentment at unsuitable political appointments.

What Pusey most feared was that politicians, whether Whig or Tory, would go on appointing to every vacant see, bishops who would not be fully disposed to resist whatever they might propose, such as even an alteration in the liturgy to placate and comprehend Dissenters. Thus, in 1837, Pusey was in full agreement with Manning in maintaining that 'the Church has a right to have bishops after her own mind, and not to have others thrust upon her'.[39] The equivocal role that bishops such as Blomfield and Maltby appeared to play in abetting the reforms proposed by the Ecclesiastical Commission first set up in 1835, gave point to Pusey's fears. However, still more alarming from a High Church point of view, was the apparent majority given to laymen on the commission. Condemning this majority in a very different tone from what he would have employed in 1828, as 'a tribute to the liberalism of the day', Pusey was led to ask:

> What had laymen to do with 'the more equal distribution of episcopal duties', or how should they know in what way 'cathedral and collegiate churches might be rendered most conducive to the episcopacy of the Church?' Duties can only be thoroughly understood practically, 'episcopal duties' by bishops.[40]

Thus far, Pusey unreservedly took up the characteristically Tractarian view of an embattled church fighting for its spiritual integrity against the tyrannical meddling of a utilitarian, secular-minded state. The Ecclesiastical Commission was but one more engine of this tyranny. The measures that it pushed through, such as the proposed extinction of the diocese of Man, could only be roundly condemned as 'Erastian acts'.[41]

Pusey's paramount concern for the spiritual rights of the Church and his fears at the apparent compromises inherent in the Church–State connection in England, predisposed him to look with favour upon episcopal branches of the Church Catholic that were not established, and had no ties with the civil power. Thus, the stand made by the Nonjurors in the previous century, and especially the witness of the Scottish Episcopal Church, had a profound appeal for him. The latter, on account of its sufferings and persecution at the hands of the English government, cast something of a spell over him, as it did over other Tractarian leaders. Above all, the fact that the Scottish Church in the previous century had appeared to draw closer towards the Tractarian ideal of the primitive Church in liturgical and sacramental teaching, as a result of her freedom from state control, was not lost upon him. As he remarked in his *Letter to the Archbishop of Canterbury* in 1842:

> It pleased God, as it seemed, almost to undo our work, that He might bring it about in His; He employed what was good in the Scottish church, as the means of purifying and restoring her; He rent from her all human aid, left her to be trodden under the foot of men, to be persecuted by the state, almost forgotten by ourselves; but a silent witness to truths which were fading among us; and now by a century of severe oppression and privation He has moulded our premature work to be a fit instrument of His Providence.[42]

Pusey's admiration for the 'primitive' witness of the disestablished Scottish Episcopal Church, led him to take an active part in promoting her interests through such schemes as the foundation of Trinity College, Glenalmond, as a school and seminary for episcopal clergy. It also led him to defend the Scottish Communion Office against attempts to remove it from its place of primary authority in favour of what he considered the less 'primitive' English Communion rite.[43]

Pusey's antipathy to the existing terms of the Church–State relationship in England was certainly heightened by the recognition and patronage afforded to Presbyterianism as the established church in Scotland. As he complained to Gladstone's friend, the Tractarian lawyer, James Hope in 1837:

> Our English politicians have much embarrassed themselves (e.g. Sir R. Peel) with the Scotch Kirk, as indeed the union with Scotland while the Kirk was established, has, I suppose been very injurious to the church. . . . The identification of

the interests of the two establishments I think, works serious
mischief; making people think our church only an establishment, and theirs altogether a sound church, because established. Hence one hears our clergymen talk of '*The* Scotch
Church' meaning thereby not their own Apostolic church,
but that which has displaced it.[44]

Pusey could have cited the example of the remarkably favourable reception given by English churchmen as well as politicians, to the abstract case for establishment put by the Scotch
presbyterian divine, Thomas Chalmers, in a popular series of
lectures, in which as Gladstone recalled, he 'flogged the
apostolical succession grievously, seven bishops sitting below
him . . . incessantly bobbing assent'.[45] Nevertheless, if one
realizes that Chalmers at least allowed the dogmatic principle,
albeit in the form of what he called 'evangelical protestantism'
so as to include Presbyterianism in Scotland as well as
Anglicanism in England, to be the basis of his defence of
establishment,[46] his views can be seen to be an advance on the
principles of Warburton and Paley. Chalmers won widespread
support from conservative Anglican churchmen precisely
because he rejected mere utility as a guide. It was in this spirit
that he had written to congratulate Pusey on his work on
cathedral institutions, and lamented that he feared 'lest every
such argument as you employ may well be thrown away on this
grossly utilitarian age'.[47] Not surprisingly, Gladstone was
especially alive to the force of Chalmers's arguments, in spite of
profound differences over the question of episcopacy.[48] However, to all the Tractarians, and not least to Pusey, they were
deeply distasteful.

Pusey's and Gladstone's paths were in a sense to cross in their
respective views on Church and State. At this time, Pusey
shared the Tractarian suspicion of Gladstone the politician
being too ready to explain away the more obvious shortcomings
of the Church–State union. For instance, while Gladstone
himself worked tirelessly on behalf of the Trinity College,
Glenalmond scheme,[49] and lost no opportunity in aiding the
Scottish Episcopal Church whenever he could,[50] even he made
apologies for the Presbyterian church being the establishment in

Scotland. Thus, to the dismay of Pusey and the Tractarians as a whole, Gladstone was reluctantly prepared to concede that the Scottish establishment ought to be supported positively, even though not apostolical, on the grounds that it represented a force for 'righteousness' and practical good.[51] As a result, Keble who, like Pusey, warmly appreciated Gladstone's stand for church principles in parliament and within the Conservative party, took sharp issue with him in his review of *The State in its Relations with the Church*. For in a striking passage, with which Pusey would have readily agreed, Keble explained such apparent blemishes in Gladstone's theory, by the fact that:

> the life of a statesman must of necessity be spent very much in calculations of expediency, and in measuring things by their visible results: and the habit of thought so generated may sometimes be unfavourable to that particular exercise of faith, the necessity of which in all church questions we have now tried to point out . . . it may do us all good to recollect that there has once been an Athanasius who 'stood against the world, and prevailed', and that he did so, chiefly by disregarding results when revealed rules and principles were at stake.[52]

Pusey steadily drifted ever further away from the world of society, the court, and church organization. His instinct was that churchmen should have nothing to do with politics. The role of Peel and the Conservative government, first in actually creating the Ecclesiastical Commission in 1835, and then in not doing more to help the church between 1841 and 1846, filled him with disillusion. Gladstone's disillusionment led him to change his mind over the Maynooth question, on the ground that the old establishment principle was no longer tenable, that religious pluralism was inevitable and that the Church could best be 'set free' by cutting her loose from remaining constitutional safeguards.[53] In taking this line, Gladstone attracted the fury of not only 'ultra-protestants' but such conservative High Churchmen as Christopher Wordsworth junior and William Palmer. For the latter, the battle of 1833 was being fought over once more. Like the opposition to the suppression of the Irish bishoprics, they regarded the opposition to the proposed extension of a government grant to the Roman Catholic seminary at Maynooth, as destructive of the basis of the Church–State union, an act of political expediency and erastianism.[54] As Wordsworth put it, the Church of Ireland had been 'placed in a state of schism by an act of the State'.[55] However, Pusey had as little time for such arguments as had Gladstone after his change of heart. It was Pusey who could claim consistency here, since in 1845 he was adopting his original refusal in 1829 to identify the interests of the church exclusively with the establishment and existing constitutional settlement. As he told his brother, Philip, at this time, 'I do not see anything amiss, or any principle violated in doing anything positive for the Roman Catholics'.[56] Moreover, he hit upon a sensitive nerve, when he reminded those who inveighed against the measure as an act of spoliation and sacrilege, that many of them themselves saw nothing wrong in the sixteenth century spoliation of church property. As he remarked:

> The spoliation of monasteries, which was a real robbery of the poor . . . is as bad as any one can make out the transfer of church property in Ireland. Let people come to such work with clean hands. If the Dukes who possess church property, Whig or Conservative, would give up what no one can doubt was wrongfully given them, they may say what they will about the church in Ireland.[57]

Other measures all served to increase Pusey's disillusionment with the existing working of the Church–State union. For instance, Lord John Russell's elevation of Hampden to the see of Hereford in 1847, in the face of vigorous episcopal protest, rekindled the earlier campaign of 1836 and the whole principle of allowing the Church the right to choose her own bishops. Pusey was in earnest on this question, and lost patience with the apparent readiness of some old High Churchmen, such as Edward Churton, not to press matters to a head. As he complained to Churton, 'we have had too much of "let alone" '.[58] However, it was the Gorham Judgement that really opened up the whole question in an acute form. Bishop Phillpotts had refused to institute George Cornelius Gorham to the living of Brampford Speke on account of what he deemed to be heterodox views on baptism. The case had gone to the Court of Arches which decided against Gorham and upheld the doctrine of baptismal regeneration. It was not simply the fact that this decision was overturned on appeal that shocked High Churchmen, but that it was the Judicial Committee of the Privy Council that had done so. After the abolition of the Roman jurisdiction, such cases had been originally tried by the Court of Delegates, which contained a preponderance of bishops and ecclesiastical lawyers. During the course of the eighteenth century, this episcopal element was gradually lost. In 1832, jurisdiction was transferred to the Privy Council. An Act of 1840 allowed bishops who were privy counsellors to sit, if cases were ecclesiastical. However, no distinction was drawn between doctrinal and other ecclesiastical matters. As Chadwick has observed, the consequence of this subtle legal change was that:

> it removed the final appeal from a court where the judges, even when junior and inexperienced, were trained in the canon and civil law; and transferred it to a court where some of the judges, though vastly more eminent, were less accustomed to the system of ecclesiastical courts.[59]

Pusey, along with other Tractarians such as Hope and Manning, responded quickly to meet this challenge, with petitions, sermons and declarations. In his speech at the great protest rally of churchmen at the Freemasons' Hall on 23 July, 1850, and in his work on the *Royal Supremacy*, Pusey castigated the apparent abuse of the civil power involved. As he put it in his speech,

> We stand . . . where two roads part, the way of the world and the way of the Church; the way of man and the way of God: the way it may be of earthly loss and heavenly gain, or the way of earthly prosperity and spiritual loss. For if the state will not, as Magna Carta pledges it, allow that 'the Church should have liberties inviolate', we must ask that the state will set us free from itself, and go forth, as Abraham, not knowing whither he went, poor as to this world's goods, but rich with the blessing of that seed in whom all the nations of the earth shall be blessed.[60]

The example of episcopal Scotland was again implicit here, and in his work on the *Royal Supremacy* written at this time, Pusey invoked those of the reviving Church of France and the Church in the United States as the path that the Church of England might, some day, have to follow.[61] In fact, by the mid-1860s, Pusey's disillusionment had become such that, like Gladstone before him, he had come to the conclusion that what he called 'denominationalism' might be a lesser evil than the continuance of establishment in its existing form. Certainly, he felt this as regards the Irish Church, and supported Gladstone's proposal to disestablish that Church. As he told Gladstone,

> I had long seen that things were driving to some sort of Denominationalism in lieu of Establishments, i.e. since the Church had lost so many of her children through her neglect, it was probable that she should be punished, at least temporally.[62]

Yet, there was another side to Pusey's teaching on Church and State that found repeated expression throughout these years. It has not been explained satisfactorily, and it needs explaining. For a careful examination of his work on the Supremacy in 1850, which as its full title suggests, was an actual defence of it and of the union of Church and State, reveals that Pusey was attacking the rising anti-establishment mentality of many followers of the Oxford Movement, just as much as the erastianism of the day. He was especially critical of the reaction of Manning, Hope, Henry Wilberforce, Dodsworth, T.W. Allies and William Maskell, to the Gorham Judgement. We will consider this aspect of Pusey's defence of Church and State against those who in clamouring for a separation, claimed to be but following out the logic of the Movement of 1833. However, to understand it, one has to go back. For this side of Pusey's 'political' thought was part of his original maturing Tractarianism in the mid-1830s, and owed much to Keble. It entailed the adoption, not repudiation, of the underlying spiritual and moral temper of that traditional High Church Toryism that had animated the Nonjurors and the Hutchinsonians.

Pusey never had to 'sing farewell to Toryism'. His emergence as a Tractarian entailed an embracing of it. The apparent

275

paradox is not as great as it might seem. A striking passage in a letter of Pusey's to Churton in 1865 has been cited to demonstrate Pusey's own 'farewell to Toryism'. Pusey told Churton,

> I could have been a Tory; but 1830 ended Toryism. I could not be a mere Conservative, i.e. I could not bind myself, or risk the future of the Church on the fidelity or wisdom of persons whose principle it is to keep what they think they can, and part with the rest.[63]

For the real implication of this passage, was that Pusey actually regarded his religious progress into a leader of the new Movement in the 1830s as a kind of substitute for that deeper Toryism as a system of moral and religious principles governing all political action. He rightly sensed that it was almost impossible to forge these principles into political reality after 1828–33. Yet, though external political conditions were changed, and as the Tractarians constantly reiterated, party politics was no longer a fitting forum for the pursuit of High Church principles, the underlying temper of the old Toryism came to exert a new appeal for Pusey. It was here that Keble's influence was paramount. Keble's deeply-held Toryism was of a totally different character from the political Toryism of popular caricature, whether of Lord Eldon's 'ultra' variant, or still less, the new, more liberal 'Conservatism' of Peel. It was the latter that Pusey was really attacking in the above passage, not Keble's brand of Toryism. It was this that had motivated Keble in 1829, and this that Pusey had then totally misunderstood. He was to feel that he knew better now.

As the controversy of 1829 illustrated, for Keble, the differences between Tory and Whig or Liberal, were far more than merely political in the party sense of the term. They implied an underlying moral difference. As Liddon justly observed:

> Keble's moral temper led him to view reform and change with distrust, if not with aversion: his faith in God's presence and guidance made all high-handed self-willed action on man's part appear more or less irreverent.[64]

It was not that politics and the life of a politician was somehow intrinsically profane. On the contrary, they were sacred. Precisely because of this, political action and matters of state had to be conducted in faithful accordance with religious principle, eschewing hasty, self-willed reform and envincing a readiness to be patient, humble and to submit to constituted authority in Church and State as representative of God's law. As Keble advanced theologically, in sympathy with Newman and the direction of the Movement, he never lost this political temper, which many later exponents of Anglo-Catholicism have found difficult to explain and have found little to their taste. For instance, as late as 1841, Keble devoted a review in *The British Critic* to castigating not simply the lax theology but what he regarded as the lax politics of the school of Warburton in the previous century. The latter's 'proud spirited' abstract notions of liberty were deemed to spring from the same false source as its claims for freedom of religious enquiry and doctrinal latitude. It was a spirit that he also saw and lamented even in the protestant Tory eulogizers of the old constitution. As Keble put it in the above review:

> in this overweening talk of human dignity and civil liberty, Warburton was but following the fashionable quasi-idolatry of that era; perhaps we might say, of our country, for a century and a half: a superstition not confined to any one school in theology.[65]

Significantly, Keble excepted not only the Nonjurors but also the Oxford Hutchinsonians from this verdict. For him, the former especially had demonstrated the true spirit of primitive Christians in first passively obeying James II and then at the Revolution refusing to compromise their principles and suffering for conscience's sake. Clearly, Passive Obedience though enshrined in the *Homilies* and standard teaching of the Caroline Divines, was still to be the only true model for a churchman in politics in the 1830s. It was a lesson that Pusey readily imbibed and took to heart.

Apart from this moral emphasis, Keble's Toryism was infused by a romantic, if not mystical reverence for the past. In this outlook, a veneration for the House of Stuart and the 'Royal Martyr', Charles I, was a potent symbol.[66] It was characteristic that Pusey should acknowledge his conversion to this brand of Toryism as a result of Keble's influence, by reference to his changed attitude to those cult symbols. As he wrote movingly to Keble in November 1837,

> It was at Fairford, many years ago, when I was thoughtlessly or rather I must say confidently taking for granted that the Stuarts were rightly dethroned, that I heard for the first time a hint to the contrary from you; your seriousness was an intended reproof to my petulant expression about it, and so it stuck by me, although it was some time before it took root, and burst through all the clouds placed upon it.[67]

Pusey's 5 November sermon in 1837, *Patience and Confidence the Strength of the Church*, symbolized by its dedication to Keble, represented the fruit of the latter's teaching on him.

At one level, the sermon appears merely political—quite untypical of Pusey, an anomaly utterly out of tune with the rest of his writings. Contemporary critics helped to foster this impression. The apparent repudiation of the 'Glorious Revolution' of 1688, led many to compare it to Sacheverell's fiery sermon of 1709, *In peril among false brethren*[68] which had led to his impeachment by the Whig ministers of the day. Moreover, the line of continuity seemed to run still wider. For just as Whig latitudinarians such as Warburton and Samuel Parr had denounced the Tory politics of the sermons of George Horne and Bishop Horsley, in the 1760s and 1790s respectively, so Arnold, in January 1838, was complaining that Pusey had quoted texts 'which appear to advocate pure despotism'.[69] However, Arnold misrepresented Tractarian 'political' as much as sacramental teaching. It is true that Pusey cited such authorities as Filmer, Overall's *Convocation Book*, Sanderson and Bishop Horsley, in favour of what he called the 'high doctrine of Non-resistance',[70] but it was moral and religious lessons, not party political points that concerned him.

Pusey's 5 November sermon was fully in accord with his other apparently more spiritual writings, and deserves to be treated as being as much integral to early Tractarianism as his Tracts on Baptism and fasting. Pusey could have readily echoed Newman's comment to Miss Giberne in 1837, 'We have

nothing to hope or fear from Whig or Conservative governments. We must trust to our own ethos'.[71] It was precisely this
trusting in the 'primitive' ethos of humility, resignation,
patience and obedience, that was the whole theme of Pusey's
teaching as bequeathed from Keble. Thus, those who accused
Pusey of wishing to restore the Stuarts entirely missed the point.
As Pusey made clear:

> With regard to the special instance of the English revolution
> of 1688, the question is now happily of practical importance
> only, as relates to men's feelings and principles, not to any
> political mode of acting.[72]

Pusey very closely linked the political doctrines always associated with the High Anglican tradition, to religious principles
and ways of acting. As he put it:

> Non-resistance or passive obedience, in the sense to which
> they are generally limited, are but two sides of the same
> doctrine, and, together, are only a particular application of a
> general principle. In religion, it is faith; under misfortune, it
> is resignation; under trial, it is patient waiting for the end;
> amid provocation, it is gentleness; amid afronts, meekness;
> amid injuries, it is endurance; towards enemies, non-requital;
> towards railing, it is 'not answering again'; to parents, it is
> filial obedience; to superiors, respect; to authorities, unques-
> tioning submission; towards civil government, it is obedi-
> ence upon principle not only when it costs nothing . . . but
> when it costs something.[73]

Given the advocacy of such a temper, Pusey had as little time as
Keble for the spirit in which even many 'ultra-Tories' lauded
1688, still less for 'mere Conservatives' ready to sacrifice deeper
truths for temporal emoluments. Pusey certainly had such
Tories in mind when he drew a distinction between, 'the
debates, doubts and palliations of those who were concerned in
it . . . [and the] exulting, or (which is more) the matter-of-
course way, in which the "glorious Revolution" is now spoken
of'.[74] On the other hand, the Nonjurors and Scottish Episcopa-
lians presented a worthy contrast. Pusey would have readily
agreed with William Copeland's comparison of 'men like

Archbishop Sancroft and Ken and Kettlewell, with the cold heartedness and semi-infidel Conservatism of many of the maintainers of our so-called happy establishment'.[75]

Another aspect of the religious Toryism which Pusey learnt from Keble was the sacral, almost mystical view of monarchy that led Keble to describe kings as the 'anointed of the Lord, a living type, of the supreme dominion of Jesus Christ'.[76] It was this high religious feeling that had always infused a traditional High Churchman's devotion to the Royal Supremacy. In accord with the famous text from Isaiah, 'Kings shall be thy nursing fathers, and Queens, thy nursing mothers' the monarch was deemed to be bound by his Coronation Oath in the service of the Church. As such, this theory of the Supremacy, even though it accepted interference in matters ecclesiastical, was not erastian. On the contrary, it was designed to counteract the purely erastian concept of a 'parliamentary Church' held by Whig latitudinarian divines. As John Reeves, a member of the 'Hackney Phalanx', put it, the monarch was obliged

> to watch over any laws, that may be proposed to him by his Parliament, for alteration in church matters, with more conscientious rectitude, than he exercises on other occasions of legislation.[77]

With Convocation in abeyance, parliament might legislate solely for the Church but only under the watchful and protective eye of the monarch. According to Reeves,

> The King is thus made more peculiarly the guardian of the church, than he is of the state; and happily, he can completely execute this office by himself, without the aid of the many advisers who are necessary towards the conduct of civil affairs.[78]

Clearly, this was the pre-1832 ideal for High Churchmen.

The early Tractarians did not readily abandon this position. Even for Newman at first, the Royal Supremacy was not deemed to be inimical to the spiritual rights of the Church. On the contrary, it was regarded as a bulwark of those rights. Thus, when parliament appeared to be enacting laws that violated the

Church's sacred rights in 1833, he appealed to William IV as 'Defender of the Faith'. As he put it,

> If it be said that the Act of Settlement secures to the people certain liberties, I reply that the Coronation oath has secured to the Church its liberties also to the utter annulment of all former precedents of tyranny—and that we stand by that oath as our law as well as our Sovereign's sanction and acknowledgment of it, and that any power in the state that innovates on the spirit of that oath tyrannises over us.[79]

When it became clear that William IV was not going to stand by his oath in the way they expected, Newman and other Tractarians became very disillusioned. Pusey shared to an extent in this disillusion, being critical of William IV's acquiescence in the Ecclesiastical Commission.[80] However, it was now that the temper of patience and resignation which he was learning from Keble, led him to continue to rest his hopes on the Crown fulfilling its divinely-ordained role of 'nursing-father'.

Pusey expounded this theme in several sermons at this time. For instance, when preaching on behalf of the SPG in 1838, he stressed the royal as well as apostolical basis of true missionary enterprise, the State's as well as the Church's integral role in it. As he put it:

> Kings and queens should be attendants upon the Church, in whose blessings they themselves share, and wherein God has placed them in an eminent post, to provide for her welfare . . . 'Kings shall be', saith God, 'thy nursing fathers, and their queens thy nursing mothers' . . . The princes of this world shall reverence the Church, and shall find their glory and their joy in ministering to her necessities.[81]

What Pusey was critical of, was not the State's meddling in the Church *per se*, but her failure positively to fulfil her duties of protection and succour. For instance, he criticized the neglect of the Church by the State in the eighteenth century, as when she failed to introduce episcopacy to America while the latter was a British colony. In fact, the old theme of American Loyalists, such as Jonathan Boucher, that this failure helped to contribute

281

to the rebellion, was reiterated by Pusey in the same sermon, when he lamented:

> Far different might the relations of that our great colony of the United States have been . . . had our state then known her duties to her colonies or to the church.[82]

Pusey was so critical of ministerial interference in church matters both in the past and present, precisely because he felt that it stifled and checked the true role of the Crown as a 'nursing father'. As Pusey complained:

> Much as the members of . . . [the] church must revere the virtues and blessed influence of George the Third, it is still certain that even he could not undo the evil which had been done by the ministers of the two first sovereigns of his line.[83]

Moreover, Pusey's desire for a veto by the chapter and consecrating bishop in the case of bad nominations was not intended to restrict the due exercise of royal authority. He agreed with Keble's view:

> His Majesty's Prerogative would gain more than it would lose by taking from him the nominal appointment and giving the real one to that party who we know are always surest to stand by him.[84]

Furthermore, Pusey's new found admiration for the old ideal of the Church–State union working in unison under effective royal authority, led him to pray and hope for its return in a spirit of patience and resignation, rather than to seek refuge in idolizing Hildebrand and Becket, as Froude and other Tractarians were to do. Thus, while he could complain to Samuel Wilberforce that the role of politicians as ecclesiastical advisers was prostituting the office of bishop, he could take comfort in the fact that, 'their interference grew only with the weakness of the House of Hanover, and even Pitt could not carry his own Archbishop of Canterbury (Tomline)'.[85] Pusey made the same point more forcefully in a letter to Gladstone at this time, wherein he remarked;

> though ministers were oftentimes (of old also) troublesome,

worldly and interfering, yet this modern plan, wherein ministers are virtually the patrons, and the king a cypher, did not come in until the middle of the last century: so I see not why we should not hope that with a struggle we might again recover the old system.[86]

The continued failure of Peel's government to set the clock back and its sanctioning of further encroachments on the Church, while it induced Pusey's strictures on the abuse of the civil power, never led him to question its legitimate and rightful use. The temper of patience, confidence and resignation, led him to part company with Gladstone, after the latter's change of attitude in the mid-1840s. For Pusey's moral temper allowed him to cling to various bulwarks of the old establishment principle, which Gladstone under the motivation of liberal theories of social justice and toleration, was increasingly happy to allow to fall. It was not the Maynooth question on which they broadly agreed, but their respective attitudes to Lord John Russell's Bill of 1847 for the removal of the civil and political disabilities of the Jews, that brought out this difference. Gladstone at once intimated to Pusey that he felt compelled to support the bill. His attitude was akin to that of his friend, James Hope, who told him:

> On the Jewish question, my bigotry makes me liberal. To symbolise the christianity of the House of Commons in its present form is to substitute a new church and creed for the old catholic one, and as this is a delusion I would do nothing to countenance it. . . . Better have the legislature declared what it really is—not professedly christian, and then let the church claim those rights and that independence which nothing but the presence of christianity can entitle the legislature to withhold from it. In this view, the emancipation of the Jews must tend to that of the church, and at any rate a 'sham' will be discarded.[87]

Old High Churchmen were scathing about this type of argument. As Christopher Wordsworth's brother, Charles, later commented,

> Is not this to do evil that good may come? Or, taking lower

283

ground, is it not reasonable to conclude that the worse the House of Commons is made, the worse are likely to be our church appointments?[88]

Pusey identified wholeheartedly with such old high church grounds of complaint. He strongly opposed not only Gladstone's and Hope's action, but still more, their apparently cynical reasons for so acting. For on hearing of Gladstone's support for the bill, Pusey immediately sent him what Liddon described as 'an almost violent protest', in which he even expressed regret at having voted for him in the University election earlier that year. As he put it:

> You would put great difficulties in the way of those who wish or are bound to pray for the Parliament as Christian: I could pray for it only as apostate, and as having prepared by this step for the coming of Antichrist. . . . Had I known that you would have joined in what I account an anti-christian measure, I could not have helped to put you in a position which would have led to such a result. I would rather, for your own soul's sake, that you had been out of Parliament.[89]

Pusey's view was utterly consistent with his deep-rooted Tory conviction of the divine origin of the State and its sacred duties towards the Church. He vigorously opposed the measure because he felt it needlessly removed another vital plank not so much of establishment but of the whole principle of a Christian as opposed to infidel or secular State. In short, it went against what Liddon called Pusey's enduring belief 'that government, like everything else, should be conducted on purely Christian principles'. The Deceased Wife's Sister Bill was another occasion for Pusey to give expression to this conviction. Gladstone opposed the measure as strongly as Pusey, but the latter felt the consequences for the Church–State ideal much more keenly. He took no comfort in it as possibly rending the two further apart. As he told Gladstone with real sorrow:

> I see, with regret, each link of the old system broken, both with regard to the state . . . and to the church; to the state, because it is dropping the relation on which our prayers for Parliament are founded, and assuming a nondescript

character which will in the end be infidel; and to the church, because having been so long forbidden in any way to act for herself, she is disabled from doing so now through long disuse.[90]

It was this element in Pusey's attitude to Church and State that explains his differences from many other advanced Tractarians in responding to the Gorham Judgement. It was in 1850 that Newman was maintaining in public lectures that the origin and whole direction of the Movement of 1833 was against the idea of a national Church or establishment. Anglo-Catholics, such as John Mason Neale, might disagree with Newman's conclusion that Rome was the terminus, but nonetheless agreed in condemning the old Tory High Church tradition, even in its Laudian form, for its 'fearful Erastianism'.[91] The impact of the Gorham Judgement undoubtedly enhanced this trend among advanced high churchmen. It had this effect on Manning, Hope, Henry and Robert Wilberforce, and Bishop Phillpott's own chaplain, William Maskell. Both Henry Wilberforce and Manning considered that the whole Anglo-Catholic position would be undermined if the Church were to accept the verdict of the Privy Council, whether favourable or unfavourable. As Manning observed to Robert Wilberforce in December 1849,

> I cannot for the life of me feel that it makes personally to me much difference which way it goes. The fact that such a case is to be decided by such a court is the one great symptom which seems far to outweigh the consideration which way they may decide it.[92]

Wilberforce likewise, actually feared a favourable decision more than an heretical one, because it might cause churchmen to overlook the real character of the court that had made the decision.

When the decision did finally go against the High Church party, Manning suddenly confessed that his 'eyes were opened' as to what he now regarded as the original and inherent erastianism of the Church of England. As he made clear in a letter to Samuel Wilberforce at this time, his allegiance to the English Church and its whole system of relations with the State, had always been granted on his part, by the assumption that the Royal Supremacy was purely civil in its bearing. He denied that it was in 'any sense spiritual, or ecclesiastical, understanding that word to mean concurrent or mixed spiritual jurisdiction'.[93] For Hope also, the Gorham appeal seemed no different in principle to all previous appeals on matters ecclesiastical. He was now convinced that the ultimate jurisdiction in spiritual matters had lain with the Crown ever since the Reformation. The Gorham appeal merely brought to light what had been implicit in the Royal Supremacy *ab initio*.[94] Thus, it was not enough simply to put the clock back to before 1828–33. There had to be a return to the state of the Common law as it affected relations between Church and Crown in the period prior to 1530. William Maskell was equally intransigent on this point. For him, the Judicial Committee was 'nothing more than the necessary organ of the Royal Supremacy as established by the statutes of Henry VIII and Elizabeth'.[95] Such a court, even if composed of bishops, had no right to sit in judgement on such a question. Such arguments and reasoning struck at the very roots of the old High Church tradition. Old High Churchmen responded accordingly.

In making this response, old High Churchmen were not being merely complacent. They were thoroughly alarmed by the doctrinal implications of the Gorham Judgement. Moreover, they were unhappy at the way in which the Supremacy was now being made to operate. For instance, Palmer of Worcester had much less sympathy than is often assumed, with the merely *laudator temporis acti* group among the old High Church party, complaining to Gladstone in 1850 that, 'men are now arguing about the Royal Supremacy as if the Crown were now in the state, or its powers were influenced by the same religious beliefs, as in the time of Elizabeth or James'.[96] Nevertheless, the abuse of the Supremacy did not invalidate its traditional role, and not only Palmer but Gladstone strongly defended it against the arguments of Manning and Maskell. Gladstone argued in favour of a strictly corrective appellate jurisdiction of the Crown in matters spiritual as a legacy of the English Reformation that was perfectly in accord with Catholic principle and practice.[97] It was only the corruption of the principle in later times that was to be lamented. Thus, Gladstone could tell Manning in April 1850 that:

> after the ordeal of this particular time . . . I feel better pleased with the Reformation in regard to the Supremacy than at former times: but also much more sensible of the drifting of the church since, away from the range of her constitutional securities.[98]

Benjamin Harrison was another old High Churchman of the younger generation who forcefully argued for this view, insisting that, 'the present Court of Appeal . . . was at variance with the ancient principles and constitutional exercise of the Royal Supremacy in the Church of England'.[99] The real significance of Pusey's attitude to the Gorham Judgement is that it was with the old High Church view of the Supremacy and role of the civil power that he took his stand, in repudiation of the advanced Tractarian position.

The context of Pusey's consistent teaching for the previous fifteen years renders his attitude both intelligible and consistent. Prior to the actual Gorham Judgement, Pusey had been at pains in private correspondence to refute the arguments of Manning and Wilberforce. He quoted at length the original Acts of Henry VIII, Edward VI and Queen Elizabeth I, to demonstrate how the Royal Supremacy initially was aimed at overruling the jurisdiction of the see of Rome and was not intended to stretch the power of any court beyond the 'ancient jurisdiction of the temporal sovereign'.[100] The power of determining heresy had not been left to the temporal sovereign. Thus, while the Judicial Committee of the Privy Council was quite inappropriate to decide such a case, this was a cause for reforming it. It did not warrant strictures against the whole ancient system of appellate royal jurisdiction as *per se* erastian. After the court had decided in favour of Gorham, Pusey did not shift from this position. In the same speech of 23 July at the Freemasons' Hall in which he attacked the abuse of the civil power, he also reminded his High Church audience that the Reformation statutes had not intended to make the State the judge in matters of Christian doctrine. Rather, those statutes had been rightly designed to protect individuals against any temporal injustice that might be inflicted upon them by ecclesiastical courts.[101] It was only the Acts of 1833 and 1834 that had introduced an entirely new situation, by unintentionally placing the decision of doctrinal questions in the hands of a final Court of Appeal which was really constituted for other purposes.

Pusey's utter rejection of the line of argument of Manning, Maskell and Allies, actually caused him to cease for a time from protesting about the Judgement and to turn on the protestors instead. This is really why he set about his work on *The Royal Supremacy not an Arbitrary Authority* in 1850. In essence, the work entailed a repudiation of those Hildebrandine notions of church absolutism that Froude had bequeathed to the Movement. In the spirit of High Churchmen of an earlier age such as George Horne, John Reeves and other members of the 'Hackney Phalanx', Pusey attacked those theories of Church and State that denied to the latter those rights which, with due safeguards, had been acknowledged in the early Church. As Liddon explained, the work 'was immediately addressed to those who held that any kind of Royal Supremacy was inconsistent with the precedents and principles of christian antiquity'.[102] Whereas Maskell argued that any royal control over ecclesiastical affairs, even when exercised through the episcopate, was indefensible, Pusey showed that emperors in early times and Anglo-Saxon kings did just this. They summoned courts and church synods, nominated episcopal judges and even sometimes suspended the judgement of a council. As he put it, after surveying the Church-State relations of antiquity,

> The principle which seems to me to run throughout these precedents is this; that the civil power called into action, regulated at times, limited, controlled, enforced by civil sanction the authority of the church, or restrained it, that it should not act independently of itself; but hardly acted itself directly, or usurped the church's place.

Thus, the Reformation introduced no novelty or innovation in Church–State relations, but only a restoration. For Pusey argued that:

> what Henry VIII and Queen Elizabeth claimed, and what

288

eminent lawyers have affirmed to be conceded, and what the Church meant to concede, was no other than the ancient prerogative of the Crown, which had been invaded, it was alleged, by the authority claimed by the Pope.[103]

Pusey insisted that his view of royal power in church matters was positive, and that it was no more erastian than the old High Church theory propounded by the Nonjurors and the Hutchinsonians had been. As he put it:

> I did not wish to maintain the prerogative of the Crown, as a mere defence of the present position of the English church. . . . On the other hand, being in a body which has owned the ancient authority of the Crown, it was my duty to observe such precedents as should justify the principles which the Church had conceded.[104]

The positive aspect, above all, flowed from Pusey's continued adherence to the sacral notion of kingship with its attendant image of the 'nursing father'. To prove his point, he appealed to the use of the title 'Vicar of Christ', as accorded to monarchs by King Edgar and 'St Edward the Confessor'. Like George Horne, his ideal remained the 'Christian King'.[105] The office of kingship was no less holy than that of a bishop. Any present failure to live up to past practice did not invalidate the ideal.

Of course, it was the Church's duty to clamour for the restoration of her spiritual rights, whether in the form of Convocation or a synod of bishops. However, a limited Supremacy with a restriction of ministerial interference could best safeguard such rights. Thus, Pusey returned again to the theme of his argument in the mid-1830s: the monarch's role would be enhanced by allowing the Church greater freedom from ministerial control. As he put it:

> The advisers of the Crown must know that its authority is mainly upheld by the Church. It has been so all along in its history. The Church gladly accepts a rightful Supremacy. To accept a wrongful one, would be falsehood to the Crown itself.[106]

It was Lord John Russell, not the High Churchman, who posed

the greatest threat not simply to the Church but the Crown. Pusey would have regarded the verdict of a reviewer in *The English Churchman* as exactly his own view:

> circumstances have forced advisers upon her [i.e. the Queen] who have not the church's welfare at heart, and, in fact, do not understand what the just claims of the church really are . . . so that practically the supreme power over the church instead of being, as the law requires, the sovereign of the realm, is a mixed body of persons of all shades of opinion and all sorts of religion. . . . We do not seek to deprive the Queen of her Supremacy. On the contrary, we desire that she should exercise it more freely and effectually.[107]

Conclusion

Clearly, Pusey was more at home on Church and State questions than his humble protestation otherwise, to Newman in 1837, would lead one to suspect. Contrary to what he told Newman on that occasion, his historical knowledge of the subject was profound. It deepened over the years, as his work on the Supremacy in 1850 bears out. Above all, a true understanding of Pusey's positive view of a union of the two powers working together, of his intense belief in the ideal of a Christian State guided by the precepts of the Church, helps to set some later views of Tractarian teaching on the subject in a somewhat different perspective. Froude set the Movement on one course, but there was always a powerful undercurrent represented by Keble and Pusey ready to regard establishment properly understood, as something more than a 'upas tree'. The path towards a so-called 'liberal Catholicism' was not as straightforward as it might have seemed. If Toryism was abandoned, it was a political and corrupt Toryism of the day that had itself cut itself loose from its earlier religious and moral principle and temper. It was Pusey who could feel himself the truer 'Tory' than Peel, rechannelling all that ancient religious feeling that lay behind a certain set of political values, to perhaps higher and nobler purposes than a mere party contest. Of course, as the State encroached even further, with the connivance of even

Conservative governments, the option of 'fleeing to the mountains' became more attractive. Yet, Pusey would only ever have considered that option as the very last resort.

Pusey's differences with Gladstone after 1845, centred on his uneasy feeling, shared by many old High Churchmen, that Gladstone appeared too ready to acquiesce in and even welcome, if not encourage, the transition from what he called 'the Catholic to the infidel idea of the state'. Even if ecclesiastical freedom and not only political Liberalism was the motivating force, this was a trend that Pusey deplored and constantly fought against. For as Pusey made clear again and again, in abandoning the State, the Church would suffer not merely temporal but spiritual loss. The conclusion to his work on the Supremacy was thus typical, and at one with his earlier writings on cathedral institutions and passive obedience.

> The loss [he wrote] would be our ancient institutions and our collegiate and parochial churches; the churches wherein our fathers have worshipped from generation to generation; the representatives of those wherein God was first worshipped here . . . We may not abandon 'the few sheep in the wilderness', so long as we can lawfully discharge our trust. We need not, because a heavy hour of trial is upon us, familiarise ourselves with the thought that we must abandon it. He hath delivered us in 'six troubles'; and 'in seven shall no evil touch' us. He who spared us in the lukewarmness of the last century, will not abandon our Church in the more devoted earnest service which He has given her the wish to render.[108]

It is a message not without relevance for those today who remain troubled and confused by the relations of the Church with the State, by the apparent anomalies and contradictions of establishment. One might heed a lesson from his abiding motto—'patience and confidence, the strength of the Church', and the text on which he loved to dwell, 'O tarry thou the Lord's leisure'.

NOTES

1 Quoted in Liddon, vol. 2, p. 25.

2 R.W.Church, *The Oxford Movement: twelve years, 1833–45*, ed. G.Best (Chicago 1970), pp. xxix–xxx.

3   W. Copeland to E. B. P., 30 October 1864 (Pusey House). According to Liddon, in later life Pusey had 'little heart for themes which did not more directly concern the well-being of souls'. Liddon, vol. 2, p. 27.

4   W. Copeland to W. N. Molesworth, 2 November 1864 (Pusey House).

5   See, for instance, Newman's comment, 'all parties ever have been Erastian'. Quoted in W. Ward, *Life of John Henry, Cardinal Newman* (London 1927), vol. 2, 117. See also, W. G. Ward's definition of 'Anglicanism' as 'establishmentism'. *The Ideal of a Christian Church* (London 1844), p. 43.

6   See W. R. Ward, 'Oxford and the origins of Liberal Catholicism in the Church of England' *SCH (L)*, vol. 1 (1964), pp. 234–9. Cf. O. Chadwick, *The Victorian Church*, vol. 1, pp. 226–31.

7   O. Chadwick, vol. 1, chap. 1; cf. O. Brose, *Church and Parliament: the Reshaping of the Church of England* (London 1959), ch. 1; E. R. Norman, *Church and Society in England, 1770–1970: an historical study* (Oxford 1976); K. A. Thompson, *Bureaucracy and Church Reform* (Oxford 1970).

8   J. P. Kenyon, *Revolution Principles: the Politics of Party, 1689–1720* (Cambridge 1977), p. 86.

9   For Paley, the best form of church government was that 'which conduces most to the edification of the people, which pleases them best, and suits with the circumstances and civil constitution of the country'. W. Paley, *Works*, ed. E. Paley, 2nd ed. (London 1838), vol. 1, p. ccliv, cf. W. Warburton, *The Alliance of Church and State* (London 1736).

10 N. Murray, 'The influence of the French Revolution on the Church of England and its rivals, 1789–1802'. (Unpublished thesis Oxford 1975), pp. 3–4; cf. H. T. Dickinson, *Liberty and property: political ideology in eighteenth century Britain* (London 1977), p. 291.

11 H. Twiss, *The public and private life of Lord Chancellor Eldon, with selections from his correspondence* 2nd. ed. (London 1844), vol. 3, pp. 488–490.

12 For examples of Hutchinsonian attitudes on church and state, see G. Horne, *The Christian King* (Oxford 1761); Horsley MSS. Lambeth Palace MSS. 1767 ff. 198–203; S. Horsley, 'Thoughts upon Civil Government and its Relation to Religion'; G. Berkeley, *An Inquiry into the Origin of Episcopacy* (London 1795); 44–45; J. Boucher, *A View of the Causes and Consequences of the American Revolution* (London 1797).

13 W. Palmer, 'The Oxford Movement of 1833', *Contemporary Review* vol. 48 (May 1883), p. 641.

14 T. Arnold, *Principles of Church Reform* [1833] ed. M. J. Jackson and J. Rogan (London 1962), pp. 109–140. For the political context of Whig attitudes to establishment, see G. Best, 'The Whigs and the Church Establishment in the age of Grey and Holland' *History* vol. 45 (June 1960), pp. 103–18.

15 W. J. Copeland to Warden of Keble 22 September 1879 (Keble MSS. Keble College).

16 J.Keble and J.H.Newman (ed.), *Remains of Richard Hurrell Froude*, (London 1838), vol. 1, p. 429.

17 *Remains* vol. 3, p. 196, 'Remarks on state interference in matters spiritual'.

18 *Remains* vol. 4, p. 223. For the whole of Froude's eulogistic treatise on Becket, see *Remains*, vol. 4, pp. 1–558.

19 Blachford, Lord Frederic, ed. G.E.Marindin, *Letters* (London 1896), pp. 45–46.

20 J.H.Newman, *Certain Difficulties Felt by Anglicans in Catholic Teaching Considered* (London 1850), p. 112.

21 Newman to Pusey, 24 January 1836. J.H.Newman, *Letters and Diaries*, ed. T.Gornall (Oxford 1981), vol. 5, p. 214.

22 J.H.Newman, *Letters and Correspondence*, ed. A.Mozley (Oxford, 1891), vol. 1, p. 441.

23 W.J.Copeland to Warden of Keble, 22 September 1879 (Keble MSS. Keble College).

24 W.Palmer, *Narrative of Events Connected with the Oxford Movement* (London 1843), p. 15.

25 This was Gladstone's complaint to Manning. W.E.Gladstone to H.E.Manning, 17 May 1835 (Gladstone MSS. British Library MSS. Add. 44683 ff. 51–52).

26 W.E.Gladstone to H.E.Manning, 5 April 1835 (Gladstone MSS. British Library MSS. Add 44683 ff. 3–6).

27 On Gladstone's ideal of Church and State in 1838, see P.Butler, *Gladstone: Church, State and Tractarianism* (Oxford 1982), 79–92.

28 Keble to Newman 31 March 1839 (Keble MSS. Keble College).

29 Liddon, vol. 1, pp. 131–2.

30 Ibid., vol. 1, p. 171.

31 Quoted in Liddon, vol. 1, p. 133.

32 J.H.Newman to E.B.P, 5 December 1832 (Pusey House).

33 See, T.Arnold, 'The Oxford Malignants' *Edinburgh Review* vol. 63 (April 1836) p. 235.

34 Quoted in Liddon vol. 1, p. 278.

35 Pusey, *Cathedral Institutions*, pp. 7–8.

36 Quoted in Liddon vol. 1, p. 229.

37 E.B.P. to H.E.Manning, 28 September 1837 (Pusey House).

38 E.B.P. to S.Wilberforce, 9 September 1836 (Wilberforce MSS. Bodleian Lib., Oxford, d.17. f.336.).

39 E.B.P. to H.E.Manning, 28 April 1837 (Pusey House).

40 Pusey, 'The Royal and Parliamentary Ecclesiastical Commissions', from *The British Critic and Quarterly Theological Review*, April 1838 (London 1838), p. 7.

41 Pusey, 'Royal and Parliamentary Commissions', p. 19.

42 Pusey, *A Letter to His Grace the Archbishop of Canterbury* (Oxford 1842), p. 124; cf. A. P. Perceval, *A Collection of Papers Connected with the Theological Movement of 1833* (London 1842), p. 49.

43 See Pusey's comment to James Hope, another Tractarian friend of the Scottish Episcopal Church: 'One should fear very seriously for the Scotch church, if they were to give up this their special deposit'. Pusey to J. R. Hope, 15 November 1843 (Hope-Scott MSS, National Library of Scotland, Edinburgh. MS. 3672 f. 220).

44 E. B. P. to J. R. Hope, 4 August 1837 (Hope-Scott MSS. N.L.S. MS. 3670 f. 192).

45 Quoted in J. Morley, *Life of William Ewart Gladstone* (London 1903), vol. 1, p. 171.

46 See, T. Chalmers, *On Church and College Establishments*, pt 2, *Lectures on the Establishment and Extension of National Churches; delivered in London . . . 1838* (Edinburgh, n.d.) Lecture 4, pp. 283–308.

47 Quoted in Liddon vol. 1, pp. 234–5.

48 On this, see *P. Butler, Gladstone*, pp. 77–78.

49 W. E. Gladstone to J. R. Hope, 8 September 1840 (Hope-Scott MSS, NLS MS 3672 f. 76).

50 See Pusey's recognition of this to Edward Churton in 1865: 'Gladstone did more for the church, by gaining the recognition of the non-established church of Scotland . . . than any other statesman I know of'. Quoted in Liddon, vol. 4, p. 199.

51 W. E. Gladstone, *The State in its Relations with the Church* (London 1839), p. 75.

52 J. Keble, 'Gladstone—the State in its relations with the Church', *The British Critic*, vol. 24 (October 1839), p. 370.

53 On Gladstone's change, see P. Butler, *Gladstone*, ch. 4.

54 See, C. Wordsworth, *Church Principles and Church Measures: a Letter to Lord John Manners, M.P.* (London 1845), p. 29, cf. W. Palmer to C. Wordsworth (Sen.), 22 April 1845 (Wordsworth MSS. Lambeth Palace MS 2143 ff. 139–41).

55 C. Wordsworth (Jun.) to H. Goulburn 7 April 1845 (Wordsworth MSS. Lambeth Palace MS. 2143 f. 132).

56 Quoted in Liddon, vol. 3, p. 171.

57 Quoted in Liddon, vol. 3, p. 172.

58 E. B. P. to E. Churton, 23 November 1847 (Pusey House).

59 O. Chadwick, *Victorian Church*, vol. 1, p. 258.

60 Quoted in Liddon, vol. 3, p. 249.

61 Pusey, *The Royal Supremacy not an Arbitrary Authority but Limited by the Laws of the Church, of which Kings are Members* (Oxford 1850), p. 212. Old

High Churchmen, such as Edward Churton, warned Pusey against setting too much store by such examples. See Churton's comment to him: 'I do not attribute quite so much of the present difficulties to our connection with the state; for those reformed churches which have no connection with the state, in Scotland and America, have scarcely any better discipline than our own'. E. Churton to E. B. P., 26 May 1843 (Pusey House).

62 Quoted in Liddon, vol. 4, p. 201.

63 Quoted in Liddon, vol. 4, p. 199.

64 Liddon, vol. 2, p. 29.

65 J. Keble, 'Unpublished papers of Bishop Warburton', *The British Critic* vol. 29 (April 1841), p. 427. See also Newman's strictures on 'the cheerful, hopeful view of human nature, which prevails at all times (especially since the "Glorious" 1688!). Such was Paley's, Addison's, Blair's, and now Maltby's and the Liberals'. Newman, *Letters and Diaries*, ed. Ker and Gornall (Oxford 1979), vol. 2, p. 35.

66 Its continued association with the Oxford Movement can be illustrated by Wilfrid Ward's account of the consternation that his father, W. G. Ward, created 'at a dinner of Puseyites and zealous worshippers of the martyr-king that the execution of Charles I was the only defensible or possible course under the circumstances'. W. Ward, *William George Ward and the Oxford Movement* (London 1889), p. 214.

67 Pusey to Keble, 15 November 1837 (Pusey House). The very words of Pusey's dedication of the sermon to Keble make explicit the nature of the influence: 'To the Rev. John Keble, M.A., Professor of Poetry, and late Fellow of Oriel, who in years past unconsciously implanted a truth which was afterwards to take root, himself the dutiful disciple of its ancient guardian and faithful witness in word and action, the University of Oxford'.

68 Liddon, vol. 2, p. 27. Even prior to Pusey's sermon, the moderate Evangelical *Christian Observer* was accusing Pusey of wishing 'to restore the doctrines and practices of Laud and Sacheverell'. Among these doctrines were included high notions of monarchical authority and non-resistance. *Christian Observer* vol. 37 (September 1837), p. 586. 'Oxford Saintology'. Pusey's sermon induced even some moderate High Churchmen to caution him against too overtly reviving Jacobite political notions. See J. Beaven, *Warnings from History, Political and Ecclesiastical: a Discourse delivered before the University of Oxford on the 30th January 1838, being the day of King Charles' Martyrdom* (Oxford 1838).

69 Quoted in *The life and correspondence of Thomas Arnold D.D.* ed. A. P. Stanley (London 1845), 4th ed. vol. 2, p. 93.

70 Pusey, *Patience and Confidence the Strength of the Church: a Sermon Preached on the Fifth of November, before the University of Oxford at St Mary's* (Oxford 1837), p. xv.

71 Letters and Correspondence of J. H. Newman, ed. A. Mozley, vol. 2, p. 241.

72 E. B. Pusey, *Patience and Confidence the Strength of the Church*, p. vi. Liddon even described the sermon as 'imbued with the old moral as well as political temper of Toryism'. Liddon, vol. 2, p. 27.

73 Ibid., p. v. See Nathaniel Goldsmid's praise of the sermon for invoking the example of 'the saints and martyrs of our own church, exhibited in all the beauty, dignity and loveliness of passive obedience and non-resistance'; 'Pusey's sermon on the Fifth of November', *The British Critic*, vol. 23 (January, 1838), p. 144.

74 Pusey, Appendices to the Sermon preached . . . on the Fifth of November, 1837 (Oxford 1838), p. 4.

75 W. J. Copeland to M. A. Copeland, 3 May 1836 (Copeland MSS. Pusey House).

76 Keble, *Kings to be Honoured for their Office Sake* [Accession Day sermon, 1836] *Plain sermons*, by contributors to the *Tracts for the Times* (London 1839), vol. 1, p. 243; cf. Keble, *On the death of a King* [9 July, 1837], Plain sermons (London 1842), vol. 4, pp. 76–7.

77 J. Reeves, *Considerations on the Coronation Oath to Maintain the Protestant Reformed Religion, and the Settlement of the Church of England* (London 1801), p. 22.

78 J. Reeves, *Considerations on the Coronation Oath*, p. 36.

79 Letters and diaries of J. H. Newman, ed. T. Gornall, p. 164. See Newman's remark to Froude in June 1835: 'Keble preached a glorious Accession sermon yesterday on "Kings shall be thy nursing fathers" etc.'

80 Pusey, *Royal and Parliamentary Ecclesiastical Commissions*, p. 6.

81 Pusey, *The Church, the Converter of the Heathen. Two Sermons preached in Conformity with the Queen's Letter in Behalf of the SPG (Oxford 1838)*, p. 23.

82 Pusey, *The Church, the converter of the heathen*, p. 56.

83 Pusey, *Cathedral institutions*, p. 96.

84 Keble to S. Wilberforce, 19 September 1836 (Wilberforce MSS. Bodleian Library. d.17 f. 338).

85 Pusey to S. Wilberforce, 9 September 1836 (Wilberforce MSS. Bodleian Library. d.17 f. 336).

86 Pusey to W. E. Gladstone, March 1836 (Pusey House).

87 J. R. Hope to W. E. Gladstone, 9 December 1847 (Gladstone MSS. British Library MS Add. 44214 ff. 322–3).

88 *Scottish Ecclesiastical Journal*, vol. 1, no. 21 (16 September 1851), p. 193.

89 Pusey to W. E. Gladstone, 13 December 1847 (Pusey House).

90 Pusey to W. E. Gladstone, Eve of St Mark 1849 (Pusey House).

91 J. M. Neale, 'The Laudian Reformation Compared with that of the

Nineteenth Century', *Lectures Principally on the Church Difficulties of the Present Time* (London 1852), p. 172.

92   Quoted in Newsome, *The parting of friends*, p. 349.

93   H. E. Manning to S. Wilberforce, 24 January 1850 (Wilberforce MSS. West Sussex County Record Office, Chichester).

94   Quoted in E. S. Purcell, *The life of Cardinal Manning* (London 1896), vol. 1, p. 527; cf. R. Ornsby, *Memoirs of James Robert Hope-Scott* (London 1884), vol. 2, p. 83.

95   W. Maskell, *A first Letter on the Present Position of the High Church Party in the Church of England* (London 1850).

96   W. Palmer to W. E. Gladstone, 7 June 1850 (Gladstone MSS. British Library MS. Add. 44369 f. 257).

97   W. E. Gladstone, *Remarks on the Royal Supremacy as it is Defined by Reason, History and the Constitution. A Letter to the Lord Bishop of London* (London 1850), pp. 14, 22.

98   W. E. Gladstone to H. E. Manning, 29 April 1850 (Gladstone MSS. British Library MS. Add. 44248 f. 39).

99   B. Harrison to W. E. Gladstone, 12 July 1850 (Gladstone MSS. British Library MS. Add. 44204 f. 132).

100   E. B. Pusey to J. T. Coleridge, 9 January 1850. Quoted in Liddon, vol. 3, p. 211.

101   Liddon, vol. 3, pp. 250–1.

102   Ibid., vol. 3, p. 258.

103   Pusey, *Royal Supremacy*, p. 162.

104   Ibid., p. 159.

105   Ibid., pp. 153–5.

106   Ibid., 210–11.

107   *English Churchman*, vol. 8, no. 409 (31 October, 1850). p. 788. For a similar view by Richard Church, see *Christian Remembrancer*, vol. 19, (January 1850), p. 509.

108   Pusey, *Royal Supremacy*, pp. 212–13.

12

Pusey and University Reform

IEUAN ELLIS

No account of Pusey's life and character would be complete without noticing his long involvement with university administration and legislation, in particular, his membership for over a quarter of a century of the Hebdomadal Council in Oxford.

Why did Pusey choose to do this, giving as much time to the often petty detail of committee business, as to scholarly work and spiritual matters? The answer lies in his reaction to the University Reform Commission, set up by Lord John Russell in 1850. The Commission's proposals, to liberalize Oxford, or (as Pusey saw it) to 'Germanize' it, were a turning point in Pusey's life. His skills as a controversialist, and his practical energies, were summoned to defend the religious ideal of the university.

Agitation for reform of Oxford was an old Latitudinarian tenet, dating from before the Tractarian period. Indeed, for the liberal party in the university, the Tractarian Movement was proof of the need for reform, for conservatism was entrenched in the collegiate system and sanctioned by the Laudian statutes. Oxford was too narrow, too restricted, the Dissenters were excluded, the rising middle-class had little claim on it. Many places in the colleges were empty, and only 22 of the 542 fellowships were said to be really open. The professoriate was only a token institution; the liberals said that it 'seemed almost impossible' that 'a university in the higher sense of the term should exist without such a class'. The situation was made crucial by the examination statute of 1850, which submerged the college tutors under a deluge of new teaching.

Pusey himself had long admitted the need for reform. In *Cathedral Institutions* he said that the universities provided only an introductory education, and, while professional studies for

298

law and medicine were provided elsewhere, the clergy were sent into the field with only the barest preparatory training. Whereas England was 'very slenderly provided with theological, or, indeed, any other professors', there were at least 125 professors of theology in Germany, with additional staff besides. How could 6 or 7 English professors be as productive of literary works as 125, even though many of the latter were ephemeral, or even rationalistic? Pusey advocated a union of the German and English systems to remedy the neglect.[1]

In 1838, in *The British Critic*, he spoke of the need to adapt 'ourselves to the altered state of society and population'. The Church had no means of 'commanding the energies of powerfully-stirred but unregulated minds . . . no means of finding nor securing any adequate knowledge in our candidates for orders, none of educating the increasing middle classes'.[2] The bearing of this on Oxford was suggested in a letter to Philip Pusey in 1845, when he said that the university should be extended 'on economical lines and on church principles': one way forward would be to open new halls, where men could live more cheaply and soberly than in the colleges, and be under proper supervision and control.[3]

The royal commission to enquire into the state, discipline, studies, and revenues, of the university, was appointed in August, 1850, with the 'liberal' bishop, Samuel Hinds, as Chairman, and A. P. Stanley, as Secretary. The Commission's Report was issued in April 1852—the famous 'blue book', which set out in 720 pages and 47 major recommendations why Oxford should be radically reformed, and given a more 'modern' tone.

The religious implications of the Report were far reaching. It was impossible to think that the Commissioners had not read Pusey's book of twenty years earlier, for they, too, pointed out the defects in the professional education of the clergy, and they were critical of the productivity of the divinity professors. Their answer was to make theology a separate subject of study, forming a final school by itself, and accordingly not required of candidates in other schools after the intermediate examination. Thus, an instant demand would arise for theological lectures. 'This demand would call the Professors into more active

Academical life', and help to establish a 'great Theological School'. They spoke of 'compelling' theological students to take first examinations in another school, so that they might relate their studies to other fields of experience.

The Commissioners proposed a modish curriculum for the school, based on the 'history and criticism of the Sacred Books'. It was certainly an ambitious curriculum: in a relatively short period of study, the undergraduate was to learn the Scriptures in their original tongues, higher and lower criticism, ecclesiastical history, dogmatic theology, including the history of doctrines, and pastoral theology.[4]

Read alongside the Commissioners' recommendations for university extension and a reformed professoriate, the scheme for a new theological school had the direst consequences for the Tractarian ideal of the Church, the ministry, and clerical education. The Report placed its faith in a new class of student, witnessing to a new educational theory: independent of college influence and tutorial control, they would be the raw material on which the new professoriate would work. The results would be more plain in theology than in other faculties, since the new school required a longer training than the others. Thus, a body of professors, who might well be lay, and would probably be 'liberal', would decide the fate of half the future clergy of the Church of England. This tribunal restricted the free choice of the bishops to select the clergy, and it also admitted political control of the Church, since the lay professors would be appointed by the prime minister of the day.

There is no need to imagine Pusey's feelings as he drew out these implications. He particularly disliked the 'pure competitive system' as an element in education, and a grave matter of principle was involved if this was admitted into a school of divinity. Sacred studies, like sacred hermeneutics, were different from other studies: they were demeaned by being made the vehicle of academical honours, and when the 'praise of men', and not the enlarged knowledge of God, was the motivation for pursuing them. 'It could only encourage a dry, hard, intellectual head-knowledge, which would be irreverent, and hurtful to religious belief', and it would be a melancholy result when professors of theology were produced by such means.

Pusey also objected to the premise that the study of doctrine ought to be an evolutionary one. He realized that the Commissioners in their desire to encourage a study of the 'history of doctrines', had used a term which (obviously) they had translated from the German *Dogmengeschichte*. This meant the 'gradual development of the fundamental truths of the Gospel, under the influence of powerful minds, or amid the pressure of heretical speculation'. But this was wholly mistaken.

I am satisfied, for myself, that there is no such real history, because there is no such reality, the faith having been, once and for all, fully made known to the inspired Apostles, and by them inserted in Holy Scripture, and committed to the Church. The name which the Commissioners have unhappily adopted presupposes, as it is commonly used, the human origin of great part of the faith.[5]

(Pusey did not mention Newman's *Development of Christian Doctrine*.) These were the aspects which fascinated Pusey, the plan to separate divinity from other studies, to liberalize religious authority, and to alter the outlook of the clergy; and he might simply have appeared before the Commission, and spoken in these terms. He approached them, as he told Stanley, 'in no unfriendly spirit . . . controversy is not a congenial element to me'.[6] However, the opportunity was denied him, or the Commission understood him to have refused it. Accordingly, what was intended to be a short paper on theological theory emerged, instead, in October 1853, as a full-scale reply to the Report.

Pusey's 'evidence', as it was called, was published with other statements of a similar nature, but it outclassed the rest, and was quickly interpreted as the most effective answer to the Commission so far. From this moment onwards, Pusey was at the centre of the debate, and looked on as the champion of the status-quo. There was a further consequence. The volume was issued by a delegacy of the Hebdomadal Board, and thus Pusey came to be allied with his old enemies, the Heads of Houses, who in previous years had persecuted the Tractarians and done their best to silence him. Some were surprised that he should accept such patronage.[7]

Pusey's objects in writing the evidence concerned, first, the government's authority for acting as it did. Either the universities belonged to the Church, or they belonged to the nation. 'If they belong to the Church, no one except members of the Church have a claim to be educated there. A Socinian has no claim. If to the nation, then I do not see how the Church can put any restriction upon it'.[8] But Oxford's whole history belied the latter interpretation. He saw the government's hand in the proposal to abolish religious knowledge as a subject in the final examination. What was this, unless an 'emphatic declaration of the uselessness of these subjects after that age?' This suggested that the search for divine knowledge interfered with the human; worse, that the 'religious knowledge required by the University would interfere, not with the healthy, but with the unhealthy study of any other branch of knowledge'. If the university admitted persons whose mind she could not form religiously, 'she abandons her office, either in theory or practice'.

He threw a novel light on the enlarged professoriate. The great question which pervaded the Report was 'whether the education given by the University shall be for the formation of the mind, or for the imparting of knowledge', i.e., whether by the college tutor, or by the university professor, or, as Pusey saw it, whether 'by the clergy of the Church, or the laity, of any religious opinions or creed'. He described at length the superiority of the collegiate system, its catechetical method of teaching, its care for the whole character; yet the tendency of the Commission's proposals would be to destroy it. In their scheme, 'the intellect and the cultivation of it have become the object of idolatry'.

Much capital was made by his enemies out of Pusey's next section, in which he claimed a German origin for the Commissioners' point of view. There is no doubt that he spent too long in discussing the German situation (as he had done in *Cathedral Institutions*), and various theories can be suggested to account for this. But the German professorial method illustrated better than anything else Pusey's understanding of the nature of truth. Christian truth was certain, unchanging, because based on divine revelation, and in a Christian university it gave a stability and coherence to all studies. In contrast to this was an idea of truth as something shifting, uncertain, the product of investigation and argument and the comparison of evidence. In a university in which the latter approach dominated, each new generation would have its favourite theories and teachers. Pusey described the calm unhurried nature of English divinity, in which the divines of the sixteenth and seventeenth centuries were still required reading. Then, in a series of undoubtedly effective pictures, he portrayed the German universities, with their succession of schools, their love of novelty which meant that (as had been confessed to him), 'no books older than 25 years were read', their violence and excitement, and the rationalism which was the natural product of all this.

'I see, then, no result, intellectual, moral or religious, for which we should be invited to imitate the plan of the German universities', said Pusey, listing the ills, which German professors since the Reformation had brought upon the Church. 'The German universities are no precedent for ours. Their whole theory is different from ours.' The results of abandoning the discipline of colleges and halls, and giving undue power to the professoriate, had been a blight upon the Germans themselves. '*The* great and *special* failure of the German universities has been, that the young man has been left unprotected, unaided, unfostered, surrounded by no religious influences . . .'.[9]

Not all Pusey's points were as effective. He overplayed the advantages of the college system, and denied what he had admitted twenty years before, that the colleges had swallowed up the university. He failed to notice that the works of foreign specialists, particularly in the classics, were increasingly used in tutorial teaching—so the fruits of the German professorial system already influenced the university. He saw the chief employment of the new professors in the teaching of undergraduates, but the Commission wished them to be a learned body engaged in research, rather than in direct education. Curiously, he allowed professors a greater role in the teaching of science, and so encouraged the rise of men who were to be the leading opponents of Christianity in years to come. His long arguments against the popularity of lectures needed a lighter touch. Pusey was a dull lecturer ('insufferably dry', said Edwin Hatch;[10] 'laborious, hesitating, iterative, involved', said the faithful but critical Tuckwell[11]), and this may explain why he doubted 'whether as to this object of advancing the knowledge of the subject, the time occupied in the delivery of lectures is not loss to the Professor'[12]—a line which gave a good deal away.

The evidence instilled a new spirit into the conservative opposition. But the liberals were angry, and suspected that the reform issue was being used by the Tractarians to settle old scores left over from 1845. 'The thing is too monstrous', said H. G. Liddell, complaining of Pusey's misinterpretation.[13] They had some discussion as to whether to make a reply. Liddell might have written an adequate answer. But the choice fell on H. H. Vaughan, Regius Professor of Modern History, and the resulting pamphlet, *Oxford Reform and Oxford Professors*, made a poor showing of their case. Vaughan concentrated on attacking Pusey; and not even Pusey as the university champion, but the once heterodox professor. The pamphlet was superficial, hurriedly written, and contained a serious misquotation from the evidence.

Vaughan enumerated Pusey's mistakes, and held that any careful reader would dismiss his entire history of the German professoriate. The better comparison between England and Germany was made, he said, when they both pointed to the need for a freer, more liberal education in the nineteenth century. He taunted Pusey with having changed his mind from his favourable impressions of Germany in 1827.[14]

The response from Pusey was a volume of 217 pages, even longer than his evidence. *Collegiate and Professorial Teaching and Discipline* was a work of polemics. It does not stand high in the Pusey canon, and it did not advance the discussion of university education very far. But, since a correspondence with Vaughan produced no satisfactory conclusion, he felt that he had to issue into print.[15]

Pusey was quite relentless, quoting author after author in over 100 pages of solid fact concerning the continental universities, so that 'ancient institutions should not be run down unjustly'. Vaughan's reliance on only one main source, and that a partial and unreliable historian, compared badly. In any case, Vaughan had misinterpreted him: he had applied to the Oxford *colleges*, what Meiners had said of the *bursae*, or halls.

Pusey's research was intended to show that the 'extra-collegiate' plan had been tried extensively on the Continent, and had failed.

He pointed out again, rather wearily, against Vaughan's 'misstatements', that his contrast was not between tutors and professors, but between collegiate and professorial systems, between 'two modes of communicating knowledge and instructing the mind'. He had opposed the plan for its 'spurious excitement', and for the prominence that it gave to the worst form of teaching, 'delivered lectures'.

As for his change of mind, 'the appalling picture which met me on my first acquaintance with German theology, at the age of twenty five', had, in fact, determined his whole subsequent life. The question, then, was the interpretation of what he had actually said in 1827, not what his opponents believed him to have said:

> I still think that the picture which I drew, and the causes which I assigned of German rationalism, were in the main correct. I have not, then (as Professor Vaughan implies,) now for a purpose 'imputed to the Professoriate at this particular crisis of Oxford for the first time', what I before ascribed to 'causes far less minute'. The statement in my Evidence is not inconsistent with those in my Enquiry. In 1827 I was speaking of the *causes* of Rationalism; in 1853, I was speaking of the *agents*.

He sought to show this by a rather elaborate analogy, which Liddon reproduces, perhaps because it is not easy to summarize, and also, perhaps, because it is not entirely convincing.

His support for Kant testified to his consistency, claimed Pusey. (But what sort of Kantian was Pusey?):

> I own now, as I did then, that Almighty God used these philosophies, to lead men back to the promised land, which their authors knew not of . . . Professor Vaughan reminds me of my hopeful language as to Germany in 1827. It is true that I have been disappointed. I watched, with many a heart-ache, over the struggles of the faith in Germany, and came to see how hard a thing it is for the intellectual mind of a country, which has once broken away from the faith, to be again won to it in its integrity.

305

Pusey did not deny that he viewed everything in its theological aspect, though, of course, he denied that he had thereby narrowed the reform issue, or saw in it implications which the Commissioners never imagined. Every faculty of the mind was some reflection of God, he said: 'without true belief in God, we shall not understand any other truth. . . . Even the intellect cannot be cultivated aright unless it be subdued to God'. Thus, there was no such ideal as a 'secular university', and to reduce the place of theology in the curriculum was evidence of an atheistic tendency. 'What we need is to strengthen our institutions, not to revolutionize them; to replace anything decayed, not to build anew; to re-form anything amiss, not to remodel them. . . . A sudden and extensive change has mostly evil in it, even because it is sudden and extensive'.[16]

As a statement of the opposition between two views of education and religion, neither the pamphlet nor Pusey's massive reply was, in the end, satisfactory. Vaughan's attitude was too aggressive, and identified the Report too closely with the fortunes of the professoriate. The anti-professorial feeling, already strengthened by the evidence, was increased, particularly among the college tutors. Pusey's closing paragraph, on the other hand, showed how limited his idea of reform went, and he was further aligned with the reactionary elements in the university.

Pusey's correspondence with Gladstone is one of the most interesting features of the reform controversy. If the literary polemics achieved little, the *entrée* to the mind of the Cabinet, provided by Gladstone, was of great value. Pusey also wrote fairly frequently to Sir William Heathcote, the other Oxford MP, but his relations with Gladstone were always closer and more cordial. He seems to have tried the statesman's patience sorely, as he bombarded him with letters in an attempt to check government action in some way. Gladstone commented on one occasion, 'I am truly grieved at your seeing ground to use language of such serious alarm', and on another, 'I am unwilling you should suppose that the language you use in your letters about the Government Bill passes me by unheeded: on the contrary, it causes me much concern'.[17]

Gladstone read the evidence 'with care', but did not think that the draft Bill would produce the evils that he described. In fact, the Report, and the heads' subsequent actions, emboldened by Pusey's statements, seem to have convinced him that government intervention was necessary. Pusey would not be satisfied: at least six letters in February 1854 (to all of which Gladstone faithfully replied), others in March, May, June, and July, were concerned with the matter of reform. Pusey deprecated the proposals in the draft Bill for altering the Hebdomadal Board, which he thought would tie their hands 'in perpetuity', the opening of fellowships to laymen, and the licensing of private halls. Gladstone thought that suitable laymen, in due subordination of numbers, would mix well with clerical fellows, 'do very great good in some respects, and not entail religious dangers in a greater degree than that in which they have been found to exist among Clergymen'. Pusey seems to have suggested that the final permission to open the private halls should rest with the colleges, but Gladstone replied that Parliament would not hear of it, well knowing that the colleges would give no such permission. Pusey tried again—why could the government not give the Vice-Chancellor the final say, in case unsuitable private persons applied? This was just as transparent to Gladstone, who asked Pusey, in turn, why a layman should not open his house as a private hall?—providing that religious instruction was given in the house, and by an ordained person.

There were continued 'mournful prognostications' in other letters. Gladstone attempted to rebuild Pusey's confidence, and warned of a 'tendency to overmuch apprehension with respect to changes, and over little confidence in the good sense and self command of our contemporaries and our children coming on after them, in succession to *work* these changes'. In another letter he wondered whether the opposition to reform also lay in that 'old disposition to rely on legal exclusiveness which has long been so unhappily characteristic of the Church of England, which has involved her in all her fearful difficulties, and has brought her, I sadly fear, near the day—may it yet be averted—when she shall find that she has bartered freedom for gold, and gold for nothing'.[18]

307

Gladstone, perhaps, mistook his man there, or his patience was wearing thin. The charge of relying on 'legal exclusiveness' could never be levelled at Pusey, though it was certainly true of others in the anti-reformers' ranks.

It is not necessary to follow the correspondence in any further detail. The character of the Bill was materially altered by the sudden amendment, proposed by James Heywood, in the Commons debate of 22 June 1854, urging admission of Dissenters to the university. But Gladstone could do little about this, and he had not expected it. He told Pusey on 14 February, 'the Government will resist . . . any attempt to force the admission of Dissenters on the University through the medium of the present Bill'. When it passed, the vote, he said, took everyone by surprise. It was one of the consequences of the 'remarkable facts' disclosed in the religious census of 1851[19]—i.e., that the majority of people in England and Wales (10,666,000 out of a total population of 17,929,000) did not attend religious services, and of those who did, nearly half were in Dissenters' chapels. If the established Church was no longer the spiritual home of Englishmen, then it could not claim exclusive right to the universities. Gladstone thought that Keble had taken insufficient notice of this in his pamphlet published at the time, *A few very plain thoughts on the proposed admission of Dissenters to the University of Oxford*. Whether this argument meant anything to Pusey is doubtful.

Gladstone had to defend the government's intentions again and again. He told Pusey, as he had told Frederick Meyrick, Charles Marriott, and others, that the provisions of the Bill were essentially conservative. More, it was an emancipating Bill, which would allow Oxford to 'exercise a far greater sway than heretofore over the mind of England', in contrast to its decline in the previous century. (Pusey had admitted this decline.) 'You anticipate from the measure of the government, ruin to the University, and ruin brought down upon it by a parricidal hand. I, on the contrary, can remember no subject in Parliament affecting the moral state and the higher institutions of the country, which I have regarded with so much hope and comfort'. Parliamentary interference was an inconvenience, but 'I submit myself to it, for the avoidance of greater evils, and for

308

the attainment of great benefits, which, as far as I can see, are not otherwise to be attained within such a time as would avert the slowly gathering storm'.[20]

So 'emancipation' was to be fairly modest, in deference to the strong feeling in the university, and to the chagrin of the Oxford liberals. Pusey, however, would not be comforted, and did not lessen the barrage until the moment of the bill's passing.

One reason for Pusey's tension and anxiety was that he felt isolated: the High Churchmen lacked a united front, partly because the younger men of the party did not see matters as he did. That was why he kept his distance from the Tractarians in the Oxford Tutors' Association; and they, in turn, realized that their relationship to him was ambiguous. They occupied a middle ground, accepting private halls, though under close supervision, and proposing that lectures in theology should be far more extensive. They did not thank Pusey for torpedoing in his evidence their plan for reformation of the Hebdomadal Board, and substituting one of his own. Pusey felt the need to consult older friends, someone who would share the burden of leadership, and enable him to keep faith with the principles of 1833. Hence, there was a stream of letters to Hursley Vicarage, asking for advice, seeking Keble's counsel on disputed matters, and giving warning of occasions when Keble's physical presence in Oxford, as a member of Convocation, was necessary to vote on a major issue.

'I miss very much not being able to ask you', Pusey wrote in a typical hurried note. 'But questions come on so quickly that I find myself obliged to decide before I should have time to put it to you'. Pusey also expected others to defer to Keble's judgement: a letter of November 1854, confesses that Keble might be able to do something more with the younger High Churchmen than himself. 'We seem to be sinking back into that timid state, before the Tracts were out. I shall be glad if you can have a good talk with Charles Marriott, for he means thoroughly well'. In May 1853, he was 'surprised and sorry' to see what obvious things the younger men overlooked, 'which they acknowledge when put before them, but, meanwhile, have written and spoken without thinking of'. That followed a plea for the 'sound judgment of matured minds, not the opinions of

young, Professor-bitten minds'. The tone of the letters conveyed his anxiety. 'I am very heavy about things'. 'I hope I have
not seemed too sad, so as to sadden you'. 'I do not wish to be
gloomy'. 'I expect any thing. I think now only of individuals'.[21]

Keble's replies were full of good sense and might be
compared with Gladstone's. His office was to soothe Pusey and
restrain any extreme action. He apparently thought that the
other's outlook was too pessimistic in his evidence, 'exhaustive'
as that was. 'I think there should be somewhere in some part of
your writings on this controversy (perhaps there may be
already, though I do not now recollect it)—a frankly drawn
good picture of a *good* Professorial system, such as one should
wish it to be, a handmaid to the Collegiate one'. Like Newman,
he wondered why Pusey had thrown in his lot with the Heads of
Houses. 'I am very sorry that you have such impracticable and
damaging allies', he wrote in March 1854, and again, a few days
later, 'I see it is reported that the Heads are to petition against
the Bill. If one must do that, I should like to be clear of *them*, and
to petition on my own grounds, with such as happen to agree
with me'. He thought that his reaction would be that of the MAs
generally: 'they will be found little disposed to come up to
support (as they will construe it) the Heads of Houses'. Finally,
Pusey's note of apocalyptic doom was entirely lacking in
Keble's reflections on the fate of the changed university. 'I
cannot but hope that we shall find matters less ruinous than they
are startling. I remember what entire confusion I and some
others expected from the Reform Bill—and now, for ought I
see, we are as well off as we were before it'.[22] That from the
preacher of the sermon on *National Apostasy*! Pusey replied
gloomily that 'the talent of young Oxford is all Liberal'. 'The
Reform of 1830 has surely done all the mischief it could. It has
spoiled the House of Commons, and I suppose that the next
reform will make it worse. But . . . the question is whether the
Universities were not rotten already. This worshipping of
talents does imply extensive rottenness'.[23]

For these reasons, there was some misunderstanding between
the two friends on the vexed question of private halls. Roundell
Palmer had proposed that MAs should be able to take in
students into their private houses, under suitable guarantees.

What was there to hinder Dissenters (he feared a 'grand Protestant hall'), and ultimately Roman Catholics, from having halls, and thus enjoying the benefits of the Bodleian and public lectures? (He told Heathcote that if private halls were permitted, 'I cannot conceive that the University can belong to the Church for ten years'[24].) Keble replied, three days later (19 February 1854) in tones which suggested that no such denominational warfare need be contemplated: the hall-masters could be affiliated to colleges, and required to attend college services with their pupils, or they could have a common service in the university church; and the final power would lie with the Chancellor and with a 'well selected Council' to sift and nominate them.

The question developed into the more specific one of the university's orthodoxy, if Dissenters gained entrance, and Keble received a letter, whose despairing tone 'saddened' him. Pusey wrote on the inevitable consequences of admitting Dissenters which, strangely, other people did not see. 'If people of various faiths have a right to be educated in the same university, they have a right to be educated, each in his own faith, by persons of their own faith; and, if so, the educators have a right to equal share of the emoluments and government. I do not see any flaw in this'. He had written in almost identical terms a few days earlier, but evidently felt the need to repeat himself. Keble thought that there was a way out; the clergy could be taught in colleges at some distance from Oxford, but affiliated to the university. Pusey replied that it would break up Oxford as a place of education, but 'it is good to put it forward, as what the University would have to resort to', once it admitted 'multifidians'.[25]

The correspondence with Gladstone and Keble provided a commentary on Pusey's practical attempts to thwart radical reform. The months between October 1853 and June 1854 saw one scheme after another put forward, as the Heads wrestled with the Report, and the developments which followed it. One of the most important schemes was Pusey's own, his plan, outlined in the evidence, for a revised university constitution, in opposition to the wholesale alteration of Congregation and the Hebdomadal Board proposed by the Commissioners. Pusey wished to save the Board, however odd that seemed to other

311

Tractarians, but placed alongside it a second body, equal in numbers and elected from the resident members of Convocation, which had the power to propose measures to Convocation. If there were differences of opinion between the two boards, these could be resolved by a joint meeting, when a majority of all the members would decide the issue: thus, a brake could be placed on the Hebdomadal Board, while there was no need to constitute the professors as a separate body, as the Commissioners wished. In February, he was trying to pilot its passage through Convocation, and asked for Keble's support: the scheme was important as 'not coming from government', and as 'more conservative than any others'. Any decided majority in Oxford in its favour would, he thought, have weight with the House of Lords, and strengthen opposition to the bill. Keble came, and induced others to travel, as Pusey asked, and the petition supporting an amended version of the constitution was passed by Convocation in February 1854. But the majority was only 51, and the Lords' unwillingness to come to Oxford's aid, when the bill arrived before them, may partly be explained by this poor response. Pusey realized that the Lords also took note of the fact that the petition of remonstrance to the Commons, against the bill, passed by only two votes in Congregation on 1 April (193 to 191). It was not, therefore, surprising that he wrote on 9 June 'All help from the House of Lords is lost; and we are handed over to the Commissioners'.[26]

Various petitions in Oxford engaged his attention at this time. One, to be presented to the Hebdomadal Board, would have seen Pusey publishing an open letter to the Vice-Chancellor, had it been passed, protesting against the unfairness of the choice that it forced on its signatories. The petition proposed that Dissenters should be excluded from places of teaching and government only, in the university. Pusey exclaimed that to support it meant admitting them to be educated and receive degrees, while to oppose it meant admitting them to everything. It was this petition which provoked various letters to Keble on the consequences of any conciliatory gesture to the government. Pusey's was an Either/Or position; either Dissenters (meaning always 'persons of any or no faith at all') must be excluded, or, if they were admitted, they must be allowed to teach and govern, and hence to change the entire character of Oxford. 'This is the old line of the Heads, persecuting to Tractarianism, cringing to Parliament or those in power'.

Consequently, he scrutinized another petition very carefully. Pusey added a rider to it: 'It is the bounden duty of the University not to admit or support any restriction of the definite faith, with the teaching of which it is entrusted'. 'I said I would not sign it without this qualification of what they had said'. The organizers, under this pressure, left out the offending preamble, and the petition stood, imploring the Lords not to make any compulsory alteration of the relation between University and Church. Ideally, what Pusey wanted was, as he admitted, a test which might be imposed on all who wished to enter the university, on the lines of one proposed in 1834: 'I ___ ___ declare that I am *bona fide* a member of the Church of England'. That would effectively block any infiltration, and secure the purity of both teachers and students. But Pusey must have realized that no Dissenting member of the House of Commons would hear of that for an instant.[27]

The early months of 1854 were busy with such plans. In the background was the constant thunder of the parliamentary debates, and the university waited to learn its fate, as the Reform Bill went through its successive stages. The parliamentary intelligence showed how much notice was taken of Pusey's evidence, and members on both sides referred to it. Lord John Russell, introducing the measure on 17 March, quoted Pusey on the present inadequacy of the university. However, he criticized the supposed antagonism between tutorial and professorial methods.

Dr Pusey has said the choice lies between the tutorial system of Oxford and that system of German rationalism which is taught by the professors in the Universities of that country. But, Sir, logical truth is entirely wanting. The system of German rationalism does not belong to the professorial system; and, if, instead of going to Germany, Dr Pusey had gone to Scotland, he would have found professors of divinity, such as Dr Chalmers, as far removed as possible in their views from the views of those German rationalists which it is the dread of Dr Pusey lest they should be admitted into this country.

Mr Horsman, a Dissenting MP, spoke of the poor state of theology at the universities. 'We have no modern theology whatever; we have failed to establish any connection between theology and the general development of learning'. Dr Pusey had warned of the dangers from Germany; yet the party which he led in the university had not produced 'any great work that can be appealed to as an authority, even in England, and much less in Europe'. If that was what the House thought of him, it was small wonder that Pusey resorted so frequently to Gladstone in his correspondence.[28]

The Bill finally passed on 29 June 1854, and with it the old Laudian university came to an end. The provisions of the Bill were to take immediate effect, and by October, the new order, by a novel and rapid transition, was in operation. The university was to retain its Anglican character for the time being, but half of the fellowships were to be open, and a quarter of them might be held by laymen; any qualified Master of Arts might open a private hall. The momentum was to be continued, since a further University Commission was promised, to oversee reform of the colleges.

Of the bill's provisions, the permission for private halls seemed an obvious defeat for Pusey. But it proved a damp squib; nothing came of it, except two small institutions, which had died a natural death by 1862. It would have been the base for the Commissioners' great 'non-collegiate plan', except that the new professoriate, which was to lead and inspire these new students never materialized, and so the students themselves were never forthcoming. The scheme of open and lay fellowships was another rebuff for Pusey, since it introduced that element of competition which he dreaded, and a college dedicated to intellectual excellence, like Balliol, could colonize other foundations: indeed, liberalize them, if the new fellows were pupils of Jowett. However, the competitive system did not work entirely in the liberals' favour, and Pusey, Liddon, and others, were able to place their own protégés in colleges, to become centres of Catholic influence.

The Bill never adopted Pusey's scheme of a second, parallel, board, but its new Hebdomadal Council reflected the Heads' proposals which were a revision of Pusey's scheme. In particular, the election of six professors was built into the constitution; and by this means, Pusey himself became a member of that supreme body in the university which, in its old form, had done so much to thwart him.

There were many who asked what he was doing in such company, that 'austere Tractarian presence', as Liddon put it, sitting among the reformers, and representing a conscious judgement on every religious statement that they made. The decision was not a long premeditated one for Pusey. A letter of October 1854 reads like an outsider's comment on the coming Hebdomadal elections: he thought that the new Council would be a 'very fair representation of the residents, whatever that may be'.[29] But he allowed his name to go forward, and in the election of 25 October, he succeeded in the poll as the second of the six professors, Robert Hussey, professor of ecclesiastical history, being placed first.

The fact that Pusey should sit as a representative of the *professors*, of all classes in the university, was an irony not lost on the liberals. By a greater irony, he was chosen instead of Vaughan, his great adversary, and the advocate of the new professoriate. Liddell thought that this was scandalous. 'For Pusey's only claim is *as* a professor. In every other point he is objectionable, and ought not to have been returned'.[30] But Pusey threw himself into the task, and found that he had energies enough for it. It was as a member of the Council that he achieved his ambition of retaining the connection of godliness with good learning. In this way, some of the ground lost by the Tractarians was recovered, and it led 'by God's mercy to the healing of some wounds of former years'.[31]

The battle went on until the end of his life, and it was maintained because Pusey missed few meetings of the Council, and agreed to serve on its committees. From the beginning there were many anxieties, and sentences like, 'everything is ended; I can fight no more', appear in the letters. In 1868 he was still filled with gloom as to the university's future. 'There is, alas! abundance of evil at Oxford', he wrote to Gladstone. 'The

315

Liberals seem to aim to revolutionize the University while they have the ascendant as the rising tutors and to fix their reign. If we could gain time, all might keep right. Theirs seems to me too ambitious a policy to be prospered'. But his final sentence showed how important his stand on the Council had become. 'As for us of the other school, we should only have to retire and leave all University affairs to the Liberals to try experiments as they will. It would be a quieter life for us'.[32]

In the first months he was occupied with the various issues, which the Bill had left to the university to decide. He said in his letter to Keble on the Hebdomadal elections, 'the real try will begin when they are elected, in the statutes for the new Halls'.[33] So he quickly became involved in an attempt to extend the collegiate umbrella—or straightjacket, depending on one's point of view—over the halls, particularly in the matter of their religious observance. 'I fear that the new Halls, if not kept to the same standard as the Colleges, will drag them down'.[34]

Another question was the religious belief of the new professors who were laymen: were they to be members of the Church of England, or Masters of Arts who signed the Thirty-nine Articles; or was no test to be imposed on them? 'I have drawn up a case', he told Keble, 'to be submitted to Counsel, to ascertain whether Professors do not come under section 44 of the late Act, and whether thereby they will not be required, by virtue of that Act, to sign the Thirty-nine Articles'. The authorities, however, preferred a less obvious scrutiny of professorial orthodoxy, and wanted a token conformity. Pusey was in anguish once more: 'I believe that we have destroyed ourselves, and that Oxford is lost to the Church of England. The dam is broken. How soon it will be carried away, God only knows. I have done what I could; now there is nothing more to fight for. The principle is gone.'[35] The question was decided finally by Convocation, and Keble waited for Pusey's summons, 'to come and vote about the Professors' Test'. When it was debated first in Congregation, Pusey appeared as a member of Council, and it may be imagined how he reacted when Bonamy Price recommended a negative, instead of a positive, test, on the lines, 'I (A.B.) declare that I will neither directly nor indirectly teach or assert anything detrimental to the doctrine and discipline of the Church of England'. G. V. Cox was present at the debate and remembered the impression given by Pusey as he rose to reply. His speech concluded with 'what was a very beautiful if not very convincing' statement, 'That it would be absurd to make a distinction between theological and non-theological Professors. All the sciences moved like planets round the sun of God's truth, and if they left their course, they would be hurled back into chaos'.[36] Cox did not realize that Pusey was merely repeating his evidence, and that to keep the continuity with his evidence, he now served on the Council.

A fresh crop of letters to Gladstone was provoked by the Coleridge Bill of 1868, which proposed the abolition of religious tests for fellowships and other college offices. Pusey took up his familiar lament: it was an even 'worse evil' than the admission of Dissenters, which he had earlier so feared. Indeed, 'I had far rather see the money of the Colleges taken, and Socinian, Baptist, Wesleyan, Presbyterian, and, of course, Roman Catholic colleges endowed with it', than permit a Bill which would expose the laity and future clergy to atheistic teaching. Once tests were relaxed, irreligious men would seek election, and propagate their views. In a curious way it brought him to see what Gladstone had always claimed, that the reform of 1854 was a protective measure. 'We were taught by the Oxford Act, twelve [*sic*] years ago, to rely on the Universities as the places of education for our clergy', and now, unlike the Dissenters and Roman Catholics who had their own seminaries, the Church of England was quite unprepared for this latest assault.[37] He told Liddon that, if the Bill passed, the bishops must set about founding seminaries, 'and the parents should look for other ways of educating their children, than by sending them to the University'.[38] Pusey could thus contemplate a rapid desertion of Oxford, if it abandoned its religious basis. It needed all Gladstone's skill to persuade him that these latest fears were unfounded, and that the power of secularism could never be as strong as denominationalism.

But, slowly, his witness began to reap its rewards. It impressed others, and the example came to be imitated by the younger Tractarian dons. There was not a 'Pusey party', as such, but the Council never became the preserve by which the

317

liberals hoped to advance their object in the university. Indeed, it has been said that by 1860, 'the liberal tide seemed to be running out'.[39] As Pusey's position grew stronger, his efforts increased. Together with H. L. Mansel, he opposed the draft of the new examination statute in 1857, and the Council was, in turn, defeated by Congregation; when the statute finally got through in 1864, it was only a shadow of its former self. Pusey was relieved when in 1858, the executive commission, appointed under the Act, finished its labours, and proposed no wholesale endowment of professorships out of college funds. He served as a member of the committee to consider professorial endowments, so perhaps the result was not unexpected. And when in March 1857, the statute was passed which, at last, set up Boards of Studies—a development which Pusey had earlier fiercely opposed—it was found that the professors had already constituted an unofficial board of their own, and Pusey was active on it.

The conservative victory is best demonstrated in the most sensitive area of all, the study of theology, which the liberals had seen as the test of true reform and the admission of new ideas into the university. The activity (or inactivity) of the divinity professors remained as before, and after Stanley's departure from the ecclesiastical history chair, in 1864, to become dean of Westminster, the run of High Church appointments was largely unbroken. (A rumour in 1869 that Stanley would return to Oxford as its bishop, sent an immediate letter hastening to Gladstone: 'a more mischievous appointment could not easily be made', Pusey warned. 'The promotion of such as he must end in the disruption of the Church of England'.[40]) The professors presented an unbroken phalanx against liberals like Jowett.

There was no talk of an honours school of theology, because of the identification of the Reform Commission with all such notions. Finally, when the matter was considered safe, it was Pusey, of all people, who proposed that a board be set up. In 1869, after much discussion, the school was at last admitted; but a comparison of the syllabus with the suggestions outlined in the 'blue book', showed how little consideration was given to the idea of theology studied in relation to other areas of human knowledge and achievement—still less of doctrine studied from the evolutionary standpoint of *Dogmengeschichte*.[41]

That not only liberals felt disquiet about the matter, is apparent from Pusey's letters. He told Liddon of meeting a young don on the train, who opposed the statute, because the school was to be 'one of mere knowledge apart from beliefs, and that if a person gave clear Arian answers, or positivist, he was to lose his honours'.[42] A petition was addressed to the Proctors, asking them to veto the statute. E. C. Wickham wrote to Liddon of his fears about the large powers given to the divinity professors: would they show the same lack of tolerance in selecting examiners for the school, as they had recently in excluding A. C. Tait, Stanley, and Liddell, from the list of select preachers? 'I cannot be a party to giving the Theological School into the absolute control of persons who, it seems to me, would ostracize half the educated laity and a third of the clergy in our Church'.[43]

Pusey, thus, played a decisive part in shaping the new Oxford, and his influence remains to this day. The amicability of the Council surprised him. 'Our first sitting went off peaceably', he reported to Keble, early in November 1854. Perhaps he felt that he would be regarded as an intruder, but 'people were very good natured to one another'. His new sense of security is conveyed in another letter, in June 1858: 'I was never listened to with more marked attention than yesterday. I was surprised at it, because of my hesitating approach. The time when I markedly lost influence was when N[ewman] left us. It was a shock to the principles which we held; and I was given to understand that I was not to look upon myself as entitled to guide or influence others, and that people meant to be independent of me, unless I would take a less "Romanizing" line'. However, there had been an obvious change. 'The whole course in the last four years has been chequered, but my own feeling has been, that I have been stemming a tide, that very few of my colleagues saw the bearings of things, and that my office was chiefly to stave off things just for such a time, at most as I am there to stave off things'.[44]

The good-natured relations meant that Pusey was able to share experiences with men whom he had previously shunned.

319

This was especially true of his new regard for Francis Jeune. The Master of Pembroke had been a member of the Reform Commission, yet Pusey was 'fascinated at their first encounter, as he told me, by the dashing talk and practical energy of Jeune'. Tuckwell, who made this comment, even thought that Pusey became, for a time, 'a weapon in that clever tactician's hands'.[45] However, Jeune himself might have been equally fascinated, by Pusey's learning, by the reputation that he brought with him, by the aura of Catholic sanctity. There was also a debt to be repaid for Pusey's help for the university cause, and Pusey evidently wished to be friends. Pusey did not need telling how useful the good opinion of a man as powerful as Jeune was, but the regard seems to have been real enough.

Others noticed the partnership. 'Pusey', wrote Liddell in October 1855, 'appears to be dominant in the Council, supporting Jeune where he can, and receiving Jeune's support in other cases'. Jowett also wrote to Tait about Pusey's role: 'In the Hebdomadal Council he appears to have great influence'.[46]

The two men—such seemingly opposite figures—began a correspondence which continued when Jeune became Bishop of Peterborough in 1864, and Pusey was able to write to him as he might to a Catholic Churchman. Thus, on Whit Sunday 1865, he spoke of the Tractarian Movement as inspired by the Holy Spirit. 'Newman and the original Tractarians saw that a work was going on, far beyond any human agency employed, which we believed to be the work of God the Holy Ghost.' That was, presumably, also the conviction which sustained his continued labours in the university. He shared with Jeune the sort of confidence which he usually kept for Keble. 'I have just been preaching for $1\frac{1}{4}$ hours on eternity of punishment. I was struck by the silence of undergraduates, as I passed them. I hope they were thinking'. The sermon was in reply to the Privy Council judgement on *Essays and Reviews*, that notorious volume in which the views of reformers like Jowett, Pattison, and Baden Powell, were revealed in their most extreme form, and which convinced Pusey that the effort to capture the university was part of a larger liberal assault on the Church of England as a whole. 'It is a death struggle', he wrote some months earlier, '—to the death, I trust, of rationalism as a power within the

Church; but they are struggling; not for life, but for victory'. Hence, it was vital for the liberals to win the university to their side—and as vital for him and Jeune to thwart them. 'It is strange to see every fresh vacancy made a battle field, in which they try to secure a post for their adherents'. The battle must be carried into political life: Pusey told Jeune that the Conservative government could only expect support from churchmen if it did not nominate liberals to high ecclesiastical preferment.[47]

The interaction between the two men led, for example, to Pusey warning Jeune away from a petition being circulated in the university in 1862, supporting the parliamentary campaign to abolish clerical subscription. Of what value were statements referring to the opinion of 'members of the Church of England', Pusey asked. 'Every infidel would make it, who did not want to break with all religious people. Colenso would. It is the very object of the Jowett school to make the Church of England a doctrineless body'. Jeune had asked whether Gladstone was 'disposed to surrender subscription'. Pusey, who had earlier spoken of 'being trained in a school of defeat', replied: 'I trust no party and scarcely any body'. A petition against the parliamentary campaign might have done some good, but 'the timidity of Convocation defeated us, as it does so often'. Then there was a direct reference to the damage done by university reform: 'The misery is, that the religious education of our undergraduates is neglected. A large proportion of the tutors seem to be clever laymen who, I fear, dread to meddle with doctrine, and the greater part of our Examiners have abjured all enquiry into it'.[48]

Jeune was in favour of boards to superintend studies, but Pusey asked him to reconsider the idea, on the ground that the boards might recommend books to students for the intellectual information that they contained, without regard to the mischief that they might do to faith:

Mill's Logic is a great text-book in the University [wrote Pusey]. I have not read it; but I know at least two able men, whose faith it destroyed. But whatever the evil of a book's being read may be, it is manifoldly more, if a Delegacy, appointed by the University and acting by its authority,

321

should recommend it. Darwin on The Origin of Species, or
Lyell on the antiquity of man might be recommended by such
a delegacy.

He thought that the power to veto the board's suggestions
should be given to the Vice-Chancellor, or Congregation, and
he asked for Jeune's opinion once more.[49] Pusey showed there
that none of the old protective instinct had disappeared.

There is one last aspect which needs examining. The period
of Pusey's crusade against revolutionary reform was one in
which important theories of the nature and purpose of
university education were being formulated. The obvious
example to cite in the Oxford connection is Newman's *The Idea
of a University*, which in its first form saw the light in 1852, the
year of the issue of the 'blue book'. Newman wrote his book
with an eye to what was happening in Oxford, and he had no
need to guess at the reaction of Pusey and his old colleagues. His
idea 'bears the marks of that clerical and humanistic Oxford
which, more or less, came to an end with the publication of the
Royal Commission's Report'.[50] It is doubtful if Newman's
theories influenced Pusey, as has been claimed,[51] for Pusey had
long published his evidence, and was in the middle of his reply
to Vaughan, when he saw the 'outside of a book of yours', about
which he had 'heard much' from Isaac Williams. That was on 7
March 1854, and Newman sent him a copy, and, in turn, asked
for a copy of *Collegiate and Professorial Teaching and Discipline*,
when it appeared. Newman seems to have helped in supplying
some information about the continental universities.[52]

In the broadest sense, the ideals of the two men were the
same. Newman in the *Discourses* of 1852 had no place for the
connection of Church and university precisely as Pusey saw it,
but he saw the hollowness of merely 'secularized' learning. The
question partly depends on what Pusey considered to be the
place of science in a university curriculum, since Newman
devotes a good deal of attention to this subject. In *Collegiate and
Professorial Teaching and Discipline*, he excluded the sciences from
the strictures that he passed on merely professorial teaching,
because he conceded that much instruction in those fields was
possible only in that form. But this did not exclude science itself

from that office of education, which was to train the spiritual, as well as the intellectual, faculties of students, and so make them fit children of God. For 'God alone *is* in Himself, and is the Cause and Upholder of everything to which He has given being. Every faculty of the mind is some reflection of His; every truth has its being from Him; every law of nature has the impress of His hand. . . . All sciences may do good service, if those who cultivate them know their place, and carry them not beyond their sphere'.[53] He told Stanley, 'In proportion as there is hope that science should be religious, I should be glad to see science established at Oxford. I have no fears from it'.[54]

To this extent, Pusey may be said to share the vision of Newman, that a proper 'liberal' education would include the physical sciences, but not restricted to their merely practical application; for to emphasize the aspect of utility excluded them from the field of liberal knowledge, and, Pusey would have added, robbed them of their true glory as the reflection of God.

Newman, however, may well have questioned the manner in which Pusey chose to defend his educational objectives. In his book, *The Office and Work of Universities*, published four years later, in 1856, he spoke of the hurt done to the university ideal when the college system usurped its functions. He quoted Pusey in support: 'The ascendancy of the college idea in the English universities [has been] to the extreme prejudice, not indeed of its peculiar usefulness (for that it has retained), but of the University itself'. He made a distinction between the two outlooks which Pusey expressed in rather different terms in *Collegiate and Professorial Teaching and Discipline*. A university embodied the principle of progress, a college that of stability, said Newman. 'The University is for theology, law, medicine, for natural history, for physical science, and for the sciences generally and their promulgation; the College is for the formation of character, intellectual and moral, for the cultivation of the mind, for the improvement of the individual . . .'. Had Pusey, in trying to stem the tide of reform, so emphasized the college aspect, that he gravely weakened the university aspect? Newman did not say so, but he plainly thought that the Oxford bill had been a botched affair, and the conservatives had been given too much. 'The late Act of Parliament . . . did not

323

dare to touch the real seat of existing evils, by restoring or giving jurisdiction to the University over the Colleges, much as it professed to effect in the way of radical reform'.[55] The Hansard record shows that the college interest proved too strong for the government, and it is worth asking whether such opposition would have been as effective, if it had not been able to cite Pusey's evidence and other writings in support, and his habit of opposing the colleges to the university, with the fatal identification of the latter with reform and 'German' theories. Newman's ideal university, it will be remembered, had no colleges on the Oxford pattern, and so the 'principle of progress' was ensured.[56]

Another theorist of the university idea was Mark Pattison, whose impressive book, *Suggestions on Academical Organization*, was published in 1868, during the period of the theological statute controversy. Again, parallels can be drawn between Pusey and someone who had once shared Tractarian beliefs with him. In his evidence before the Commission, Pattison had criticized the old Oxford for being simply a place of elementary instruction, and he warned them against compounding this by introducing a purely professorial system which 'aims at, and is the readiest and easiest way to, a very inferior stamp of mental cultivation, but a cultivation which, from its showy, available, marketable character, is really an object of ambition in an age like the present'.[57] The words were very like Pusey's, and Pattison knew why the other rejected the spurious authority given to professors. Their popular image was superficial, inconsistent, limited to the tenure of their Chairs. In contrast to this was the solid authority of a literary tradition, which required students to work on the standard texts. For Pusey the authority of religion rested on the same principles, on a proper acquaintance with the documents of the faith, in a spirit of scholarly obedience to the literary heritage of the Catholic past. Pattison also echoed his dismissal of a syllabus which provided merely professional or useful knowledge. The Commissioners' plan, Pusey had said, 'falls in with the tendency of the present day to look to mere knowledge, not to the discipline and training of the powers of the mind, as the one end to be attained'. The plan coincided with the 'practical side of the

English character, which goes directly to its end, and which hardly understands how any thing can be of use which does not directly bear upon it'.[58]

By 1868, though allowing that the Act of 1854 was a useful beginning, in avoiding sweeping change, Pattison held that the time was ripe for further reform. The English desire for useful instruction had proved stronger than the Commissioners' recommendations: revenues had been voted away for practical, non-academic purposes; 'the public could not see the use of higher knowledge'; and Pusey himself, in Pattison's eyes, seems to have become a symbol of the opposition to progress. He had already pointed out that reliance on a venerable literary tradition must be accompanied by a proper historical method; no 'sound and enlightened study of scientific theology' would be possible at Oxford, if it continued to be restricted to a 'blind getting up of the divinity of the seventeenth century which Dr Pusey still wishes to enforce as the standard of the English Church'.[59] Pattison now contrasted the paucity of the Oxford achievement with the 'brilliant lecture list' at Leipzig, adorned by 110 professors, including eleven in theology, or the 38 courses given in the theological faculty of Berlin in one semester alone. Did he intend a deliberate comparison with the similar argument, and battery of Teutonic names, which Pusey had given in *Cathedral Institutions* 35 years previously? On the question of the state of Oxford theology, he commented: 'the difficulty of touching this matter at all can hardly be overestimated'. 'Dr Pusey has painted, for our avoidance, a picture of a German sophist preaching some wild and novel theory, in order to attract a crowd of unfledged enthusiasts round his chair. That theories have power to attract, implies at least enthusiasm for knowledge, an enthusiasm with which we cannot but sympathize, however much we regret its malappropriation. No professor here in Oxford need fear to become dangerously popular by a similar course'. He thought little of the theological statute, and preferred a more radical alteration, including lay professors of divinity, and the creation of junior lectureships in the faculty.[60]

These last factors suggest how the reform controversy left its mark on Pusey. It is easy to criticize Pusey for divorcing the university from the wider concerns of life, for not relating education to social needs and skills (except in the matter of ministerial training), and for misunderstanding the class issues in the University Bill.[61] But who else (including the liberals) in Oxford, at the time, had any real grasp of these matters which are so important in the modern discussion of higher education? His rejection of a superficial and diffused learning based mainly on lectures, and his suspicion of professorial control of teaching and administration, need no underlining in the experience of many university teachers today. Certainly, his warnings against governmental interference and manipulation have never seemed so relevant as in the present crisis of British universities.

But there were elements in Pusey's antagonism to the University Commission, which revealed the darker and more problematic side of his character. Reform was psychologically alien to him, and this explains the highly-charged correspondence with Gladstone and Keble, and the despair, which at times overwhelmed him, conveyed in it. The psychological aspects combined with the more intellectual antipathies which he felt for 'liberalism', Locke's philosophy of mind, and German 'rationalism' —the latter, as he recalled, having used the universities, when constitutionally altered to suit its purposes, for the transmission of its ideas. But whatever it was that he chose to see in the Report, his response was intense and personal.

Tuckwell, in his gossipy reminiscences, thought that the later Pusey was 'not so *great* as the imposing hierophant of the Forties', and he meant the busy man of affairs and university legislator.[62] Tuckwell concentrated on the change in Pusey's demeanour, his loss of *gravitas*, but the effect on the evolution of Tractarianism was hardly less important. The decisive event seems to have been Pusey's willingness to accept the patronage of the Hebdomadal Board, when it proposed to publish his evidence. Pusey chose to work with the Heads, and his election, in due course, as a member of the Hebdomadal Council, and involvement in university government, was the logical consequence. The surprised reaction of Keble and Newman has already been noted. For them the question was the wisdom of accepting so readily the friendship of those old enemies who had shown such contempt for the Catholic Movement in the past. But, on a deeper level, it was the wisdom of allying the Tractarian pioneers with discredited and notoriously reactionary forces in the university which had regarded them as dangerous innovators. The Tractarians in the thirties had seemed the party of advance, standing for a new religious enthusiasm and scholarship, turning their back on the moribund churchmanship of the past, inspiring the Church with a sense of fresh movement and growth. The question is, how much of that spirit survived what Tuckwell called the 'transitional period' in Pusey's life, given the manner in which he had already expressed his reaction?

NOTES

1 Pusey, *Cathedral Institutions*, 2nd ed. (London 1833), pp. 18, 21, 24, 63.

2 *The British Critic*, vol. 23 (1838), pp. 455f.

3 Liddon, vol. 3, p. 79.

4 *Report of Her Majesty's Commissioners appointed to inquire into the State, Discipline, Studies, and Revenues, of the University and Colleges of Oxford* (London 1852), pp. 71–4. (Hereafter cited as *Report.*) Pusey wrote to Liddon on 25 February 1854, 'Oxford is on the eve probably of a revolution. God guide it. . . . It is very narrow-minded to destroy a Constitution, on the grounds that it has been ill-administered. The Fellows ought to be the élite of the University; the Heads, of the Fellows. If Fellows have abused their trust and have elected Heads unequal to their office, then Fellows are those who need reformation. . . . For myself, I do not expect the University of Oxford to belong to the Church twenty, if so long, years'. (Pusey House, 'Correspondence of E. B. Pusey with H. P. Liddon', vol. 1, fo. 20).

5 *Report and Evidence upon the Recommendations of Her Majesty's Commissioners for inquiring into the State of the University of Oxford* (Oxford 1853), *Evidence*, pp. 102–6. (Hereafter cited as *Report and Evidence.*) Pusey also objected to the Theology School, lest it be regarded as a refuge for academically poor students. 'Others say, there are a number of young men, who will never learn any thing of the Classics. It is better that they should learn something which will be useful to them. This is [B.P.] Symons' language. So they are dunces, who are to get first classes in Theology'. (Keble College, 'Correspondence of E. B. Pusey with J. Keble', vol. 2, fo. 8, 15 June 1854.)

6 Liddon, vol. 3, p. 391.

7 Cf. Newman's letter of 11 March 1854: 'I have read the Report of the

327

Heads of Houses, and smiled to find that after all the rubs they had given you, they were at last obliged to have recourse to you as their best champion . . .'. (Liddon, vol. 3, p. 394, and Newman, *Letters and Diaries* (London 1965), vol. 16, pp. 80–1.)

8   Keble College, 'Correspondence of E. B. Pusey with J. Keble', vol. 2, fo. 13 (5 July 1854).

9   *Report and Evidence*, pp. 1, 63, 77, 101f, 139. Cf. Liddon, vol. 3, pp. 381–6. The conversation on Oxford reform and German professors, at Mrs Proudie's reception, in *Barchester Towers*, suggests that Trollope had read Pusey's evidence. A. Trollope, *Barchester Towers* (London 1963), pp. 104–5.

10   Literary Estate of Miss Ethel Hatch. MS 'Life of Edwin Hatch', vol. 1, fo. 99.

11   W. Tuckwell, *Reminiscences of Oxford* (London 1900), p. 141.

12   *Report and Evidence*, p. 18.

13   E. G. W. Bill, *University Reform in Nineteenth-Century Oxford: a Study of Henry Halford Vaughan* (Oxford 1973), p. 136, and cf. pp. 137–46.

14   H. H. Vaughan, *Oxford Reform and Oxford Professors* (London 1854), pp. 72, 76, 94.

15   Pusey asked Vaughan to correct *Oxford Reform and Oxford Professors*, which contained a quotation, allegedly from the *Report and Evidence*, naming R. D. Hampden as an example of a mistaken professorial appointment by the prime minister. Pusey had not mentioned Hampden, and evidently meant J. A. Ogle, Regius Professor of Medicine. Vaughan refused to make a retraction in the form asked for by Pusey, and published the correspondence in a *Postscript to Oxford Reform and Oxford Professors*. Bodleian Library, MS Eng. Lett. d. 44, fo. 57–76.

16   Pusey, *Collegiate and Professorial Teaching and Discipline* (Oxford 1854), pp. 4, 43, 53–5, 63, 64, 179–87, 212, 216; cf. Liddon, vol. 3, pp. 386–91.

17   Pusey House, 'Correspondence of W. E. Gladstone with E. B. Pusey', vol. 1, fo. 459–60 (17 February 1854), 471 (13 March 1854).

18   Ibid., fo. 435–44 (7 February 1854), 451 (15 February 1854), 459–60 (17 February 1854), 483–4 (13 March 1854).

19   Ibid., fo. 455 (15 February 1854); cf. *Correspondence on Church and Religion of William Ewart Gladstone*, ed. D. C. Lathbury (London 1910), vol. 1, p. 217.

20   Pusey House, 'Correspondence of W. E. Gladstone with E. B. Pusey', vol. 1, fo. 473–81 (13 March 1854).

21   Keble College, 'Correspondence of E. B. Pusey with J. Keble,' vol. 1, fo. 253 (May 1853), vol. 2, fo. 2 (16 February 1854), 7 (9 June 1854), 14 (July 1854), 28 (November 1854).

22   Pusey House, 'Correspondence of J. Keble with E. B. Pusey', vol. 3, letters of 12 March, 19 March, 27 March, 12 June 1854.

23 Keble College, 'Correspondence of E. B. Pusey with J. Keble', vol. 2, fo. 8 (15 June 1854).

24 Pusey House, 'Correspondence of E. B. Pusey with Sir Wm. Heathcote', letter of 9 May 1854.

25 Keble College, 'Correspondence of E. B. Pusey with J. Keble', vol. 2, fo. 2 (16 February 1854), 13, 14, 15 (all July 1854). Pusey House, 'Correspondence of E. B. Pusey with J. Keble', vol. 3, letter of 19 February 1854. Keble and Pusey also seem to have differed slightly on the question of altering college founders' wills; cf. Keble College, 'Correspondence of E. B. Pusey with J. Keble', vol. 1, fo. 261 (22 December 1853), and Liddon, vol. 3, pp. 401–2.

26 Keble College, 'Correspondence of E. B. Pusey with J. Keble', vol. 1, fo. 250 (May 1853), vol. 2, fo. 2 (16 February 1854), 7 (9 June 1854).

27 Ibid., vol. 1, fo. 11 (? June 1854), 15 (July 1854).

28 *Parliamentary Debates*, 3rd series, vol. 131, pp. 893–9, vol. 132, pp. 942–3, and cf. vol. 134, p. 628.

29 Keble College, 'Correspondence of E. B. Pusey with J. Keble', vol. 2, fo. 19 (October 1854).

30 E. G. W. Bill, p. 192.

31 Liddon, vol. 3, p. 405.

32 Pusey House, 'Correspondence of E. B. Pusey with W. E. Gladstone', vol. 2, letter of 17 June 1868. Pusey found that the length of the meetings taxed him; cf. his comment to Liddon, 'We have just had a time-wasting Council' (Pusey House, 'Correspondence of E. B. Pusey with H. P. Liddon', vol. 1, fo. 180 (5 June 1868)).

33 Keble College, 'Correspondence of E. B. Pusey with J. Keble', vol. 2, fo. 19 (October 1854).

34 Pusey House, 'Correspondence of E. B. Pusey with J. Keble', vol. 3, letter of November 1854.

35 Ibid., letter of June 1854. Liddon, vol. 3, p. 408.

36 G. V. Cox, *Recollections of Oxford* (London 1868), p. 390.

37 Pusey House, 'Correspondence of E. B. Pusey with W. E. Gladstone', vol. 2, letter of 24 March 1868.

38 Pusey House, 'Correspondence of E. B. Pusey with H. P. Liddon', vol. 1, fo. 222 (13 April 1869).

39 W. R. Ward, *Victorian Oxford* (London 1965), p. 217.

40 Pusey House, 'Correspondence of E. B. Pusey with W. E. Gladstone', vol. 2, letter of 20 August 1869.

41 W. R. Ward, pp. 250–2. J. W. Burgon, *Plea for a fifth School* (Oxford 1868).

42 Pusey House, 'Correspondence of E. B. Pusey with H. P. Liddon', vol. 1, fo. 197 (17 December 1868).

43 Ibid., fo. 188 (autumn 1868). Pusey's pamphlet, *The proposed Statute for a*

Pusey Rediscovered

Theological School, envisaged a board consisting of four divinity professors, with the Vice-Chancellor and Proctors. The clerical majority was needed, he argued, because the removal of religious tests no longer safeguarded the orthodoxy of the other members. The liberals held that this would make Theology the one school not accountable to Congregation, but they were defeated when the statute was finally passed in May 1869.

44 Keble College, 'Correspondence of E. B. Pusey with J. Keble', vol. 2, fo. 27 (November 1854). Pusey House, 'Correspondence of E. B. Pusey with J. Keble', vol. 5, letter of 11 June 1858.

45 Tuckwell, p. 149.

46 E. G. W. Bill, p. 192; cf. Liddon, vol. 3, p. 405: '"I have made a discovery", said Dr Jeune . . . "since I have been in Council: I always thought of Pusey as a mere theologian; I find he is an admirable man of business" . . . [Pusey said] "Jeune is not the sort of man some of our friends have thought him: he is a person of clear and strong, if somewhat narrow faith, and brings an acute and powerful mind to the support of positive truth"'.

47 Bodleian Library, MS Eng. Lett. d. 193, fo. 143 (20 June 1864), 151 (autumn 1864), 186 (Whitsunday 1865).

48 Ibid., fo. 127 (6 August 1862).

49 Ibid., fo. 169 (26 April 1865).

50 J. H. Newman, *The Idea of a University,* introduction by C. F. Harrold (London 1947), pp. xx–xxi; cf. F. McGrath, *The Consecration of Learning* (Dublin 1962), p. 153.

51 F. McGrath, *Newman's University: Idea and Reality* (London 1951), p. 177.

52 J. H. Newman, *Letters and Diaries,* vol. 16, pp. 80–1, 88.

53 Pusey, *Collegiate and Professorial Teaching and Discipline,* p. 215.

54 Liddon, vol. 3, p. 391. This view of science was similar to Newman's view that Theology must be the basis of all studies in the university, and without it no true knowledge was possible. Newman's denial of the utilitarian approach to education, and his criticism of Locke, were also echoed in Pusey, cf. *Report and Evidence,* pp. 38, 39, 101, 110–11, 173, and *Collegiate and Professorial Teaching and Discipline,* pp. 215–16, with J. H. Newman (ed. I. T. Ker), *The Idea of a University* (Oxford 1976), pp. 91–3, 140–6.

55 J. H. Newman, *The Office and Work of Universities* (London 1856), pp. 339, 345, 359–60.

56 Cf. J. H. Newman, *The Idea of a University,* ed. I. T. Ker, p. xxvi.

57 *Report,* p. 94.

58 *Report and Evidence,* p. 73.

59 *Oxford Essays 1855,* p. 305.

60 M. Pattison, *Suggestions on Academical Organization* (Edinburgh 1868), pp.

176–7, 244, 325, 341–8; cf. *National Review* (January 1868), p. 213. Pusey's 'Germanic' manner of teaching was described by Stanley: 'The whole atmosphere of the Professor's lectures breathed the spirit of Germany. . . . I heard there the names of more German writers than in the whole course of the instruction given in my whole stay in Oxford. . . . Of all the Professors in Oxford, there is none who has more frequently recurred to me as the example of what a German Professor is, and of what an English Professor might be, than the present Regius Professor of Hebrew' (Bill, pp. 252–3). But Stanley was apt to see correspondences when none existed; cf. Pusey's letter to Jeune in June 1864, 'Perhaps it is another case of his [Stanley] being able to see similarities, but not to see differences' (Bodleian Library, MS. Eng. Lett. d. 193, fo. 142).

61 Pusey admitted in the evidence that the 'weakness of the Church in these later years has been, that it has not known how to employ the talents of the middle ranks'. He had observed how many English divines were the 'sons of tradesmen', but a 'good and religious education, after a few years, will leave no traces of this distinction of birth' (!) (*Report and Evidence*, p. 81); cf. Pattison, p. 325, 'Oxford has lapsed into a School for the Upper Classes', and Liddon, vol. 3, p. 396 1 n, 'Pusey does not appear to have anticipated one great mischief of this [Reform] measure: its transfer of endowments, intended for the poor, to the sons of parents who could pay for forcing tutors and so secure University prizes. Its effect was to make a present of the endowments of Oxford to the upper middle class'.

62 Tuckwell, p. 150.

13

Reflections on a Controversy: Newman and Pusey's 'Eirenicon'

RODERICK STRANGE

1

In the September of 1865, John Keble's wife, Charlotte, who had suffered a great deal from ill-health, was unwell once more. Newman had been planning to visit the Kebles for some time. Although they had not actually met since Newman had been received into the Roman Catholic Church in 1845, nor corresponded between 1846 and 1863, their friendship remained undimmed. However, the plan almost went awry. Charlotte Keble's ill-health and the news of an unexpected visit by Pusey to Hursley Vicarage tempted Newman to postpone his call. He had not seen Pusey for nineteen years and to meet two such dear friends together after such a lapse of time was, he felt, more than he could bear. But at the last moment he changed his mind, reversed his plans, and arrived on Keble's doorstep unannounced. Thus it happened that these three friends, who had been so united and later so separated, dined together 'simply by themselves', according to Newman, 'for the first and last time'.[1]

The incident is noteworthy here because of Pusey's reaction to it. The meeting had been reported in the press. Pusey protested. He wrote to the editor of the *Guardian*, the Tractarian newspaper, on 9 October 1865:

> I much regret having to obtrude upon the public my own private feelings, but the statement which you copied from some local paper (inaccurate in every particular, except that I spent some happy hours with my friend Dr Newman) is so intensely painful that I cannot help myself. The statement is, that Dr N. and myself were '*reconciled* after twenty years'. The

deep love between us, which now dates back for above forty
years, has never been in the least overshadowed. His leaving
us was one of the deep sorrows of my life; but it involved
separation of place, not diminution of affection.[2]

This declaration by Pusey of his bond with Newman supplies a
natural and illuminating starting-point for a study of their
controversy.

At the time of their meeting, Pusey was writing a new book.
It was to be addressed to Keble and called *An Eirenicon*.[3] The
work was in answer to a pamphlet of Manning's, who became
archbishop of Westminster at about that time. Manning in turn
had been prompted to write because he had been identified
popularly as one of those Roman Catholics who were, in a
phrase of Pusey's, 'in an ecstasy of triumph' over certain
troubles within the Church of England. He wanted to make his
position clear. His pamphlet, though not unsympathetic, was
marked by his characteristic vigour and aggressiveness. He
rejoiced in the workings of the Holy Spirit within the Church of
England, lamented when truth gave way before unbelief,
rejoiced at the unfolding of more perfect truth, but could not
'regard the Church of England as "the great bulwark against
infidelity in this land"'.[4] During his conversation with Keble
and Newman, Pusey was full of his work in reply to these
charges,[5] and at that time Newman had neither desire nor
inclination to become involved in the debate. Within three
months, however, circumstances had changed. By December,
despite a painful illness, he was composing at great speed his
own answer to Pusey.

Their controversy is an unusual one for three main reasons.
First, it is relatively rare for two people, who have so close and
affectionate a friendship, to be locked in public debate. They
disagreed sharply, but without acrimony. Secondly, their
friendship meant that they were able to discuss their separate
positions in private letters as well as by the exchange of public
pamphlets.[6] Thirdly, the sympathy between them created the
most favourable climate for resolving their disagreement
satisfactorily. However, it will be instructive to consider why
the outcome was in fact a disappointment. Here, therefore, is a

controversy whose strategy can be uncovered, examined, and assessed. Let us start at the beginning.

2

Manning's pamphlet appeared in the middle of November 1864, ten months before the three friends were to meet at Keble's vicarage. Pusey and Newman were corresponding at the time about the prospect of Newman establishing an Oratory in Oxford. Pusey mentioned in passing the pressure that was being placed on him to reply to Manning. Newman's reaction was rather off-hand. In a postscript he commented: 'Of course I do not see things on your side sufficiently to be able to say that you should not answer him—but I am tempted to ask, Why should you?'[7] Soon after this, however, Pusey began work on the *Eirenicon*. The next year he produced his book. It is long and not easy to read. His friend, R. W. Church, reviewed it for *The Times* on 12 December 1865 and observed:

> Dr Pusey's views or hopes appear to undergo a modification as his work goes on. He does not end in quite the same mind as he was in when he begins. He is, it must be said, loose in his way of writing, and there is a want all through of gathering up and bringing to a point what he means to urge, which is embarrassing to a reader.[8]

Pusey felt the need to write not only because of Manning's attack. He nurtured a longstanding desire to promote the reunion of the Christian Church. He did not presume that the goal could be achieved in his lifetime, but he insisted that it should be pursued. 'Is there then', he asked, 'no issue to the present division of Christendom? Is disunion to be the normal state of the Church, for which we all pray that God would give her unity, peace, and concord? God forbid! I have never expected to see that external unity of intercommunion restored in my own day; but I have felt it to be an end to be wished for, and prayed for.'[9] And he judged the main obstacle to be Rome's practical system. He could feel no great difficulty over the theory of the Council of Trent, but was thrown back by the way he saw the theory put into practice.

Accordingly, the strategy of his argument followed two main

lines of thought. In the first place, he was anxious to establish the compatibility of the Thirty-nine Articles with the Decrees of the Council of Trent, and in the second to elicit from the Roman authorities some statement of practices which were not *de fide*. Soon after he began working, on Christmas Eve 1864, he explained his intentions to Newman:

> The Council of Trent seems to me to have drawn the line as to the minimum which is to be believed: the English Articles seem to me (speaking generally), especially Art. 22, to condemn a maximum, as not being to be believed. So we are at cross-purposes. Only, while there is no explanation on the Roman side, what is the practical system of the Roman Church everywhere would become the practical system here, in case of the reunion of the Churches.

He wanted a Council of the Roman Church to say, '"Such and such things are *not de fide*," as well as what is *de fide*.'[10] There was naturally much else besides in the *Eirenicon* itself, and in particular a lengthy and detailed reply to the charges levelled by Manning, but strategically these two issues remained paramount. And indeed, to speak of the compatibility between Trent and the Articles was to echo in part the argument of Newman's *Tract* 90. In the same letter, Pusey called it a 'reawakening' of the *Tract*, while in his book he was to observe: 'The interpretation which he [Newman] then put forth, and which in him was blamed, was at the time vindicated by others without blame.'[11] Pusey had been himself one of the vindicators, and now he spoke once more without rebuke. At the same time, the other issue, his concern to establish what was not *de fide*, led him in his book into long-drawn-out illustrations of Roman excesses in devotions to Mary and a discussion of Papal authority. It may well be that these are the passages, which explain Church's reference to a lack of precision in the writing.

Before continuing, however, there is a passing point of interest which it might be most natural to mention here. The controversy as a whole is difficult to assess nowadays because it is so dated. Manning's pamphlet champions the view which identifies the Roman Catholic Church simply and exclusively as the One, Holy, Catholic, and Apostolic Church of the Creed.

That is not surprising. At that time there was no alternative available for someone of his convictions. Pusey in debate argues against this position. His interpretation of the unity of the Church lays stress particularly on the organic union enjoyed by Christians with one another through their union with Christ; even interruptions of intercommunion, he maintains, cannot destroy that unity.[12] Newman, for his part, adopts the same viewpoint as Manning. That also should be expected. It is, however, noteworthy because when writing to Pusey in November 1864, and speaking of his agreement with Manning, he also points out where they disagree: 'In this respect I differ from Manning, because he attempts to define the classes, who are, and who are not [invincibly ignorant and so members of the Church or not].'[13] It is a remark which anticipates an idea of the distinguished Orthodox theologian, Evdokimov, quoted by Bishop Christopher Butler in his Sarum Lectures on *The Theology of Vatican II* in 1966: 'We know where the Church is; it is not for us to judge and say where the Church is not.'[14] Newman's remark stands out as a rare beam of light in the ecclesiology of this controversy.

3

From the time Pusey started work on his book until Newman began his reply, various letters passed between them. One reason for writing was reinforced by coincidence.

Pusey's letter of Christmas Eve 1864, it will be remembered, spoke of his work reawakening *Tract* 90 in people's minds. Some days earlier Newman had received an unexpected letter from a man named John Giles, requesting permission to reprint the Tract. Newman wrote to Pusey asking for information about Giles,[15] and Pusey replied, unsure of Giles' identity, but asking if he might not reprint the Tract himself.[16] Newman agreed on 4 January 1865, 'You may publish when you will',[17] and with publication imminent for Advent of the same year, he wrote to reassure an anxious Pusey on 14 November: 'It is impossible I can dislike any thing you do about it . . . I am far *more* than safe in your hands.'[18]

Newman's confidence in Pusey's treatment of his old Tract did not arise from perfect agreement between them. In part it was an expression of their warmth of common feeling; Newman was confident he could trust in Pusey's kindness towards him. And in part it arose, as he mentioned in the same letter, because his own views on the subject were known so well, no confusion was possible. The difference in their views is of interest. Newman had argued in the *Tract* that those who composed the Articles intended to be vague so that a Catholic interpretation could be included; Pusey believed that that was the interpretation actually intended. Newman had explained this difference in a letter to the Jesuit, Henry Coleridge, some weeks earlier.[19] And when he came to write his public *Letter* to his friend, he decided to be sure that no mistake was made. He pointed out that Pusey's object was different from his own. 'Its [The Tract's] original purpose was simply that of justifying myself and others in subscribing to the Thirty-nine Articles, while professing many tenets which had popularly been considered distinctive of the Roman faith.' Pusey now was taking up an idea, already aired by Cardinal Wiseman, 'that the decrees of the Council of Trent should be made the rule of interpretation for the Thirty-nine Articles'.[20] Throughout this discussion the friendship of the two men was undisturbed by their contrasting opinions. The same was true when they turned their attention to the status of teaching which was not *de fide*.

Newman expressed his misgivings just once. He wrote to Pusey on 4 January 1865, and commented on his Christmas Eve letter:

> You indeed want the Church to decide what is *de fide* and what is not—but, *pace tua*, this seems unreasonable. It is to determine the work of all Councils till the end of time. . . . No one on earth can draw the line between what is *de fide* and what is not, for it would be prophesying of questions which have [not] yet turned up. All we can say is that *so much* actually *is de fide*; and then allow a large margin of doctrine, which we accept as *de fide* implicitly, so far forth as God by His Church shall make it known.[21]

Liddon noted that this view revealed a serious divergence between Pusey and Newman as to what could be achieved, particularly, he observed, because Newman acknowledged 'the power of unlimited future definition . . . to lie in the Church'.[22] It is easy to understand his apprehensions. On the other hand it is possible to sympathize with Newman who felt it was unreasonable 'to ask for more than *liberty* to hold what is, (though not defined), contrary to the *general* belief of the faithful'.[23] In spite of Newman's dissuasions, Pusey continued to press the argument both in further letters and in his book.[24] Newman does not appear to have been drawn on the subject again.

Pusey and Newman exchanged letters on 9 and 10 February 1865 in connection with the Oxford Oratory, but did not write again until early September, when Pusey offered Newman a copy of his new book and Newman accepted it. A week later they met at Keble's vicarage. After that the correspondence intensified.

4

Early in October 1865 Pusey left for France. He visited various French bishops in the hope of arousing interest in his plans for reunion. While abroad and after his return letters were arriving, full of praise for his book, but Newman was silent because he felt profoundly disappointed. He wrote to Keble to express his sadness:

> I really marvel that he should have dreamed of calling it an Irenicon . . . if Pusey is writing to hinder his own people from joining us, well and good, he has a right to write as he has done—but how can he imagine that to exaggerate, instead of smoothing contrarieties, is the way to make us listen to him? I wish I were not obliged to say that his mode of treating with us is rhetorical and unfair.

And after giving a detailed example of his meaning, he concluded: 'The first duty of charity is to try to enter into the mind and feelings of others. This is what I love so much in you, my dear Keble; but I much desiderate it in this new book of Pusey's—and I deplore the absence of it there'.[25]

Keble in turn was saddened. His reply to Newman illustrated clearly his own sense of the actual unity of the branches of the Church, a unity which was obscured only by the need to protest against 'the practical application and popular construction of certain statements'. He was appalled to think that Newman himself might be the one to cut such ground from under their feet.[26] Newman replied two days later unrepentant. The *Guardian*, known for its sympathy and moderation, had reacted with horror to the account of Roman practices reported in the *Eirenicon*. How could it be eirenical to provoke such a response? He objected to Pusey's unbalanced presentation. There was no attempt, he pointed out, 'to soften the impression he leaves on the reader, of the *universality* of' extreme views. 'The whole tone is antagonistic'.[27] Some days later Keble reported this correspondence to Pusey.[28] It is plain that he had missed the main point. He said that Newman seemed to have conceded Pusey's ground by speaking of the difference between formal and popular doctrine. But Newman was not denying certain abuses; he was rather protesting against the unfairness of Pusey's exposition and so questioning its effectiveness as an eirenicon. By this time, however, Newman had written to Pusey himself. His letter, as he had promised, was gentler than the one he sent to Keble. All the same, his disappointment is evident.

'It does seem to me,' he told his friend, 'that Irenicon is a misnomer; and that it is calculated to make most Catholics very angry—And that because they will consider it rhetorical and unfair.' He complained about the way Pusey had built his case by indiscriminate quotation from authors of different status; he acknowledged certain excesses, but doubted their influence; and he indicated certain extravagances, such as the teaching about the Virgin's presence in the Eucharist, which had actually been censured in Rome. 'An Irenicon,' he observed, 'smooths difficulties; I am sure people will think that you increase them.'[29]

Pusey, of course, was pained by this reaction and anxious not to appear hostile in fact under the guise of speaking peace. He explained that he had hoped all the authors he had used were either men of weight, particularly Alphonsus Liguori on whom he relied heavily, or favourite popular authors, like Faber. And he cherished the desire that what was not *de fide* might be set aside. He told Newman, 'I thought, "There it is; if any of it is disowned, it is a gain"'.[30]

Newman wrote back the following day, 3 November, reassuring Pusey that this intention had not been lost on him. But he feared that most people would miss that point and settle down to the parts they could understand more easily. He put it more colourfully still in a draft preserved at Pusey House, 'My great anxiety is that I consider the substantial framework of it will not strike the mass of readers, but they will go off into those other parts of it, its muscles and flesh, which is to Protestants such good food'.[31] In this letter too he mentioned to Pusey that he had no present intention of publishing anything, but that, if he did, it would be in the spirit of an Eirenicon.

At this point, perhaps the most significant question in the whole controversy emerged. Pusey brought it out in his next letter on 6 November. It is the question of the way in which real disagreements should be handled in a dispute.

Pusey's letter expressed the dilemma well: 'if I do not state difficulties, I seem unreal; if I state them, I seem controversial.'[32] He was expressing a genuine problem. Where there is a division and the need consequently to reconcile those who are divided, it is necessary to show sufficient cause for the conflict. It would be an exercise in futility to labour to unite two parties who have no reason to be at odds with each other. But it is difficult to give a satisfactory account of such a sufficient cause. It means usually indicating faults on the other side, besides perhaps owning up to some on your own. And to indicate faults is to appear antagonistic. No one should doubt Pusey's kindly intentions. In his letter on Christmas Eve 1864, he had stated his hope that Newman would 'not much dislike' his answer to Manning;[33] and he explained his approach in the long letters he wrote on 2 and 6 November 1865. Three interwoven lines of argument can be detected.

First, in pursuit of his desire for a declaration of what was not *de fide*, Pusey brought attention to extreme Catholic expressions in relation to Mary. R. W. Church, reviewing his book in *The Times*, recoiled: '. . . there is something absolutely bewildering, like the imaginations of a sick dream, in this audacious extravagance of dogmatism, unfolding itself inexhaustibly into ever stranger and more startling conclusions'.[34] It was the kind of reaction Pusey wished to elicit from Catholics, followed, he hoped, by the disavowal of such extravagance. Secondly, it has been noted that he took care to select his examples, although extreme, from authoritative representatives, whether weighty or popular. Quotations from St Alphonsus Liguori, Bernardine of Siena, Eadmer, Faber and others were pressed into service. He did not want the case he presented brushed aside as peripheral. Finally, he pointed out to Newman that the popular aspect was also an important one. To submit to a faith, he said, while criticizing its practical system was quite inconceivable, and he reminded Newman of a lady to whom he had made such a remark many years previously; she had replied by confirming that Newman held exactly the same view. He had told her, 'Dr P. is quite right; a person ought not [to join the Church of Rome] unless he can receive the system taught by Liguori.'[35]

In reply, Newman doubted the reality of the dilemma. He did not feel it was a matter either 'of *not* stating your difficulties, *or* of *offending* Catholics'.[36] In his view, Pusey had failed to take account of two vital distinctions. First, he had not distinguished between doctrine and devotion. Newman discussed the matter in various letters to his friends, observing that while doctrine was settled, devotion was various. He put the matter to Pusey succinctly, 'Suarez teaches dogma, and dogma is fixed. St Bernardine is devotional, and devotion is free'.[37] Furthermore, he had failed to observe the distinction between the practical system, and its local colouring. Newman acknowledged readily that it would be wrong to enter a Church and not take up its practical system, namely what is presented in its popular catechisms and books of devotion. That was what he meant by accepting the system of Liguori. But he insisted that it was still necessary to discriminate. For example, it could be correct to adopt a moral theology, like that of St Alphonsus, while not holding its doctrine of equivocation. 'The practical "system"', he commented, 'remains, quite distinct from the additions or colour which it receives in this country or that, in this class, in this school, or that.'[38]

The result of this failure to observe these distinctions was, Newman argued, confusion. When devotion and doctrine are simply mixed up together, and a practical system presumed to imply any idiosyncracy that might be expressed, casual comments or flights of devotional fancy seem to possess an authority which in fact is groundless. He referred to one outstanding example in several letters.[39] He indicated how Pusey had quoted Suarez quite properly in favour of the intercession of Mary, but then glided on through quotations from Bernardine of Siena and the English historian and theologian, Eadmer, who was a companion of St Anselm, to illustrate the view that it was necessary to invoke her or to be devout towards her in order to be saved.[40] But intercession and invocation are very different matters. And Newman objected to a way of writing which implied that acceptance of the one was advocacy of the other. With Pusey he was blunt: 'When you say or imply that Suarez said what Eadmer said, whereas he only said what St Irenaeus says, you startle us, because, instead of stating an existing difficulty, you make one, which you do not show to exist. Suarez's name is authoritative all over the Catholic Church; not so Eadmer or St Bernardine'.[41]

In brief, Newman was resolving Pusey's dilemma by appealing for a higher standard of scholarship. He said as much in answer to his friend, T. W. Allies, who wrote the following February to compliment him on the publication of his *Letter to Pusey* and who referred to Pusey's 'untruthfulness'. Newman replied: 'As to Pusey, it is harsh to call any mistakes of his, untruthfulness'. He at once explained what he meant, 'I think they arise from the same slovenly habit which some people would recognize in his dress, his beard, etc. He never answers letters, I believe, which do not lie in the line of the direct *work* which he has on hand. And so, in composing a book, he takes uncommon pains about some points, as in his analysis of the Episcopal Replies *in re* Immaculate Conception; but he will combine this with extreme carelessness in respect to other statements'.[42] Throughout the dispute, Newman felt that Pusey did nothing to smooth away difficulties. It was this omission which, to his mind, made the claim of 'Eirenicon' so inappropriate.

At this juncture, however, it is possible to detect clearly the rare atmosphere of their exchanges. Pusey has been gently but firmly arguing his case and Newman has been replying directly and frankly. Did their relationship cool, as Keble had feared? 'I do hope he [Newman] will not waver in his friendship for you,' he had remarked to Pusey.[43] The fear was unfounded. At the very time of disagreeing with him, Newman was also writing enthusiastically, offering to co-operate with suggestions for the French translation 'most gladly', advising Pusey to delay so that he could take into account any comments from Manning,[44] and rejoicing at an encouraging notice of the *Eirenicon* in the *Weekly Register*.[45] Pusey, for his part, was wondering whether Newman 'could draw up something which I might put before the English Church, as firm to offer'.[46] They were most cordial disputants.

5

On 24 November 1865 Newman wrote to Coleridge in a way that suggested he had still not decided to join the debate publicly. Four days later he left for Rednal, the Oratorians' house in the country outside Birmingham, to prepare to write. Various factors had swayed him. He felt keenly the harshness of Rome's dealings with Catholic members of the Association for the Promotion of the Unity of Christendom. Membership had been prohibited the previous year and an appeal by 187 Anglicans had elicited only a condemnation of the branch theory of the Church. Such events created an impression that all Catholics were like Ward and Faber.[47] Newman wished to qualify that impression by his own moderate treatment of the subject, if he could write without causing Pusey pain;[48] and in the event he wished also to correct the notion which was becoming popular that he was the person, quoted by Pusey, who had called the Anglican Church the great bulwark against infidelity in England.[49] Such a description compromised his position.[50]

At Rednal he wrote at great speed. He also sent letters to both Keble and Pusey on 8 December, the feast of the Immaculate Conception, so that they knew what he was doing. He stressed to them his wish not to cause pain and his desire to preserve the eirenical spirit.[51] Pusey replied the next day. The controversy had gathered momentum and he was relieved that Newman was taking a part. He noted, 'This discussion is taking too wide a range, for me to wish you to be silent'.[52] And indeed Newman wrote in a manner which exemplified the advice he was to give to Coleridge some months later. He warned him that 'Abuse is as great a mistake in controversy, as panegyric in biography'. He should rather try 'to say a word in season to *his* [Pusey's] followers and to *his* friends—to dispose them to look kindly on Catholics and Catholic doctrine—to entertain the possibility that they have misjudged us, and that they are needlessly, as well as dangerously keeping away from us'.[53]

Nor is it surprising that Newman was able to write so fast. He soon decided to limit his remarks to Marian teaching and devotion and he adopted in general a patristic line. Accordingly, he needed only to throw into more popular form material he had already discussed in his *Essay on Development*. The rest was largely a matter of distilling thoughts which he had expressed previously in his letters: the question of bulwark and break-water; the difference between Faber and Ward, on the one hand, and himself, on the other; the significance of Tract 90; the distinction between doctrine and devotion, intercession and invocation. In a famous passage he repudiated foreign extrava-gances as 'a bad dream': '. . . as spoken by man to man, in England, in the nineteenth century, I consider them calculated to prejudice inquirers, to frighten the unlearned, to unsettle consciences, to provoke blasphemy, and to work the loss of souls'.[54] His *Letter* was published on 31 January.

After publication, Keble wrote within days, gracious and grateful as ever, but overcome by the sudden deterioration in his wife's health. He had not opened the book.[55] Within two months, quite unexpectedly, he was himself dead. Pusey wrote soon also. He was grateful for Newman's kind words about himself, but took the opportunity to explain various points which he disputed. The controversy continued, both men receiving praise and rebuke from their own communions as well as each other's. Pusey was to write two further volumes of *Eirenicon*, both addressed as *Letters* to Newman, while Newman was eventually able to continue his reply to Pusey, almost ten years later, when he wrote about authority and the papacy in his *Letter to the Duke of Norfolk*. It is necessary to draw to a close.

6

The outcome of this debate may well seem disappointing. It had so much to encourage optimism: friendship and sympathy between Pusey and Newman, a common objective, and a readiness to co-operate as their dispute unfolded. Yet they could not reach an agreement. Indeed, at the end they do not seem any closer than they were at the beginning. Various reasons suggest themselves.

First, it may well be that the very understanding of the Church which they employed defeated them from the start; Newman held to the claim of the Roman Catholic Church to be exclusively the Church of Christ, while Pusey worked with the branch theory of the Church with all the complexities and questions which that begs. Again, although both desired reunion, both were prompted to write by different factors. Pusey, in the first instance, was concerned to answer the charges levelled by Manning; his work grew out of that concern. Keble was to remark that, when Newman spoke of Pusey attacking Catholics, he was in danger of forgetting that he was actually defending Anglicans.[56] Newman did not write mainly to answer Pusey. He had done that already in the series of private letters which had passed between them. His purpose, although intended as an answer, was primarily to make public and establish openly an English disposition to certain Catholic doctrines and devotions which at that time were suffering from an excessive amount of continental colour and influence. In the circumstances, it is hardly surprising that their exchanges were not more fruitful. Were they, therefore, a waste of time? Are they bereft of significance a century later? Not necessarily.

One sentence from this controversy has become famous. At the beginning of his public *Letter*, Newman took Pusey to task for calling his book *An Eirenicon*. He went on, 'There was one of old time who wreathed his sword in myrtle; excuse me—you discharge your olive-branch as if from a catapult'.[57] Liddon acknowledged the turn of phrase, but called it unjust, for it 'cleverly diverted attention from the fact that the sting lay in the obstacles themselves and not in their enumeration'.[58] Church, on the other hand, reviewing Newman's *Letter* in *The Times* on 31 March 1866, agreed wholeheartedly: 'This is, no doubt, exactly what Dr. Pusey has done'.[59] Such reactions are instructive.

Liddon's meaning is plain enough. In fact Church's was the same. He argued that Pusey had no alternative but belligerence. He had given more credit to Rome than most people would have thought possible, and so it was necessary to state the obstacles also, openly and courageously. Church was pleased that Newman had detached himself from these obstacles, the extravagances of the extremists, but he went on to observe, 'it seems to us much more difficult for him to release his cause from complicity with the doctrines which he dislikes and fears . . . the question is whether he or the innovators represent the true character and tendencies of their religious system'.[60] It is a telling point. It cuts to the heart of ecumenical discussions. It is not answered by distinctions between doctrine and devotion, however necessary and proper those may be in their place. Whether Pusey was confused or not, makes little difference. He had articulated a suspicion, and aroused a prejudice, and Church's reaction bore witness to it. All their sympathy and friendship—and Church too was a good friend—could not erase that uncertainty. The only antidote could be a widespread, popular trust, an ease and confidence in the other.

At the very least, this controversy is a cautionary tale. It warns us that Agreed Statements on our shelves, on the Eucharist, ministry, and authority, on the nature of the Church, Mariology, and justification by faith, and on many other subjects besides, will count for nothing, *even combined with love, sympathy, and friendship*, unless there exists amongst us this deeply-felt, unequivocal trust.

NOTES

1   Newman, *Letters and Diaries*. Ed. C. S. Dessain *et al.* (London & Oxford, 1961–), vol. 24, p. 142; see also ibid., vol. 22, pp. 51–3.
2   Quoted in Liddon, vol. 4, p. 112.
3   Pusey, *An Eirenicon in a Letter to the Author of 'The Christian Year'* (London 1865).
4   See H. E. Manning, *The Workings of the Holy Spirit in the Church of England: a Letter to the Rev. E. B. Pusey, D.D.*, 2nd ed. (London 1865), pp. 6–7.
5   See *Letters and Diaries*, vol. 22, p. 52 n. 6.
6   That can be a delicate task, as Newman was aware. He warned off the Jesuit, Father Henry Coleridge, who had written about Pusey's book in *The Month*. 'As to your writing to him,' he remarked, 'there is a difficulty

in keeping up consistently two characters at once—that of a private acquaintance and that of a stranger.' (*Letters and Diaries*, vol. 22, p. 120.) On account of their friendship, of course, Newman was better placed.

7 *Letters and Diaries*, vol. 21, p. 315.
8 R. W. Church, 'An Eirenicon', in *Occasional Papers* (London 1897), vol. 1, p. 351.
9 *Eirenicon*, p. 98.
10 Quoted in Liddon, vol. 4, p. 99.
11 *Eirenicon*, p. 30.
12 See *Eirenicon*, pp. 46, 59.
13 *Letters and Diaries*, vol. 21, p. 315.
14 See Christopher Butler, *The Theology of Vatican II*, rev. ed. (London 1981), p. 119.
15 See *Letters and Diaries*, vol. 21, p. 360.
16 See Liddon, vol. 4, p. 101.
17 *Letters and Diaries*, vol. 21, p. 372.
18 *Letters and Diaries*, vol. 22, p. 103.
19 See Newman to Coleridge, 20 October 1865, *Letters and Diaries*, vol. 22, pp. 78–9.
20 Newman, *A Letter Addressed to the Rev. F. B. Pusey, D.D., on occasion of his Eirenicon*, in *Certain Difficulties Felt by Anglicans in Catholic Teaching*, uniform edition (Westminster, Maryland, 1969), vol. 2, pp. 13, 14.
21 *Letters and Diaries*, vol. 21, p. 370.
22 Liddon, vol. 4, p. 100.
23 *Letters and Diaries*, vol. 21, p. 370.
24 Pusey to Newman, 5 January 1865; and 2 November 1865; and *Eirenicon*, p. 99 ff.
25 *Letters and Diaries*, vol. 22, pp. 67–9.
26 Keble to Newman, 30 October 1865; see *Letters and Diaries*, vol. 22, p. 91, 3 n.
27 *Letters and Diaries*, vol. 22, pp. 91–2.
28 Keble to Pusey, 8 November 1865; see Liddon, vol. 4, pp. 124–5.
29 *Letters and Diaries*, vol. 22, pp. 89–90.
30 Liddon, vol. 4, pp. 121–3.
31 Draft of Newman's reply of 3 November 1865; copied after Pusey's letter for 2 November, in Pusey House.
32 Liddon, vol. 4, p. 124.
33 See Liddon, vol. 4, p. 99.
34 Church, *Occasional Papers*, vol. 1, p. 354.
35 See Liddon, vol. 4, pp. 121–4; quotation at p. 123.
36 *Letters and Diaries*, vol. 22, p. 100.

37 *Letters and Diaries*, vol. 22, p. 90; see also Letters to Keble, 8 October 1865, ibid. vol. 22, p. 68, and to J. R. Bloxam, 6 November 1865, ibid. vol. 22, p. 98.

38 *Letters and Diaries*, vol. 22, p. 100.

39 See, for example, Letters to Keble, 8 October 1865, *Letters and Diaries*, vol. 22, pp. 67–9; to J. R. Bloxam, 19 October 1865, ibid., vol. 22, p. 78; to Pusey, 31 October 1865, ibid. vol. 22, p. 90; to J. R. Bloxam, 6 November 1865, ibid., vol. 22, p. 98; to Pusey, 10 November 1865, ibid., vol. 22, p. 100.

40 See *Eirenicon*, pp. 101–3.

41 *Letters and Diaries*, vol. 22, pp. 100–1.

42 *Letters and Diaries*, vol. 22, p. 158.

43 Keble to Pusey, 8 November 1865; see Liddon, vol. 4, p. 125.

44 *Letters and Diaries*, vol. 22, p. 102.

45 *Letters and Diaries*, vol. 22, p. 106. The notice was by William Lockhart. For a discussion of his view, see H. Christopher Budd, 'Dr Pusey's Eirenicon: a Study of an Anglican Scheme for Reunion, its Background, its Principles, and its Effect' [unpublished thesis, Pontifical Gregorian University, Rome 1966], pp. 133–49.

46 Pusey to Newman, 13 November 1865; printed in R. D. Middleton, *Newman at Oxford* (London 1950), pp. 250–1.

47 See Newman to Coleridge, 24 November 1865, *Letters and Diaries*, vol. 22, p. 110.

48 See Newman to James Hope-Scott, 26 November 1865, *Letters and Diaries*, vol. 22, p. 112.

49 *Eirenicon*, p. 8.

50 The saying was confused with his remark in the *Apologia*, describing the Church of England as 'a serviceable breakwater against errors more fundamental than its own'. Newman explained that he thought a bulwark integral to an object, a breakwater accidental; and the reference to 'more fundamental' errors implied the presence of some fundamental errors within the Anglican Church (see *Letter to Pusey*, pp. 9–11).

51 See *Letters and Diaries*, vol. 22, pp. 118–19.

52 Liddon, vol. 4, p. 131.

53 *Letters and Diaries*, vol. 22, pp. 211–12; also ibid., vol. 22, pp. 306–7.

54 See *Letter to Pusey*, pp. 113–15.

55 Keble to Newman, 3 February 1866; see *Letters and Diaries*, vol. 22, p. 147, 3 n.

56 See Keble to Pusey, 24 November 1865; see Liddon, vol. 4, p. 130.

57 *Letter to Pusey*, p. 7.

58 Liddon, vol. 4, p. 136.

59 Church, *Occasional Papers*, vol. 2, p. 406.

60 Ibid., p. 415.

14

Leader of the Anglo-Catholics?

PETER G.COBB

To be a leader 'has been altogether foreign to all the objects of my heart', Pusey declared in 1850,[1] and almost at the end of his life, in concluding a letter to *The Times*, he said, 'I write this simply as an individual, never having been a "leader" '.[2] Yet in popular history and indeed during his own lifetime, Pusey was widely regarded as the leader of the Catholic party in the Church of England: its members, in fact, were usually known as Puseyites. Pusey himself was aware of the anomaly.

> I am in this strange position [he told Bishop Tait] that my name is made a byword for that with which I never had any sympathy [i.e., Ritualism]. . . . I have had no office in the Church which would entitle me to speak publicly. If I had spoken, it would have been to assume the character of one of the leaders of a party, which I would not do.[3]

He had no wish to encourage party-spirit. He believed in the Catholic nature of the Church of England and it was this he was concerned to defend and make manifest. This explains his fluctuating relationships with the various Catholic societies and organizations. It also explains the main weakness of the Catholic party in the Church of England, its lack of direction. Pusey was its only possible leader but he had no wish to act as such. As a rule he intervened in church politics only when some doctrinal point was at stake.

The role of Pusey in the Gorham crisis in 1850 is typical of his involvement in the doctrinal controversies of the nineteenth century and well illustrates the nature and extent of his influence and the means by which he brought it to bear.

He was always ready to put his learning and scholarship at the disposal of those trying to defend Catholic doctrine and

349

practice. The Gorham case involved various issues: the doctrine of baptismal regeneration, the legitimacy of the exercise of the Royal Supremacy and the revival of synodical action to counteract the Judgement. Pusey advised Bishop Phillpotts in the latter part of his conduct of the case, helped him to draft his Pastoral Letter in response to the Judgement and to organize a diocesan synod to reaffirm the disputed doctrine. He also published a learned tome crammed with historical facts and quotations on the Royal Supremacy. Like his later volume on the Real Presence (1857), the product of the eucharistic controversy in the Denison case, it was only a fragment of a much larger projected work which was never completed.

Pusey also used the controversial weapon, familiar in academic circles, of a declaration or protest signed by influential names. In the Gorham case there were many of these protests and the original one, a list of resolutions, was actually drawn up by Manning and some of his more extreme friends. Pusey and Keble were 'alarmed at the thorough going tone' of them, and fearing the reaction, got them considerably modified.[4] This did not please some of the extremists and neither Pusey nor Keble was consulted over the drawing up of a second Declaration about the Royal Supremacy.[5] Pusey learnt from all this and in later controversies drew up declarations on the Eucharist (1856) and on Confession (1873),[6] which were framed to attract as wide a spectrum of support as possible. The object was also to 'make themselves marks for others to shoot at'.[7] Several times Pusey urged the ultra Protestant Church Association to prosecute him or associate him in the current prosecution.[8]

Pusey's intention was always irenic. Whilst fighting to reaffirm the truth as he saw it, he had no wish to alienate the Evangelicals or to narrow the comprehensiveness of the Church of England. He opposed putting out what he called 'a new and more stringent statement on the doctrine of baptism than any now contained in our Formularies', such as Dodsworth wanted, for the sake of the Evangelicals, who, he was convinced, misunderstood the theological issues 'and believe better than they speak'. The misunderstandings had to be removed and the affirmation of belief in baptismal regeneration to be balanced 'by the statement of other truth'.[9] He was opposed to any exaggeration of the seriousness of the crisis and was quite prepared to use the threat of resignation to enforce his own views. When the Committee of the London Church Union was discussing the implication of the Judgement on the Church's right to decide controversies of faith, a very exaggerated statement of the claims of the Crown was put forward. Pusey threatened to withdraw if it were not modified, and was indeed on the point of leaving when Marriott persuaded the proponents of the resolution to compromise.[10]

This stance led to Pusey's being accused of betrayal by some of the more extreme Catholics like Dodsworth and Allies, who eventually seceded to Rome. On the other hand, it led to his being equally misunderstood by the moderates like Denison and Palmer. As a consequence of secessions and rumours of secessions to Rome, and in the heated atmosphere engendered by the announcement that the Roman Church intended to set up a hierarchy in England, many felt that opposition to the exercise of the Royal Supremacy in the Gorham case had to be accompanied by some sort of anti-Roman declaration. Even Keble thought that 'a *very moderate*, but *quite real* disavowal of Rome' was necessary.[11] When Palmer framed such a declaration and proposed putting it to a meeting of the Bristol Church Union, Pusey was adamant against it:

> Such a Declaration is adding to the Articles of the Church of England; and what business has a private body . . . to lay down as a fundamental Article what the Church of England has not laid down?

The declaration included a statement that intercommunion with the Roman Church could not be restored until the Roman Church had reformed itself. Pusey singled this out as an example of the presumption of a small body attempting to determine the policy of the Church of England. 'The English Church has never said anything of the kind about non-intercommunion with Rome'.[12] Despite his misgivings, especially in view of Keble's opinion, Pusey determined to oppose it because of the seriousness of the consequences. 'I fear that it will be a hard struggle; but it is one of very great moment. It is one to determine the whole course of the movement.'[13] 'An anti-

351

Roman declaration will hopelessly split us.'[14] In the event, the Declaration was not adopted by the Bristol Church Union, nor by the London Church Union. As a result Palmer and Denison and their supporters left the Bristol Union. Nevertheless, after Pusey's death, Palmer, reflecting on the course of events, magnanimously conceded that Pusey's policy had been right. He had conciliated the 'semi-Romanizers', steadied them in the Faith and enlisted their energies and abilities which would otherwise have been lost to the Church. This was no mean task. 'He had to control a very uncertain party, open to Newman's influence for some time—a party which was unsettled in principle and might easily be driven into secession.'[15]

Pusey was thus very actively involved in the Gorham crisis and exerted himself, writing, publishing, speaking at public and private meetings, advising, even threatening, in order to defend the Catholic position of the Church of England. The position he adopted was essentially conservative, a defence of the status quo. He was content to accept patiently some of the anomalies arising from the Reformation. Although at one point he spoke vaguely of disestablishment, in his book on the Royal Supremacy he backed away from it. 'It seems to me a duty not to contemplate a disruption of the relations of Church and State, until it should be forced upon us. . . .' 'We should not, on every fresh offence of the Legislature, speak of the separation of Church and State.'[16] Again although he advocated the revival of provincial synods in theory,[17] he played no active part in the actual revival of Convocation, which in some ways was the most significant result of the crisis. He thought it would be 'a very anxious thing' if it were to be restored, 'except that the Bishops are so cautious'.[18]

In the ensuing years Pusey's reputation grew enormously. He was persecuted by the bishops, singled out by Bishop Blomfield of London, in his 1851 Charge, for the spirituality, which he inculcated by his adaptation of Roman Catholic devotional books and his use of the confessional, and privately inhibited by his own bishop, Samuel Wilberforce, from preaching in the Oxford diocese because of the tone of his teaching. This made him a martyr in the eyes of the Catholics, yet he was not a 'party man'. He came to the defence of Catholic eucharistic doctrine in the Denison and Bennett cases and in the trial of Bishop Forbes but he was not a member of any of the Catholic societies which were formed in the fifties and sixties until he joined the English Church Union in 1866. He never belonged to the Association for the Promotion of the Unity of Christendom (founded 1857) or to the Confraternity of the Blessed Sacrament (1862) or to the later Society for the Maintenance of the Faith (1873). The one exception was the Society of the Holy Cross, SSC, whose object of promoting holiness in the lives of priests was particularly dear to Pusey. He joined within a year of its foundation in 1855, helping to draw up its Rule for celibates. One of its first retreats was held in his house.[19] He soon parted company with the brethren, however, over the question of ritualism and had ceased to be an active member by 1858. He was never a great reader of the religious press. He ceased to subscribe to the moderate High Church *Guardian* (f. 1846) in 1862 because of its doctrinal 'laxity' and his dislike of its 'flippancy', professing to be shocked 'that it should be supposed to represent us'.[20] He had an even lower opinion of the more avowedly partisan Anglo-Catholic *Church Times* founded in 1863 and never addressed a letter to the editor. Both failed the Catholic cause in the controversy over *Essays and Reviews*. 'The *Church Times* seems worse than *The Guardian*. *The Guardian* represents respectable, the *Church Times* Pharisaical and conceited indifference.'[21] He found it impossible to keep to his intention of not allowing letters of his to appear in *The Guardian* and on several occasions did in fact write to the editor but it is significant that when he wrote to the Press, he usually chose to write to *The Times*. As an Oxford professor and canon of Christ Church, Pusey was obviously heavily involved in the business and politics of both University and college and in his own academic and literary work, but, apart from these considerations, he stood somewhat aloof from church politics because he had little sympathy with Ritualism, with which the Anglo-Catholics were increasingly identified.

Of late years [he said in 1860] when Ritualism has become more prominent, I have looked out for a natural opportunity of dissociating myself from it. . . . Altogether I have looked with sorrow at the crude way in which some doctrines have been put forward, without due pains to prevent misunderstanding and ritual has been forced upon the people unexplained and without their consent.[22]

In 1866 he joined the English Church Union, an amalgamation dating from 1860 of the local Church Unions with the Church of England Protection Society, of which most of the leading Ritualists were members. This somewhat surprising move was in part an act of piety towards Keble, who had recently died. He was asked to take Keble's place in the Union by Robert Brett, one of the lay Anglo-Catholic leaders, and some of his friends. He probably felt that he could not refuse such an invitation, but he also professed himself satisfied with 'the prudence and wisdom of the chairman [Hon. Colin Lindsay], and the proceedings of the Council'.[23] Another possible reason for his joining was the exoneration of the liberal theology of *Essays and Reviews* by the Judicial Committee of the Privy Council which had revived agitation for the revision of the Court of Appeal and made Pusey appreciate the value of organized opposition to the Establishment. He was immediately elected a member of the English Church Union Council and was soon clerical Vice-President. Thus he was thrown headlong into ecclesiastical party politics.

The great issue of the day was the Ritualist question and Pusey's effectiveness as a leader must to a large extent be judged by the extent of his success in influencing and guiding the Ritualists through his position in the English Church Union. The difficulty was that Pusey had no interest in Ritualism or understanding of it. His concerns were doctrinal and spiritual. Hence his original attitude to Ritualism. As he explained in his first speech at the English Church Union.

We had . . . a distinct fear in regard to ritual; and we privately discouraged it, lest the whole movement should become superficial. . . . We felt that it was very much easier to change a dress than to change the heart, and that externals might be gained at the cost of the doctrines themselves. To have introduced ritual before the doctrines had widely taken possession of the hearts of the people . . . would have been like children sticking flowers in the ground to perish immediately. Our office was rather . . . to plant the bulb where by God's blessing it might take root, and grow and flower beautifully, naturally, healthfully, fragrantly, lastingly.

Now circumstances had changed. There was no longer any 'danger of superficialness'.[24] When the Bishops in Convocation criticized the Ritualist movement, he defended it because he believed that 'the object of that movement has been to set before the eyes Catholic truths in regard to the Holy Eucharist, which have been ever received in the Church', and it was for those truths that he pledged himself to resign his preferments should any of them be declared contrary to the doctrine of the Church of England 'by a competent authority'.[25] He wanted to keep the Ritualist question quite distinct from the doctrinal. He proposed that the Council of the English Church Union should acknowledge that vestments were not essential to the validity of the consecration or even the dignity of worship, but failed to carry it with him. The prosecution of Bennett, the vicar of St John's, Frome, by the Church Association in 1868 for his eucharistic teaching looked like being the crucial test case. 'It is the existence of the whole High Church body, which is aimed at, and which is at stake' Pusey told Gladstone.[26] Moreover, he felt himself to be on trial because Bennett had substituted Pusey's words for his own in his statement of his beliefs. What made it worse was that Bennett refused to defend himself. The case eventually came before the Judicial Committee of the Privy Council. Pusey was confident of the support of the English Church Union. At the Annual General Meeting of the English Church Union in 1869 he declared that the case had united the Ritualists and the non-Ritualists. The Church Association had over-reached itself, thinking that the Ritualists would be an easy victory and that at the same time 'a thrust would be given to those who held the same faith, but used not the same modes of expressing it'.[27] He solemnly pledged both the English Church Union and the Catholic Union for Prayer, of which he was Warden, to ignoring the judgement when it was made.[28] In the event Bennett was acquitted and the doctrine of the Eucharist, for which Pusey had contended, acknowledged as consonant with the formularies of the Church of England.

Pusey could now rest secure as far as the doctrine of the Eucharist was concerned. He and the Anglo-Catholics had been united in its defence. But Pusey had become very disillusioned about the Ritualists on other doctrinal issues. The English Church Union failed to support him in his opposition to the appointment of Temple as Bishop of Exeter. Temple was one of the contributors to *Essays and Reviews* which, in Pusey's eyes, undermined the authority of Scripture. 'To fight for Ritualism and allow the wolf to be a shepherd would be hideous', he told the President of the English Church Union. He tried to resign and complained bitterly:

> I threw away a good deal of trust which some Bishops had reposed in me, by taking the part of the Ritualists: they have in requital deserted me on the first occasion in which I felt much to be at stake. I fear that they idolize themselves.[29]

Even worse, in Pusey's opinion, was the indifference of some of the Ritualists to the attack on the Athanasian Creed by the liberals, who were supported by Archbishop Tait. Pusey and Liddon both threatened to resign their offices in the Church of England if the Creed were omitted or mutilated but the Ritualists, Pusey said, would not be shaken. They would 'take their own line of caring for nothing', and hold the episcopate 'all the cheaper . . . as having betrayed the faith'.[30]

One of the main reasons that Pusey had allied himself with ritualism was that he had become convinced that it was 'from its very centre a lay movement'.[31] He believed the pressure for ritualist advances came from the laity. Indeed, he once said, 'the clergy need to be defended against the choirs who give them no rest'.[32] He constantly supported Mackonochie, one of the most extreme Ritualists, at St Alban's, Holborn, because he had the backing of his people.[33] On the other hand, he was totally opposed to priests, who introduced changes in worship without preparation and without the acquiescence of their people. This was what first brought him into serious conflict with the English Church Union. At a meeting on 20 November, 1867, whilst supporting the motion to oppose any proposed alteration in the law on ritual, he spoke strongly on this issue. He thought there was a danger that some priests were being 'Presbyterian towards their bishops and Popes towards their people'. He wanted ritual to be introduced first into the early services 'when those only were present who could be edified by it', and the 11 o'clock service left unchanged 'to old-fashioned people, who might worship God at the old-fashioned hour in the old-fashioned way'. He was content to go very slowly:

> I believe it would be better to wait almost any time, except for the Bread of Life Itself—I mean the weekly Communion—rather than introduce changes against the wishes of the communicants, expecially in this matter of reviving obsolete laws.

He felt that three-quarters or four-fifths of the meeting were against a sentence of his 'disclaiming the forcing of ritual on an unwilling congregation'. Only when he threatened to resign did they give way but he 'could tell from the scraping of feet throughout the discussion that [his] opponents had the hearts of the meeting'.[34] This conciliatory attitude was the same as he had shown in the Gorham crisis. He did not wish other sections of the Church of England to be alienated by ritualistic practices, whilst at the same time he wanted to keep the Ritualists within its fold.

Besides his wish to subordinate ritualism to doctrine, and his anxiety not to have it forced on unwilling congregations, Pusey's third concern in the Ritualist question was the maintenance of discipline and law. Pusey was himself in a vulnerable position on this because he did not accept the judgements of the court of final appeal, the Judicial Committee of the Privy Council, in the case either of Gorham in 1850 or of the Essayists in 1864. Indeed, after the latter case, he had helped found the Association for the Reform of the Final Court of Appeal. The difficulty was to decide what ought to be done to improve the situation. He described Wilberforce's scheme for excluding the bishops from the final court as 'perfect insanity'.

> This would indeed be hugging our chains and making the Queen Summa Episcopa, Episcopa Episcoporum. . . . It is

one thing to say, better to have a Court which should be wholly civil than one with an insufficient sprinkling of Ecclesiastics, another deliberately to agitate or vote for a thoroughly bad Court.[35]

The Mackonochie Judgement in 1868, in which the Privy Council presumed to impose a spiritual penalty, made Pusey change his mind about the all-lay character of the court but he nevertheless advised submission. At a private meeting convened by Denison, the extremists such as Bennett, Chambers and Shipley carried the day in favour of resistance, but at an English Church Union meeting Pusey successfully proposed taking the line of denying the competence of the Court but submitting under protest. When the final Court of Appeal was reformed by the Supreme Court of Judicature Act in 1873, it was composed solely of lay judges with all the bishops, not just the Privy Councillors, eligible to act as assessors.[36] Pusey thought the compromise should be accepted. He agreed with Liddon: 'I should think it just as good a judge of facts as myself or any of us probably except a few experts'.[37]

The situation had meantime been complicated by the Purchas Judgement in 1871, which gave such a manifestly forced interpretation of the Prayer Book rubrics that Pusey himself had been driven into open defiance. In protest he adopted the eastward position and used a mixed chalice when celebrating in the cathedral at Oxford, and publicly advocated 'passive resistance'.[38] Taking his stand on a literal interpretation of the Prayer Book rubrics, he was also convinced of the legality of eucharistic vestments, and although he was very cautious about their introduction, from 1868 he occasionally wore them himself in private chapels.[39]

Pusey was thus in a rather anomalous position in that he wished to be law-abiding and yet refused to accept the law on the grounds that it was bad law. He was very sensitive to the charge of lawlessness and very critical of the Ritualists for their apparent indifference. The whole issue came to a head over the new court set up to replace the old Court of Arches by the Public Worship Regulation Act in 1874.

Pusey had already been alienated the previous year by a

petition to Convocation about licensing Confessors, organized by SSC, which had precipitated a crisis about the place of Confession in the Church of England. He considered it 'ill-advised' and confided to a friend that it gave him 'a thorough mistrust of the ultra-Ritualist body'.[41] Nevertheless when Tait floated the idea of a bill to put down Ritualism, he wrote several letters to *The Times* against it. At the same time, however, he spoke out against 'this love of Ritual for its own sake' at an English Church Union meeting[42] and tried to restrain the Ritualists privately. In a letter to Beresford Hope he gives a pessimistic estimate of the extent of his own influence.

> I cannot speak for any Ritualist. . . . Only the most moderate Ritualists would listen to me. The rest would think it a great honour to me, to be the figure-head of the vessel which they steer—I fear, on the rock.[43]

He became very embittered, blaming the Ritualists for bringing down on them all, the Public Worship Regulation Act. He accused them of 'fussiness, pettiness, self-consciousness', 'restlessness', 'arbitrariness', 'infallibilism' and 'pedantry'. They were 'inebriated with the imagination of their own wisdom'. They were behaving like 'stragglers from an army, who [had] got into a defile . . . [and] instead of retreating to the main body' were begging for assistance from that main body 'at whatever cost'.[44] He determined 'not again to come forward in any meeting nor to mix myself up with them'.[45] The Ritualists on their side became impatient with Pusey. Even so moderate a ritualist as Archdeacon Denison could not agree with him. He compared him to 'a man who has lit a fire, and is surprised and vexed because it does not confine itself to the bottom of the grate'.[46] In May 1875, Pusey's own protégé, Charles Wood, the President of the English Church Union, proposed a resolution committing the Union to defending six points (lights, vestments, incense, the eastward position, the mixed chalice and unleavened bread). Pusey immediately objected and wrote to him 'only wishing that I had never joined the English Church Union and . . . that some one could take my place'[47] but the only modification he secured was a statement that there was no wish 'to go beyond what recognised Anglican authorities warrant'.

The final trial of strength came the following year. All along Pusey had recognized the jurisdiction of the new court under Lord Penzance, set up by the Public Worship Regulation Act, in relation to the temporalities of the Church. Ritualists such as Fr Tooth refused to acknowledge its jurisdiction at all and declared they would neither plead before it nor accept its decisions. Pusey professed not to understand their position:

> There ought to be an answer to the Bishop of Lichfield's question, 'Whom, or what would you obey?' I suspect that most of the Ritualists would be at a loss for an answer. Their line seems to me to be '. . . We shall obey our own consciences . . . and shall obey no authority, spiritual or temporal, which contravenes this'.[48]

Then Phillimore, the ecclesiastical lawyer, moved a resolution at an English Church Union meeting, pledging support for any priest suspended or inhibited by the new court. The debate was adjourned, but Pusey immediately protested. Wood supported Phillimore. Pusey therefore submitted his resignation from the English Church Union on 26 December 1876. He explained his reasons privately to the President. The resolution shifted the ground of objection from 'a particular wrong decision', the Purchas Judgement, 'to all authority'. In 'impugning the existing Courts as created by the Public Worship Regulation Act'[49] the English Church Union was 'disavowing all existing law'. Wood begged him to change his mind but Pusey stood firm, taking his stand above party politics.

> There is a large body of real High Churchmen outside [the English Church Union], whom I must not seem to compromise by allowing myself to appear to agree to what I do not think.

The English Church Union was 'not a representative body'. Its purpose was practical, to defend the oppressed not 'to put out abstract principles for the guidance of Churchmen'. 'I think we have been giving ourselves airs for some time, laying down the law in matters where we have no call'.[50] Wood was determined not to lose him, however, and the resolution was modified. The Union's denial that the secular power has authority in matters purely spiritual was balanced by statements that 'it distinctly and expressly acknowledges the authority of all Courts legally constituted in regard to all matters temporal', and that it 'submits itself to the duly constituted synods of the Church' in regard to rites and ceremonies and controversies of faith. With this Pusey professed 'complete satisfaction'[51] and withdrew his resignation, remaining Vice-President of the English Church Union until his death. In practice he enjoyed a virtual veto over the decisions of the Union 'through the affectionate loyalty of the President' whose influence 'was sufficient to prevent anything being carried of which Pusey did not approve'.[52]

Although Pusey succeeded in asserting his leadership of the Anglo-Catholics only by the extreme measure of threatening to resign from the English Church Union, the distance between his position and that of the Ritualists was soon narrowed because of the course of the legal proceedings against them. The progress of the Ridsdale case had already made Pusey change his mind about the reformed Final Court of Appeal. Lord Penzance had felt himself bound by the earlier judgements of the Judicial Committee of the Privy Council and therefore summarily condemned Ridsdale on all points dealt with by the Purchas Judgement. The case was taken to the highest court and the fact that the episcopal assessors were to be the two Archbishops who had helped condemn Purchas made Pusey realize the court was still not secular enough.[53] The final judgement allowed the Eastward position but still condemned vestments. Pusey consequently joined in a petition against the Judgement as being a non-natural interpretation of the Ornaments Rubric although he was anxious not to be understood as defending 'ritualism *en masse*'.[54] However, as the Church Association continued its relentless persecution of the Ritualists, Pusey identified himself more and more with their cause until, finally, early in 1881, he published a forthright defence of ritualism as the legitimate development of Tractarianism, in an open letter to Liddon with the characteristically involved title *'Unlaw in Judgments of the Judicial Committee and its Remedies'*. The continued imprisonment of one of the ritual martyrs, Sidney

Green, caused him much distress in the last months of his life. On 24 August 1882, he penned a letter to *The Times* on the subject, the effort contributing to precipitate his final illness.[55]

Another momentous ecclesiastical issue in the nineteenth century was the question of reunion. Pusey early saw that the practical outcome of the Tractarians' deeper understanding of the nature of the Church should be its reunion. From 1839 he was expressing a longing and prayer for it in his published writings. 'To feel what the Church should be, is to long that it be so'.[56] After 1845 and Newman's secession, he concentrated more exclusively on the reunion of the Church of England and the Church of Rome. Pusey was not alone in his desire. The Association for the Promotion of the Unity of Christendom, founded in 1857, is said to have attracted 16,000 members, the majority of whom were Anglo-Catholics. But Pusey did not try to take a lead in its councils. He did not join it; he even refused to subscribe to its paper. At one point he began to doubt the wisdom of ignoring it. In February 1865, he wrote to Keble:

> I wonder whether, when you are better . . . we could put that Society on a better footing, if we were to join it; i.e. not to leave it so entirely in the hands of the Secretary [F. G. Lee].[57]

But in the end he never did join, for fear of what Lee might commit him to.

With the announcement of the summoning of the Vatican Council, an approach of some kind to the Roman Catholics became more urgent. Pusey pursued his own course, writing a three part *Eirenicon* and engaging, together with his friend, Bishop Forbes of Brechin, in a secret correspondence with a Jesuit theologian, Victor De Buck. The English Church Union gave enthusiastic support to the line which he had taken in his *Eirenicon*, of reunion on the basis on the Council of Trent and the Thirty-nine Articles explained, but the initiative was entirely his. Some of the Anglo-Catholics wished to do more, but Pusey refused to co-operate in an address to the Pope, organized by Gerard Cobb, a Fellow of King's, Cambridge, and dissuaded the English Church Union against a proposal to present a memorial to the Council about Anglican Orders.[58] One of them complained to the Bishop of Orleans who was sympathetic to the cause of reunion.

> Talk about the infallibility of the Holy See! It is nothing compared with the necessity of making absolute abandonment of faith, reason and everything else into the hands of the great Dr Pusey in person, who reigns supreme amongst us Anglicans.[59]

It is doubtful whether Pusey's refusal to put himself at the head of the Unionists or even to try to moderate their efforts really prejudiced the cause he had at heart. Certainly their activities, as he ought to have foreseen, brought about the condemnation by the Holy Office of what were essentially his own ideas for corporate reunion before he had himself adequately expressed them.[60] But the time was not ripe. Manning, the archbishop of Westminster, had no sympathy for the cause and indeed schemed to get the Association for the Promotion of the Unity of Christendom condemned.[61] Moreover, the Council quickly became too engrossed in the issue of Papal Infallibility to consider reunion.

Pusey was then, leader of the Anglo-Catholics only in a very qualified sense. His position in the Church was not dependent on his following. He had an authority of his own, partly due to his personal connections and his professorship, but even more to his own character. His saintliness, his generosity, his integrity, gave him a power uniquely his own. He could afford to stand aloof from the pettiness of party politics. The Anglo-Catholics on the other hand, could scarcely act without him, and certainly not against him. There was a massiveness and immovability about him which his opponents called obstinacy and which even his friends, from time to time, found irritating. But it was this quality which, in a crisis, made him 'one of those fulcrums and stays about which people gather', as J. B. Mozley said perceptively about him.[62]

NOTES

1 London Union on Church Matters. A reprint from the *Guardian* of Pusey's address in St Martin's Hall on 15 October 1850, with a Postscript, p. 12.

2   8 January 1876.

3   26 April 1860. Liddon, vol. 4, pp. 211 f.

4   E. S. Purcell, *Life of Cardinal Manning* (1895), vol. 1, pp. 528–30; cf. 'I fear as they stand, they will shake people thro' and thro'.' Pusey to Dr Mill [14 March 1850] (Lambeth Palace).

5   Purcell, vol. 1, pp. 540–1.

6   See Liddon, vol. 3, pp. 440 ff; vol. 4, pp. 266 ff.

7   Pusey to Keble, 27 August 1856. Liddon, vol. 3, p. 436.

8   e.g., Liddon, vol. 4, pp. 215, 217, 318 ff., 366; cf. vol. 3, p. 319.

9   Letter to the *Guardian*, 17 June 1850.

10 Liddon, vol. 3, p. 220.

11 Keble to Pusey, 17 September 1850. Liddon, vol. 3, p. 276.

12 Pusey to Keble, n.d. [September 1850]. Liddon, vol. 3, p. 275.

13 Pusey to W. J. Copeland, n.d. [September 1850] (Pusey House).

14 Pusey to Keble [17 September 1850]. Liddon, vol. 3, p. 277.

15 William Palmer, Supplement to *A Narrative of Events* . . . (1883) pp. 240 f.

16 *The Royal Supremacy* (2nd ed. 1850), pp. 212, n. 1, 211.

17 p. 168.

18 Pusey to Keble [7 August 1850] (Copy, Pusey House).

19 [Maria Trench] *Charles Lowder* (1881) p. 96; SSC *Minute Book 1855–60*, pp. 158–62.

20 Pusey to Keble, 9 May 1862, 24 September 1862, 10 February 1864 (Copies, Pusey House); cf. Liddon, vol. 4, p. 50.

21 Pusey to George Williams, 28 September 1864 (Copy, Pusey House).

22 Pusey to Bishop Tait, 26 April 1860. Liddon, vol. 4, p. 212.

23 G. B. Roberts, *The History of the English Church Union* (1895), pp. 12, 260.

24 Liddon, vol. 4, pp. 212 f.

25 '*Will ye also go away?*', Appendix (1867), p. 25.

26 Pusey to W. E. Gladstone, 6 December 1868. Liddon, vol. 4, p. 218.

27 *Church Times*, 18 June 1869.

28 *Church Union Gazette*, 1 January 1872.

29 Pusey to Charles Wood, 23 December, 28 December 1869 (Copies, Pusey House).

30 Pusey to Liddon, 2 January 1872, to Samuel Wilberforce, 27 July 1872. Liddon, vol. 4, pp. 240, 246.

31 Speech to ECU, June 1866. Liddon, vol. 4, p. 213.

32 Pusey to Liddon, 25 May 1874 (Pusey House).

33 e.g., Pusey to A. H. Mackonochie, 28 June 1874. Liddon, vol. 4, p. 277.

34 *ECU Monthly Circular* pp. 3, 343 f. Liddon, vol. 4, p. 216.

35 Pusey to Liddon n.d. [3 October 1864] (Pusey House).

36 P. T. Marsh, *The Victorian Church in Decline* (1969), pp. 129–132.

37 Pusey to C. L. Wood, 1 January 1874 (Copy, Pusey House).

38 Liddon, vol. 4, pp. 223 f, 366; *A Letter to the Writer* published with *The Purchas Judgement* by H. P. Liddon (1871), pp. 61 f. On Pusey and the ablutions, see F. L. Cross *Darwell Stone* (1943), p. 440.

39 Sister Clara, MS 'Anecdotes of Dr Pusey', p. 13 (Ascot Priory).

40 e.g., Pusey to Liddon, 29 December 1873. Liddon, vol. 4, pp. 272 f.

41 Pusey to Editor of *The Times*, 28 March 1874, to W. Bright, 28 July 1873, Liddon, vol. 4, pp. 271, 275; cf. Trench, p. 499.

42 Liddon, vol. 4, p. 276.

43 n.d. [1874] (Copy, Pusey House).

44 Pusey to T. T. Carter, n.d. Trench, p. 488; to C. L. Wood, 2 January 1875. Liddon, vol. 4, pp. 279 f.; Pusey to C. L. Wood, 14 October (1874) (Copy, Pusey House); Pusey to Liddon, 31 December 1874 (Pusey House).

45 Pusey to R. W. Randall, 25 October 1874. Liddon, vol. 4, p. 278.

46 G. A. Denison to C. L. Wood, 7 September 1874 *Fifty Years at East Brent* ed. Louisa E. Denison (1902), p. 161.

47 n.d. (Copy, Pusey House).

48 Pusey to C. L. Wood, 4 December 1876. Liddon, vol. 4, p. 285.

49 Pusey to C. L. Wood, 28 December 1876, 5 January 1877 (Copies, Pusey House). Liddon prints the whole of the first, vol. 4, pp. 286 f.

50 Pusey to C. L. Wood, 31 December 1876 (Copy, Pusey House).

51 Pusey to C. L. Wood, 13 January 1877 (Copy, Pusey House).

52 Liddon, vol. 4, p. 288.

53 Pusey to Archbishop Tait, 21 November 1876. Liddon, vol. 4, pp. 283 f.

54 Pusey to C. L. Wood, 10 June 1877. Liddon, vol. 4, p. 289.

55 Liddon, vol. 4, p. 381.

56 *Letter to the Archbishop of Canterbury* (1842), p. 26.

57 [19 February 1865] (Copy, Pusey House).

58 Pusey to H. P. Liddon, 9 July 1869 (Pusey House); Church Union Deposit 10, 31 May, 7 June 1869 (Lambeth Palace).

59 [Cobb?] 29 July 1869 cited by F. Mourret *Le Concile du Vatican* . . . (Paris 1919), pp. 126 f.

60 Letter of the Congregation of the Holy Roman and Universal Inquisition to English Reunionists 8 November 1865, printed in Purcell *Life and Letters of Ambrose Phillips de Lisle* (1900), vol. 1, pp. 417 ff.

61 Purcell *Life of Cardinal Manning*, vol. 2, pp. 280–4.

62 *Letters of the Rev. J. B. Mozley DD* edited by his sister (New York 1885), p. 330.

15

Pusey: the Servant of God

A.M.ALLCHIN

Of the three unquestioned leaders of the Oxford Movement Pusey is perhaps the least known. Neither he nor John Keble have received in the last fifty years the attention which they deserve. In the course of this essay we shall consider a little why this should be so in the case of Pusey. Let it be said at the outset that in him we face a complex, many-sided character, a man of great ability, of great perseverance, of great depth, and yet to many of his contemporaries, as to us, an enigma. Preaching in St Mary's pulpit, shortly after his death, Dean Church remarked, 'No man was more variously judged, more sternly condemned, more tenderly loved'.[1] More than fifty years before, John Henry Newman had remarked on the elusive quality of Pusey's mind, when, commenting on his book on the theology of Germany, he wrote, 'it will be sadly misunderstood, both from his difficulty in expressing himself, the largeness, profundity and novelty of his views, and the independence of his radicalism'.[2] A man, who was often misunderstood; a man with a large, profound, independent, radical mind, a man of a powerful and volcanic spirit, who saw things in light and in darkness, a man with a capacity for grief, self-reproach, self-condemnation which may frighten or repel us; a man marked at times in his life by a sadness, an austerity, a lack of flexibility, which we find it difficult to accept. And yet above all, a witness to the reality of God, a man wounded by the divine love. Not a harmonious radiant character like Edward King; rather a saint who has been tried in the fires of dread and anxiety, one who has known the dissonance of life, and yet a man in whom sadness is constantly turning into joy. It is not customary for Regius Professors to spend their Long Vacations tending cholera victims in Bethnal Green; I suppose an equivalent today would be working with the dying in the streets of Calcutta or Beirut; yet that was what Pusey did in 1867, and the descriptions of him during that memorable episode, are accounts of a man full of resource, gentleness and humour in face of appalling suffering and loss.[3]

I do not use the word 'saint' in relation to Pusey lightly or conventionally. I am fully aware of the charges made against him by various writers in his own time and in ours. I do it in the conviction that men and women have been recognized as saints not on account of some supposed ethical perfection that they have achieved, still less on account of the fact that they never made errors of judgement about people and events, at times tragic ones. Neither Jerome nor Thomas of Canterbury would be in the calendar if this had been the case in the past. Nor would Newman's cause be so far advanced at Rome if this were the case now. Recognition of sanctity in Christian history has involved two things above all else; first, the belief that a man or woman has been called by God to play a decisive role, open or hidden, in the life of God's people and that he or she has responded to that call; secondly, that the life of such a person has shown them to be touched by God; men and women whose very being has borne witness to the overpowering reality of God's claim on human life. That they were people who bore the marks of the wounds of the world's suffering and sin has never been a disqualification in the followers of a crucified Lord.

To return to Dean Church and to his judgement on Pusey, a judgement which carries the more weight in so far as the two men had by no means always found themselves in agreement in the course of the years:

First and foremost, he was one who lived his life, as above everything, the Servant of God. . . . When our confusions are still, when our loves and enmities and angers have perished, when our mistakes and misunderstandings have become dim and insignificant in the great distance of the past, then his figure will rise in history as one of the high company who really looked at life as St Paul looked at it.[4] . . .

So I intend in this essay not to look at the extent and scope of

Pusey's interests and concerns, educational, social, ecclesiasti-cal, the spread of his involvement in many aspects of the life of his time, but to concentrate on what is the central point of his life and teaching, the witness which he bears to the reality and mystery of God's judgement and God's love. The clue to his life and thought, as to that of the greatest of his disciples, Fr R. M. Benson, is its God-centredness. As in the case of Benson, we cannot say that Pusey is either a mystic or a theologian; we must if we are true to him, recognize him as both; a man devoured by the mystery of God's love, whose whole life is offered to that mystery, a man who finds himself ill at ease amongst his contemporaries on this account.[5]

But when we speak of Pusey's God-centredness, we speak of something which in varying ways is common to Pusey, Keble and Newman alike. At the heart of the Oxford Movement was a passion for holiness, a longing for the knowledge and the love of God, revealed in Christ Jesus, imparted in the Holy Spirit. This passion for scriptural holiness was characteristic of both the Oxford Movements, that which began in the 1730s, no less than that which began in the 1830s. That is a fact which demands to be long and seriously pondered. Not the indepen-dence of the Church from the State, not the doctrine of Apostolic Succession, not the assertion of clerical privileges, not even the recovery of a living understanding and experience of the sacraments, was at the heart of the Tractarian movement, but the longing for 'holiness without which no man shall see the Lord', a longing 'to be found in Christ, not having a righteousness of our own, . . . but that which is through faith in Christ', to apprehend what it is to be apprehended by him, and in him, to enter into the circulation of life and love which is at the very heart of the Triune God.

I intend then to concentrate my attention on a number of Pusey's sermons preached during the 1840s, which contain what seems to me the heart of his message for us. In one sense they are typically Tractarian utterances. They enforce convictions which were shared by all the leaders of the Movement. But they do it in a way which is very personal to Pusey, a way which, as Owen Chadwick pointed out more than twenty years ago, makes us think of the word 'ecstatic', a way which helps us understand why Brilioth could speak of Pusey as the *Doctor Mysticus* of the Movement.[6]

But before we come to the text of the sermons, let us reflect for a moment on the decade, the forties in which they were preached. It had been for Pusey a time of many griefs. It opened with the aftermath of his wife's death in 1839. In 1843 there was the condemnation of his University sermon on 'The Holy Eucharist, a Comfort to the Penitent'. In 1844 there was the death of his favourite daughter, Lucy. The departure of Newman came in 1845. In the years following Newman's conversion, Pusey was constantly the centre of controversy and debate, and at the very same time, as we know from his letters, he was entering into the uttermost depths of self-condemnation and reproach. As we study his development during these years we see a man living through a series of tempests, intellectual, spiritual, psychological; a man accomplishing an astonishing inner journey, which left him in some ways hampered, apparently paralysed in face of some lines of intellectual reflection and research, but in other ways astonishingly free of conventions, ecclesiastical, social, theological, free to be creative and original in many facets of spiritual life, to initiate changes in Anglican ways of prayer and devotion, which have had far reaching consequences, in the subsequent years. We may think of his part in the rediscovery of the Religious life, of retreats, of sacramental confession, of the frequent celebration of the Eucharist. In his unshakeable conviction that the Anglican tradition could assimilate and profit from elements of Catholic faith and life which were at that time foreign to it, he has been over the years proved triumphantly right, even if he was sometimes unwise in the choice of particular devotional practices. All these developments were not purely a matter of 'a devotional life', which had no relation to thinking and reflection. They presupposed the Catholic doctrine of grace. They were a realization in practice of the Tractarian claim that the Church of England was truly part of the one Catholic Church, and were thus a living and not merely an institutional sign of its continuity with, and faithfulness to the Catholic whole. When in the last decade of the nineteenth century the *Lux Mundi* group took up again the work of constructive theology, which had been to a considerable extent abandoned after 1845, they had to make a decisive and painful break with Pusey's views on biblical inspiration. There was, however, no trace, on their part, of a desire to abandon the sacramental and spiritual tradition which he had done so much to revive. They remained, in the Anglican sense, Catholic to the core.

It has sometimes been remarked that in the years leading up to 1845 Pusey was less perceptive than others of the changes which were taking place in Newman. When we consider the inner transformations which were taking place in himself during this time, in their own way as profound as those which were altering the shape of Newman's convictions, we need hardly be surprised that this was so. It is an indication of how much we tend to judge the development of those years in relation to John Henry Newman that it is very seldom remarked on the other side that the ever deepening relationship between Pusey and Keble was something which wholly escaped the attention of the recluse of Littlemore. Pusey and Newman alike were undergoing profound spiritual changes, and engaged in profound spiritual conflicts which were to bear fruit in the lives of millions who were then unborn. The fact that in one case a change of outward Church allegiance was involved while in the other it was not, should not make us underestimate the reality and significance of the second and more hidden journey.

The sermons preached at this time seem to show signs of a certain intensity and stress on the part of the preacher. Pusey, we may be sure, always preached with emphasis. As J. B. Mozley put it, 'Pusey seemed to inhabit his sentences', or as Liddon comments, 'Each sentence was instinct with his whole intense purpose of love, as he struggled to bring others into communion with the truth and Person of him who had purified his own soul. . . .'[7] But the impression of strain is perhaps in some ways an erroneous one. It was not like this that Pusey sounded to an observer who heard him preaching in a village church at the beginning of 1847. His description is worth quoting, because it suggests not only something of the quality of the preacher, but also something of the unexpected ecumenical quality of his words:

Never before did I hear so beautifully evangelical a sermon as this from the man who has given a name to a party which is supposed to represent a different principle in the Church. It had but one fault, it was fifteen minutes too long. Nevertheless it was listened to throughout by that little crowded church-full with fixed and rapt attention, though it was neither declamatory, noisy, nor eccentric; but plaintive, solemn and subdued, breathing throughout, I may say, a beauty of holiness and a Christian spirit so broad and catholic, so deep and devotional, that while the most zealous Protestant could find nothing in it he might not approve, the most bigoted Roman Catholic could not entertain an exception to a single expression it contained.[8]

The ecumenical achievement of these sermons was in some ways incidental to their purpose. It was not, however, accidental, or by chance. In the introduction to the volume 1 of his *Parochial Sermons*, published in 1848, Pusey declares that they have been gathered together with two main aims in view. First, to try to show to Evangelicals that the Tractarian insistence on the importance of the sacraments and structures of the Church was not in any way intended to take away from the Evangelical insistence on the absolute centrality of Christ, and that similarly, the Tractarians' emphasis on good works was in no way intended to undermine the scriptural teaching of the all-sufficing of God's grace. In these pages, Pusey quotes St Augustine at length to show that the good works which we do are more God's work than ours, even though God acts in us, not as automata but as free and responsible agents. Always Pusey was to insist in relation to Evangelicalism, that while we may teach more, we never teach less than our Evangelical brethren. The second purpose of Pusey's publication of these sermons is perhaps even more pertinent to our present situation than his desire to show the biblical basis for his teaching. Man's longing for God, he declares, is so ineradicable that if it is not assuaged by an experience and understanding of the perfect union of man with God in Christ through the Spirit, it will search for satisfaction through other and less adequate paths.

The doctrine of the life of the Christian as being from and in

Christ, as it is the safeguard against any shade of Pelagianism, so, in conjunction with the rest of the Catholic Faith, it satisfieth the cravings of the soul for a life united with God, which if not lawfully satisfied may readily become a prey to fanaticism, a spurious mysticism, or, ultimately Pantheism.[9]

Anyone who is acquainted with the syncretistic 'new religious movements', which have proliferated over Western Europe and North America in the last quarter of a century will recognize the prophetic truth of what Pusey says.

But it is time to turn from these considerations to the sermons themselves, and first to one preached at St Barnabas Pimlico, in the summer of 1850, on a text from the Song of Songs, and with the theme 'God withdraws in Loving-kindness also'.

Christ is ever knocking at the heart, in those who have not received him, that they may receive him; in those who have received him, that they may receive him more fully; in those who are negligent or who relax, that they may rouse themselves; in those who are holy that they may be holier still. 'Behold I stand at the door and knock.' Christ is within the heart, else we could not open it. He is without, because it is finite, he is infinite. And so in love and grace he may through the Spirit dwell in us ever more largely, because however he fills, yet he must overflow. The blessed are immersed in the ocean of his love; yet the ocean embraces them, fills them; it is not contained by them. He is within the heart, but the heart has many folds, many recesses, inner chambers, corners and angles; some perhaps unknown to itself; some, on which it does not dare look; some which it would keep closed, and with which it would have none to interfere. Our Lord, as the Lord, the Maker, the Husband of the heart, to whom the whole heart's love is due, claims it all. All must be opened to him, to be purified by his grace, enlightened by his Spirit, warmed by his love. . . . He knocks by all things which teach us to choose him; that he is all, and all else nothing, except as he is in it, and comes with it and makes it anything. He knocks by all things, within or without, which scare us or sicken us of things out of him. . . . By all things, good or evil, vanity or verity, nothingness or truth, remorse at evil or peace in good; the fading of this world, or glimpses of his own endless, abiding beauty; . . . by the dryness of the ashes whereon we feed for bread, or the sweetness of his hidden manna; the dreariness of his absence, or the light and life of his presence, in something done for him; by his Word, his preachers, his sacraments, he stands at the door and knocks.[10]

It is a very characteristic passage. Pusey may be passionately opposed to pantheism and to any tendency to equate God with the totality of things, but he is very clearly a panentheist. God is in all things, all things are in God, God comes to us in all things, good and bad indifferently. With an almost Islamic exaggeration he declares all things created to be nothing, except as God is in them. Similarly he insists that God who is immanent, is at the same time transcendent, within and without the heart, entering into it, plumbing its unseen depths, yet always overflowing, always going beyond its limitations. The doctrine of *epektasis*, of the soul's infinite progress into God, comes to life again in these pages. In our inner experience, in the preaching of his word, in the sacraments of the church, in the events of everyday, in the feeling of his presence, in the perception of his absence, in all things God comes.

But especially he comes to us in times of suffering and loss, in times when the soul feels out of itself in longing for God. In a passage which clearly reflects his own experience he declares:

Few understand the state of such a soul as this; one who burns for more love, yet finds no comfort. 'My soul' she says, 'failed', literally 'went forth' out of herself to him whom she loved, 'when he spake'. She was out of herself for longing and for love. The world thinks such an one mad; they advise the soul to distract itself; they speak of over-much religion; they would send it back to the swine-husks of this world to satisfy its immortal longings after God. But even 'the keepers of the city', those whom God has set as watchmen over the city of God often wound such a soul. Some wound her healthfully, some unskilfully. She *must* be wounded by all things, who is so keenly alive to sorrow. . . . The holy apostles in the divine Scriptures, who guard the heavenly city from error or mischief pierce her. They take away the veil and laying her open to herself, set her gaze freer to behold her Lord.[11]

But even this pain of longing is preferable to the pain of feeling totally abandoned, cut off from God's presence. But this too comes to God's servants.

They feel far off from God, and fear, being what they are, to approach him; they feel bad and dare not come nigh his majesty; cold and distracted, and dread to offend him by their coldness and distractions. . . . All faith, hope, love, contrition seem to be gone, or never to have been. All things of earth seem sternly real; all of heaven unreal. They pray, but as to one who is not. The heart will not melt in tears, even over its own misery. It seems like a rock, and no rod touches it to make the waters flow. Nothing feeds its affections. . . . Such an one walks in darkness which may be felt, and is shrouded in it. Everything is parched to his touch. . . .[12]

In a passage in another sermon Pusey shows himself very much a contemporary of the romantic poets, who considered our perception of the world to be dominated by our inner condition;

The world is one great mirror. As we are who look into it or on it, so it is to us. It gives us back ourselves. It speaks to us the language of our own hearts. . . . Our inmost self is the key to all. Our ruling thought or passion, the thought or love, that is, which has the mastery of us, and governs us, and occupies our soul, is touched by everything around us. In grief, all things alike, the most joyous or the most sorrowful, suggest to the mourner thoughts of grief; yea, joyous sounds and sights speak mostly, most heavily to it of its own heaviness, or of the absence of the lost object of *its* love.[13]

But it is in a sermon preached on the feast of the Circumcision, on the text of Job 13, 'Though he slay me, yet will I trust in him', with the theme 'Joy out of suffering', that Pusey speaks most fully on this theme of pain and death.

Merciful and very good are all the scourges of the all-good and all-merciful. The deeper, the more merciful; the more inward, the more cleansing. The more they enter into the very soul, the more they open it for the healing presence of God. The more they slay its very self, the more do they convey to it the virtue of Christ's death. The less it lives, the more Christ liveth in it. Hence it has been seen that God mostly doth not send these trials at first upon the soul, but when it is somewhat strengthened by his grace. . . .[14]

These are words which remind us irresistibly of the lines of Charles Wesley:

> Deepen the wounds thy hands have made
> In this weak helpless soul
> Till mercy with its kindly aid
> Descend to make me whole.
>
> The sharpness of thy two-edged sword
> Enable me to endure
> Till bold to say: My hallowing Lord
> Hath wrought a perfect cure.
>
> I hear th' exceeding broad command
> Which all contains in one.
> Enlarge my heart to understand
> The mystery unknown.[15]

At times the conflict becomes acute. We are pulled down into the depths of hell.

> If thou canst see nothing but hell before thee, shut thine eyes and cast thyself blindly into the infinite abyss of God's mercy, and the everlasting arms will, though thou know it not, receive thee and upbear thee. . . . 'Though he slay me, I will trust him'. Seemeth this a great thing, brethren? The great holy words will mean yet more. 'Lo, if he slay me, I will trust in him,' not 'although' only but *'because'* he slayeth me. It is life to be touched by the hand of God; to be slain is, through the cross of Christ, the pledge of the resurrection.[16]

In one of the most perceptive comments on Pusey to have been made in recent years, John Saward has written:

> It is not sufficiently appreciated . . . to what extent the Catholic Revival in the Church of England in the nineteenth

375

century was undergirded by martyrdom, by faithful witness
in the face of vilification and mockery, of legal harassment
and discrimination, and, as we now see in the case of Pusey, in
the face of deep psychological suffering, of a kind of
madness. . . . The word of Our Lord to Staretz Silouan in our
own century, 'Keep thy mind in hell and despair not,' was
conveyed to Dr Pusey in the reign of Victoria by a
seventeenth-century Jesuit (Jean-Joseph Surin) who for
twenty years endured a dark night without ever abandoning
his love for God.[17]

The life giving quality of this journey through death and hell
is well conveyed by Pusey in a passage where he speaks yet more
clearly of the paradoxical way in which man is called to go
beyond himself into God, to be and yet not to be, to live and yet
not to live, because it is God who lives and is within them. In
this paragraph we see too how firmly the great themes of
Christian mysticism are rooted in the teaching of St Paul:

O blessed passage of the soul through the valley of death;
which dies to live; which hopes, though in a way she is not;
which *is* and is not; is slain and trusts in him who slayeth her;
'dieth and behold she lives'. For the soul lives, not in herself,
but 'by faith in the Son of God, who loved her and gave
himself for her.' Not she lives, but 'he liveth in her'; and so
death to all but him, yea, to and in her very self also, is his
enlarged life to her. It is the very life of the blessed, to be
nothing in themselves, but vessels wherein God can pour in
the fulness, and bliss, and richness, and transporting,
overpowering, overwhelming sweetness and tenderness of
his love, and they, not of themselves but through and with his
own love, shall love himself. It is the very joy of their Lord
wherein they shall enter, to joy not with their own joy, but
with his; to be themselves, only to be not themselves; to *be*,
only to have within them the Being of God, which is his
love.[18]

We are far indeed here from the 'plaintive' tone, of which we
heard in the description of Pusey's preaching from 1847. That
his sermons could at times have this quiet, pleading, wistful

quality we need not doubt. But it is evident that they could also strike a note of triumphant awestruck affirmation:

> This only we know, that he himself will be our portion. He himself has said, 'Son, all that I have is thine'. . . . He giveth it to thee, not to be held as an outward thing; not to *have*, as it were, created knowledge, or wisdom, or love. This were a small thing for the Love of God. But God will be himself all in all. Thou shalt know with his knowledge, he wise with his wisdom, be holy with his holiness. . . . Their being shall be his being, and they shall be themselves only to be not themselves, only that there may be beings, to be ever filled with the thrilling, pure, holy ecstatic love of God. They shall be out of themselves in the absorbing love of God, and God in his boundless love shall dwell in them.[19]

The passages at which we have been looking so far have spoken to us in highly personal terms of God's coming to man and man's coming to God. They have plumbed the depths and secrets of man's heart, have told us of his subjectivity. But for Pusey, all this was never merely inward, never merely an experience and aspiration of man. It was always grounded in God himself and in the mystery of his love for man. In this sense it was an utterly objective, given, transcendent reality, always beyond the limitations of the human heart and mind, always leading the soul forwards into a new discovery of God's love. What was most intimately personal was at the same moment most joyfully open and Catholic. It was the rediscovery of the doctrines of the Trinity and the incarnation, not as abstract metaphysical formulae, but as living powers of truth which bring God down in love for man, and raise man up in love for God.

Nowhere are these great truths affirmed more strongly than in two remarkable sermons on the resurrection to be found in the 1848 volume of *Parochial Sermons*, the one entitled 'The Christian's Life in Christ', the other 'Christ Risen our Justification'. In these sermons we see the co-inherence of all the articles of Christian faith. In proclaiming the glory of the resurrection, Pusey also proclaims the glory of the incarnation and of Christ's redemptive death and passion. In them we also see a striking realisation of the ecumenical ideal of the Oxford Movement. With the aid of the Greek fathers, we are introduced into a Catholic fulness of faith and life, which is rooted in the Scriptures, has made its own all that is positive in the witness of the sixteenth-century Reformers, and is no longer limitingly Latin, or English, or German, or Greek, but is open to the fulness of humanity restored in Christ, transfigured in the Spirit.

But all this begins in a reaffirmation of the faith of the Fathers of the Church, that God became man, that man might become god. Our coming to him, depends upon his coming to us. There is a mutual indwelling, but the initiative is always his.

> These two are spoken of together in holy Scripture. 'He that dwelleth in love, dwelleth in God and God in him,' and 'he that keepeth his commandments dwelleth in him, and he in him'; and in the service for the Holy Communion, we pray that 'we may so eat the flesh of Christ and drink his blood, that we may evermore dwell in him and he in us.' For we can only dwell in God by his dwelling in us. To dwell *in* God is not to dwell *on* God only. It is no mere lifting up of our affections to him, no being enwrapt in the contemplation of him, no going forth of ourselves to cleave to him. All this is our seeking, not his taking us up; our stretching after him, not our attaining him; our knocking, not his opening. To dwell in God must be by his dwelling in us. He takes us out of our state of nature, in which we were fallen, estranged, in a far country, out of and away from him, and takes us up into himself. He cometh to us, and if we will receive him, he dwelleth in us, and maketh his abode in us. He enlargeth our hearts by his sanctifying Spirit which he giveth us, by the obedience which he enables us to yield, by the acts of faith and love which he strengthens us to do, and then dwelleth in those who are his more largely. By dwelling in us, he makes us parts of himself, so that in the ancient Church they could boldly say, 'he deifieth me', that is, he makes me part of him, of his body, who is God. . . .[20]

In this sermon which began with the text 'As in Adam all die, even so in Christ shall all be made alive', the preacher has passed swiftly and imperceptibly from the future to the present. The resurrection is a reality now, a present consequence of the mystery of God's taking flesh.

> This is the great present fruit of the great mystery of Godliness, 'God manifest in the flesh', that he, by sanctifying our flesh might fit for his indwelling all who would receive him, might come secretly to us, to be hereafter in us manifested for ever. It was a commencement, a practising, as it were, of what was to be for ever.[21]

Certainly it is a reality which is here known only in part, in a hidden, sacramental way, but none the less triumphantly and joyfully made known. And this mystery of God's indwelling in man is precisely a fruit of the new relationship between God and man established in the resurrection of Christ and the coming of the Spirit at Pentecost. In a passage where we see something of the biblical nature of Pusey's thinking, he contrasts the new covenant with the old, showing us how even then God had had to make himself very small in order to communicate with man, implying the still greater divine *kenosis* involved in this new gift of God in the coming of the Spirit. As we read these words we may well think of the action of the prophet, Elisha, cramping himself on the body of the child, eye to eye, mouth to mouth, in order to restore it to life.

> Great it is that he should speak with man, as with a friend, talk with him face to face, know him and call him by his name, as one with whom he was familiar and one familiar with himself. . . . Great is it that he, the Lord of heaven and earth, the infinite, all-wise, all-good, who 'upholdeth all things by the word of his power', should narrow himself (so to say) so as to speak, as one with one, with the human soul he had made, that he, whom no space holds, who contains in his infinity all which ever was, is or shall be, all which could be, even if they never shall be, should, as it were, eye to eye and mouth to mouth, make himself known to one, such as ourselves. Prophets, patriarchs and apostles, seem to us, as it were, different beings from ourselves, that they should have been brought into such aweful, tender nearness to Almighty God.[22]

But in Christ, through the gift of the Spirit, we have still more. What then is the character of this new presence of God within us?

It is not a presence to be touched, handled, seen, heard, felt by our bodily senses; yet nearer still, because it is where bodily senses fail, where the outward eye cannot reach, the outward ear cannot hearken; but when the outward senses fail, then the inward eye sees a light, brighter than all earthly joy; the inward ears hears his voice; the inmost soul feels the thrill of his touch; the 'heart of hearts' tastes a sweetness, 'sweeter than honey and the honey comb', the sweetness of the love of the presence of its Lord and God.

But whether or no he giveth to the faithful soul, to feel its own blessedness, or in whatever degree he maketh the soul to hunger after him, and so satisfieth the hungry soul with his own richness, the inward, unseen presence of God in the soul is *the* gift of the Gospel. This is its great, its one all-containing promise.[23]

And after this passionate utterance of personal conviction, there follows a kind of public statement of faith, a re-affirmation of the Church's tradition, where in a way without parallel in his *Parochial Sermons*, Pusey feels that he must cite his patristic authorities in full, and where almost every line of his text is supported by a page of citation from Cyril of Alexandria.

The everlasting Son, for our redemption, took our flesh, to be one of us; he came in our flesh, he cometh by his Spirit, really and truly to dwell in us. He dwelleth not as he doth in the material heavens, nor as he sanctifieth this house of God, nor as he did in the Tabernacle, but united with the soul, and, in substance, dwelling in her as he did personally in the man, Christ Jesus. In him dwelt 'all the fulness of the Godhead bodily'. In him the incarnate Word dwelt, becoming one with his holy manhood, 'by unity of person', by taking it into himself. In his saints, he dwelleth partially, by the gift of his Spirit, in different degrees, according to their measure; but still his union with them is a shadow of that ineffable union of the ever-blessed Trinity, the mode in which he dwelt in our ever-blessed redeemer. For so our Lord himself prayeth for them, 'as thou, Father, art in me, and I in thee, that they also may be one in us.' And this he bestoweth upon them by, himself, dwelling in them. Thus again, is he the Mediator between God and man, receiving of the Father to impart to us. The Father dwelleth in the Son and the Son in the Father; and so, both the Father and the Son dwell [in him] in whom the Son dwelleth, as he saith, 'I in them, and thou in me, that they may be made perfect in one;' and this through him, in whom the Father and the Son are one, the Holy Spirit. For so saith the holy Scripture again, 'Hereby know we that we dwell in him, and he in us, because he hath given us of his Spirit.' And both through the great mystery of the incarnation. The Son, as man, received into himself the life of the Father, that he might with himself, impart it to us. 'As the living Father hath sent me, and I live by the Father, so he that eateth me, even he shall live by me.' This then, as it is the special mystery of the gospel, so it is of the resurrection—to be in Christ.[24]

In a later sermon Pusey affirms that God the Holy Spirit comes to dwell

really, truly, substantially, in the souls of men. Not of course that he so dwelt in any man, as God the Son was united with the Man Christ Jesus; this were blasphemy; but he does really and truly dwell in man, not by mere gifts and graces, however great, but by himself. . . . His gifts are the fruits of the Spirit, not without us but within us. His gifts stream forth from his Gift, himself. His Gift is himself. He giveth us not only, if we will, his various graces; he *is* to us 'Wisdom and Righteousness and Sanctification and Redemption,' and that by indwelling.

Man stands amazed before this super-abundant generosity of God.[25]

If in the text of his sermon on the resurrection, Pusey seems to insist primarily on the personal relation of the believer to the Father in Christ, through the work of the Holy Spirit, in the lengthy quotations from St Cyril's commentary on the Fourth Gospel which fill the lower part of the page, the ecclesial dimensions of this teaching are made very plain. The Lord 'prays then for the bond of love, and one-mindedness and peace, bringing believers to spiritual unity, so that the concurrence in unity, through the universal consent and undissevered harmony of soul, should imitate the character of that natural and essential unity in the Father and the Son'. We do not of course share in that natural and essential unity which is within the Godhead. The unity of the Church is a reflection, an imitation, an image of it. It is its manifestation on earth, and this unity as St Cyril understands it, is both in flesh and in Spirit. It is in flesh because through Christ's taking our flesh we become members of his body, and *concorporate* with him, and with one another in him. It is in spirit, since 'we all, having received one and the same Holy Spirit, are, in a manner, mingled together with each other and with God. . . . For as the power of the holy flesh maketh those in whom it is concorporate, in the same way the one indivisible Spirit of God, dwelling in all, bringeth all together into spiritual unity'.[26] We see again how this living realization of the teaching that we are truly made partakers of the divine nature carries with it ineluctably an urgency of ecumenical concern. How can those who are members of the one Christ, sharers in the one indivisible Spirit, be at enmity with one another, hostile and indifferent to one another's condition? The effort towards Christian unity and reconciliation springs from the very heart of the faith of the Oxford Movement.

In this sermon on 'The Christian's life in Christ', Pusey turns pre-eminently to Cyril of Alexandria; in the previous sermon, on 'Christ risen our Justification', it is more the presence of Augustine whom we feel. The irenic intentions expressed in the preface of the book are taken up here. Here too we see very clearly how much the Tractarians learned from one another, for here, in his own way, Pusey expresses the central theme of Newman's *Lectures on Justification*, perhaps the greatest constructive theological work produced during the years of the Oxford Movement. 'This is really and truly our justification, not faith, not holiness, not (much less) a mere imputation; but through God's mercy, the very presence of Christ.'[27] It is this which is ours through the gift of the risen Lord. In himself he brings all his gifts.

These are indeed, all one gift, variously applied and spoken of, according to our various needs, or decays, or deaths. . . . He doth not *shew* us the way, nor *give* us wisdom only, nor *cause* us to be sanctified. He himself, by the condescension of his living presence in us, *is* our way to the Father, our righteousness, and wisdom, and acceptableness in him. These are the gifts which, as man, he received, to shed down abundantly on man, through his risen and glorified humanity. Yea, they are all his one gift, his ineffable presence. . . . And this is the special greatness of his sacraments, that they are the channels whereby, through union with him, he conveys these exceeding gifts to us. They are his death and life in one. . . .[28]

This presence of Christ within us, is not an inert or lifeless thing. How could it be? Rather it is living, and life-giving, it creates within us new capacities of life and action, drawing out the freedom of our response of love. For as Pusey declares in another sermon 'God advances his kingdom through man,' it is in and through his creature that God chooses to work.

Everywhere, in our own souls, towards our neighbours, towards the Church or the whole race of his redeemed, he wills to blend in one our poor love with his boundless ocean of love; our weak efforts with his own almightiness; our petty abilities with the depths of his wisdom; our little mercifulness with his own endless loving-kindness; our poor human words with the fire of his Spirit which he came on earth to kindle.[29]

For it is finally in the coming of the Spirit at Pentecost that the mystery of Christ is fulfilled. Towards the end of the volume, from which we have been quoting, there comes a sermon for Whitsunday, which fittingly crowns the teaching of the Easter homilies:

Every festival of the mysteries of our faith is, in time, the greatest, and all alike are equal. Each seemeth, for the time, the greatest, because each bringeth to our nothingness the Infinity of God. All are alike equal, for all relate to that infinity, in which there are no degrees, no parts, no more or less, no bounds, no beginning, no end, no time. But God in himself, infinite, unchangeable and one, shows himself to his creatures in degree and measure, and divides, as it were, his ineffable light in the bow which is around the throne; so may we, who cannot behold his glory who sitteth thereon as HE IS, behold his beauty and love, parted in the varied hues of that mercy which droppeth from above. In each separate mystery is the operation of the Trinity, although for us the Son alone took flesh, suffered, died, rose again, ascended; the Holy Spirit alone is 'shed abroad in our hearts', although through him, the Father and the Son come and make their abode in the faithful. Each mystery is, at once, a stooping down of his unchangeable majesty, and a raising up of our deep-sunken misery. The earlier mysteries presuppose what is in time the later; the later crown the earlier, yet all is one in God.[30]

As we have already seen in the sermon on Christ our Justification, it is the living presence of Christ at the heart of man's life which constitutes the blessing and fulfilment of man's existence:

How could any Comforter be better for us than he? [the preacher asks, and replies] 'Not better, but nearer. Not better, but his very self again, only in a nearer, dearer way. Himself, 'not to go in and out among you', but if we admit him, 'to abide with us for ever'; not to join himself to us by the way, but to be himself our way; not to eat and drink with us, but to be himself our food; not only to talk with us, even as at that blessed moment when the hearts of his disciples burned within them, but himself to be the fire of love within us; not even 'to have the words of eternal life' and to impart them to us, as our master, but himself to 'create', yea, himself to 'be the law in our hearts;' not to be without us, our friend, to call us (amazing words) 'friends', speak to our hearts, but to unite himself to us; . . . He would be himself the very life of our souls, himself the love wherewith we love himself, himself the righteousness, through whose presence we keep his commandments; himself the holiness whereby we are holy; the wisdom, whereby we know his will; himself our joy wherewith we joy in him; himself our peace, whereby, 'at peace with God the Father', we rest in him; himself our hope, himself whom we hope for; himself the fountain of eternal light, whereby we see his light; himself the earnest of our everlasting inheritance; himself our portion, and possession, and inheritance of which he is the earnest. For so he saith, 'My Father will love him, and we will come unto him and make our abode with him.' And how do the Father and the Son come and make their abode in any? Even by the Spirit who is of the Father and the Son, the inseparable bond of both. 'In whom,' says holy Scripture, even in the Lord Jesus Christ, 'ye are builded together for an habitation of God through the Spirit.'[31]

In such a torrent of expressions of God's presence in us, we may be reminded of passages in the works of the great Byzantine saint of the eleventh century, Symeon the New Theologian, a writer whose work Pusey almost certainly did not know. Is there in such a stylistic excess an attempt to express the overwhelming nature of the impact of the divine? Is there perhaps a reflection of his readings in Arabic? Unlike most of his contemporaries Pusey was awake to the existence and the attractions of what he calls 'Soufic poetry'? However we regard it, there can be no question of the reality of this evocation of the contact of man with the divine.

At the end of an essay on the recovery of the doctrine of deification in the teaching of the Oxford Movement, Andrew Louth cites a phrase of Yves Congar, where he speaks of 'the immediacy of contact with spiritual realities', which we find in many of the writings of the Fathers of the Church. They are we feel, 'the writings from an eye-witness about the country of his birth', and Andrew Louth comments, 'In the Oxford Movement we find not so much recourse to the Fathers, as a rediscovery of the patristic tradition, in that in the lives and writings of those whom we may well call the Oxford Fathers, we rediscover that immediacy of contact with spiritual realities'.[32] In them the one tradition lives and grows and becomes more accessible to us here in Western Europe, now in the late twentieth century.

   Such a theology as we find in these sermons of Pusey, is a theology of Trinity and incarnation, in which faith and experience, love and knowledge have come together into one. It is a theology which sees the doctrine of the deification as a necessary corollary to the doctrine of incarnation, and as the fitting way to express our entry into the life and love of the Triune God. It is a theology which sees man's nature as essentially ec-static, self-transcending; man discovers himself by going beyond himself in love and in knowledge of his fellow-beings, but above all in love and knowledge of God. He is a being made for God, restless till he finds his rest in him. It is not only the theology of the Fathers of the Church, both of East and West, but also that of classical Anglicanism from a Richard Hooker and a Lancelot Andrewes at the end of the sixteenth century to a Michael Ramsey and a David Jenkins at the end of the twentieth. It is emphatically not the theology of that dominant liberal Protestant school which in the last hundred and fifty years has had so much influence throughout the English-speaking world. In that tradition, ever since the time of Kant and Schleiermacher, it has been judged that 'nothing whatsoever can be gathered for practical purposes from the doctrine of the Trinity . . . ', that this doctrine 'cannot count as being the direct statement of the devout personal consciousness', and that therefore 'it is unbiblical. It does not belong to Jesus himself. It is speculation, superfluous for faith and harmful for morals'.[33] That is why the book from which that quotation is taken, Jürgen Moltmann's *The Trinity and the Kingdom of God* is so important in this connection. It expresses from within that German tradition of theology, a determination to recover the trinitarian nature of Christian thinking and living. It is a book which contains much insight gained from that other way of approach to the Christian reality, and which explores areas highly relevant to a renewed understanding of the importance of Pusey for today. In relation to our understanding of human nature as essentially ec-static, there is, for example, the analysis of the meaning of experience in the realm of personal knowledge. Is our experience, Moltmann asks, something basically self-centred, self-regarding? Or is it something which opens up to the knowledge and the love of the other?

> From time immemorial experience has been bound up with wonder or with pain. In wonder the subject opens himself to a counterpart and gives himself up to the overwhelming impression. In pain the subject perceives the difference of the other, the contradiction in conflict and the alteration of his own self. In both modes of experience the subject enters entirely into his counterpart.

In such a description we recognize at once the kind of experience to which Pusey bears such powerful testimony. Again Moltmann speaks of 'knowing in wonder. By knowing or perceiving one participates in the life of the other. Here knowing does not transform the counterpart into the property of the knower; the knower does not appropriate what he knows. On the contrary, he is transformed through sympathy, becoming a participator in what he perceives. Knowledge confers fellowship. That is why knowing, perception, only goes as far as love, sympathy and participation reach'. For Moltmann, 'a modern discovery of trinitarian thinking will involve a fundamental change in modern reason—a change from lordship to fellowship, from conquest to participation, from production to receptivity'.[34] These are certainly today, even more than they were one hundred and fifty years ago, matters of life and death, questions which touch on the very possibility of a human future on this planet.

We live at a moment when many despair in the face of the problems which confront humanity, and our apparent inability to change. 'Concentration camps like Belsen and Dachau, remain with us as symbols of the value we attach to human beings.'[35] Has human life any meaning at all? Is man nothing more than a bundle of random and frustrated sensations? Can there be a God we can know and love? Is there any possibility for man in his fragmentedness to rise to such love and such knowledge? In face of such questions the life of the Church often seems superficial and unworthy, absorbed in trivialities, neglecting the deepest fears and longings of the human heart and mind. The tradition within the Church of England, which stems from the events of 1833–45, at the present day, often seems lacking in depth of commitment, in breadth and creativity of vision. Christians need to grow if they are to be in any way equal to the demands this century places on us. They need to learn again from those great original moments of vision which we recognize in men, such as Pusey, Newman and Keble.

Only one who has felt in his flesh and in his bones the acute disproportion between the infinity and holiness of God, and the littleness and misery of man; who has himself been through the hell of doubt and despair, of self-reproach and self-condemnation, of the sense of loss and the sense of abandonment, can have a word to speak which can be heard in a time such as ours; and Pusey is such a one. His presence is a disturbing one. He troubles us, by the violence of his penitence, by the violence of his joy; by his intensity, his unrelenting insistence on the claims of God on human life. But through the very intensity of his vision he offers us a word of life and a word of hope. He speaks of man's ineradicable longing after God; of God's unquenchable desire for the wholeness and restoration of man. He gives us the hope that our human life may not be doomed to ultimate frustration and waste, but may find its unimaginable fulfilment in the knowledge and the love, the presence and the joy of the one by whom and for whom we were made. He is, as Dean Church told us, 'one who really looked at life as St. Paul looked it', confident that nothing can separate us from the love of God, constantly leaving the things that are behind, and stretching out towards the things which lie before us, towards the high calling of God in Christ Jesus. As he wrote in the last weeks of his life, to a friend:

> You, I hope, are ripening continually. God ripen you more and more. Each day is a day of growth. God says to you, 'Open thy mouth and I will fill it.' Only long. He does not want our words. The parched soil, by its cracks, opens itself for the rain from heaven and invites it. The parched soil cries out for the living God. Oh! then long and long and long, and God will fill thee. More love, more love, more love![36]

NOTES

1 Liddon, vol. 4, p. 389.

2 *Letters and Diaries*, vol. 2, p. 74.

3 Liddon, vol. 4, pp. 141–4.

4 Ibid., vol. 4, p. 390.

5 *Benson of Cowley*, ed. M. Smith, ssje (Oxford 1980) *passim*.

6 The judgement of H. C. G. Mathew is interesting as regards the sermons. He considers them, 'much under-rated as spiritual exhortations . . . [They] constitute perhaps the chief testament to the force and temper of the Oxford Movement in its post-Newman form'; this from an article, which is not notably sympathetic to Pusey's religious concerns, but is highly perceptive about the historical and intellectual background. H. C. G. Mathew, *JTS, n.s.* vol. 22 (1981), p. 119.

7 Liddon, vol. 2, p. 61.

8 Ibid., vol. 3, p. 139.

9 Pusey, *Sermons during the Season from Advent to Whitsuntide* (1848), p. xviii.

10 Pusey, *Parochial and Cathedral Sermons*, pp. 303–5.

11 Ibid., pp. 310–11.

12 Ibid., pp. 313–14.

13 *Advent to Whitsuntide*, pp. 109–10.

14 Ibid., p. 100.

15 Methodist Hymn Book, No. 556.

16 *Advent to Whitsuntide*, p. 103.

17 John Saward, *Perfect Fools: Folly for Christ's Sake in Catholic and Orthodox Spirituality* (1980), p. 207.

18 *Advent to Whitsuntide*, p. 97.

19 Ibid., p. 119.

20 Ibid., pp. 252–3.

21 Ibid., p. 235.

22 Ibid., p. 237.

23 Ibid., p. 239.

24 Ibid., pp. 239–44.

25 Ibid., pp. 344–6.

26 Ibid., pp. 241–3.

27 Newman, *Lectures on Justification*, p. 167.

28 Ibid., pp. 219–21.

29 *Parochial and Cathedral Sermons*, p. 322.

30 *Advent to Whitsuntide*, pp. 342–3.

31 Ibid., pp. 348–9.

32 *Essays Catholic and Radical*, ed. K. Leech and R. Williams (1983), p. 79.

33 J. Moltmann, *The Trinity and the Kingdom of God* (1980), p. 62.

34 Ibid., p. 9.

35 A sentence of J. Saunders Lewis in his essay on the Welsh hymn-writer, Ann Griffiths, in J. Coutts (ed.), *Homage to Ann Griffiths* (Church in Wales Publications 1976), p. 29.

36 Liddon, vol. 4, p. 376.

Bibliography

A bibliography of Pusey's own published writings is to be found in Liddon's biography (see below) IV 395–446. His *Spiritual Letters* were edited and prepared for publication by J. O. Johnston and W. C. E. Newbolt, 1898.

BOOKS

Grafton C. *Pusey and the Church Revival* (Milwaukee 1908).

Liddon H.P. *Life of Edward Bouverie Pusey*, edited and prepared for publication by J. O. Johnston and R. J. Wilson, 4 vols (1893–7).

Lough A.G. *Dr Pusey: Restorer of the Church*, privately printed (Newton Abbot 1981).

Prestige G.L. *Pusey* (1933).

Richards G.C. *Dr Pusey* (Frome 1933).

Russell G.W.E. *Dr Pusey* (1907).

Savile B.W. *Dr Pusey: an Historic Sketch. With some account of the Oxford Movement during the nineteenth century* (1883).

[Trench M.] *The Story of Dr Pusey's Life* (1900).

ARTICLES

Booth S.P. 'Essays and Reviews: the controversy as seen in the correspondence and papers of Dr E. B. Pusey and Archbishop Archibald Tait', *Historical Magazine of the Protestant Episcopal Church*, vol. 38 (1969), pp. 259–79.

Donaldson A.B. 'Edward Bouverie Pusey', *Five Great Oxford Leaders* (1900), pp. 149–226.

Forrester D. 'Dr Pusey's Marriage', *Ampleforth Journal*, vol. 78 (1973), pt 2, pp. 33–47.

Gorce D. 'La spiritualité d'Edward Bouverie Pusey . . . d'après ses lettres inédites à sa fiancée', *Revue des Sciences Religieuses*, vol. 26 (1952), pp. 30–58.

Griffin J.R. 'Dr Pusey and the Oxford Movement', *Historical Magazine of the Protestant Episcopal Church*, vol. 42 (1973), pp. 137–53. 'Dr Pusey' *The Oxford Movement: a Revision* (Front Royal, Virginia, 1980), pp. 58–70.

Hopkins J.H. 'Edward Bouverie Pusey', *American Church Review*, vol. 41 (1883), pp. 61–88.

Matthew H.C.G. 'Edward Bouverie Pusey: from Scholar to Tractarian', *Journal of Theological Studies*, n.s. 32 (1981), pp. 101–24.

Mozley J. 'Dr Pusey's Sermon', *Essays Historical and Theological*, 3rd ed. vol. 2, (1892), pp. 149–63.

Oxenham H.N. 'Dr Pusey', *Short Studies in Ecclesiastical History and Biography* (1884), pp. 376–84.

Russell G.W.E. 'Edward Bouverie Pusey', *Household of Faith* (1902), pp. 44–59.

Shairp J.C. 'Dr Pusey and the Oxford Movement', *Good Words* (1883) pp. 25–32, pp. 202–7.

Talbot E.S. 'Dr Pusey and the High Church Movement', *Fortnightly Review*, n.s. vol. 33 (1883), pp. 335–48.

Wilberforce R.G. 'Dr Pusey and Bishop Wilberforce', *The Nineteenth Century*, vol. 38 (1895), pp. 57–67.

Index of Names

Dawson, Christopher   120, 136n
Denison, G.A.   350–3, 358–9, 365n
Denison, L.E.   365n
Dessain, C.S.   182n, 346
Dickinson, H.T.   292n
Doane, G.W.   206n
Dodsworth, W.   70n, 76, 183n,
   225–6, 228–30n, 275, 350–1
Dodwell, Henry   212
Donaldson, A.B.   391
Driver, Sir Godfrey R.   73, 113
Driver, S.R.   89, 110–11, 113,
   115n, 118n
Drummond, A.L.   31n
Dupuis   5–8

Eadmer   340–2
Eichhorn, Johann   9, 60, 75–6,
   78–9, 86, 91, 107, 115n, 120,
   151
Eldon, Lord   259, 276, 292n
Elkin, A.P.   208n
Ellacombe, Jane   223, 253n
Ellis, I   31n
Elton, O.   xi n
Emerton, J.A.   73, 113n
Eusebius   76–7
Evans, H.J.   205n
Evdokimov, P.   336
Ewald, Heinrich   77–9, 97,
   114–15n

Faber, Geoffrey   10, 31n, 161n,
   339, 341, 343
Fairchild, H.N.   69n
Ffoulkes, E.F.   30n
Fletcher, Clara   121, 136n
Forbes, A.P., Bp   353, 362

Forrester, David W.F.   2–3, 22, 27,
   29n, 33n, 186, 206n, 252n, 391
Freytag   75, 77–8
Froude, Hurrell   3–5, 7, 24, 29n,
   119, 137n, 141, 261–6, 268,
   282, 288, 290, 293n, 296n
Froude, James Anthony   27

Gaisford, Dr   108
Gandell, Robert   110
Gaume, Abbé   215, 222–3, 227–9n
Gesenius, H.F.W.   20, 74, 78–9,
   82, 86, 93–4, 98–9, 101, 104–5,
   109, 113, 114–15n
Gibbs, Josiah W.   82–94, 98, 102,
   112–13, 115n
Gidney, T.W.   116n
Gilberne, Miss   278
Gilbert, Ashurst Turner   255
Giles, John   336
Gillman, Ellen   96
Gladstone, William Ewart   144,
   160n, 199, 202, 208–9, 224,
   263–5, 271–3, 275, 282–4, 287
   and n, 291, 293–4, 296n, 306–8,
   311, 314–15, 317–18, 321, 326,
   328–9n, 355, 364n
Gleig, G.R.   159n
Goldsmid, Nathaniel   296n
Golius, Jacobus   75, 77
Gorce, D.   391–2
Gorham, George C.   273–4, 357
Gornall, T.   293n, 295–6n
Graves, Richard   75
Gray, G. Buchanan   111–12, 118n
Gray, Robert, Bp   186, 193–5,
   204–5, 207–9n
Green, Sidney   362
Grey, C.N.   207n

Saravia, Dr 211–12
Saward, John 375, 389n
Schleiermacher, Friedrich 9–10, 13, 15, 16, 31n, 120, 151, 386
Schroeder, N.G. 75
Schultens, Albert 75, 86, 94
Selwyn, George, Bp 186, 188, 195, 198–9, 237, 253n
Semler, Johann Salamo 17, 19
Sewell, William 214
Shaffer, E.S. 69n
Shaftesbury, Lord 120
Shairp, J.C. 392
Shaw, G.P. 205n
Short, Augustus 205n
Silouan, Staretz 376
Simonis, J. 75, 79, 86, 91, 115n
Sleidan, J. 77
Smith, Payne 109–10
Speller, J.L. 113–14n
Spener, Philipp Jakob 10, 15, 164
Spinoza, Baruch 31
Stanley, A.P. 159–60n, 295n, 299, 301, 318–19, 323, 331n
Steinschneider, Moritz 109, 116n
Stock, Joseph 76
Stone, Darwell 70n, 365n
Storr, V.F. 68n
Strauss, David Friedrich 21, 33n, 106
Stuart, Moses 97–105, 113n, 116n
Sumner, J.B. 194
Surin, Jean Joseph 239–40, 253n, 376
Svaglic, M.J. 29n
Symons, B.P. 327

Tait, A.C., Archbp 319, 349, 356, 359, 364–5n, 391
Talbot, E.S. 392
Talboys, D.A. 116n
Taylor, Jeremy, Bp 212
Temple, William, Bp 356
Thirlwall, Connop 9
Tholuck, August 9, 11, 13–15, 17, 20–1, 23, 31–3nn, 76, 101, 151
Thompson, K.A. 292n
Thorndike, Herbert 173
Torrey, C.C. 116n
Trench, Maria 161, 228n, 364–5n, 391
Trevor, Meriol 119
Trollope, Anthony 139, 328
Tronson 241, 250
Tuckwell, W. 303, 320, 326–7, 328n, 330–1n
Tulloch, John 2, 29n, 31n
Twiss, H. 292n
Tyrell, William 204

Ussher, James, Archbp 212

Vaughan, H.H. 304–6, 315, 322, 328n
Vincent, William 76
Volney 5–7

Walton, Izaak 211, 227n
Warburton, Bp 258, 268, 271, 277–8, 292n, 295
Ward, W.G. 292n, 295n
Ward, W.R. 26, 256, 292n, 295n, 329n,
Watson, G. 49n
Watson, Joshua 259, 263
Wellhausen, Julius 77
Wellington, Duke of 94, 128, 134
Wesley, Charles 11, 375

Whately, R. 5, 24, 30n, 122, 129
White, Blanco 16, 32n, 265
White, Joseph 71–2
White, R.J. 69n
Wickham, E.C. 319
Wilberforce, Henry 285
Wilberforce, R.G. 228n, 285, 392n
Wilberforce, R.I. 94, 112, 137n
Wilberforce, Samuel 186, 190,
  193, 198–9, 206–8n, 216, 226,
  228n, 270, 275, 282, 285, 287,
  293n, 296–7n, 352, 357, 364n
Williams, Edward R. 253n
Williams, George 364n
Williams, Isaac 51–3, 69n, 223,
  226, 229n, 230n, 322
Wilson, Thomas, Bp 212

Winer, Georg Benedict 78–9,
  114–15n
Wiseman, Nicholas, Cardinal 224,
  337
Wolf, J.C. 106
Wood, Charles (Lord
  Halifax) 360, 364–5n
Wood, George 359, 361
Wordsworth, Charles 283–4
Wordsworth, Christopher 272–3,
  294n
Wordsworth, William 56–9, 61,
  67–8, 69n

Yarnold, Edward 70n
Young, Isobella 224